Radical Territories in the Brazilian Amazon

NATIVE PEOPLES OF THE AMERICAS

Laurie Weinstein, Series Editor

Radical Territories in the Brazilian Amazon

The Kayapó's Fight for Just Livelihoods

Laura Zanotti

THE UNIVERSITY OF
ARIZONA PRESS

TUCSON

The University of Arizona Press
www.uapress.arizona.edu

Printed in the United States of America
21   20   19   18   17   16   6   5   4   3   2   1

ISBN-13: 978-0-8165-3354-1 (cloth)

Cover design by Miriam Warren
Cover illustration based on a topographic map by Nicole Kong

Publication of this book is made possible in part by the proceeds from a permanent
endowment created with the assistance of a Challenge Grant from the National
Endowment for the Humanities, a federal agency.

Library of Congress Cataloging-in-Publication Data
Names: Zanotti, Laura, author.
Title: Radical territories in the Brazilian Amazon : the Kayapó's fight for just livelihoods /
    Laura Zanotti.
Other titles: Native peoples of the Americas.
Description: Tucson : The University of Arizona Press, 2016. | Series: Native peoples of the
    Americas | Includes bibliographical references and index.
Identifiers: LCCN 2016007086 | ISBN 9780816533541 (cloth : alk. paper)
Subjects: LCSH: Cayapo Indians—Brazil—Social conditions. | Cayapo Indians—Politics
    and government—21st century. | Cayapo Indians—Government relations.
Classification: LCC F2520.1.C45 Z36 2016 | DDC 981/.13—dc23 LC record available at
    http://lccn.loc.gov/2016007086

♾ This paper meets the requirements of ANSI/NISO Z39.48-1992 (Permanence of Paper).

Contents

Illustrations

Acknowledgments

This work would not have been possible without the continuing support and vision of the community of A'Ukre. I have been honored by the invitation of the community of A'Ukre to share in their pursuit of just livelihoods, and I have learned from all whom I have worked with how to consider alternative futures. I want to express my deepest gratitude and debt to the community, who have opened and continue to open their lives to me and others. My adopted family, invited me into their home, and spent countless hours helping me learn what it means to be beautiful and Kayapó. I want to thank many for offering time spent in the forest and savannah, others for teaching me how to fish, and all the other countless community members who took me to their gardens, fields, or enjoined me to dance in the festivals. I have continued to share friendship, gentleness, laughter, and humor throughout the years with friends made since 2004, and I continue to be inspired by the Kayapó peoples' vision of a good life.

I received a National Science Foundation Dissertation Improvement Grant and a University of Washington's Chester Fritz Grant for Research and Exchange for financial support for this research. A Purdue Research Foundation Grant and College of Liberal Arts, Purdue University Engagement Grant made subsequent work possible. Since I joined Purdue University, the Department of Anthropology, The American Studies Program, and the Center for the Environment have all been important strongholds that anchor and ground intellectual engagement and inquiry. I would like to thank in particular Ellen Gruenbaum, Evie Blackwood, Michele Buzon, and Melissa Remis for their welcoming comments and conversations over the years. Leigh Raymond, Linda Prokopy, Kimberly Marion Suiseeya, and Zhao Ma at the Center for the Environment have been instrumental in helping me keep my nose to the ground, and Shannon McMullen, Rayvon Fouche, and Susan Curtis have been supportive of humanities social science hybrids. I'd like to thank my students, who have inspired me to be a better mentor, scholar, and community partner. Many conversations during my political ecology and methods seminars serve as a catalyst for ideas and inspiration.

I began what was to become a longstanding partnership with Dr. Diego Soares da Silveira on a trip down the Xingu river in 2008. Diego has helped to facilitate ongoing research permits and cross-institutional dialogue. He has been an indispensible intellectual interlocutor over the past several years. In Brazil, I would also like to thank Julio Cezar Melatti, Marcela Coelho de Souza, Denny Moore, and Luis Barbosa. Barbara Zimmerman, at the Wild Foundation's Kayapó Program and Adriano Jerozolimski and Valdeis at the Associação Floresta Protegida deserve my heartfelt appreciation and respect. Their logistical support at various points during fieldwork and openness and kindness to share their mission and goals have been unparalleled. Moreover, I would not have been able to conduct research without the National Indian Foundation (FUNAI) and the Ministry of Science and Technology (CNPq) granting permission to conduct this work.

This project was seeded at Colgate University where I was an undergraduate. I owe many things to Mary Moran, Nancy Reis, Peter Balakian and Leila Philip, who were four inspirational mentors. Mary and Nancy made a professional career in anthropology seem like a viable and fruitful post-graduate career and life path. Without their mentorship, this work would not have materialized. Peter Balakian's modernist poetry class inspired a life-long interest in Elizabeth Bishop's work, which for reasons I was not able to put my finger on at the time, crystallized my eventual work in Brazil.

As a book emerged from my doctoral experience, Stevan Harrell, Janet Chernela, Carol Jolles, and Jonathan Warren were invaluable advisors at the University of Washington and the University of Maryland. The advice, proverbial wisdom, and guidance from Stevan Harrell fortified an interest in environmental anthropology. His astute editorial comments and assistance have greatly improved my theoretical, methodological, and personal ethos as an engaged anthropologist and a scholar. Without Janet, I would not have had the chance to become personally acquainted with the Kayapó, an experience that would determine the course of my future community partnerships. I am deeply grateful for the energy, opportunities, support, and scholarly counsel Janet has offered. Carol Zane Jolles continued to push me on decolonizing, participatory, and feminist work—a dominant strand that is still present in the way I practice and advocate for respectful researcher–community interactions.

The environmental and sociocultural anthropology program at the University of Washington, Seattle, provided a unique interdisciplinary-minded intellectual home. Ismael Vaccaro, Brooke Scelza, Courtney Carothers, Megan Styles, Heather Lazrus, Amanda Poole, Askel Casson, Karma Norman, Teresa Mares, Leila Sievanan and many others were formative in this regard. Their friendship and, for many, insightful critiques on earlier and later drafts of this manuscript were indispensible.

The Society for Lowland Amazonian Anthropology and the Anthropology and Environment Society have been homes away from home, providing conviviality and an important space to exchange and generate new ideas. In particular, William Fisher, Juliet Erazo, Jeremy Campbell, Carlos Londoño-Sulkin, Laura Graham, Beth Conklin, and William Balée, among many others, have been wonderful colleagues to work with and build an exciting, ethical, and reflective community of practice.

Above all, I would like to thank my partner, my parents, sisters, brothers, cousins, and extended family, who, despite not knowing much about my career path, have only offered their love, compassion, and support over years. Their encouragement and patience have been immeasurable, and this work would have been impossible without them.

A Note on Orthography

Despite decades of research with Kayapó communities, no standard orthography of Kayapó terminology exists across the villages. The orthography was developed by the Summer Institute of Linguistics phonetic notation. However, while I was in A'Ukre, Kayapó schoolteachers who taught the written Kayapó language to schoolchildren were not satisfied with the writing system they currently had and were trying to transition from previous traditions of orthography to ones that conformed more to Luzo-Brazilian orthography and the Latin alphabet. As I wrote important words or phrases down I would check spellings with Kayapó schoolteachers and other leaders in the village, which often produced conflicting results. For example, the word for fruit—*pidjô*—was alternatively spelled *pidjô* and *pidj'y* or the word for work, *âpeii*, was spelled *âpei*, and *apex*. Inter and intravillage variation seemed prevalent. In this manuscript I have tried to use the spellings that were most common in A'Ukre while I was there. In general, though, I have used consonants, vowels, and nasal vowels as outlined by Jefferson (2009 [1974]): Consonants, p t k 'b d g x dj m n nh ng w r j; Vowels, i e ê a à o ô u y ỳ; Nasal Vowels, ĩ ẽ ã õ ũ ỹ.

For further reference, one can consult Thomson and Stout (1974a) who describe the following use of consonants and vowels: "p, t, k, b, d, g, m, n, w, r, y, i, a, u, ĩ, ẽ, ã, ũ, e, õ indicating the usual phonetic qualities. The other letters follow with the indicated phonetic qualities: x [tš], j [dž], nh [ñ], ng [ʔ], ê [e], e [ʔ], ô [o], ò [Ê], o [Í], ù [à], ü [á], à [ñ], a [ò], e ' [glottal stop]." However, please keep in mind that in 2014 an initiative began to standardize spellings. I have attempted to change and modify spellings of words to reflect these changes, although not all words reflect the most up-to-date usage of the spellings.

Radical Territories in the Brazilian Amazon

Introduction

This is a story of lives entwined and of new places of being and belonging.

—Bawaka Country, *Telling Stories in, Through, and with Country*

Losing hope is the same as dying. Recovering hope as a social force is the fundamental key to the survival of the human race, planet earth, and popular movements. Hope is not a conviction that something will happen in a certain way. We have to nurture it and protect it. . . . It is not about sitting and waiting for something to happen; it is about a hope that converts into action. In movement we can change things.

—Gustavo Esteva, *Planet Earth: Anti-systemic Movements*

Introduction

We were beaders the afternoon Nhakprikti (Nhak), looked at me and exclaimed, "Sit!" I followed her inside her house and watched as she tucked her dress under her legs and plopped down on the concrete floor. I was particularly fond of this dress of hers; it was faded red, with blue and yellow piping and two front pockets. I made myself comfortable across from Nhak; freshly bathed, my wet hair stuck to the back of my neck. Resting her head against the wall, Nhak grabbed a balled-up, old floral-print dress and then carefully unwrapped it and spread the fabric across her lap. In it were brightly colored glass beads and a bracelet in the making. She got right to work. Picking up the fish line where she had left off, she placed one end of the line in her mouth as she continued to weave the bracelet, which bore geometric shapes made of orange, green, and blue.

Her other family members walked in and out of the house, their sandals crunching and clicking against the thin layer of red earth on the concrete floor as they swiftly moved on to other tasks. Every once in a while Nhak would flatten out the wristband on her thigh and even out the beads to count how many rows until Nhak moved on to the next color. Weaving as she worked, she held beads between her thumb and index finger, swiftly stringing them, pulling the line through the beads again, and then adjusting the piece. Nhak was making wristbands for her son, who was to be in a naming ceremony later that month, participation in which is one of the highest honors in the community. However, she very well could have been making a bracelet for the handicraft market that the community was involved with, which takes Kayapó beaded objects to cities for sale.

It was shortly after midday, one of the sun-choked moments of the afternoon. I picked up some beads and line and began to work as well, but quickly my mind flitted around. I looked longingly at the patterned hammock that was strung between the walls but knew that slipping into it would not help. From where I sat, outside seemed unbearably bright. Water from a spigot dripped into a blue plastic barrel. Coconut and mango trees sheltered the still yard. I could just make out some community members walking on the path that skirted behind her house.

In retrospect, nothing particular about this moment seemed different from any other day. We had started out as usual with a quick but laborious trip to the fields to harvest manioc and sweet potatoes, followed by a dip in the river and an afternoon of beading. As Nhak and I sat together, we talked about the latest film shown on the village TV, and Nhak asked,

"Do you know the movie?"

"What was it about?"

"It was about a large monkey that was in love with a woman," (she said and looked up at me), "the woman in the movie looked a little bit like you, a *kuben kajaka*" (a white, foreign woman).

"I think I know that one, maybe *King Kong*?"

"Next time you come to the village, can you bring *Titanic*, the one with the big boat and the love story?"

"Sure, I will try to remember."

I made a mental note.

But there was something about the moment of that day, what Canessa (2012, 32) calls the "small spaces of everyday life" that continued to grab me; that what was extraordinary, was that this remained entirely ordinary: us in the house, Nhak beading, her kids in the backyard, her father on the front porch carving, her husband out fishing, her mother elsewhere, and her sisters down at the river washing clothes and dishes. Such activities reflect the daily rhythms of Mebêngôkre-Kayapó (Kayapó) village life that are dependent on healthy lands and waters but also demand creative entrepreneurship and political acumen to generate income and foster pathways to success. Nhak was intimately aware of all of this. Indeed, she knew that her capabilities—to raise her kids, to continue to sponsor naming celebrations, to take pleasure in the creation of beaded ceremonial items, and to relish evenings with her family watching films from Hollywood or made by Kayapó documentarians—correspond to choices that she could make owing to the successful struggles of her peoples over the past several decades to demarcate a federally recognized indigenous homeland: the Kayapó Indigenous Lands.

In the late 1970s, the Kayapó began to fight for land recognition and rights through the political, legal, and activist avenues available to them. By the early 2000s, Kayapó communities seemed to have achieved their goals when they demarcated more than 11 million hectares of their current homeland. The results were astounding, as their lands comprise one of the largest protected spaces in the Americas. Today the heart-shaped territory, with its adjacent but unconnected northeastern portion, lies in the southern portion of the state of Pará, Brazil, with a small, but not insignificant, area that edges into northern Mato Grosso (figure 1). Unevenly bisected by the Xingu River, a major tributary of the Amazon, and veined by many others, the federally demarcated lands contain both neotropical forest and savannah habitats. The lands boast plentiful fishing grounds, game hunting areas, fruit and nut collection sites, savannah resources, and zones for agricultural production.

Yet, these lands are located on a particularly powerful borderland. The area is physically marked by agro-industrial interests, gold mining, illegal timber operations, public–private energy consortiums, nongovernmental organizations (NGOs), and multinational mining enterprises—all of whom have stake in the area. Satellite imagery of the area confirms the lands as a "forest island" hugged, perhaps too intensely, by severe deforestation and extractivist economies. Bordered on the west by the BR-364 (Cuiabá–Porto Velho) and BR-163 (Cuiabá–Santarém) highways, on the north by BR-230 (Trans-Amazon) and PA-279, and on the east by PA-150 and BR-010 (Belém–Brasília). Contiguous with the Xingu National Park to the south, the borders of the territory are increasingly threatened by the expanding soy frontier, hydroelectric development, and a resurgence in gold mining. These industries contrast against federally demarcated Indigenous Lands and protected areas connected to robust civil society movements: localized and transnational indigenous activism and conservationist concerns. Within these lands, Kayapó peoples support village life, construct their homes, and forge their livelihoods. In doing so, the Kayapó peoples are redefining what sustainability and development mean not for conservation agendas but for the future of indigenous peoples and their lifeways.

Kayapó livelihoods also have been shaped by an invisible but equally powerful, imagined border that separates indigeneity from modernity, forests from development, tradition from progress, and conservation from extraction. As I will argue, these dichotomies are fictions of a bygone era. Yet, despite the multicultural and democratic turn in Latin America and the participatory era of environmental governance, Kayapó communities continue to endure critiques of their practices and lifeways. For example, national discourses continue to finger indigenous communities and cultural difference as obstacles to development and some environmentalist narratives suggest Kayapó peoples are failed environmental stewards because of their engagement in market activities. These discourses remain firmly entrenched in the way in which indigenous peoples

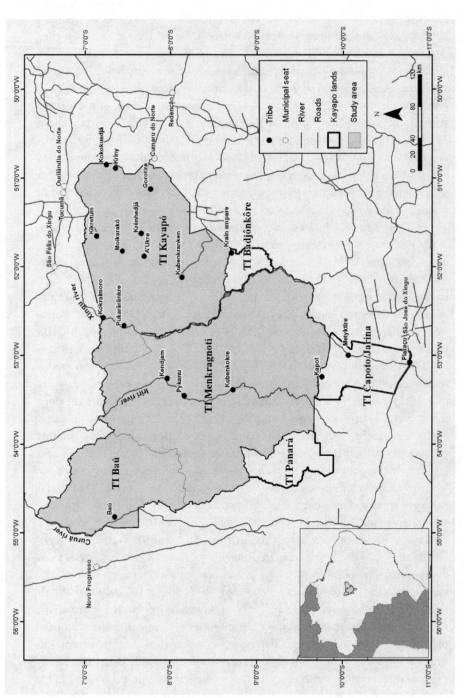

Figure 1. Map of the Kayapó Indigenous Lands. A'Ukre is located in the upper right-hand portion of the territory.

persist in (wrongly) being understood as antithetical to globalization, cosmo-politanism, and living a good life.

In this book I offer up a different story. *Radical Territories in the Brazilian Amazon* foregrounds how Kayapó peoples use diverse strategies to actively construct landscapes in the Amazon region that support indigenous lifeways, nurture indigenous identities, and address justice concerns. I move beyond binary framings to show that by negotiating complex territorialities, Kayapó peoples have carried out strategies in cooperation with or in opposition to environmental organizations, corporate interests, and state mandates in their area. They have sought to retain diversified foodways, experiment with nontimber forest products (NTFPs) projects, forge strong community–conservation partnerships, and become well-known cinematographers, cultivating media practices of their own. This is a story of how protests can be filled with songs, how household fields are emblematic of the struggle for food sovereignty, how foraging for Brazil nuts is reflective of historical connections to place and routes to alternative economies, and how flights connecting community to urban centers can simultaneously be a mode of transportation and an activity that supports vigilance and monitoring. For the Kayapó, these landscapes are dominated neither by agro-industrial interests nor by protected, uninhabited landscapes. Rather, Kayapó peoples see their homeland as a multifaceted, plural landscape where indigenous, conservation, and development interests coexist—albeit all the while continuing to fight against the uneven and unjust geographies that these plural landscapes engender.

Through a focus on territoriality and indigeneity, I thrust questions about territory, identity, place, space, landscape, and home into the spotlight to make sense of the "small spaces" of everyday life and their geopolitical and socioeco-logical entanglements. In the late 1980s, Foucault (1986, 22) commented that while the "great obsession of the nineteenth century, as we know, is history," the "anxiety of our era has to do fundamentally with space." Following Foucault's observation—or perhaps in spite of it—several sociospatial concepts have emerged in the past three decades to capture the global, late liberal, and post-colonial world in which the Kayapó and all of us live: heterotropias (Foucault 1986), hyperspace (Jameson 1991), rhizomes (Deleuze and Guattari 1987), networks (Callon 1986; Latour 2005; Law and Hassardh 1999), routes (Clifford 1997), lines (Ingold 2007), nonplaces (Augé 2008), lived space (Lefebvre 1991), third space (Bhabha 1994; Soja 1996), and territories (Escobar 2008; Harvey 1990; Moore 2005). Tsing (2005) asserts that global processes—the freeing up of labor markets and the rise of multicultural politics—generate friction-filled "zones of awkward engagement." Appadurai (1996) describes the rapidity and connectivity of media, technology, people, and real and virtual worlds with terms that indicate different circulatory "-scapes" that crisscross the globe.

Emerging from postcolonial scholarship, science and technology studies, and political ecology work, these theories show the limitations of western epistemological approaches to space grounded in Cartesian–Newtonian philosophies, as well as the force from which the processes of late liberalism has both deepened historically sedimented ideologies of the world order and simultaneously ruptured their moorings thereby creating new networks of belonging. While these scholars also point to the spatiality of local practice and the unsettled geographies of capital accumulation, they also suggest, as feminist political ecologists do, that spatial practices coupled with power and history impact bodies, landscapes, and scales differently. This highlights the salience of cultural difference and shows both the top-down, as well as diffusive forms of material and discursive powers that operate within these contested and risky geographies. What *Radical Territories in the Brazilian Amazon* foregrounds is the way in which new expressions of spatiality have accommodated what indigenous groups have been advocating for centuries: a notion of territoriality that is not based simply on Eurocentric notions of space resting on capital logics. Rather, it is an approach to place, space, and being that is at once affective, material, cosmological, and brought to life through a relational practice that involves both human and non-human beings.

Almost two decades ago, Gupta and Ferguson (1997a, 1997b, 37) suggested that postmodernity is marked by reterritorialization, a concept that called into question fixed notions of cultures, identities, and peoples while at the same time troubling the notion of nation-states as solid, bounded units. Quoting James Clifford (1996), Gupta and Ferguson (1997b, 37) take up a question that Clifford posed: "What does it mean, at the end of the twentieth century, to speak . . . of a 'native land?' What processes rather than essences are involved in the present experiences of cultural identity?" What Gupta and Ferguson raise here echoes the basis of this analysis of Kayapó territorial concerns in the twenty-first century: the ongoing question of sovereignty of indigenous peoples and nation-states, the role of identity politics in struggles for justice, the ways in which indigenous notions of self and personhood are translated and represented nationally and internationally, the ability of Kayapó communities to continue their livelihoods in ways that support rather than essentialize their ways of being, and the different scalar territorial (and Indigenous/Native) politics, given the de- and reterritorialization of the global political landscape and the new ecologies of a post-neoliberal society.

This analysis emerges out of critiques to development, modernity, and progress that were seeded in the 1950s (Goldman 2006).[1] The territorial politics of development regimes and late liberal capitalism are characterized by the weakening of national boundaries, the decline in the Fordist era and rise of flexible specialization, the exponential growth in the rapidity and heightened connectivity across the globe, the devolution and deregulation of governmental intervention, the rise in social movements, an increased sense of the precariousness of life itself, and the emphasis and reliance on the free market politics and economics. Subsequently, the late liberal moment, especially in Latin America, is being fueled by what Lievesley and Ludlam (2009) have identified as "pink tide" progressive politics and neoextractivism, the latter a term coined by Eduardo Gudynas (2009) (see also Povinelli 2011). Pink tide politics capture what some have called the Post-Washington Consensus moment, an era characterized by social democracy and socialist parties in Latin American countries, including Brazil, that combine multicultural platforms with pro-poor programs. Liberal democratic recognition of cultural difference as expressed through pink tide politics are taking place in tandem with a growth in hydro-carbon investment, or neoextractivist agendas, a term that describes development projects across Latin America where "endogamous growth" based on extractive economies are used to fund different social projects and poverty alleviation measures (Bebbington 2012).[2]

Radical Territories in the Brazilian Amazon analyzes Kayapó activism and diverse strategies for making their livelihoods in their new homeland as they intersect with and resist against the spatial politics of neoextractivism and neodevelopmentalism. By deploying the term territorialities, I evoke the multiple ways through which Kayapó peoples creatively and strategically produce landscapes that are all part of the fabric of indigeneity, conservation, and development in the Amazon. As Moore (1998, 347) highlights, "Rather than conceiving of localities as inert, fixed backdrops for identity struggles, we need to see them as products of those contestations." State-driven unification efforts to define territorial sovereignty, corporate land-grabbing practices in the name of development, international measures that transform local spaces into conservation hotspots, and indigenous struggles for homeland demarcation are all fundamentally linked to different conceptualizations and contestations of spatial practices. While intently focusing on the discord borne out of conflicting epistemologies and agendas, I show that "being indigenous" or "making territory" or "governing conservation" is not simply a top–down process where Kayapó villagers become environmental subjects or governed citizens. Rather, these processes happen synergistically where Kayapó peoples are also the drivers of change as they emplace cooperative and experimental forms of entrepreneurship, conservation initiatives, and the expressive politics of indigeneity into locally relevant frames and ways of being. As such, decolonizing knowledge, nature, and place, play a central part in this story.

Radical Territories in the Brazilian Amazon also foregrounds a political ecology and feminist political ecology approach to Kayapó livelihoods that seeks to counter dominant development, late liberal, and neoextractivist models. While pink tide politics and neoextractivism are fashioned as positive nationalist movements that support multicultural citizenship, national sovereignty, and social equity—what it seems the Kayapó peoples are struggling for—other possibilities for the future that are not predicated on capitalist expansion remain viable and sometimes radical alternatives. Attentive to the territorial, cultural, ecological, and economic facets of local livelihoods, I analyze the sociospatial and political ecological terrains that current Kayapó communities navigate to make a living in this "post" world. For example, Gibson-Graham (2008, 614; 2011) proposes that we are in a "new moment" where "projects of economic autonomy and experimentation are proliferating worldwide," with an attendant "cultural infrastructure" that is disseminating and supporting them. Similarly, in his monograph on Cofán peoples and environmental politics in Ecuador, Michael Cepek (2012, ix) counsels for an anthropology of hope where, "hope is an essential element in the imagination, investigation, and realization of alternative futures." A degrowth society is one that centers on shared notions of "democracy, justice, meaning of life, and well-being" (Asara, Demaria, and Corbera 2015, 377). Escobar (2015, 451) suggests that as a collective these alternative approaches to late liberal logics are "transitional discourses," which "call for a significant paradigmatic or civilizational transformation."

The following quotes from well-established leaders in their respective tribes, nations, or countries, capture the pulse of what now is being referred to as a movement for zero growth or de-growth, which when coupled with long-standing struggles for self-determination honors indigenous cosmovisions and ways of being in the world: "In nature's economy and sustenance economy the currency is not money, it is life" (Vandana Shiva 2005, 33). "In the time of the sacred sites and the crashing of ecosystems and worlds, it may be worth not making a commodity out of all that is revered" (Winona LaDuke 2013, np). Finally, Mayalú Txucarramãe, a young Kayapó leader who is the daughter of renowned chief Megaron and is also related to Chief Raoni, was quoted in an *Amazon Watch* (2013, np) feature article on her activism to have exclaimed, "Resistance is in my blood!"

An "effective politics for transformation" is historically and spatially situated, and Kayapó peoples offer possibilities for new geographies of well-being and living well through a mosaic of livelihood practices (Escobar 2015, 452). While the Kayapó's political actions certainly can be framed as addressing "environmental issues," more importantly Kayapó strategies are about efforts for self-determination that acknowledge and honor indigenous ways of being in the world. I argue that Kayapó visions for their livelihoods are rooted in the similar sensibilities proposed by proponents of de-growth and postdevelopmental paradigms: (1) robust and creative local economies and relational practices that are guided by indigenous cosmologies and notions of exchange; (2) new transactional economies based on a mixed portfolio (NTFP markets, state-based poverty alleviation programs, wage labor) that derives from complex alliance building (civil society movements, NGO partnerships, alliances with institutions of higher education and research, celebrity activism, governmental entities); and (3) self-determination, sovereignty, and justice demands critical to their well-being (e.g., land, food, water, health, education, land and media). Kayapó strategies align with a politics of transformation, in that these practices honor Kayapó ways of being in the world, support livelihoods that are not predicated on capitalist expansion, and reflect Kayapó notions of what it means to live well. However, while finding kinship with transitional discourses, these approaches also are not blind to political and economic realities of a neodevelopmentalist and neoextractivist state. Kayapó peoples continue to create strategic alliances, adopt NGOs, individuals, and organizations into community life, and draw upon different forms of cash-generating activities.

It is also important to remember that late liberal expansion and neoextractivist states incise different hierarchies onto the landscape where particular peoples—whether it is because of their race, ethnic status, socioeconomic status, or marginalized position—experience historical and widespread systemic and structural violence and disruption (Asara, Demaria, and Corbera 2015, 375). Gordon (2006, 40) argues that although the predatory nature of colonial histories has threatened to transform everything in its stead—people, things, society and nature—its limits can be found in Kayapó cosmologies, which hold that the incorporation of non-Kayapó things, objects, and beings can strengthen, not weaken, Kayapó social life. Certainly, over the decades Kayapó leaders carved out a homeland and continue to strive for justice as their peoples thrive despite the violent processes of colonization, pacification, statecraft, and neodevelopmentalism. Yet, West (2012, 252) argues that dominant narratives are persistent global imaginaries that continue to position people and places as fluid—and often disposable—nodes in a complex system of uneven capital circulation and simplified citizen-subjects occupying calcified positions marked by the complicated terms of "Native," or "impoverished." In this book, I remain wary of these essentializing and entrenched orthodoxies that blame or victimize local, undifferentiated resource users ("bad actors") and instead emphasize the broader structural issues that are relevant to analyzing the persistent devaluation of cultural difference, local livelihoods and multicultural worlds (Anguelovski and Martínez Alier 2014; Elmhirst 2011; Forsyth 2003).

Accordingly, new imaginaries emphasize place as central to dynamic conceptualizations of indigenous livelihoods. Dirlik (2011, 48) opines that "one of the most important and ironic products of the most recent round of economic globalization has been to enhance, foster, and render visible consciousness of place." Yet as early as 1977, Yi-Fu Tuan (1977, 73) explained, "when space feels thoroughly familiar to us, it has become place," capturing what was to become an often-cited, but contentious definition of space and place. Tuan proposed that whereas space is abstract, place is the center of different life worlds. Henri Lefebvre (1991), later argued that the ideologies that underpinned capitalist modes of production instigated a notion of alienated, and abstracted space, as Tuan suggested, which opened up new pathways for domination and control (see also Massey 2005). Lefebvre's Marxist perspective on space, adapted and modified also by the anthropologist Edward Soja (1996), shows a tripartite construction of space or the trialectics of space, where first space (physical and perceived space) and second space (perception, cognitive maps, and conceived) conjointly create third space, or lived space (see Kahn 2000, 7). Both Tuan and Lefebvre stress that embodiment, experiential practice, mythic time and phenomenological worlds comprise and cocreate place. This conceptualization aligns with many ways indigenous peoples envision place and place-making. Keith Basso (1996) with the Western Apache, and Davi Kopenawa (Kopenawa and Albert 2013) writing from his own Yanomami perspective, for example, show that many indigenous peoples' cosmologies conceptualize place as process, a process that is brought into being by the transformative relationships between different human and nonhuman beings.

Throughout this book, I echo Hubbard, Kitchin, and Valentine's (2004, 6) definition of place, where place is "relational and contingent." I also agree with Escobar (2008, 3) that "the examination of place-making and region-making from multilevel economic, ecological, and cultural perspectives affords novel opportunities for understanding the politics of difference and sameness that accompanies enactments of globality." Finally Little (2001, 5) suggests that the territorial politics in Amazonia are best understood through the concept of cosmographies, which captures the "collective, historically contingent identities, ideologies, and environmental knowledge systems developed by a social group to establish and maintain a human territory," as well as the affective, symbolic dimensions of space. In highlighting the Kayapó peoples desires for a good life as it intersects with territorialities of rule, indigenous projects of citizenship and political efficacy, and questions of governance, this book is a story written with these territorial sensibilities in mind. I offer a framework for considering different ways in which Kayapó lives are not simply controlled or shaped by late liberal or neodevelopmental discourses while at the same time make visible the obstacles the Kayapó peoples face in the "small spaces" of their daily lives that are constantly positioned against the backdrop of power relationships, territorial control, and identity politics.

Moreover, the case that I describe here raises important questions about the possibilities for the Brazilian Amazon to accommodate alternative, in this instance Kayapó, self-determination strategies into the future. On the surface, the Kayapó success in demarcating the majority of their homeland in the 1990s and fight for the recognition of their territory provides a striking counterexample to the worldwide trend of protected-area delimitation largely disconnected from or in contradiction to local livelihoods. Through the frame of making indigenous territorialities, I expand this discussion to emphasize the polysemous identities that the Kayapó Lands simultaneously hold as an indigenous home-land, a conservation stronghold in the Xingu corridor, a federal territory, and one of the largest protected areas in the neotropics, a critical part of the global commons. I show how Kayapó peoples have translated customary political prac-tices into the multiscalar landscape of territorial governance, creating radical new geographies that accommodate for Kayapó ontologies at the same time it embraces new notions of citizenship, rights, and knowledge systems. This has resulted in a "scaling up" and pluralistic approach to coordinate decision-making across their territory and enter in alliances with other groups that are supportive of their goal to continue to create communities for and by Kayapó peoples. Because state-defined pathways for representation have often limited the Kay-apó, Kayapó peoples have formulated a political space that recognizes difference and indigenous authority. In this way, Kayapó livelihoods and political agendas are best understood as a process of making indigenous territorialities.

"Making" references the active, embodied ways the Kayapó engage with place and their constant struggle to retain their lifeways through their culti-vation of indigenous-driven activist efforts and other place- and space-making activities. Being indigenous for Kayapó peoples means being *tycht* (strong, alter-native spelling *tyx*) in the face of seemingly insurmountable obstacles. It means protecting their lands and waters for future generations. All that is *metire* (beau-tiful) or about life—raising children, circulating names and objects, perform-ing ceremonies with relatives and friends, carrying out subsistence activities, going to school, and experimenting with different forms of visual expression and self-determination—depends on the continuation of their lifeways in these spaces. In the complex terrain of the southern Pará and northern Mato Grosso states, Brazil, where the Kayapó live and where conservation and development violently collide, being indigenous also means that Kayapó communities nego-tiate different market opportunities, develop strong activist and political plat-forms, and continue to explore, exchange, and create, as they have long done, through their entanglements with other groups and practices. It is this sense of making worlds and making lives I refer to throughout the book.

Johnson and Larsen (2013, 8) hold that "place speaks to the holistic totality of human and nonhuman relations situated in a particular locale or region." In the remainder of this chapter, I introduce A'Ukre, the place that is central to this work and the community with whom I am forever indebted to for sharing their lives and worlds with me. Then, I expand upon several of the concepts presented in this introduction, further detailing why making indigenous terri-torialities serves as a central concept of this book. I discuss how work with the community of A'Ukre began and, in the same vein, how ethnographic practice also has the possibility of being "transformative." Finally, I offer a road map to the rest of the book, a book that is a testament to the complex terrain that the community of A'Ukre navigates to make home and place.

A'Ukre

The Mebêngôkre-Kayapó people's self-reflexivity identifies themselves as the Mebêngôkre, the name that is theirs, that refers to their people. I heard repeatedly and constantly, "We, Mebêngôkre" or "The Mebêngôkre way is this way," while in A'Ukre. Mebêngôkre means "People of the Watery Hole" or "People of the Watering Place." This name is an important one, as it indicates the relationship between the Mebêngôkre and outsiders, whether indigenous, nonindigenous, or nonhuman. Many community members I talked with did not know the origin of the term, but the connection to water always struck me. Contained with the name for their peoples were the diverse terrains that make home: water, land, rivers, and lakes. When I came to A'Ukre, an elder often talked about an old cave in the savannah that had a river underneath where they used to visit long ago. The cave has large, beautiful rooms beneath and traces of other peoples living there. Not many that were still alive had seen the cave; only a handful of community members had been there. This description of a cave made sinuous by underground rivers always reminded me of the word Mebêngôkre, people of the water hole or watery place. When asked, though, no one was sure of any connection. Years later, the elder still talked of the same place.

While Mebêngôkre is the name of the people I worked with, I have chosen to use the term Kayapó throughout the book. Kayapó is a name that was designated by outsiders during colonization, but also one that the Mebêngôkre-Kayapó use in political contexts. It is the name used that identifies their demarcated territory, the name that is on many maps, and the name used in official identity documents. Many villagers have accepted the term Kayapó and have expertly used it in different political situations for environmental and social justice efforts. When I refer to the Kayapó or Kayapó individuals in this book, I do it with the understanding that it is a powerful political and legal marker of identity, one that individuals and leaders have embraced as part of the "slot" within which they locate themselves for their efforts at self-determination and autonomy (Li 2000). The term *Kayapó* should not be read as a way to homogenize individuals or overlook the heterogeneity of the experiences, divisions, personal biographies, and situated identities within the group. Since the world has come to know and recognize the Mebêngôkre as the Kayapó, I have kept Kayapó throughout. I do so with conflicted and unsettled feelings, acknowledging the colonial history it bears, as well as with the desire that readers will come to understand through this work how Kayapó peoples are the Mebêngôkre.

In 2010, the estimated total population of Kayapó peoples ranged between five and seven thousand individuals located in more than forty villages.[3] Kayapó peoples are sometimes referred to as the Northern Kayapó and belong to the Gê speaking linguistic group.[4] They live in villages in the middle and upper regions of the Xingu River valley in Brazil (figure 2). A'Ukre, where Nhak makes her

Figure 2. Aerial View of A'Ukre. This photo was taken during the dry season. The community was in the middle of Olympic Games, which is why there is a pronounced volleyball court in the center. Note the school, clinic, and project houses on the way to the river.

home, is located east of the Xingu River, in the northeastern portion of the Kayapó area. The lands of A'Ukre are varied. Hillocks rise and undulate in the distance, unfurling a blanket of mottled greens; rivers and streams ribbon outward, softly etched into the landscape, expanding and contracting with the rainy and dry seasons. The area surrounding A'Ukre is part of the *terra firme* lands in the Amazon Basin that have long been distinguished from the fertile *várzea* soils of the Amazonian floodplains, both for ecological and cultural reasons (Roosevelt 1989). The environment is composed of seasonal dry forests, semideciduous liana forests, transitional forest/savannah corridors, and woodland and grassland savannah areas ([both *cerrado* and *campo cerrado*] Malcolm et al. 1999). All of these land covers are considered endangered and encompass two of the eight major vegetation types found in Amazonia (Hames and Vickers 1983). Ungrazed but anthropogenically modified savannah composes approximately 15 percent of the area surrounding A'Ukre, although the dominant land cover near A'Ukre is the seasonal dry forest (Malcolm et al. 1999).

A'Ukre was established in 1979. The village founders thought the locale was a good place to make a home. Migrating from the larger village of Kubenkranken with a dwindling population, the founders found the forested environment on the small curve of the Riozinho River inviting. The origins of the village have been told and retold to me many times. *A'Ukre tum* (A'Ukre velho) was the original location. The name A'Ukre was given to the locale a long time ago; it is a name that refers to the sound the fish make under the rocks in the early evening, and it still remains a favored fishing spot. The founders soon found it difficult to make gardens on the hilly landscape and rocks in old A'Ukre. Moving the village a little bit upriver to another gentle bend became what is now referred to as A'Ukre. The forest provided productive lands for growing manioc, sweet potatoes, bananas, and other crops. The river offered a passage for travel, but its rapids promised a refuge from easy access to city life, which is approximately a three-day boat passage that always is long and dangerous in the dry season. The villagers were already familiar with this place. Brazil nut groves were abundant here, as well as certain fruit trees. A number of them had collected nuts for trading in years past. Trails made here would be easy to connect to other well-established routes in the savannah, less than a day's journey away. Situated not far from growing frontier towns as the crow flies, a landing strip would render the services provided by those towns easy to access. Fertile fishing grounds were close, and game animals promised to be abundant.

The group of initial founders began work at once, as I am told. They cleared the land in a small circle not far from the river's edge and were gifted seeds, such as the mangos that currently ring the village, to make the home. The area would offer easy access to the water for bathing, hunting, fishing, and other daily chores. They built houses around the circle and placed a men's house in the center. They began to plant fruit trees surrounding the houses, and then cleared more ground for their horticultural fields. It was a good start, yet not enough. The ground, once cleared, was riddled with rocks that made it hard to weed, maintain, and expand the settled area. The houses were moved a bit farther inland, where the village has remained over the decades. At night, when the sky is jet black and the stars are piercing bright, the houses became dark silhouette cutouts. The sky above looks like it was tailored to the village's size. Family hearths or lights burning bright would give the village a magical, warm glow in the darkness. On such days, while looking up, I would momentarily feel as if I were in a snow globe, with the borders of the world around me almost, but not quite, close enough to touch.

I came to regard A'Ukre as a handsome and familiar village, but first-time visitors to the place often have different reactions. A slightly misshapen plaza area defines A'Ukre, and the village bulges with its growing population, which is approximately 390 residents. When the rainy season comes in August and September, the plaza's hard-baked dirt, which accommodates dancing, turns brown and muddy. Water carves out puddles, and impromptu streams streak across the celebrated central space of the village. Despite its seasonal variability, the plaza,

Figure 3. Village leaders in the men's house.

the homes, and the men's house are the canvas upon which everything else sits, serving as the anchor point from which life radiates inward and outward. In the heart of the village is the men's house, also fondly referred to as the community house; it is a large open building with concrete floors and a fabricated roof. In the past, some of the larger Kayapó villages had two men's houses, one in the east and the other in the west, but at present, most have only one, as in A'Ukre. Many political, ceremonial, and community activities take place here. The men's house, described as akin to "a congress," is an important space for the women, men, and families to gather for ceremonial activities, briefings, radio communication, and many other types of meetings. Young kids have marked their names and phrases as graffiti on the inside. The men's house, as its name suggests, is also a gendered space where men meet daily and routinely but also where kids play soccer, women sometimes—but infrequently—gather, and the community has meetings (figure 3).

When I think of A'Ukre, I think of one particular bright blue house that stands out against all the other weather worn houses, all of which were made of store-bought wood and materials with logging money that flowed in during the 1990s. Families have added porches, verandahs, woodsheds, clotheslines, chicken coops, solar panels, parabolic antennas, and outdoor cooking spots to their rain-stained, gray homes. These modifications distinguish one home from another, and more importantly, are functional open-air additions that provide respite from the almost unbearable midday heat. Outside of this initial ring of homes, more homes populate the area. These houses, a testament to A'Ukre's growing population, are on the east and south sides of the village, uncharacteristically hugging the edges of the main plaza in irregular clumps. But the blue house is the same color as a deep turquoise, similar to the blue yarn that has replaced the crushed bird eggs that the Kayapó used to decorate the faces of small children and others during ceremonies. The house pops with color. Located on one side of the village, it is just one of over thirty-eight houses that are more or less equidistant from the men's house, forming the plaza area and making the village a whole, contained unit.

The house that I lived in during my longest stay in A'Ukre was located near the river across from the pharmacy. Conservation International (CI), an international environmental NGO that had a long-standing presence in the area, built the wattle-and-daub house, which hosted researchers and other visitors. The house had a palm-thatched roof, a large brown window that I could open and close with a hitch, a wood burning stove, a two-burner gas stove, a plastic sink without running water, a pair of shelves, a bench, and a painted tapir on a sign out front. I slept in a small two-person dome tent in the back.

The house was also on the way to the river, a well-traversed path that split 20 m from the river's edge, slicing the bank in two. Tall gray-barked trees with forked branches straddled the two banks and often hosted black vultures, or how community members described them, "those that made the earth good again." In the dry season, the upriver spot was a rocky place where the boats docked and women liked to fish and wash clothes. Downriver, the water was glassy and smooth with deeper cool and warm pockets—also a good spot to fish and bathe. Mist rose from the water in the early morning, one of my favorite times to visit, bathe, or take photos. The river was luxurious; the water was warm in the cold morning air, and in the afternoon it sliced cold on your skin under the baked heat. "Gwaj 'ỳrỳ djwa," I often heard my friends call from my window. And I would see Nhak with her kids and a metal basin full of colorful plastic plates and aluminum pots stacked above, ready for washing. Sometimes, we took a bucket of roasted sweet potatoes down and a couple of spools of fishing wire to fish by the river.

Along the path from the village to the river sits a defunct Brazil nut processing area, a brightly painted pharmacy, and the NGO house I lived in. Today, this space includes a pink and yellow elementary school, a large house built by a local NGO, and a raised Brazil nut drying hut. A payphone that seldom works stands here, too. I was told that an old missionary house used to exist in this spot, as well as a school building that burned down long ago.

Sleeping next to the main village, I often heard their hens and roosters crowing and shuffling in the early morning. One time I found a newborn dog sleeping in the path between the houses; someone's daughter had accidently left it behind. I was often wary of the leaf litter from the mango trees that piled up behind the houses. During the rainy season a bushmaster traversed the path, and during the nights as I moved back and forth from the house to the village, my flashlight often did not penetrate beneath the leaf piles. During the day, though, I welcomed the way the fruit trees provided shady areas so that chairs, blankets, and hammocks could be set up to bead, body paint, or work on other daily tasks.

Flights intermittently but with frequency came in and out of the village. I often went toward the landing strip to greet the pilots, visit the soccer field to watch practice, or get to the fields. The path from my house to the landing strip took me by the chiefs' houses, one of my favorite master craftsman's home, and the house of a lovely elderly couple that helped found the village, who were always up for a visit. All of these houses were made out of locally harvested or sourced materials: wattle-and-daub-brick, palms, or posts, with palm-thatched roofs. As one chief would say, "it is cool and nice in these houses, not hot like the ones the loggers built." Similar to the houses that abutted against mine, the elders and chiefs had mango and coconut trees in their yard. One chief had planted açaí (*Euterpe oleracea*) and buriti palms (*Mauritia flexuosa*). I would walk past genipapo trees (*Genipa americana*), homemade chicken coops, manioc drying on orange tarps, and urucum (*Bixa orellana*) drying on black tarps. I would sometimes see ducks and always bump into sleeping and wandering dogs. I would bob under hanging laundry that crossed between the old houses and the new ones. The satellite dishes gleamed in the sun. Water sparkled as it came out of the spigots where women would wash dishes and clean their feet, and young men freshen up, passing their fingers through their quick-soaked, black hair. The red, blue, and yellow macaw pets always took my breath away— their long, vibrant feathers beautiful wherever they were. From the airstrip, I could cut across to the soccer field to get to the gardens or circle to the top left of the village where the *chakra* was, a location where there were a few houses and lime trees.

The insides of the homes are modest, even sparse, by Anglo-European standards. Matriuxorilocal residences are often multifamily dwellings that provide homes for one to four families. Most have three bedrooms and one to two open areas. The bedrooms have hammocks, tents, or foam mattresses as sleeping areas. Lines are strung up in the homes and filled with the families' clothes. Many have ceremonial necklaces, headdresses, and armbands carefully hung on different nails on the walls. If a firstborn child has been recently born, *pute* (or *Inajá* [*Elaeis oleifera*]) sticks are in the rafters as a constant reminder of the day and the growth of the child. Family photos, catalog cutouts, movie posters, local music shows, and certificates of completion are pasted, stapled, and hung from the walls. Other personal and family items, clothes, shotguns, pipes, handicrafts, fishing materials, oars, and daypacks are also placed here. Mirrors are at times perched on a wall, such as the distinctive one in the house of Nhak.

It was a small mirror framed by orange-colored plastic. I had the same kind, which I had picked up in a nearby town prior to moving to the village.

Open windows filled in by green mosquito netting only let streaming sunlight dimly in. Families might have a car battery powered by solar panels for irregular TV viewing, radio use, or lights in the evening. At times, homemade wooden shelves hold TVs, DVD players, and electronic gadgets. Other shelves hold metal pots, colorful and large multiuse plastic bins, buckets of water, and harvested food. Hand-woven baskets in a variety of sizes hang or lie on the ground. Sweet potatoes and firewood often spill in segmented areas on the floor. The adjacent kitchen hearths often fill the air with a light, smoky smell along with whatever is in the cooking pot. Noise from the plaza area filters in, and murmurs of voices can always be heard in the distance.

To live in A'Ukre was to live in a rich soundscape of life. It is a life marked by ceremonial songs, the clatter of firewood when it hits the ground, radio chatter on one of the Kayapó frequencies, *forró* (Northeastern genre of music in Brazil) and popular hit music, macaw calls, parakeet chirps, and ceremonial crying. Fish splash in the water, and women pound açaí in large pestles and grate manioc. Frogs start to sing at sunset, howler monkeys call in the morning, and planes buzz overhead. Roosters caw and dogs bark. Hammocks creak as they sway, men whoop as they go out to hunt, and women sing to their children. The rich background noise reminds us not to judge affluence by the seemingly spare material surroundings. The wealth that the Kayapó have, both material and immaterial, is not measured by brand names, but by beautiful names along with leadership abilities, expertise in particular and general skill sets, and knowledge of different worlds and ways of being.

Behind the intimate spaces of the household interiors, interconnected backyard gardens form a well-shaded area. In A'Ukre, the long, slender, drooping leaves of mango trees, the fruit-studded crown of the genipapo tree, and the occasional bushy crown of coconut palms dominate. The ground in this area is kept clean, similar to the plaza area, unless some have lapsed on weeding or piling leaf litter. Women maintain *ki* (hearths), spots where they roast sweet potatoes and yams or cook meat or fish with manioc in banana leaves. During the late afternoon, it was common that I would spend time with and see sisters, mothers, and children sitting on blankets, stools, or chairs to chat, body paint their kids, or work on their beads together in the shade of the larger fruit trees. In the dry season or dry moments in the wet season, this area is the preferred space for women to paint each other or paint their husbands or relatives. Families also use the edge of this space to dispose of household garbage, by piling manioc skins, banana peels, cornhusks, and other food and now store-bought debris. Another prominent feature that marks this area are the places set aside for roasting bitter manioc. Three open-air, palm-thatched structures shelter large *fornos* (pans), which rest on top of wooden posts where community members can roast dried bitter manioc. Manioc preparation and cooking areas emit strong smells, a mixture of the smoke and the acrid odor of three-day-old soaked manioc, but the resulting kernel size farinha (roasted bitter manioc) is easy to take on a trek, throw in açaí broth, or eat with Brazil nut milk and bananas.

The health, education, and NGO buildings and their attendant services are part of the daily routines of community members in A'Ukre. Basic services in the community as of this writing include a clinic and sanitary system, and a school, whose educational program is under the purview of municipal governments. In addition, each village has a Fundação Nacional do Índio, or National Indian Foundation (FUNAI), post in a nearby urban center, which addresses financial needs, administrative concerns, or any other business. Not surprisingly, these buildings are symbolically clustered in the same area outside of the village plaza on the way to the river and port areas.

Many colonial and missionary programs in Brazil and elsewhere were designed to destroy the spatial patterning of indigenous villages and required indigenous peoples to organize their village in a way that fit with Western notions of space. For the Church, this enabled priests and pastors to regulate individual souls by undermining cosmological and ceremonial spaces. At the same time, state functionaries could survey, order, and control the population. These "pacification" efforts no longer exist in the same form, but new relationships between indigenous groups and extralocal actors, mostly mediated through FUNAI and the Fundação Nacional de Saúde ([FUNASA] the National Health Foundation), have made certain spatial alterations in villages like A'Ukre that have become permanent fixtures in the landscape. Missionaries have been in A'Ukre in the past, but at this time, there are no outside missionary organizations permanently stationed within the community of A'Ukre, although there are somewhat regular church gatherings in the community led by a local community member, to sing songs and read from the bible.

During the school year, an early morning bell summons young children to the schoolhouse where students receive bilingual instruction and instruction in other areas: science, history, and math. Women and children crowd the clinic at dawn and twilight when it is open. Villagers on their way to and from the river, pharmacy, or school often stop to linger at the NGO house to chat with researchers or visitors who may be in residence. The familiar low hum of an airplane usually gives the villagers enough warning so that someone from each household can meet the plane as it lands on the airstrip and send or receive packages. The most frequent flights are medical in nature, but FUNAI, the local NGO, and other visitors to the area also charter planes to fly in and out.

The well-trafficked areas in the village (the men's house, plaza, households, backyard gardens, school, pharmacy, soccer fields, and landing strips) are hugged by a transitional area where ceremonial preparations take place and where the cemetery is located as well. On one side of the village, trails lead to different riverbanks, bathing areas, and close-by fishing spots. On another, similar trails lead to camping sites, footbridges, impromptu dams from fish-poisoning events, or structures left from forest-based rituals. These spots are reachable by paths that jut out from the central village plaza area or from the river and landing strip. Frequently trafficked areas that require villagers to cross seasonal streams to reach swidden fields or other places need upkeep. Villagers build more permanent, longer-term bridges made of several logs, as well as single-log footbridges. In the height of the dry season, these bridges are barely used. However, as the inland streams swell during the wet season, they are initially welcome and then ultimately indispensable, as the water can reach up to the neck and shoulders, even when traversing the logs several meters above the ground. In conjunction with land-based trails, the river is a well-traversed trail where men of various ages go fishing, families travel, or it can be an access point for hunting, foraging, or ceremonial camps. These trails are likewise seasonal. Beyond and within this area are the swidden fields. The field mosaic is more established and complex, relative to the age and size of the village. Indeed, for more than two decades, villagers in A'Ukre have made this spot their home, laboriously planting, creating, and maintaining the patchy landscape of swidden fields, hunting zones, nearby backyard gardens, and fishing areas that are life-giving today. Past the fields are trekking trails, traveling routes, fishing spots, and hunting areas.

When I try to describe A'Ukre, I often think of sitting with Nhak. I hear her instructing me on how to formally joke with a man across the village. "Louder" she would say if she thought my words did not carry. I recall seeing the outlines of men in the men's house in the early evening or their attentive gaze at the chiefs during different afternoon gatherings. I hear another friend (Iredja) laugh, and I recall how she would poke me in my ribs to make me smile when I was struggling with something, how she would grab my arm to walk across the village, or how she used to sing to me, slowly, so I could learn the song and remember too. I also recall the worried discussions I had with friends about complications for registering for Bolsa Família (a governmental cash-transfer program for young families), hydroelectric construction to the north, illegal miners in the area, uneven cash flow, healthcare, city life, or the state of the United States post-9/11. I recall the names of many Kayapó family members that became part of my extended family network, where they live in A'Ukre or elsewhere, and how they are related to me.

I also find it difficult to write about A'Ukre without mentioning one of its former leaders, Paulinho Payakan. Payakan's story is what initially drew me, thousands of miles away, to A'Ukre. As an undergraduate, in a short but life-changing conversation, my advisor recommended that I consider the Kayapó-Body Shop case as a potential topic for an honors thesis. The Body Shop is a UK-based cosmetic chain that touts "natural" and "ethically produced" products.[5] Body Shop's "Trade Not Aid" Brazil nut oil project became the focus of my undergraduate thesis and started what later was to become a long relationship with the residents of the village of A'Ukre. Paulinho Payakan figured largely in that story and, I learned, in many others. His life history has so captivated scholars and media officials alike that Laura Rabben wrote a book about him and another famous indigenous leader in a work published in 2004. While I have only had a few occasions to meet Payakan in person, to me his presence and the events that surrounded him in the 1980s and 1990s marked A'Ukre as a distinct village in the Kayapó Lands.

Payakan, whose name in Kayapó is a reference to a savannah bird, was born the son of a chief in 1956 (Blanco 2006, 2). Together, Payakan and his father are credited with initially founding A'Ukre in the late 1970s, although others in the village also claim to be village founders. A little over twenty years old when he helped establish A'Ukre, Payakan had come of age at an interesting time in Brazil's history. Along with the usual things that boys and young men learn growing up in a village, Payakan had also worked on the Trans-Amazon Highway, lived in frontier towns in the region, such as Altamira, learned Portuguese, and interacted closely with missionaries (Blanco 2006, 4–5; Rabben 2004). Not long after the creation of A'Ukre, Payakan was among the indigenous leaders who participated in helping draft the 1988 Brazilian Constitution. Payakan was also part of and instrumental in protests that halted the construction of a large-scale hydroelectric dam in the 1980s. Beginning with his visit to Florida and Washington, DC, in 1988 and culminating in a 1989 Altamira protest, his and various groups' efforts briefly stopped the construction of one of the largest dams in the world.

Payakan's active career as one of the leaders from A'Ukre helped forge partnerships and cutting-edge programs that reflected several conservation and indigenous rights trends that had taken hold worldwide in the 1980s and 1990s. When briefly tabulated, these achievements are remarkable. Anita Roddick, the founder of The Body Shop, was so taken by the Kayapó that her company selected two communities to start a Brazil nut oil project. Payakan helped establish an ecological research station near A'Ukre called Pinkaití Ecological Research Station (Pinkaití). This move eventually resulted in a Kayapó program funded by CI. While this program no longer exists in the same form as it did in the early 1990s, it persisted for almost two decades and resulted in a series of projects in the Kayapó Lands meant to benefit communities and conservation alike. Finally, the state legally recognized major portions of the Kayapó Lands through an official process of demarcation, including lands where the village of A'Ukre is located. Even more noteworthy is that these programs were set up when the village was in the middle of experimentation with logging and mining. During those same decades, A'Ukre and many other villages illegally engaged in the sale of broadleaf mahogany (*Swietenia macrophylla*), which brought a substantial and unprecedented amount of wealth to the community before a federal moratorium stopped all illegal logging activities in the area (Zimmerman 2010).

This well-publicized history drew me to the village. Payakan lived in A'Ukre when I traveled there for the first time in 2004, but in subsequent visits, he had moved away. The blue-gray Body Shop building, set between the houses and the river, was a reminder of the project that once was. In 2004, I visited the village as a student in a course jointly hosted by the University of Maryland, CI, and the Kayapó, a testament to relationships built from 1988 onward. The main rectangular ring of the village with homes made of store-bought materials was also a potent reminder of the logging years. Later, after village elders invited me to make A'Ukre my home, Payakan appeared repeatedly on the radio, in newspapers, and in glossy magazines. Certainly, although he was not physically in A'Ukre, his presence was not altogether absent. When the village was initially founded in the late 1970s, many residents had probably not imagined that A'Ukre soon would be instrumental in the subsequent decades that saw advances in indigenous rights, conservation efforts, and sustainable development alternatives, but indeed it has.

For me, A'Ukre is a place between worlds, a borderland where my life and the lives of so many who have become my friends and family have become entangled. And every time I move from there to here or here to there, I find that tears always come. I am saddened as elder women keen when I arrive, I cry with my closest friends as I leave, and I spend many sleepless nights before and after every journey. When I long for A'Ukre, I try to reach Kayapó friends traveling on Skype or I open my desk and take a deep breath in of smoky, urucum- (*Bixa orellana*) dyed wristbands in my drawer. The bands still slightly stain my fingers red when I touch them, the smoke fills my nostrils for the rest of the day, and it is hard to forget A'Ukre, another home.

Making Indigenous Territorialities

Mejkumrei (alt. spelling *Mexkumre*) is a word I frequently heard in A'Ukre, and to a certain extent it captures the way in which the Kayapó peoples make their world meaningful. Mejkumrei means many things; it can signify "great," "good," "hello," or "how are you?" Mejkumrei can be used in a passing phrase to say good-bye or as an adjective to positively describe an event, thing, or experience. It is the first word I teach the students who are traveling to meet the Kayapó. *Mejkumrei* can capture those qualities—*mex* or *mêtch* (beauty), *tycht* (strength), and *âpeii* (work)—that make up a good life and well-being for the Kayapó.

Making

Radical Territories in the Brazilian Amazon brings together three powerful and interlinked frames (making, indigenous, and territorialities) to call attention to what it means to have a mejkumrei life for Kayapó peoples and their pursuit of self-determination during this latest wave of economic liberalization, neo-extractivism, international capital investment, and identity politics. Kayapó peoples make A'Ukre their home through different productive and generative practices that comprise the social, economic, and political fabric of daily life. Throughout the book, I expand on what "making" means in practice and how making occurs through the mutually constituting processes of capital expansion in the region, the rise of sustainable development economies, the persistence of local productive practices, and Kayapó notions of personhood and home. From a political ecology and a feminist political ecology approach, how the Kayapó make their livelihoods and construct personhood is inevitably tied to but not limited or structured by broader landscapes of power, capital, labor, and hierarchical relationships (Blaikie and Brookfield 1987; Robbins 2012; Rocheleau and Roth 2007). This analysis of the Kayapó experience will set the stage for a discussion of the transformative processes that make personhood and place, the intimate geographies of resistance and belonging, the interactions between the state and indigenous populations, the transnationalization of the geopolitical landscape, and, ultimately, the power-laden aspects of the overlapping and complex matrix of territorialities in the region. One central mission of transitional discourses is to redefine the terms well-being and livelihoods in a way that aligns with indigenous cosmovisions, and this is a story of how the Kayapó are doing just that (Escobar 2015; Kallis, Demaria, and D'Alisa 2015).

A legally and constitutionally recognized, indigenous conceptualization of good living has been a platform that many indigenous peoples have struggled for since the late 1980s and early 1990s in Latin America. For instance, in Bolivia, Ecuador, and elsewhere in Latin America the concept of *buen vivir* (good living) has been particularly visible. *Buen vivir* is based on indigenous principles and encompass Quechua (*Sumak Kawsay*), Aymara (*Suma Qamaña*), Guarani (*Ñandereko*), Ashuar (*Shiir waras*), and Mapuche (*Küme Mongen*) worldviews. Yet, despite gains that recognize indigenous lifeways, several critiques to *buen vivir* exist. Those that find fault with *buen vivir* typically do so on two fronts: (1) scholars note that distilling diverse indigenous cosmovisions into a unitary concept proves to be problematic, and (2) *buen vivir* is a practice that has met through engagement with extractivist economies and therefore antithetical to indigenous worlds (Vanhulst and Beling 2014, 56). For example, the extractivist position proposes that social equality and national sovereignty should be strengthened by "endogenous development," and pro-poor governmental programs that promote energy, food, and financial sovereignty instead of a conceptualization of *buen vivir* based on alternative notions of growth and well-being (Guardiola and García-Quero 2014, 178). Despite these critiques, those scholars and activists who envision *buen vivir* as a transformative discourse continue to argue that the concept embraces indigenous worldviews that are "based on the indigenous conception that nature, community and individuals all share the same material and spiritual dimensions" (Guardiola and García-Quero 2014, 177).[6] On a regional level, strong opposition to dominant development paradigms have consolidated in Latin America around the notion of *buen vivir*.

Kayapó peoples' current attempts to make a good life, while arguably situated in similar projects as those of *buen vivir* divorced from large-scale extractivism, are also part of a longer, more violent, engagement with the circulation of capital, all of which have been predicated on extractive economies that serve to transform worlds into different forms of property. The circumstances that created capitalist expansion in the Amazon—remote, "uninhabited" lands in the region; conditions to engage in the cash economy but limited access to markets; and powerful stakeholders who can grab land and make it their own with little to no consequence—provide different opportunities and obstacles for indigenous peoples, such as the Kayapó (Li 2014; Little 2001). People, goods, and labor have remained structured into different processes of production and exchange, generating pronounced racial, ethnic, and spatial consequences. Expansions have been founded upon prejudices that meant to assimilate, eradicate, erode, or dismiss indigenous lifeways. In "frontier" regions, Li (2014) proposes that expansions tend to create unstable but highly lucrative markets, short-term relationships based on labor and extraction rather than long-term stewardship, and a desire to keep the ownership of forest commodities, including the lands where they are located, in the hands of a few.

Capital expansion and restrictive labor can easily become a mechanism for the eradication of local livelihoods and indigenous conceptualizations of well-being. This was argued by Marx, who noted capitalism is a process with transformative power that irrevocably changes the relationships of humans among one another and with other nonhuman beings and objects (Kamenka 1983). Marx anticipated that the rise of capitalism would result in the unilateral proletarianization of labor, which would culminate in a class-based revolution. More than a century later, Marx's analysis of capitalism has provoked a rich canon of literature analyzing modes of production, consumption, and distribution, as well as class-based struggles and commodities, even if his forecast for a class-based revolution has been dimmed by the complexities of the market economy. Yet, in maintaining a focus on sites of production to those of consumption and discard, revisionary notions of Marxism have continued to provide key insights on the marginalization of certain livelihoods over others. Neil Smith (2008, 2) describes, "Marxist theory attempts to explain the specific economic, political, and social structure of society in a given period as the result not of supposedly universal forces (for example, human nature), but as the result of historically specific and contingent process."

In the Brazilian Amazon, capitalist relations have been menacing as their short-term bursts over centuries produced relationships to markets that do not honor customary landscape use or social and spiritual ties to those same places and serve to commoditize the very relational networks that serve as the foundation of social life. Kayapó interactions with outside stakeholders (e.g., state functionaries, extractivists, short-term laborers, and missionaries) were caught up with other projects of pacifying or assimilating indigenous peoples that ultimately devalued their livelihoods and ways of being in favor of opening up landscapes for more powerful actors and capital expansion. William Fisher (2000) characterizes this history as one market by "hollow frontier" politics, where social groups have different access and control over natural resources, which in turn impacts governance, rule, and cyclical economies in the region.

The Kayapó peoples with whom I worked had differing opinions on access to the market and its transformative effects on their livelihoods. The circulation of capital has not always been positive, and many Kayapó leaders and elders see too much emphasis on accumulation and individual gains as dangerous. For example, many elders explained to me that the Kayapó word for money (*pi'o kaprin*) roughly translates as "sad leaf." They said that the word originated from all the pain initially brought by the monetary economy and its associations—dislocation, demoralization, disease, and death. This prominent memory of such associations reflects what the Kayapó peoples have endured as they moved, voluntarily and forcibly, postcolonization. From pacification by attraction methods in the early 1900s that brought exchanges in beads, machetes, and other items for Brazil nuts to experimenting with illegal logging industries in the 1990s, informal and extractive economies have circulated among and influenced Kayapó communities for decades.

Development in the region around where the Kayapó live, and what has caused them much pain, has in part followed a worldwide pattern of development, or development with a big "D" as Lawson (2007) describes it. Originally part of modernization projects in the post-World War II era, development schemes were considered universal panaceas that would alleviate poverty, inequality, and marginality in what was then referred to as the Third World. James Scott (1998) argues that during this period, which he called the high modernist era, nation-states began to organize locales into a standardized grid as part of an attempt to homogenize the cultural terrain into a unified national project tied to a ready-made national, territorial homeland. Many of these programs helped create new types of spatial marginalization. Certainly, the Kayapó in the 1900s were entangled in Brazil's modernization process, which did not account for the heterogeneity of lifeways and worldviews practiced on the ground (Escobar 1995; Vandergeest and Peluso 1995).

Yet, market engagement has also become a highly contested part of a larger project for sustainable futures where the retention of local lifeways are seen as compliments to developing robust local economies in the face of dramatic change. More recently, Kayapó communities have created sustainable development programs and indigenous media projects; they have also sent their youth to cities to receive a high school education to eventually land employment in their village. Their employment opportunities and cash-income opportunities remain diverse: salaried positions with local NGOs and governmental agencies, sale of NTFPs and handicrafts, participating in governmental welfare or conditional cash transfer programs, and other occasional seasonal activities that bring them income. Capitalist relationships in this way do not always result in a loss, and the Kayapó with whom I worked envisioned entry into and access to markets as a mixed, if dangerous, relationship (see DeHart 2010; Fisher 2000; Gordon 2006; Kramer 2006). This is similar to other scholars who have also highlighted how local groups are agentive in their market practices—what Larson (1998) identifies as "adaptive vitality" and Greene (2009) "customization" in other Latin American contexts. For the Kayapó, market engagement often has been part of a process of incorporating Western goods into locally relevant frames of meaning and signification, thus informing self-determination projects.

As the Kayapó have come to make the homeland that is theirs today, their land has been a terrain shaped not only by these top–down agendas—pacification and developmentalist efforts—but also by subsistence and other economies of well-being that provide the resources and context that make Kayapó communities and people whole. Bebbington (2000, 498) reminds us that "making a living, making living meaningful, and struggling for the rights and the possibility of doing both are all related." The production of Kayapó livelihoods and the concept of being Kayapó—beautiful and whole—are tied to another process wholly outside of projects of modernity, development, and late liberalism. In spite of dramatic shifts, Kayapó communities have continued to diversify their foodways and rely on local productive practices that guide harvest cycles but also intersect with individual rites of passage and community-wide events. Kayapó peoples have continued to persist, forging their livelihoods in a way that aligns with local sensibilities of personhood and the production of community life. Harvesting found or cultivated plants, nuts, and fibers and then creating baskets, weaving cotton bands for children, applying body paint, and crafting ceremonial items are critical skills that mark an individual's passage from a young child into an adult. Similarly, practices that comprise daily life— planting sweet potatoes, manioc, beans, corn, and papaya; cultivating mango in backyard gardens; foraging for açaí, Brazil nuts, and other fruits; fishing in the rivers for *tucunaré*, *pintado*, and *ibê*; and hunting for peccary, tapir, and deer— are defined by the rhythms of the wet and dry seasons. An elder chief once noted to me that founding villages and making a supportive landscape for the community require *àpeii tycht* (hard work). *Mari mêtch* (those that know well) know their land well; they know how to fish well, how to garden well, and how to make valued ceremonial and quotidian objects; they are valued members of community life, cultivating a rich nexus of lifeways for their people.

In making their worlds mejkumrei, Kayapó communities also fabricate their social lives where material and immaterial objects are part of the production of personhood and conviviality over time and space. Kayapó personhood is made over the course of a lifetime; villagers complete important rites of passage, learn new skill sets, become name-recipients and name-givers, and potentially rise to new leadership positions. In part, this lifelong journey is encoded in the social relations that make the bonds of daily life—the *ĩ* or substance that is shared between parents, children, and other relatives, and *karon*, the vital substance of people (Fisher 2003; Lea 2012, 405). *Karon*, which can be translated as "image is the soul" as Lea (2012, 47) points out, can also be a photo, a map, or a shadow. The complex system of those ceremonial prerogatives that belong simultaneously to individuals and matrihouseholds (such as *nekrêtch*, alternative spelling *nekrej*, *nekretx*), as Lea (2012) illustrates, also offers a complex web from which social life is produced and sustained. *Kukradjà*, which glosses as "culture" or "knowledge," is a term that captures the traditions, songs, dances, and things that make up Kayapó worlds. *Kukradjà* is experiential and performative, circulated, and transmitted, especially in ceremonies and is what makes the Kayapó Mebêngôkre. *Kukradjà* also are the rules and norms that pattern exchange, whether from a particularly large harvest, within the confines of ceremonial practices, or within the context of diplomacy and warfare. Naming ceremonies are perhaps the most pronounced example of intersubjective relations, which animate the production of personhood, the domestication of objects, and human–nonhuman relations. Kayapó lifeworlds then are made of situated biographies, local cosmologies, and experiential practice gained by transformative interactions with human and nonhuman beings (supernatural and other) over time.

The materials and materialities of everyday life also serve as substantive contributions to personhood for Kayapó individuals. In a review of indigenous peoples' engagement with objects, Santos-Granero (2009b, 3) proposes three ways to understand the materiality of making life in the Amazon region: the subjective, social, and historical lives of things. These three frameworks, namely, object subjectivities, human–object interactions, and histories of objects (source materials, fabrication, giving, and exchanging), encompass the many ways through which objects, and their residual and agentive capacities, circulate within indigenous communities. For the Kayapó peoples, the domestication of objects from other external actors, whether they are indigenous groups, non-indigenous outsiders, or other beings and entities, occurs in multiple ways to produce the sociality of village life and personhood over time. This process is part of passing down *nekrêtch* and nonmaterial and material things that relations give to future generations through a complex process of the transference of ownership (see Lea 2012). It is rooted in the creative process of incorporating new objects, ideas, and practices into village life, such as songs, exterior goods (e.g., beads), animal bones and teeth, forest nuts, and shells from rivers.[7]

Kayapó sensibilities of being Kayapó, human, and whole, and the "production" or making of self and communities are distinct from but inevitably connected to productive practices and broader-scale processes in the region. As described in the next section, expressions of indigeneity play upon these local significations within wider frames of legibility.

The examples described here complicate the assertion that indigenous pathways to justice will inevitably be overwhelmed by the uneven landscape that economic liberalization, neoextractivist regimes, and globalization engenders. Kayapó peoples make their livelihoods by cultivating livelihood activities that accommodate for different market, nonmarket, unpaid, wage and cash-income opportunities whether gained from the state, NGOs, corporations, informal venues, or a complex assemblage of interactions among these different sectors (See Gibson-Graham 2008). Productive practices that guide daily life, whether subsistence or market based, and the fabrication of personhood are dialogic, relational processes that guide each other. At present, the Kayapó's intention to explore different market opportunities and diversify their livelihood strategies are caught up in the processes of conservation, extraction, and cultural recognition, all of which are part of development, sustainable or otherwise, in the Amazon region.

Indigenous, Indigeneity, Índio/a

For the Kayapó, being indigenous is a complex reality. Shuttling between using the terms *povos indígenas* (indigenous people), *índios* (Indians), Kayapó, and Mebêngôkre, Kayapó peoples engage in the global panindigenous movement, regional indigenous networks, local politics of identification, as well as legalistic identity claims that are directly linked to territorial rights. The cultural politics of identity, then, bears strongly on the outcomes of territorial recognition and contested geographies of self-determination. As a politically active group in Brazil, Kayapó leaders and community members draw from global conversations on being indigenous in their activism, both within and without the community. Being "indigenous" for the Kayapó today reflects a shared political and legal positioning among many different indigenous peoples over the past several decades that has been established by international and national networks, grassroots movements, and even the common histories of violence and displacement (Field 2009; Shanley 2015). In Latin America and elsewhere this has fostered a "racial resurgence" of "indigenousness" after years of assimilationist policies to make way for indigenous republics, multiethnic states, and hard-won rights (Postero 2007; Warren 2001).

In *Origins of Indigenism*, Ronald Niezen (2003, 4) describes how "indigenous peoples" developed as a legal term and a recognized identity in the international sphere. He, like Shanley (2015), has argued that the United Nations and the International Labour Organization's Convention No. 169 have played an especially important role in creating a global "indigenism" where communities who share histories of exploitation, ethnocide, and marginalization have come together in an international movement. For example, in July of 2000 the United Nations created the Permanent Forum on Indigenous Issues, a working forum proposed as early as the 1990s, to serve as an advisory body that raises awareness on a range of topics. The United Nations also proclaimed the first international decade of Indigenous Peoples in 1993, and in consideration of the pressing issues that indigenous peoples continuously face, declared a second in 2005. In 2013 the Summit of the Peoples of Latin America, the Caribbean, and Europe took place in Santiago, Chile. During the past several years, The Centro Latin Americano de Ecología Social (The Latin American Center of Social Ecology) also has become a key site for activism (Escobar 2015, 455). In September 2014, the first World Conference on Indigenous Peoples was held and indigenous peoples are now granted observer status at major global environmental governance meetings, such as the annual Conference of the Parties to the United Nations Framework Convention on Climate Change (UNFCCC) meetings. These are a few of the ways that indigenous rights and recognition have taken place in the twenty-first century to forge a web of regional and international movement of concerned groups and citizens as well as create multilevel governance regimes that acknowledge indigenous participation.

Carneiro da Cunha and Almeida (2000, 316) applaud the way in which indigenous groups have been expert at negotiating these contemporary legal challenges and labels that they have brought with them.

> Terms such as "Indian," "indigenous," "tribal," "native," "aboriginal," and "mixed blood" are all products of the metropolis, generated by encounter. And yet, artificial and generic as they were at the time of their creation, these labels have progressively come to be "inhabited" by flesh-and-blood people. This has sometimes been the outcome of the elevation of these terms to a legal or administrative status. What is remarkable, however, is that as often as not, the forced inhabitants of them were able to seize these highly prejudiced categories and turn them into banners for mobilization.

Inevitably, projects of sovereignty and self-determination remain a story of inclusion and exclusion for indigenous peoples. For the Kayapó, the question of being indigenous in Brazil, as Carneiro da Cunha and Almeida pointed out, is complicated. Contrary to other colonial regimes, in Brazil, miscegenation or "mixing" was encouraged to "civilize" indigenous individuals early on (Warren 2001, 69). While these ideas fell out of favor by the mid-twentieth century, the impacts of miscegenation have persisted in different ways. Today, indigenous peoples simultaneously occupy multiple contradictory positions as citizens and as tribal nations in legal, material, and ideological arenas. Since the twentieth century, Brazil has marshaled the past to cultivate a national narrative of where "racial democracy was to be displayed, but indigenous socioeconomic marginality obscured" (Garfield 2001, 134). Acculturation often has been proposed as a redemptive pathway to productive citizenship for indigenous individuals, similar to other Latin American *indigenismo* policies (Peña 2005).

In spite of popular discourses surrounding a shared racial past, indigenous peoples have a particular legal status in Brazil. Since Brazil's independence and up to the 1970s, many policies toward and everyday discourses on indigenous groups have highlighted their distinctive position in society. For example, the 1916 Civil Code and subsequent statutes outlined the concept of *tutela* (guardianship), which states that the FUNAI has legal responsibility over indigenous groups, who are considered "relatively capable" citizens (Carneiro da Cunha and Almeida 2000). This clause and FUNAI's role in indigenous affairs is still under debate today, but it legally treats indigenous groups differently from other nonindigenous Brazilian citizens, which diverges from a national discourse that promotes an identity founded on racial mixing.

As in other Latin American countries, Brazil moved from authoritarian rule to a postauthoritarian state in 1988. For peoples like the Kayapó, democratic rule and the embracement of neodevelopmental policies have been mixed. The post-1980s period in Brazil is one that has been "productive" for indigenous groups, as they gained political clout through special provisions for indigenous rights outlined in the newly ratified constitution, but also "difficult" and troublesome (Conklin 2002, 1051–52). This productivity manifested itself in the formulation of several civil society organizations and governing bodies, which represented individual peoples in specific regions, as well as agencies that coordinated across indigenous peoples in vast areas of the Amazon and Latin America. For example, the Coordinator of Indigenous Organizations in the Amazon River Basin was founded in Lima, Peru, in 1982. In 1989, the Coordination of the Indigenous Organizations of the Brazilian Amazon was launched, and as of the current writing, it has more than 160 different indigenous groups as members. A number of organizations also emerged to address specific concerns of indigenous women. In the 1990s, Kayapó communities developed their own associations and community–NGO partnerships; they also deliberated on whether to join larger, regional organizations.

Kayapó communities and then-emerging associations sought to achieve different types of recognition and gain traction on different projects to secure their futures, including rights-based recognition, territorial security, and market possibilities. Kayapó peoples directed most of their efforts at territorial rights, although goals to demarcate additional parcels of land continue today. The same federal policies that supported indigenous demarcation efforts aided in these successes coincided with federal and state policies in Pará and Mato

Grosso that sought to expand the reach of the market and state farther, thereby exacerbating deforestation and entrenching corporate interests in the region (Hecht 2011). What is more, during this time, the government was downsizing, and FUNAI was broken apart; it is currently under the purview of various ministries. This decentralization and diffusive politics of governance has made it extremely tricky for indigenous individuals to navigate the fragmented bureaucratic system to solve pressing and often critical and time-sensitive service needs and promote self-administration (health, education, food, etc.). The Kayapó I worked with repeatedly said that the era when FUNAI was "strong" was over; current FUNAI representatives have to be particularly savvy in helping Kayapó peoples with their desires as the agency has limited funding.

As a politically active group in Brazil, Kayapó leaders and community members draw from these state-defined and international recognized conversations about being indigenous in their activism both within and without the community. Top-down notions of "development," and "modernity" are often considered in direct opposition to indigenous interests or equated with corruption or the slow erasure of indigenous identities. As described previously, Kayapó negotiations of market possibilities, access to cash income, and tense but ongoing relationships with the state show that these relationships do not necessarily negate indigenous identities or projects. Many Kayapó consultants in A'Ukre consistently told me that they "have not forgotten" their culture or their traditions, and that they are still Kayapó despite decades of change. Kayapó leaders have also cultivated a strong visual language of "being indigenous" in different public spaces and venues of protest, and in many cases, are popularly referenced as some of the most recognized indigenous peoples in Brazil. This type of politicking has become effective at garnering public attention and has created spaces where Kayapó concerns are heard; simultaneously, it has offered different images and imaginings, both positive and troublesome, of what indigenous peoples should look like.

Yet, the Kayapó, while aware of the legal implications of indigenous identification, they also consider their identities determined by much more than the state or international conventions. Andrew Canessa (2012, 4) argues that indigenous identities and their associated politics are "highly contingent" and "thoroughly imbricated with gendered, racial, and linguistic identities and informed by historical consciousness." Similarly, Michael Cepek (2012, 66) shows that for Cofán peoples "the structure of Cofán identity is not static or constraining. Rather there is an active effort to add essential elements to it without losing what is already indexed." Whereas national and international indigenous movements often conceive of "being indigenous" as an identity that one does or does not have, for many indigenous people, identity is a lifelong process and not merely a legal term or a contemporary moment. Identities are influenced by the historically entrenched relationships between the colonizer and colonized that still permeate daily life, the racially charged landscapes of state-making and conservation programs, and the gendered politics of activism. Importantly, for the Kayapó, their notion of identity is based on a series of practices and relationships (material and immaterial) over time that creates personhood. Personhood is the collection of aspects that make up individual lives, "gender, generation, names and *nekretx*, matrihouseholds, relatives, formal friends, etc." (Lea 2012, 53) as well as different practices, individual and collective, that constitute the conviviality of daily life.

The framework of making indigenous territorialities presented within *Radical Territories in The Brazilian Amazon* draws on this history and these recent trends in indigenous politics to illuminate how current struggles are inevitably entangled in the politics of identity and indigeneity, the current conservation–development matrix, environmental governance strategies, and Kayapó notions of personhood. From the landmark case of the United Nation backing the rights of indigenous peoples in 2007 to a new Kayapó website that supports the efforts (e.g., see www.raoni.com), these multinational, multicultural, and multimedia imaginings of indigenous peoples represent the complex landscape of "indigenous alterity," as Bessire and Bond (2014, 441) put it, and its linkages to justice efforts, rights, and self-determination. Part of what I show in this book is that land, home, territory, space, and place are all part of the fabric of the contemporary politics of indigeneity, and the Kayapó have become astute "border crossers," fluidly traversing through these layered politics of identity on a daily basis.

Territorialities

In a 2012 YouTube interview, a famous Kayapó chief, Raoni, declared that the "main issue in my region [is to] secure our land and get it demarcated." While pithy, Raoni pinpointed in this statement that Kayapó efforts at addressing justice concerns have largely been through a struggle for territory. In highlighting indigenous land rights, Raoni outlined a broad trend that has taken place within Latin America's democratic turn and pink tide politics, in which specific forms of territorial control is awarded to indigenous, Afro-descendent, and other marginalized populations. That the Kayapó are still attempting to demarcate swaths of their territory more than twenty years after the ratification of the 1988 constitution reflects the hold of spatial politics on indigenous geographies. Neodevelopmentalist and post-neoliberal policies in the region have supported the conversion and privatization of land for agro-industrial and extractive industries, which rely on policies that are predicated upon what Harvey (2003) calls "accumulation by dispossession." In this sense, Raoni's statement amplifies the exclusion of indigenous voices in key policy decisions, including the Kayapó's, and their persistence in guaranteeing a more inclusive politics through engaging with municipal, state, and international stakeholders, as well as their creation of counterspaces and contentious politics that make room for indigenous political authority. Raoni's vision, which is an appeal to global audiences vis-à-vis a common multimedia platform, is reflective of postauthoritarian and post-neoliberal natures where indigenous leaders often frame land rights in multiscalar contexts to assert their distinctive position in articulating an indigenous vision of sovereign futures. In this case, Raoni's statement could be linked to global concerns on environmental governance, carbon sequestration, biodiversity protection, best forestry practices, or the conservation of international human patrimony. What Raoni did not address, and what might not be as readily apparent, are the corresponding epistemological and ontological tensions inherent between indigenous cosmovisions of place and jurisdictional understandings of enclosure, property, and rights that are embodied in demarcation efforts.

As such, Raoni's statement captures one of the arguments put forth in this book: the territorialities that shape geopolitical and socioenvironmental landscapes remain essential to understanding Kayapó projects for self-determination and sovereignty. Territorialities are not simply about land and resources but also about the histories and practices that constitute a place, as well as the jurisdictional and legal realities of these place-making practices.[8] Chandra Mukerji (2002, 1) sums it up nicely: "Looking at where land becomes visibly enrolled into culture . . . is fundamental to social analysis—not just for doing cultural history but for analyzing regimes of power." Uncovering these different territorial projects, and their material, symbolic, and ideological dimensions, draws attention to the political, economic, and historical realties that have privileged certain types of territorial expressions and their associated imaginaries. At the same time, an attention to territorialities has the potential to rupture the forces behind hegemonic spatializations of land, territory, and home in order to make Kayapó visions for sustainable futures and alternative forms of development legible. Within this context, I ask this: who makes, owns, produces, and imagines territory and place?

In the late 1980s, the answers to these questions seemed to be rooted in the already mentioned postauthoritarian context in Latin America, where new democracies, under the watchful eye of burgeoning and vibrant social movements, constitutionally recognized indigenous and communal land rights while also emphasizing protected units as key to combating deforestation and conserving national patrimony. Legal recognition of collective land rights and the ramping up of the demarcation of conservation units have had significant impact on land use and land change. Across Latin America, an estimated 2,344 Indigenous Territories and 610 protected areas cover the region (Walker et al. 2014). From a conservationist perspective, indigenous land demarcation overlapped with projects to reduce deforestation, protect biodiversity, and manage natural resources. This trend was especially true in the Brazilian Amazon, where Indigenous Lands in certain states became key conservation units. In the case of the Kayapó, their successful demarcation of a large portion of their lands in the mid-1990s buffered widespread deforestation in the state of Pará, amid the state's favorable conditions for intensified agricultural expansion and land privatization. Offen (2003) and Bryan (2012) call this phenomenon the "territorial turn," where recognition of land rights has been the centerpiece of neoliberalism and post-neoliberal politics in Latin America.

Neoliberal projects have been processes that have spatially reshaped land, labor, and peoples across the globe. According to Deleuze and Guattari (1987), globalization produces different injustices through reterritorialization and deterritorialization processes centered on the privatization of land, expropriation of territory, and transformation of livelihood patterns (Elden 2006). In Brazil, massive development projects carried out in the past four decades have had pronounced spatial consequences on indigenous livelihoods. At the same time, as policies in Latin America have turned toward post-neoliberalism and neoextractivism, we have seen the region blossom "as a focal region with respect to political and intellectual 'resistance' and the articulation of alternatives" (Harris and Roa-García 2013, 22). These twin and seemingly contradictory agendas (neoliberalism and resistance) reflect different projects of de- and reterritorialization.

In Brazil, the 1988 Constitution reflects this "territorial turn" of Latin America in different ways. On the one hand, the constitution embraced an agenda that sought to reduce deforestation, convert land to protected units and indigenous reserves, promote alternative development strategies, and strive for socioecological sustainability. On the other hand, structural adjustment programs, the transformation of state enterprises into private or multinational conglomerates, and privatization of resources and land have accelerated investment in agriculture, silviculture, mining, logging, oil, and other industries (Hecht 2011). Renewed interest in green energy linked to national sovereignty reinvigorated large-scale development plans; these plans have roots in the 1960s and have now been transformed into neodevelopmental concerns about state security in the crisis-driven age of risk societies (Beck 1992; Smith 2008). These initiatives are fueled by national projects for the patrimonialization of resources, pricing of nature, and historical processes of dispossession and fragmentation. This instance is but one case showing the new global mosaic as being patterned by intensified extraction and dramatic territorial transformations countered by robust participation and resistance.

From the conservationist perspective, the "territorial turn" in Brazil reflects the transformation of a militarized frontier zone driven by forest product markets to one that is dominated by large-scale extractivist and agro-ranching economies, as well as by protected zones, alternative economies, and diverse livelihood strategies. It has also provided a space for indigenous and conservationist concerns to be linked through different dreamtimes of environmentalism, to borrow Heatherington's (2010) phrase, which is how statements like Raoni's above is inevitably entangled with broader conversations on climate change, water sovereignty, and energy security. Moreover, the "territorial turn" has corresponded with a trend toward the devolution and deregulation of forestry and natural resource governance to community control; a trend that Erazo (2013) identifies as key to understanding indigenous politics. These processes have placed heavy emphasis on community conservation alliances, cooperative and community-based forestry, and natural resource management regimes.

In 1987, the Brundtland Commission report closely followed by the 1992 United Nations Conference on Environment and Development in Rio de Janeiro marshaled a new era dominated by the theme of sustainable development, which linked poverty alleviation with conservation concerns. Post 1990s, community–conservation partnerships, comanagement regimes, and integrated conservation and development programs became more common (Kremen, Merenlender, and Murphy 1994; Wells and Brandon 1993). In Brazil, the decentralization of natural resource management governance from federal to state and municipal also set the conditions for a rise in participatory approaches to conservation, especially those mediated by NGOs (Larson and Soto 2008).

Beth Conklin and Laura Graham (1995) note that indigenous–conservation relationships have been possible because of a "shifting middle ground" that has emerged as a space upon which indigenous and other stakeholders draw clear directives of mutual concern.[9] The "middle ground" denotes the "shifting" positions that enable diverse actors to make temporary, mutually beneficial arrangements among all interested parties. In this case, the governance of indigenous territories has resulted in indigenous groups drawing upon nationalistic and environmental discourses to strengthen or advocate their claims to their lands and the natural resources they depend upon for their livelihoods. In the process, many communities have countered romantic imaginings of their territories with local understandings about their home, or what they have come to call their homeland after centuries of forced relocation, discrimination, and demoralization. The recognition that resource-dependent communities are constrained by, but also actively alter, their environments has also highlighted the different values and spiritual practices that cultural groups assign to the same biophysical setting. Further, a global concern for human rights has energized discussions over indigenous issues, collective rights, and possibilities for more equitable livelihoods (Brown 2003). As mentioned above, international institutions, such as the United Nations Permanent Forum on Indigenous Issues, and other governing bodies on the establishment of rights have launched new international governance norms, in which states can be held accountable for illegal activities (see Harris and Roa-García 2013, 21). In the process, cultural rights have emerged as a critical political platform, and the spatial aspects of those rights, such as sacred spaces, monuments, and ceremonial practices, are increasingly recognized.

Steven Rubenstein (2001) argues that excavating these different territorialities inevitably demonstrates that indigenous sovereignty, state-making territorial projects, and conservation-based governance are not mutually exclusive of one another.[10] Instead, the intertwined histories of state-defined legal homelands and indigenous efforts to maintain or demarcate a homeland involve a process in which multiple stakeholders and indigenous peoples fight for the determination of land use, ownership, and management. As Rubenstein pointed out, simply considering indigenous lands as bounded homelands or federal protected areas is inherently problematic. The sharp lines of protected area boundaries that now contour the Earth tend to flatten the lived realities of everyday peoples and define their livelihoods within the confines of conservationist concerns, state agendas, or market logics.

Leilani Holmes (2000, 46) argues, "political/social history does not exist in a different realm from indigenous cosmology; rather it intersects with that cosmology." Holmes (2000, 46) explains that in Hawaii, relationships to land is expressed through notions of *aloha a'aina* (love of the land) and *malama 'aina* (taking care of the land). Among the Mamaindê peoples, Miller (2013) notes that it was a child that opened a gourd to release the night patterning the world that we see today. Gregory Cajete (2000, 186) counsels that Native peoples see their relationship with place as one "that [can] only be described as 'ensoulment.' . . . it is from this orientation that Indian people developed 'responsibilities' to the land and all living things." While working with Australian aboriginal peoples, Deborah Bird Rose (1996, 8) found that "country is multidimensional—it consists of people, animals, plants, Dreamings; underground, earth, soils, minerals and waters, surface water, and air. There is sea country and land country; in some areas people talk about sky country." While these quotes, as presented here, are incomplete representations of the many cosmologies of indigenous peoples, they remind us that late liberal logics are not the only way of being in the world. The postauthoritarian turn in Latin America then is one that is more than the legal recognition of territory but also about recognition of indigenous cosmovisions, which structure their engagements with territories and territorialities.

For Kayapó communities and individuals I worked with, their *pyka* (homes and lands) in A'Ukre were part of separate but overlapping projects of making place in the Amazon region. These projects were embedded in their own cosmovisions of place that linked sky to land, which oriented the spatial composition of the village, as well as patterned relationships among people, objects, animals, and plants. Kayapó peoples saw their territory as a vast expanse of lands and places that were not and could never be captured within the confines of their current homeland. As Simpson (2014, 11) has argued, "like Indigenous bodies, Indigenous sovereignties and Indigenous political orders prevail within and apart from settler governance." At the same time, the individuals I spoke with placed great value on the gains they had made to secure their current legally recognized territory and the futures it promised. They forged community–NGO relationships to embark on projects of territorial surveillance and enforcement. Community members also initiated sustainable development projects to bolster alternative development strategies. Kayapó efforts were, as Holmes noted, one in which the cosmological is not separated from the political. Kayapó projects aimed at territorial recognition are resonated in the statement that Mapuche leaders Pablo Marimán, Sergio Caniuqueo, Jose Millalén, and Rodrigo Levil (2014, np, italics in original) made: "We are currently undergoing a process that some have dominated the reconstruction of *territorial identities*. . . . They span the gamut from the repositioning of traditional *Mapuche* leadership, to a process of cultural reconstruction that embraces ceremonies in their more original meaning and structure, in order to create a public space where *Mapuches* can express their religiosity and transmit modes of learning as a People."

Similar to the finding of Marimán et al. (2014), territorial demarcation for the Kayapó peoples is a much larger project than legal recognition but one that hinges on making indigenous territorialities. It is tied to local cosmovisions for sustainable futures; it is part of a challenge to monolithic narratives of the Amazon region. It problematizes place-bound notions of indigenous peoples and also pushes for a reconsideration of indigeneity that removes the concept from the constraints of an oppositional binary of indigenousness as inextricably linked to a singular, static locale or to a pan-indigenous identity removed from the particularities of place. It is a fight for self-determination and justice.

Worldwide transformations in spatial configurations certainly have not gone unnoticed by the Kayapó, and they have not gone unnoticed by other indigenous groups around the globe, all of whom have collectively endured violent and demoralizing histories of ethnocide, the material conversion of territory into property, and the ideological transformation of territory into imagined elsewheres. This book is also about understanding how Kayapó peoples negotiate a political process to decide the fate of their land (space and place), their resources, and their place-making practices. Kayapó efforts to live in and retain their territory continue to be fueled by a wide range of changing actors and political and economic restructuring, but the Kayapó's efforts are increasingly performed against the backdrop of ideas that cement together concepts of territory, home, place, memory, and identity. The success of these efforts is largely a result of the new tensions between indigenous territorialities reflected in global processes and local sensibilities.

Loose in the World

By noting that this research centers on territorialities, I am also referring to the many "places" that research takes place (Zanotti and Palomino-Schalscha 2015).

Influenced by Gloria Anzaldúa, bell hooks, and Mary Louis Pratt's seminal works on borderlands, spaces, and the contact zone, many scholars seeking to define the research experience draw upon spatial metaphors to describe a new terrain of practice (See Larsen and Johnson 2012). For example, using the concept of the "contact zone," Manathunga (2009, 166) argues that postcolonial theory has the power to address "symbolic violence, exploitation, and assimilation that occur when researchers or the research system do not work sensitively and equitably across these cultural borderlands." Haig-Brown (2003, 416) presents the concept of "impossible knowledge" or knowledge "that is beyond our grasp because of the limits of our language and our lived experience." Impossible knowledge is part of the pathway to conducting respectful and meaningful research, where research participants do not have to conform to the Western research protocols but rather create a mutual space for sharing. Hermes (1998) argues that research with indigenous communities should be a "situated response" rather than a prescribed formula for culturally sensitive or community-based work. In proposing "Circle as Methodology," Graveline (2000, 364) emphasizes being self-reflective, culturally located, listening respectfully, and "to "choose words with care and thoughtfulness." Marisol de la Cadena (2015) calls for "co-laboring" to create relational spaces of engagement. The relationship that researchers have with the people whom they work with is a complex topography and frequently calls up questions of representation (either via written or more visual forms), and power. Many anthropologists who write texts today, myself included, grapple with the positivist and essentializing past where anthropology was questionably the handmaiden of colonialism (Di Leonardo 1998). Even when drawing from decades of intellectual grappling, poststructural examination, and textual experimentation set to decolonize the field, scholars find the anthropology's history to be tense and the practice itself to be, as Donna Haraway (1988) suggested, a "partial" endeavor. Language and power can never be completely decoupled. The relationship exists, no matter how experimental the final product becomes or reflexivity pronounced.[11]

I consider stories powerful things and anthropological works as texts that translate, interpret, and voice life experiences (Asad 1975; Behar 1996; Chakrabarty 2000; Hymes 1974; Viseweswaran 1994). I do not use the term "story" lightly. Working alongside the Kayapó peoples, one is quick to learn what Thomas King said so succinctly, that "the truth about stories is that's all we are" (King 2003, 3). King further advised that stories are at once wondrous and dangerous. You "have to be careful with the stories that you tell. And you have to watch out for the stories that you are told" because "once a story is told, it cannot be called back. Once told, it is loose in the world" (King 2003, 3). I consider this book both wondrous and dangerous. Wondrous because at its core it celebrates the way in which Kayapó resist, subvert, and negotiate dominant structures of power as they forge their livelihoods in a postcolonial, democratic context that seems to be simultaneously celebratory and hostile to their life-ways. Dangerous because, as with any work suspended in words and pages, it is caught in time and crafted in a form of storytelling that is antithetical to many living, breathing, storytelling traditions. It is true that this work is inevitably a product of my own positionality and life experiences, disciplinary expectations, and community commitments as much as it is the result of a scholarly pursuit.

Following the impulses of critical ethnography, my approach to writing can only be described as one of hope and care. Coombes, Johnson, and Howitt (2014, 95) suggest that research has the possibility to create "a new relational ethics which unsettles any remaining binaries that survived the qualitative revolution in human geography: ethics becomes method; data become life; landscape becomes author; participants become family." Drawing attention to the "affective, performative, and emotionally invested research," they show how research is relational and that there are different types of labor required to partner with communities—preparations, ethics, emotional labor, and other considerations involved (ibid.). In Brazil, this is a multistep process that can take several months to accomplish and in other cases, several years. The Brazilian government requires foreign researchers, such as me, to acquire a research permit and research visa. The research permit is granted after submission of a lengthy application to FUNAI, the National Council for Scientific and Technological Development (CNPq), and more recently, Council for Genetic Resources (CGEN). A foreign researcher must collaborate with a Brazilian scholar from her/his same discipline to apply for these approvals and permits. Once the research permit is approved, the next step is to apply for a research visa. This step demands another application process with several supplemental documents, including those received from FUNAI, CNPq, and CGEN.

In addition to completing these steps, anthropologists are bound by different professional and institutional ethical requirements. The American Anthropological Association outlines a series of ethical guidelines that anthropologists should follow (see http://www.aaanet.org/issues/policy-advocacy/code-of-ethics.cfm). Moreover, universities require researchers working with people to apply to an Institutional Review Board (IRB). The IRB approval of an application deems "human subjects" research appropriate and culturally sensitive, and approves different methods of informed consent. The language that researchers are required to comply with during the application process is highly technical, and more often than not it fails to reflect the way in which anthropologists approach working with communities. The term "human subjects" seems to beckon comment from Vine Deloria, Jr., a scholar and activist, who has criticized anthropologists for making American Indian groups the "zoo" from which they conduct research (Deloria Jr. 1969; also see Biolsi 1997). Discussing people as "subjects" rather than individuals relegates them to objects—people to be "targeted" and samples to "recruit." This aspect, too, shows a language of power.

Nevertheless, IRBs are required, and for important reasons, even if the language used is less than desired. Other preparations are also required. Prior to research, most anthropologists have already read the relevant literature, learned another language, obtained grants and other funding, and sought the advice of knowledgeable individuals. Before all of this, researchers should be in touch with the community and individuals with whom they would like to collaborate. In my case, I talked with the community of A'Ukre. I asked for their support and guidance on working with them. Without their express permission, I could not have participated in their lives the way that I did. Certainly, I could not have had the honor to participate at all.

I chose to include the steps required to conduct research and the vulnerabilities involved to make legible to the readers the jagged process in which knowledge, which is separate from but linked to committed scholarship, is categorized, justified, legitimized, and produced. Additionally, all of the forms, permits, preparations, and codes, which regulate my capability to perform my work, are well-ordered procedures that are borne out of, but also mask, a chaotic and uneven history of complicated relationships that cross the borders of North/South, anthropologists/Others, researchers/institutions, male/female, field/home, and many other malleable dichotomies. These practices, like writing, are vital parts of work and require critical reflection and ethical consideration. By turning the gaze not only outward but inward and then understanding the micropolitics of the practice, anthropologists can confront the strange business of being vulnerable observers caught within the webs that history and power have spun (Behar 1996; Grenier 1998; da Col and Graeber 2011, xii). The politics of practice that dictate anthropologists' lives force individuals into many subject positions, identity proclamations, and personal reflection prior to the start of a research project. Even here, the institutions that fuel our lives remind us that identities are intersectional and articulated across multiple zones of difference. I am at once a woman, a cultural anthropologist, a U.S.-born-and-based researcher, and a social scientist working with "human subjects." I, too, am a governed body working within and against the biopolitics of power.

Meanwhile, I also occupy multiple and different positions to the Kayapó men and women who invited me to their lands and still welcome me into their homes. As a white female foreigner, I was a *kuben* (foreigner), *kuben kajaka* (white foreigner), or *kubenire* (female foreigner). After I became close to a family, many friends and consultants in the village became a *tabdjwy* (cousin), *kanikwỹí* (sister), and a multitude of other kin terms. As a childless, postadolescent woman, I was in the age grade of *mekurere* and painted as such. As I worked and was friends mostly with women who had children, I was an honorary member of the *mekrabdjire* age grades (women with kids). As an anthropologist, I was a *pesquisadora* (researcher). An elder woman early on gave me a Kayapó name, *Bekwypỳ*, but only a few called me by it. It did not quite stick. Most often, as

I conversed in either Portuguese or Kayapó—or a hybrid of both—I answered simply to Laura.

In this book, I use pseudonyms for individuals I worked with, including my relationships and relatives in A'Ukre. As is customary in the village, I chose both Brazilian and Kayapó names as pseudonyms. The only exceptions I make to pseudonym use are when referencing already published works about Kayapó leaders, such as Payakan or Raoni.[12] I spent the most time with six women, three of whom are married, and an ever-growing number of children. Out of the six women, I chose to highlight my interactions with Nhak and Iredja, both of whom were of *mekrabdjire* status at the end of my lengthy stay in the village; they were my main teachers and friends. From Nhak and Iredja, I learned the rigors of what they referred to as "women's work" and "women's knowledge" in the village. Nhak was in her early twenties when I met her and had several children (which soon expanded). Nhak and Iredja lived with their children, husbands, fathers, and sisters. Much of the subsistence work fell on the shoulders of Nhak and Iredja.

Nhak, who I opened this chapter with, loved playing soccer, but I rarely saw her on the field on the women's team, as she would be out fishing, gardening, or preparing food. She also enjoyed watching the news, telenovelas (soap operas), films (Hollywood and Kayapó-produced films) on the village television that was intermittently in states of repair and disrepair. Nhak and I conversed about an unending amount of questions about life in the United States or in Brazilian cities from what she saw on the television, and our conversations ranged from discussing Armstrong's steps on the moon to the fact that my first name was the same as the then-current U.S. president's wife (Laura Bush). Nhak was also interested in my life as an American woman, and we had ongoing discussions about expectations for marriage, children, and work. Nhak became my de facto teacher of different aspects of Kayapó life.

My days were also filled with time spent with Iredja, who was only a little bit younger than Nhak. Iredja would often invite me down to the river to wash clothes, go to the garden, or bead. Iredja was quieter than Nhak, and Nhak would often instruct her on paintings she needed to know for her youngest child or when to serve food to her husband. Iredja was also a fierce competitor in soccer and volleyball, although her participation was also infrequent on the women's team. Iredja taught me Kayapó songs at night, which she sang to her children. She would patiently repeat her children's names to me, encouraging me to remember them all, as names have many meanings, as identity and ancestral markers for the Kayapó peoples. Mothers are the keepers of those names. "Write it down," she would say to me, "so you don't forget." Encouraged to reciprocate, I often found myself singing campfire songs of Woody Guthrie or joining in with Kayapó in singing Bob Marley songs. Iredja, like Nhak, also taught me how to prepare Kayapó foods, make rice over an open flame, roast fish with manioc, and use urucum in pasta. Nhak and Iredja were the ones who encouraged me to paint their kids and instructed me with the skill sets required for such an endeavor.

In many ways, Nhak and Iredja embody what life is like as young but adult Kayapó women in A'Ukre. They live at a time when they are as conversant about the Brazilian dance style *forró* as they are about body-painting patterns. While they both have grown up in A'Ukre, they have traveled to see relatives in nearby villages and visited cities and towns for medical treatment or for shopping trips. They were present when CI began its program in A'Ukre, saw a Body Shop cosmetic Brazil nut project come and go, and witnessed the strife caused during the logging years in the 1990s. The ease by which Nhak befriended me is a testament to her ability to maneuver among different types of actors involved in Kayapó livelihoods. Iredja and Nhak also participated in all the ceremonies in the village, were called upon as ceremonial friends to participate, and were recognized body painters. These changes point to different ways in which Kayapó men and women have incorporated foodways, technologies, and tastes into their lives and built strength from within the community, what Gordon (2006) describes in his work with the Xikrin Kayapó as an economy of predation. As discussed in more depth in the chapters that follow, individuals are constantly negotiating change in this complicated landscape where indigenous, private, conservation, and state interests meet.

In addition to the Kayapó women with whom I became close, other villagers appear in this book, some more frequently than others. Marcio, a young leader, was a close confidante and expert consultant who guided my time in A'Ukre in several ways. His role in this work has been fundamental, and his voice is threaded through the chapters, an anchor on which many stories pivot. In carrying out different subsistence and other ceremonial tasks with Kayapó consultants, I tended to work with young women with kids, such as Senna, Iara, Marcia, Panh, and Prytupi, when harvesting different fruits, collecting firewood, going to fields, or carrying out various household chores. Other individuals in this book are only featured briefly, but their experiences are meant to capture the dynamic aspects of daily practices and the multitude of perspectives present in villages like A'Ukre. I reference older women, such as Ireti, who appears in chapter 3, always keen on instructing me about Kayapó livelihoods. The life experiences of young men whom I joined on fishing and hunting trips or consulted with during festivals are represented throughout the chapters. Finally, several of the older men and chiefs whom I worked with, including Tonti, who appears in chapter 5, have in many ways exposed the current complexities of the political, social, cultural, and environmental challenges that villagers face today, as well as the often little understood non-Western perspectives that continue to drive and shape their livelihoods. Many other individuals appear in this book and should be a reminder that more than three hundred people with their own particular histories make up the heterogeneous place of A'Ukre.

Although not all voices are represented here, through the summation of interview responses and highlighting of stories relayed by particular consultants, I aim to present the current challenges and opportunities faced by A'Ukre villagers today. To some, it might seem curious that in a work devoted to complicated notions of territory and territoriality, I locate this research within the classic, spatial arena of anthropologists, a village called A'Ukre. Although centered on A'Ukre, as the pages that follow will show, the book scatters outward and takes a "multiangular" approach to demonstrate the way through which current commodity chains, visual economies, rights-based efforts, and daily routines make villages multisited (Rupp 2011). Working with a Gê group also challenges this further. The spoked-wheel configuration of the village plaza complex already described is deceptive. It seems too easily confined and contained. I write this with a commitment to the village to reintroduce dynamism and everyday experience within the discourse of working with what traditionally has been described as "bounded" and "mappable" sites. In this sense, I take a cue from Patricia Spyer's assertion that ethnography is a fruitful space from which to examine entanglements. Spyer (2000, 6) suggested that the Aruese Islands in eastern Indonesia are more accurately described as a place deeply marked by "runaway topographies" rather than a singular place. Similarly, Tracy Heatherington (2010) noted that her research in the Sardinian town of Orgosolo is reflective of revisionary notions of space within anthropological research. Heatherington explained that "fieldwork is no longer bounded by place but guided instead by thematic engagements and particular questions" (2010, xiii). While an increasingly common practice for anthropologists is to avoid working in only one locale, the practice does not preclude from, as Heatherington and Spyer suggested, asking meaningful questions that challenge normative notions of place, nature, and space even in the context of a singular village.

Just Methods

In the opening of *Vulnerable Observer*, Ruth Behar (1996, 5) queried, how do you "stand up, dust yourself off, go to your desk, and write down what you saw and heard," when perhaps the only thing that you wish to do as an author is "tear up a clump of earth with a hoe and put that on the page and publish it?" In lieu of a clump of earth, I offer the just methods used in this study that formed the corpus of text from which this book is written.[13] The data that comprise this work are an amalgamation of the more signature, cultural anthropological approaches to fieldwork combined with methods particular to visual and engaged anthropology. I organized this research accordingly, where methods, such as interviews and participant observation, were interspersed with and undergirded by participatory approaches (e.g., participatory mapping or guided field walks), where community members as experts taught me about their lifeways. As one leader said to me while he was visiting A'Ukre, "There are all sorts of experts always coming into our territory trying to find something out about our environment. I am an expert as well. I just do not have the degree to show it."

Throughout this work, I relied heavily on participant observation, in which the researcher works closely with a community through participating in their daily lives. Out of all the disciplines, anthropology is unique in that through participant observation, it relies on the body as a site of knowing (Bernard 2011; Conquergood 1991, 180). Whether an active participant or full observer, the researcher is one of the main "instruments" relied upon during field experiences (Johnson, Avenarius, and Weatherford 2006). As such, in the past several decades, scholars have urged a move away from the distant observer to an embodied experience guided by decolonizing and participatory principles (Tuhiwai Smith 1999). Anthropological research, in this sense, is a haptic and sensory experience. "Thick" field notes are made starchy out of bodily sensations (sights, sounds, smells, and tastes) and tasks of daily life. Many who have worked with Amazonian communities have noted similar ways in which participant observation was indispensable.[14] As an embodied way of knowing, participant observation, coupled with becoming a member of the community, charted my daily activities. I sat on the dusty floor of the men's house during community meetings, took up a machete to harvest sweet potatoes in gardens, made brightly beaded medals for soccer tournaments, peeked in on classes at the school, nursed blisters after weeding, slipped into the river to bathe and wash clothing, carried bundles of glossy banana leaves and irregularly shaped rocks for upcoming ceremonial events, collected firewood, soaked manioc, trekked to the savannah, listened to radio chatter, and watched TV with Nhak.

My body, too, began to record my relationship with the wider community. When a friend, Bekwy, had her first child, I was painted head to toe in urucum with the other young, unmarried women and, per ritual requirement, walked to the river where we scrubbed the oily red dye off one another. At the men's coming-of-age ritual at the end of a Bemp naming ceremony, I participated in the inversion of gender roles, during which time a young man sloppily covered my face with genipapo. I frequently received compliments on my friend's intricate body-painting designs practiced on me and nods of approval when I requested designs meant for *mekurere* women. I also enjoyed the intimacy and soothing relief of sitting in the shade, surrounded by friends, feeling the cold, clumpy genipapo–charcoal mixture being applied to my arms.

An assortment of different interviews patterned my time in A'Ukre: open-ended, unstructured interviews, household surveys, guided field walks, and participatory mapping. These conversations, which sometimes took place *in medias res*, were conducted in a mixture of Portuguese and Kayapó, depending on the type and content of the conversation and with whom I was conversing. I have translated all of these conversations into English in this work, and all errors in translation are entirely my own. I talked with an array of individuals (men and women) over the age of eighteen years with varied life experiences that ranged in terms of political involvement, employment history, subsistence skill sets, collaboration with conservation efforts, interest in health and education opportunities at home and away, leadership goals within the community, and many other distinctions. A number of those interviewed had always been residents of A'Ukre, others were part of the founding group of the community, and still others had recently moved to the area.

Interviews, when they were in the form of guided field walks and participatory mapping efforts, took me across the village, into the swidden fields, onto the rivers, and through the forest.[15] Indigenous peoples have always had "geography of oral tradition" with excellent cognitive maps and "paths of observation" of their different landscapes (visible and invisible) and place-naming practices (Gibson 1979 quoted in Ingold 2000, 226; also see Basso 1996; Brody 1985; Feld and Basso 1996). These types of interview methods, guided field walks and participatory mapping, which I suspect are common in anthropology, have recently been named and labeled within anthropological works to reflect the growing interest of research that engages with space and place in participatory ways. In a small sampling of Amazonian ethnographic work, one can see the prevalence of this type of ambulatory interview. Consider the following.

> During my two periods of fieldwork among the Yanesha, whenever I drove or walked along the roads and trails that crisscross their "traditional" territory, my Yanesha companions would point out different sites or features of the landscape, readily connecting them to past events, whether personal, historical, or mythical (Santos-Granero 1998, 130).

> I herein present transcripts of interviews that include some extended consideration of a topic. I do want to emphasize that I also learned much in less-structured situations, particularly when *droghing* (trekking) between villages and other sites (Whitehead 2002, 108, emphasis in original).

> It is walking through the forest with informants that I came to realize that there was no clear boundary between wild plant foods and cultivated crops or between gathering and cultivating (Rival 2002, 2).

Although not all the interviews collected in this way are presented in this work, the incorporation of more participatory, active ways of interviewing generated an overview of current land use, resource use areas, and different ways of being-in-place. It also demonstrated to those interviewed that I was genuinely interested in learning more about their ways of life and was not afraid to spend mornings harvesting and porting manioc in the hot sun or spend hours traveling to the savannah. This type of experiential knowledge corresponds with how Kayapó communities envision the learning process, which involves a combination of seeing, listening, and doing, or in the words of Tim Ingold, a "total sensory experience" (Ingold 2000, 99). Consultants drew maps by hand, discussed colored satellite images, and helped with inputting place names into GIS coordinates.

As A'Ukre is a relatively new village, participatory mapping techniques were critical to the spatialization of daily activities in a way that resonated with Kayapó everyday practices and cosmovisions. The identification of place names, resource use areas, land use, land cover, and other storied information about the landscape provided valuable information on how places become landscapes charged with cultural, symbolic, and ancestral meanings. Guided field walks also yielded a series of map biographies, which refer to a particular type of interview that solicits information on places used and known within living memory of an individual. Most importantly, all interviews expressed the experiential knowledge place, as held through memory, embodiment, and historically informed practice that different community members related as they told their life histories, thoughts about home, and the changing practices of being Kayapó.[16]

As an engaged anthropologist, I deemed it incongruous to think that anthropological research can be separated into precise categories of being "there" or being "here." This double vision polarizes the field, where research is separated out from other professional and personal aspects of our livelihoods. Diane M. Nelson understands how interweaving your life with others—people and places—as a research inquiry lays bare the difficulties of anthropological work. After fifteen years of living in Guatemala, she confesses, "I have experienced the 'epistemic murk' that Michael Taussig discerns . . . the great steaming morass of chaos that lies on the underside of order and without which order could not exist" (Taussig 1987, 4 quoted in Nelson 1999, 31). I consider the words that follow in this book as polished versions of the "chaos that lies on the underside of order."

The Exhibition of Chapters

Eric Wolf (1982, 4) said in his famous work *Europe and the People without History*, "If there are connections everywhere, why do we persist in turning dynamic, interconnected phenomena into static, disconnected things?" Accordingly, I begin this book by drawing attention to diverse spatiotemporal conceptualizations of and historical transformations in the Amazon region—by its indigenous and settler inhabitants—and how it has impacted the Kayapó peoples across time and space. The colonial encounter, followed by subsequent waves of planned and spontaneous political-economic and infrastructural growth in the Amazon, marginalized and dispossessed indigenous peoples of their lands and livelihoods, dramatically reconfiguring notions of property, ownership, and wealth in the region. Kayapó peoples weathered indirect and direct contact through different strategies for survival, which increasingly was based on securing territorial recognition, acknowledgement of rights-based claims, and countering dominant, often state-produced, narratives about indigenous peoples as backward, ignorant, or animal-like (Slater 2002). Drawing from oral histories and ethnohistorical work, I use the frame of making indigenous territorialities in chapter 1 to argue that the question about land in Brazil has been as much a geospatial project as one about racial politics and competing ontologies.

In the multiethnic context of pink tide citizenship in Latin America, indigenous communities' struggles for different rights-based claims and self-determination efforts have been also accompanied by a suite of resistance strategies that range from the highly visible to invisible. For more than three decades now, the Kayapó peoples have established themselves as experts in the visual politics of representation where ceremonial regalia, distinct dress, and body modifications are employed for political traction, collective action, and community well-being. Chapter 2 draws attention to these forms of resistance as but one part of a series of strategies the Kayapó employ. I turn to a naming ceremony to highlight that political activism is rooted in indigenous expressive forms that have complex levels of signification and meaning for their indigenous participants, which are often unintelligible to widely viewing publics. Naming ceremonies are honored among the Kayapó, as they reflect the most cherished Kayapó values of beauty, strength, and power (Turner 2003b). In many ways naming ceremonies are sacred performances that establish how villagers emplace themselves within time and space in ways that diverge from Western epistemologies. At the same time, the Kayapó have used the aesthetics of ceremonial practices as powerful symbols in their activist and resistance efforts. By revealing the dynamic linkages between ceremonial life and political activism, I show how naming ceremonies are an example of Kayapó navigations of competing notions of place, space, and identity. In this instance we see the interconnections between political protests for territorial retention and a vibrant ceremonial life based on local cosmologies operating alongside one another.

Across the globe, environmental governance and local (and transnational) grassroots efforts increasingly employ the term "justice" within different themed socioenvironmental contexts—for example, as demonstrated by food justice and water justice—to incite political action and alternative modes of existence. As global debates over indigenous rights, food security, and preservation of heirloom seeds and cultivars intensify, tropical deforestation rates remain a persistent concern. In chapter 3, I turn to food justice and food sovereignty narratives to explore the multidimensional strategies Kayapó communities employ to make their livelihoods. While I could highlight any one of the diverse food-gathering or productive practices of Kayapó peoples—hunting, foraging, fishing, horticulture, and store-bought food stuffs—in this chapter I find swidden agriculture a particularly powerful entry point to analyze place-making and personhood in Kayapó communities. As Vaccaro, Dawson, and Zanotti (2014, 2) emphasized, "territoriality, as a consequence of its conceptual complexity, is a concept that summarizes a significant part of the processes involved in the social translation of space as an abstract category into territory as a socially meaningful quotidian reality (Delaney 2005; Storey 2012)."

Examining swidden practices provides not only a lens to understand their contributions to well-being, but also the possibility of their sustainable applications for the future. The first of two chapters that showcase local livelihoods, I use ethnoecological and ethnobiological approaches to address the politics of swidden cultivation in contrast to large-scale, land-use transformations, such as the predominance of intensive ranching and industrial agricultural practices that have often favored large landholders. Ethnographic research with residents of A'Ukre provides grounded data on the way in which swidden agriculture remains key to food sovereignty, or locally controlled foodways, in A'Ukre. Despite an influx of and increased access to store-bought foods, residents of A'Ukre retain strong preferences for subsistence foods and foodways, which remain part of the fabric of social relationships, sense of belonging, and an increasing mixed-market economy. Weaving in ethnographic experiences from a variety of field visits, I show the way in which shifting cultivation and swidden management pattern community life and shape territory in ways distinct from conservationist or state-driven visions of the same locale.

As emphasized above, entry into and negotiation of market participation into a multidimensional subsistence practice enables individuals, families, households, and communities to diversify their livelihood strategies while maintaining activities, practices, and positions that affirm their values, belief systems, kin networks, personal goals, and career interests. Chapter 4 analyzes the successive waves of engagement A'Ukre villagers have had with informal and formal NTFP markets and their relationship to generating robust local economies that have a regional and transnational reach. A'Ukre villagers have experimented with a variety of community company and community conservation projects to develop cash-based economies. An analysis of the dual subsistence and cash economy in A'Ukre reveals the diverse strategies the community uses in order to serve market, dietary, and other daily needs. A focus on NTFPs, in particular, unravels these complex entanglements of market and nonmarket activities and their relationship to the lived experiences and the dominant imaginaries of Amazonian peoples.

Environmental globalization, a term coined by Karl Zimmerer (2006), is a form of global territoriality that is defined by the increased coordination among different institutions, knowledge systems, and efforts positioned to influence and govern nature. Using this frame in chapter 5, I examine community conservation programs in the Brazilian Amazon to reveal how the multiple processes of making territory have in certain instances provided new contexts for contestation and rights-based struggles. While an uneven terrain, the Kayapó peoples' experience and interaction with conservation NGOs has created a mutually beneficial program in the region that is supportive to competing conceptualizations of place and space. Creswell (2013, 5) suggests that "all over the world peoples are engaged in place-making activities," and the place-making activities of conservation programs with the Kayapó have produced multiple exchanges and alliances among villagers, chiefs, young leaders, researchers, NGO staff members, students, and others. In particular, this chapter explores the jointly agreed upon practices that have emerged within the context of the alliances. The many different territorialities that the Kayapó homeland encompasses also have been a boon to Kayapó leaders as they forge ahead with political and other interests. For example, an ecological research station or a study abroad project becomes short-term or long-term revenue sources as changing political alliances help fortify border surveillance and ongoing support for enforcement of protected area boundaries.

As a collection, these chapters highlight the transformative strategies that Kayapó peoples use to retain control over their livelihoods in the face of widespread and dramatic change: countermapping projects that foreground the visibility of indigenous peoples across time and space, political action built from sites of community strength, community well-being fortified by control over local foodways alongside experimental market engagements, and dense community–outsider networks built out of concerns for territorial retention and control. Kayapó peoples have surfaced from developmentalist agendas, neoliberal reforms, and neoextractivist regimes and with this robust platform of action and self-determination. *Radical Territories in the Brazilian Amazon* reveals these complicated and intertwined histories, economies, and practices in relation to Kayapó self-determination efforts. The complex temporalities of a mixed-market lifestyle heavily based on subsistence practices, the place-making strategies that animate villages, the political institutions behind new governance strategies, and the growing digital media worlds of activism and cultural expression all drive the Kayapó's current struggle for sustainable and just futures. These multiple valences of making indigenous territorialities play an important role in how indigenous groups participate in the politics of homeland demarcation and defense.

Yet, stresses, including climate change, political-economic realities of clean energy platforms linked to national security and sovereignty, and tumultuous national politics threaten to erode the advances that Kayapó peoples have cultivated over the last three decades. I close the book by turning to some of these challenges, including the development of the hydroelectric dam, Belo Monte, which is currently being built on the "Big Bend" of the Xingu River in Pará State, Brazil. The Kayapó people's struggle against the Belo Monte Dam has been more than thirty years in the making, and Belo Monte will be the world's third largest dam. I also point to the recent introduction of the Proposed Constitutional Amendments (PEC), like PEC 215, which seeks to undermine indigenous territorial demarcation throughout Brazil. Despite some of these looming and real threats, the Kayapó have, with incredible strength, shown the world that their struggles are at once theirs and everyone's in offering an alternative vision of landscapes and livelihoods for sustainable futures that is supportive of indigenous cosmovisions. It is the Kayapó who continually recognize the importance of conflictive histories and how to strategically deploy them in ways that nurture rather than stifle their lifeways and the lifeways of peoples across the globe. Their experience should be an example for all of us.

1

The Making of a Border
and Territory

> Outsiders may never fully understand traditional narratives,
> because the meanings are embedded in prior cultural knowledge
> and words that only a speaker of the language can completely
> appreciate. Nevertheless, stories can have some wider interpretation
> and understanding in other cultures, and perhaps this is why some
> themes transcend cultural and linguistic boundaries.
> —Nancy Turner, *The Earth's Blanket: Traditional Teachings for
> Sustainable Living*

Introduction

In the 2012 independent documentary, *Belo Monte Announcement of a War*,
which chronicles the conflicts that have occurred regarding the construction of
the highly politicized Belo Monte Dam in the Xingu region, an indigenous activist, Abacamu Kamayurá implores: "They must look at the past. Who has lived
here in Brazil long ago were the Indians. The Indians are the owners, they must
consider this" (available at https://www.youtube.com/watch?v=ZoRhavupkfw).
In Abacamu Kamayurá's attempt to articulate the injustices that the Belo Monte
Dam would have on his people, Kamayurá reminds the viewer of indigenous
habitation of Brazil that predates any settler societies. Facing the destruction of
their lands or possible relocation, Kamayurá's position is one that also is reflective
of indigenous struggles since colonial times, where colonial and now new developmental geographies have privileged propertied policies that serve to benefit
the public good or the elite rather than particularly situated but cosmologically
expansive indigenous conceptualizations of place.

Belo Monte Dam is a perfect example of this ongoing struggle as part of
Brazil's neodevelopmental "accelerated-growth" program, which combines concerns for reducing poverty with "green" alternatives (Zanotti 2015, 4). Some
argue that the dam project will bring energy, infrastructure, and security to the
Brazilian nation-state in order to fortify the country and its populace. Plans
for improvement that ostensibly are crafted for the public good like this one
continue to privilege dominant discourses of place, territory, and home—
which emphasize land as national patrimony or propertied wealth for a leading

agricultural and industrial class all the while overlooking other social and environmental impacts of massive hydroelectric infrastructures. Yet, as Kamayurá reminds us, different "owners" of these lands have long existed, and indigenous well-being should be considered as part of renewable economies rather than antagonistic to energy alternatives.

Kayapó efforts and the efforts of leaders like Kamayurá to secure their lands within neodevelopmental regimes, whether it is from hydraulic futures or otherwise, are best understood as a "movement in defense of life and culture that demands territory instead of land—self-determination instead of property" (Baletti 2012, 593). In this way, making territory for the Kayapó means at once defending and retaining their demarcated homeland with strategic governance strategies while at the same time embarking on a process of countermapping the region in a way that weaves Kayapó conceptualizations and understandings of place into broader cartographies and imaginaries (see Chapin, Lamb, and Threlkeld 2005). Conceiving the relationship to the landscape as one that is relational, temporal, and spatial, the Kayapó's fight for land thus is inevitably tied to their desire for recognitional justice or justice that "acknowledg[es] people's distinct identities and histories and eliminat[es] cultural forms of domination of some groups over others" (Sikor 2013, 7).[1]

Using the concept of territory as a point of departure, in this chapter I build on Kamayurá's comments to examine the material and ideological processes that have made indigenous territories and racialized bodies over time. As Escobar (2008, 56, italics in original) reminds us, making territory is part of the "*production* of territoriality." Kayapó peoples with whom I worked, like Kamayurá, often emphasized their historical presence and cosmological ties to homeland and territory through myths, oral history, personal biography, place-making activities, and performative politics. The statement "The Kayapó are the original inhabitants of Brazil" was something I heard from Kayapó interlocutors when asking about territory, place, and home. "People say that Cabral discovered Brazil, but he, a white man, was not the one that discovered this place. We were already here," Teodoro, a village leader, said to me. Far from passing comments, in a political, legal, and economic system that recognizes land rights as one of the pathways to protection, at least above the subsoil, claims to originary rights to landscapes and resources are weighty arguments.

Kayapó individuals see themselves, as the Mebêngôkre who have walked, lived in, and dwelt in vast parts of Brazil. This geography of belonging, embedded in Kayapó origin stories, cosmologies, and historical movements across the landscape, points to a more generous vision of territory that is not restricted to a demarcated homeland or propertied notions of being in place. In this chapter, I show that the making of Amazonia in Brazil was part of making indigenous peoples and certain types of territoriality while at the same time, it was a process by which Kayapó peoples sought to reaffirm local senses of place as they simultaneously adjusted to new territorial norms.[2] I acknowledge that, "geographies of belonging privilege particular subjects' positioning while simultaneously rendering other bodies vulnerable to violence" (Moore, Pandian, and Kosek 2003, 14). However, like Jean Dennison (2012, 11), I see colonial and historical processes postcontact as entangled, where "agency and endurance" constitute key responses to the violent suppression of and attempt to erase, control, or dominate indigenous peoples, their lands, homes, bodies, and identities.

In this vein, I take up Deborah McGregor's (2004) charge that scholars should pay attention to creation myths and stories of origin as a way of respecting indigenous peoples and honoring their lifeways. I begin this chapter with Kayapó myths, and in sharing these stories I describe how the Kayapó emplace themselves in the landscape as the originary inhabitants of Brazil and otherworldly landscapes both in historical and mythic time. Moving away from, and problematizing the customary depiction of indigenous communities as "isolated," "static," and inhabiting specific locales since "time immemorial," the history presented is one of visibility and heterogeneous change, dotted by purposive movements, circulations, and mobilizations that took place long before colonization. Here I shift the emphasis from "written to embodied culture, from the discursive to the performative" to emphasize different ways of making, knowing, and becoming that pattern human and nonhuman actors together (Taylor 2003, 16).

In the second part of the chapter, I turn to the series of relations that have marked Amazonia since contact. Simpson (2014, 127) characterizes the colonizing process as a dream of "Indigenous pacification, containment, and demobilization." Likewise, the jerky, colonial frontier history of Amazonia similarly emphasized erasure, assimilation, and destruction of indigenous peoples and politics that unevenly but powerfully transformed labor, property, and work into different expressions of territory and territoriality. In this vein, Paul Little (2001) argues that diverse set cycles have pulsed through frontier Amazonia: missionary, mercantile, national developmentalism, and more recently, environmental economies.[3] Relatedly, Susanna Hecht (2011) compresses the history of Amazonia into three analytical categories that point to political and discursive shifts over time: Ür natures, neo-natures, and socio-natures. Ür natures mark the colonial and empire-building moments, where indigenous groups, their lands, and the wealth that was contained within were seen both as a boon and a problem. Neo-natures emerged in the mid-1950s, as the Brazilian Amazon was being positioned as part of a number of modernist projects associated with state-building. Finally, socio-natures describe the current moment, which is a "mosaic" patterning of large-scale extractivist and agro-industrial interests in the region alongside small-scale, sustainable development ventures and inhabited forested landscapes. I show how these shift from extractivist mercantile economies and agro-industrial and mega-development strategies to a mosaic socioenvironmental landscape, to what I argue are current neodevelopmental economies. These transitions have coincided with tense but enduring strategies by Kayapó peoples to continue to make place and home *mejkumrei* all the while confronting social inequalities and the fetishes and dreamtimes that empire- and nation-building bring with them (Heatherington 2010; Taussig 1997).

Aletta Biersack (2006, 23–24) argues a reorientation of history can reveal these tensions among diverse territorialities as expressed in entanglements of culture and place. Taking a "place-based approach stipulates the limitations of capitalocentric and Eurocentric analyses" and "acknowledges the presence of grassroots agents . . . contributing to a postcolonial historiography that renders 'subalterns' subjects of their own history." Indigenous notions of territory that have taken on the material forms of maps and the discursive forms of counter narratives have long served to counter hegemonic, often state and colonial forms of violence, surveillance, dispossession and containment (Scott 1998). Feminist Cindi Katz (2001, 1216) identifies counter-topographies as sites that "might encourage and enable the formation of new political-economic alliances that transcend both place and identity and foster a more effective cultural politics to counter the imperial, patriarchal and racist integument of globalization." These counter-topographies, she continues, highlight the "specific ways globalization works on particular rounds" (Katz 2001, 1216).

While the Kayapó's history is one of theft, as Kramer (2006) so simply but profoundly put it in her ethnography of Bella Coola art, it is also one of *sobrevivência* (survival) and struggle. In the middle of it all are Kayapó men, women, families, and children, their wishes, fears, and desires. What follows is a history of the Kayapó Indigenous Lands, and the making of a border and a territory. I begin with Kayapó myths that are trailed by a discussion of the precontact era and the "discovery" of Brazil. I then follow the intersections of rubber, mining, and timber economies with Kayapó "pacification" efforts, move toward capitalist engagements, and conclude with the democratic turn in Brazil and a look toward future concerns that will shape the region for years to come.

Origins

The Village in the Sky

Before I plunge into the many decades of matted intersections with settler societies, I open with two Kayapó myths. In an attempt to decolonize academia, several indigenous scholars and activists have criticized nonindigenous accounts of indigenous origins as scientific narratives that are not attentive to, or respectful of, local histories of origin (Deloria 2003, 2004; McGregor 2004). Indigenous peoples call upon and find strength from their own creation stories—rooted in local cosmologies and animated by rich storytelling traditions—which offer mythic and historical interpretations of human and nonhuman relations that continue to guide relational interactions with outsiders today (Cruikshank

2005). These histories are truths that are core to different notions of reckoning time, the way in which spiritual, moral, and ancestral events are lived and practiced, the relationality among human and nonhuman beings, and dwelling in place. In this section, I trace how Kayapó myths and histories underlie and index the past, present, and future, which guide their beliefs, behaviors, and actions of being in this world. As both colonial and contemporary politics in Brazil have hovered around questions of land, resources, and territory, the stories told in this section provide a representation of oral forms of knowledge, embodied histories, and the experiences of Kayapó peoples beyond the spatial and temporal confines of a colonial encounter. In other words, they are formative to making indigenous territorialities and to remapping settler lands.

Lea (2012, 215) proposes that Kayapó myths are similar to Claude Lévi-Strauss's (1966, 17) concept of bricolage, which refers to aggregated and composite practices, beliefs, or objects, or "whatever is at hand" that produce new products and "contingent" results. For Lea, myths can be formatted and reformatted, and micro-adjustments take place as they are passed from one member to another over the generations. Furthermore myths are but one manifestation of indigenous cosmovisions in which shamanic practices, the life course, and ceremonial performances transform, mark, and regulate. Likewise, Viveiros de Castro holds that indigenous mythologies accept "that each living species is human in its own department, human for itself (*humano para si*), or better, that everything is human for itself (*todo para si é humano*) or anthropogenic. This idea originates in indigenous cosmogonies, where the primordial form of the being is human: 'in the beginning there was nothing,' say some Amazonian myths, 'there were only people.' Thus, the different types of beings and phenomena that populate and wander the world are transformations of this primordial humanity" (Viveiros de Castro quoted in Fernadez Brazo 2013, np).

Johannes Wilbert and Karin Simoneau (1978), who put together a compendium of Gê myths, also note that most Gê groups, including the Kayapó, have origin stories detailing these transformations on three planes of being: the upper world, the earth, and the underworld. The Kayapó peoples I worked with also told me many stories that all point to the origins of human and nonhuman beings, where "different types of beings" populated the world through their relation with one another. For the Kayapó peoples, there are stories about the acquisition of fire, a celestial vault, a sky girl, a mythic tree, the sky people, and of O Òróp and Bira, among many others.[4] Of all these stories, two predominated while I was in A'Ukre; that is, these two were most often told when asked about origins. Although as Lea (2013) suggests, by evoking the concept of bricolage, they by no means represented the only origin stories.

I relate two myths here alongside a previously recorded one. As stories continue to be passed down, they are a fount from which Kayapó individuals continue to find a source of strength, as storytelling practices fortify and affirm being human in a way that is distinctive from Western understandings of boundaries, edges, borders, and worlds (see also Fabian 1992). Furthermore, as I will detail later in this chapter, the myths that the Kayapó tell about their past have also become powerful narratives in a political context where laying claim to territory and home remains vital to the future of their peoples. These stories, as Li (2014, 30) put it, signal "the spatial elements of . . . relations, and the entanglement of topography with identities, practices, and powers."

During my time in A'Ukre, I was told and retold the story of the Sky People over firelight on nights when the cold nipped at my arms and settled in my bones, with youth as I walked to the river, among elders in their homes, in the house where I lived, on the rickety wooden bench that sat in front of my door, and later in new NGO houses when I brought students to the village. Below is a version of one myth that Lukesch recorded in the mid-1900s. I relate the first part of the myth, as recorded by Lukesch and presented by Wilbert and Simoneau (1978, 107–8), here:

> Long, long ago the Cayapo lived in the sky, where they had everything they could possibly want. They had every type of food imaginable: sweet potatoes, *macaxeira*, yams, manioc, maize, inaja fruits, bananas, game of all kinds, and land tortoises. One day one of the experienced *mebenget* [elder] warriors discovered an armadillo hole in the forest. He wanted to catch the animal and therefore he began to dig. He kept on digging all day until the evening came, but he did not find the armadillo. Early the next morning he went out into the forest to continue digging, and again he dug until evening without success. Suddenly, on the fifth day, when he had already reached a considerable depth, he saw the giant armadillo. But at the same time, in the excitement of digging, he broke through the celestial vault. The armadillo fell into the depths; it kept on falling until it landed on the earth. The old warrior also fell. On the way down, however, a strong wind caught him and threw him back up, and he flew back into the sky. Through the hole he looked down on the hearth and saw a forest of buriti palms, a big river, and a vast plain. A deep longing, a burning desire for the world he saw below, arose within him.

In A'Ukre, talking with a middle-aged man named Marcio, I listened to an alternative, shorter telling of these same events several decades later. Marcio began the story in the sky by describing a village that existed long ago and then suddenly: "One day, the villagers saw 'good land' below the clouds through an armadillo's hole. After much discussion, half of the Kayapó decided to stay in the sky, and the other half descended to the earth with the wind. The stars that current villagers see at night, much like the ones you and I see on clear nights in A'Ukre, are the fires made by those Kayapó who decided to stay in the sky villages. The Kayapó communities who remain on the earth today are descendants of the group that was carried down with the wind."

In contemplating life above earth and following Viveiros de Castro's wish for the decolonization of thought, Cymene Howe (2015, 203) relays, "wind finds itself with no terrestrial home, no borders to maintain, no ownership to be claimed. Its pressured and oscillating gases are the kinetic energy of the sky. Wondering into the wind leads us upward." Where Howe (2015) finds that wind has "no terrestrial home" and "no borders," wind, for the Kayapó has the opposite effect—a force that is not positioned upward but in-between, carrying the Sky people both up to the sky and down to the earth, grounding human beings in this world as it also links them to other worlds in star-studded night skies. Within Kayapó stories, traveling and making place, whether it is through wind-based travels or the actions of elders and shamans, often are the source of transformative journeys that create Kayapó worlds.

The story of O Òróp also points to formative relationships among humans and nonhumans. While the details and the content of this story changed, depending on the person with whom I was speaking, they shared many similarities. One version was as follows:

In the past, there were no Indians, only O Òróp, his brother, his wife, and his brother-in-law. In the past, there were a lot of good shamans, but there were only three men and one woman. They asked the shaman why there were only the four of them, and told the shaman that they wanted more people to be with them. At night, they talked this over with him. He said that if they really want to know they were going to make a men's house. The men went to the forest and, by that time, the shaman had already made a house out of palm fronds and wood. It was good wood and the shaman began to sing. At night, the family came and there was the house. They then heard music. They listened, and the Kayapó were asking how this could be. The shaman knew. The people sang and decided to make a headdress. And they saw that there were already other people in the house the shaman built and there was a Kayapó camp. Men were in the house planning a festival. There were already a lot of Kayapó.

Some of the versions told by other villagers talked of O Òróp as the shaman and that he was married to named woman's sister. Others who told this story commented on different place-names from historical events, combining mythic time with precontact and colonial encounters, affirming the Kayapó's place in making the world and the disruptive aftermath of contact. These versions oftentimes extended the Kayapó territory, placing ancestral characters in important political and financial centers of Brazil. One was as follows:

At the beginning, in the capital of São Paulo, there was a man named O Òróp, his wife, his wife's sister, and two children. The two children grew up and asked their father why there were not many Indians, because they wanted to see more people. Afterward, there were a lot of Indians. Later, the white man came and started attacking the Indians near the Araguaia River, and the Indians left to find good earth. In São Paulo, many Indians left because many others had been killed. A shaman told them to migrate, and for that reason, there are a lot of different Indians now: Catete, Tapirapé, and Parque Nacional Xingu. An old man from Kapot told me this story. He was from Pykatôti. After Pykatôti, some left to make the village of Mekrāgnoti, and others to make Gorotíre. The Xikrin also looked for good land and decided to stay nearby. O Òróp's two children were happy, because there were already a lot of Indians. The next day O Òróp made a headdress, and told the story to his people.

The myths of the sky, as well as the story of O Òróp, emphasize that places and things (wind, stars, etc.) are made meaningful by the actions that individuals endow in them over time to activate the creative potential of the land and peoples to comingle and produce one another (see also Coelho de Souza 2010, 113). I suggest, instead of envisioning these transformative processes "as peripheral to the village–plaza complex, central to political ideologies, or constrained by environmental adaptations," these stories should be understood as a discursive practice that "continue[s] to make place in a charged region where land and territory are often in question and serve as a stimulus to knowledge creation and transmission" (Zanotti 2014b, 113). While making place and affirming personhood occur within storytelling traditions, myths also serve as oral cartographic traditions that remake territory in a way that aligns with Kayapó cosmovisions and sensibilities of space and time.

Moreover, the Kayapó's attention to the production of community life in these stories is consistent with the emphasis on movement and dynamism as part of making place. The stories remind us that the formation of Kayapó villages and of personhood, in general, are part of a long-term process of creating, maintaining, adding, and abandoning villages over time and space where men's houses, plazas, and houses formulate a space from which ancestral ceremonies can be carried out, food harvested, and "good life" sustained through the sharing of substances and generative practices (Fisher 1991; Lea 1986; Turner 1965, 1995b; Werner 1983). In this way, Kayapó stories show how place-making practices are, in part, founded on the processes of fissioning (one group breaking away from another) and trekking, which link "new or 'alien' spaces to familiar ones through trail-making, practice, and storytelling" (Zanotti 2014b, 116). For example, fissioning plays a significant role in the myth of the sky village. In this myth, individuals from the village in the sky either purposefully or accidentally broke away from a larger group to form a village on earth. The story shows how villages experience and sustain fissions over time, and the current practice of fissioning and creating new communities are part of longer-held histories about Kayapó relationships to making their *iñho pyka* (lands). Lived spaces produce landscapes that are marked by shamanic, ceremonial and quotidian activities generative of community life and beautiful people. Later, in this chapter, I will show how fissioning and trekking have played another, but distinctive, role in the Kayapó histories as a response to colonial encroachment on their lands.

The sky village myth also suggests that, although villages might be spatially connected (current populations can still "see" where previous populations came from in the night sky), new villages or places can be incorporated into the landscape and built autonomously from one another. In both sets of stories, mobility and exploration of new topographies are stressed, for spaces have the unending capacity of becoming and being. I have many field jottings recording community members' comments that note repeatedly how critical the ability to scout and settle or camp in a place with *pyka mex* or *pyka mej* (good land) was to establishing villages or reconnecting spaces together over time. The ability to establish villages and move through the landscape remains a vital practice for Kayapó livelihoods today, even within a demarcated, bounded homeland.[5]

On the other hand, some of the stories recorded and retold also refer to a variety of spaces and places of origin. The myths note the sky, the forest, the savannah, or important Brazilian cities as initial sites of occupation, whether they are worldly or otherworldly. These sites situate Kayapó peoples as the original inhabitants in the current external centers of power (São Paulo), place Kayapó peoples in different neotropical environments (forest and savannah), or locate communities in separate but interrelated planes of being (sky and earth). For example, in the first O Òróp myth, individuals lived in a forest space without other Kayapó. In the second O Òróp myth, the Kayapó lived in São Paulo, near the Araguaia River, and in several other key areas identified by place-names that reflect a settler presence in the contemporary Brazilian nation-state. Not only emphasizing ongoing place-making practices that are important to the transformative aspects of contemporary lifeways, these events also emphasize the extension of notions of territoriality and their embeddedness in different social relationships, notions of national belonging and indigenous citizenship. For example, the story of O Òróp describes a family that is isolated and estranged from desired social ties and camaraderie, but soon is joined by others through ceremony, song, and shamanic intervention, which is cause for celebration. This aspect of the myth places weight on the relationships that constitute social worlds, and is telling of the importance of ceremonial life for villagers, as an expression of the values of beauty and wholeness.

All of these histories, including those told and those untold, are truths that animate and connect Kayapó understandings of their journeys from other planes of being to their current homeland. It is my hope that these events will serve as a grounding point, from which the rest of this chapter unfolds, and a key starting point for understanding the Kayapó Lands today. The myth of the sky and the myth of O Òróp represent characteristics of Kayapó worlds that index Kayapó notions of place and home. They show how human and nonhuman relations, nonhuman actors (e.g., wind), and fissioning, and its antithesis, consolidation, emerge as significant elements in the production and sustenance of life. As I will show below, these myths are representative of the broad trends that have shaped the Kayapó's different migrations across the landscape as they interacted with others, and they point to the layered territorialities that the Kayapó navigate and, in turn, produce to support alternative modes of living and being in the world today. These myths are now mobilized in political spaces to legitimize territorial claims and to rewrite colonial narratives to show that indigenous peoples were the original "owners" of the land as Kamayurá stated. Kayapó peoples are creating new discourses of power based on storytelling traditions that "make myth, indigenous perspectives, and discourses styles relevant to contemporary events" (Graham 2002, 211). The visibility of indigenous narratives are much needed, as the history of encounter was and still is a dramatic rip in the fabric of making a good life. As Povinelli (2011, 11) states, these moments are tense, but also "help shape how social belonging, abandonment, and endurance are enunciated and experienced."

Traces of the Past

Aligned with the Kayapó's conception of historical events and mythic time, non-Native pre-Columbian history of the Amazon characterizes the landscape as one dominated by movement and mobility, not stasis. Where today indigenous territorial demands associated with self-determination and sovereignty rely upon fixing a space on the map, in the pre-Columbian landscape the need to demarcate particular homelands as part of state-led legal processes simply did not exist—as the Kayapó myths just told attest. While other indigenous territorial patterns and relations to the land did exist, they conformed to a spatial reality that often contrasts with, rather than follows, Western notions of land and property. Scholars are only now beginning to understand the scope and scale of the roles that migration and mobility played in both the pre-Columbian past and the colonial past through new information that has become available on landscape modifications, demographic collapses, ethnogenesis, extensive trade networks, and similarly extensive shamanic journeys (Erikson 2008; Heckenberger 2005, 2006; Hornburg 2005; Schaan 2011).

According to non-Native histories, initial human occupation in Amazonia dates back to the late Pleistocene (13,000–10,000 BP) when the biophysical characteristics of Amazonian landscapes would have approached similar levels of diversity as today (Neves and Peterson 2006, 281). In the Holocene era (after 10,000 BP), the area was most probably in a constant state of disequilibrium with hydrological changes, such as rising sea levels, and the inundation of large portions of the Amazon creating deep lakes (Neves and Peterson 2006, 281; Roosevelt 1989, 2000). Current archaeological data indicate early occupation in the Amazon was probably in *terra firme* or "upland areas" rather than in the *várzeas* or "seasonally flooded forests," contrary to a long-standing belief that the floodplain was the initial area for settlement (Denevan 1992, 2001, 2006; Lathrap 1977; Neves and Peterson 2006; Roosevelt 2000). The development of forest farming is dated 2000–4000 BP, and, at this time, indigenous forest management formed many of the palm forests found in the upland areas today (Balée 1989; Roosevelt 1989, 2000).[6]

Indigenous peoples, and there were many diverse groups, also cultivated forests and encouraged the growth of specific species, like Brazil nuts, that are now found in *castanhais* or "groves," which are abundant in the southern and southeastern regions of Pará (Denevan 2001, 2006). The anthropogenic soil type, *Terra preta do índio*, or Amazonian dark earth (ADE), is highly concentrated in this time period (Graham 2006). Linguistic evidence indicates that some of the major groups of the Amazon region, the Arawak, Tupi, Carib, and Gê peoples, began significant migrations during this time as well. Arawak peoples dispersed along rivers and coasts, and Tupi-, Carib-, and Gê-speaking peoples migrated into the uplands (Heckenberger 2005, 2006). At the same time, some peoples adopted unique Arawakan cultural characteristics. The Gê peoples' ritual plaza complex and village spatial arrangement were possibly adopted from the Arawakan model through contact with the southeastern-most populations of the diaspora (Heckenberger 2006, 329). Gê peoples, including the Kayapó peoples, probably migrated from the southern and southeastern Amazon region (Urban 1992 quoted in Heckenberger 2006, 317).

Beyond these broad brushstrokes, charting the Kayapó peoples' history prior to colonization has been quite difficult for scholars. Julian Steward made some of the earliest attempts to understand this history. Steward characterized the Kayapó peoples as culturally "marginal" in comparison to those groups living along the floodplains.[7] Lacking ceramics, hammocks, or canoes, which were present among Arawakan groups, for example, the Kayapó were labeled according to the academic norm at the time, equating elaborated material culture with an associated cultural complexity. Numerous ethnographers already have commented on this misleading classification of indigenous groups according to the material complexity of their lives that took place in nineteenth-century ethnography (Gordon 2006; Lea 2012; Viveiros de Castro 1992). In particular, Viveiros de Castro (1992) and later Lea (2012) also write about Steward's *Handbook of South American Indians* and its privileging of those groups that produced durable structures and goods, mistaking longevity with technical acumen and an equally complex social and political economy. The Kayapó peoples reportedly made short-term, makeshift structures in the forest and used degradable forest products for household items. Similarly, European visitors to the region noted that the Kayapó peoples, like many Gê-speaking groups, had a complex social organization with "simple" subsistence practices. This observation led several scholars to hypothesize that the Kayapó peoples must have devolved from more culturally complex tribes and migrated from what were then thought of as ecologically "rich" areas (Lévi-Strauss 1967; Lowie 1963; Steward 1955). The logic behind this argument was that, according to cultural evolutionary models, a complex social hierarchy was linked to equally complex economic and material cultures. This kind of labeling, while following the scientific standards of the moment, has, in retrospect, been harshly criticized as contributing to, rather than upending, racial and ethnic stereotypes about indigenous groups, their past, and their place-making practices. Unfortunately, we continue to see some of these histories repeating themselves in popular narratives of the region. Moreover, describing indigenous groups as highly mobile people without homes was also convenient way to envision Amazonian landscapes as uninhabited and unproductive—which was far from the case.

Later, scholars suggested that the Kayapó (Northern) migrated from the southern flanking scrubland areas (also called the Brazilian Highlands, which are composed of the *cerrado* and *caatinga* ecoregions) and occupied their present area after the 1750s.[8] This was based on written sources from the 1800s and 1900s, and on some archaeological projects in the Araguaia River area (Bamberger 1967). Anthropologists Terence Turner (1965), Gustaaf Verswijver (1992b), and William Fisher (1991) argue that the Kayapó migrated, at least since the nineteenth century, from the Tocantins-Araguaia River to their current territorial setting. This reconstruction, based on ethnohistorical and oral history research, fits with what we know about Kayapó settlement patterns, indigenous responses to colonization, and, importantly, Kayapó oral histories. Many indigenous groups fled or migrated during the contact period, and the Kayapó are known to abandon villages and areas where an uncommon amount of death has occurred (Turner 1965; Posey 2002a). Even those groups that had always shown strength during times of upheaval, like the Kayapó, could have sought refuge in the interior of the country and moved away from the encroaching settlers because of concerns about disease and death. In addition, the Kayapó might have willingly moved westward because of their preference to remain in indirect contact with settlers.

Furthermore, the Kayapó peoples were probably connected to aboriginal trade routes among other Gê-speaking tribes, the Arawak (as mentioned above), the Karajá, and the Guaraní (Lowie 1963, 477; Posey 2002a, 18). There is also some evidence that the Kayapó were trading with other groups and launching skirmishes (warfare and raids) during the precontact and contact periods against the Panará, Juruná, Mundurucú, Arara, Tapirapé, and other groups, which resulted in the constant circulation of peoples, things, plants, and animals (Bamberger 1971; Giraldin 1997; Posey 2002a; Wagley 1977).[9] In an earlier time period, however, the Kayapó peoples might have had indirect contact with disease from colonists, or heard oral accounts about the colonists in the area, through already established networks (Posey 2002a). Today, at least one group within the Kayapó Indigenous Lands has preferred to remain relatively hidden from the settled Kayapó villages, still preferring a seminomadic lifestyle. Other Kayapó factions in the past might have had the same reaction to the colonization process. Even with the research presented, it has been difficult to examine the precolonial history of the Kayapó from a Western academic standpoint. Most of what is presented in the Western record, as noted above, charts migrations and practices after the 1500s.

Contact

Invasion

As noted in the introduction, many Kayapó claims to their lands point to the erroneous historical retelling that Pedro Álvares Cabral was the "first" person to discover Brazil. Cabral, has certainly been revered as the "founder" of Brazil in most history books, and his landing on the Brazilian coast in 1500 is the classic date for the beginning of Brazilian colonial history, although several navigators explored parts of the Amazon in the fifteenth century. The French, English, and Dutch had early footholds and explored some of the major tributaries of the Amazon near the river delta but were quickly expelled by the Spanish and Portuguese. The Portuguese had, by chance, gained most of their territory in Brazil from the 1750 Treaty of Madrid, a renegotiated version of the 1494 Treaty of Tordesillas. Between the first and second treaties, the Portuguese set up some forts, notably Belém in 1616, now the capital of Pará, where the Kayapó Lands sit, and Manaus in 1669, now the capital of Amazonas. What is most relevant to the Kayapó's history, and that of frontier economies in Amazonia, is the post–1750 time period that reconfigured land and labor in important ways. This period is characterized by the Pombal Era, named after José de Carvalho e Mello, Marquis de Pombal (Schmink and Wood 1992, 39; Sommer 2005).

Pombal sought to promote trade and set up coastal cities as centers for markets based on *drogas do sertão* (wild forest products), and he was also interested in the promotion of plantation economies (Hecht and Cockburn 1990, 66; Schmink and Wood 1992, 40; Sommer 2005). Miscegenation was also encouraged. This resulted in the continued growth of a *mestizo* and *caboclo* demographic, which Pombal supported, and the ongoing rapid decline of indigenous populations that had sustained direct contact with settlers near the riverbanks and cities. The Pombal reforms were meant to transform indigenous peoples from captives to wage laborers and to use enslaved Africans instead to fuel his envisioned plantation economies of sugar, cotton, coffee, and cacao (Hecht and Cockburn 1990,

66–67). Pombalian reforms anticipated many of the subsequent development initiatives, albeit on a smaller scale, that marked the Amazon region during the military regime of the 1960s (Hecht and Cockburn 1990, 67).

During Pombal's time, most colonial settlements were concentrated near the coast or on the Amazon River, and relied heavily on an export economy. Missionaries had set up centers in the area, and the military was busy with the creation of forts and posts to protect their newly established territory. Reforms created many class-based distinctions that were later complicated during the rubber boom of the nineteenth century and the drive to the west in the mid-twentieth century (Hecht and Cockburn 1990, 71). Those indigenous groups that formerly lived close to the coast and the major tributaries of the Amazon were first exploited as slaves, and then as laborers. Seventy-five percent of indigenous languages became extinct after contact, and the groups that suffered most were the ones closest to the coast (Moore 2006). Still, in this era, the interior was largely unexplored by settlers. Peoples like the Kayapó lived on smaller tributaries of the Amazon and were affected by colonization in a different way than indigenous peoples who lived near coasts or major rivers. A few travelers and nonindigenous others did penetrate the region where Kayapó peoples lived, chronicling some of the first reports on the Kayapó.

In the early years of colonial Amazonian history, Kayapó peoples appear relatively seldom in written records, and their story is not well-known beyond information contained in oral histories. As time passed, and the population in the newly founded colony increased, written records of indigenous groups became more and more frequent. It would be remiss to believe that the several centuries of colonization did not affect Kayapó peoples. The ongoing process of settlement in the Amazon area more than likely did reverberate among Kayapó peoples, through different forms of direct and indirect contact vis-à-vis trade with other indigenous groups, and sporadic interactions with nonindigenous travelers in the region.[10]

As has been mentioned, historically the Kayapó fissioned or abandoned villages because of disease, death, disputes, or the desire to create a new home. It is likely that many Kayapó communities splintered and fragmented during the intensified contact with non-Kayapó groups in the region. Indeed, the earliest memories of many of the elders I spoke with in A'Ukre, as well as their retellings of their parents' and grandparents' histories, was of a highly transitional period during which they were constantly moving—albeit this history of course retells personal experience that took place centuries after Cabral's landing. For example, an elder woman recounted.

> I was born in the Kapot—a village in Mato Grosso, and when I already had kids I moved to Pará, to Kubenkranken. In Mato Grosso, in the cerrado, there was a big village—like a capital, and one person separated from this village. When

I was a small child I was part of this group, and they moved and made a new village, but all the warriors and all the elders died. Then, when I was already a bit bigger, part of this group moved to Kubenkranken—about ten of them— and then all became dispersed and no one was really together anymore. . . . In the past, people didn't live like they do today. They would move every day and make a camp, and in the morning move again—this was the way of the Kayapó. They would eat meat from the forest (*mry*), and the fruits of the forest, and they wouldn't get sick like today. . . . They were only walking and walking and they wouldn't get sick from the food. They would eat cacao, açai, honey, and be fine. In the past no one knew how to make farinha—they only knew how to make *beiju* [a type of manioc dish], because that took only a day. . . . My grandmother explained the history to me and I learned with my grandmother. Because of this I am explaining everything to my grandkids as well.

An elder leader remembered.

We were only walking and walking and we didn't stop because of fighting. There was a chief [name], that was only walking and there wasn't a village or a place to make a garden, because we were afraid to fight and be killed. We walked very far, and we returned one way and went another way. We were walking and we stopped at a river. My mother and father went to the forest. And at that time another chief came, and took me and my brother with him, and took us to his village. My mother and my father stayed at that place. I stayed . . . six years until the white people started threatening us. . . . We stayed with the white man while the others were menaced [at another village]. And the white man told us that our parents were there.

These personal histories certainly reflect the sustained and abrupt shifts Kayapó peoples endured in the past century, and potentially reflect the endured experiences of their peoples since colonization. Many early accounts of the Kayapó were often based on contact with groups that had dispersed from larger villages (such as Pykatôti), who were living in a constant state of fear of settlement because of warfare among other tribes, related groups, and outsiders. In the early 1900s, the states of Pará and Mato Grosso, where initial "direct" contact took place, were still underdeveloped and relatively unknown in comparison to the coastal and southern regions of Brazil. Those indigenous groups, like the Kayapó, who fled to, or had originally inhabited, the interior, had large tracts of land at their disposal. As these stories show, fissioning was a common and easy option for intravillage conflict among the Kayapó in the early twentieth century. But this process was also heart-breaking and confusing, all the while Kayapó peoples retained the defense of their peoples and lands they wished to continue to call home.

Rondon

After the Pombal Era (1750–1777), the Amazonian economy changed relatively little until the rubber periods (1850–1920, 1942–1945). In the interim, things began to change rapidly for the Kayapó peoples. Brazil became independent from Portugal between 1822 and 1824, and at that time, the northern "Amazonian" colony (*Grão-Pará*) of the country reaffirmed its alliance with the new independent nation (Schmink and Wood 1992, 41). The first rubber period established a lucrative, but short-lived, booming economy in the Amazon region based on one commodity (rubber), overlaid with previous markets based on a range of forest products, mercantile exchanges, and experimentation with agricultural goods. Beginning as early as the 1800s, the rubber trade escalated rapidly after 1839 when Charles Goodyear, the American inventor, discovered the vulcanization process, which transformed rubber into a more durable commodity. In the Amazon, the profitable rubber trade again organized people, goods, and markets into an unequal system, where wealth was concentrated in the hands of a few (Weinstein 1983).

The trade spurred a debt/patronage system of *aviamento*, by which *seringueiros* (rubber tappers) would trade their goods at the local trading post, owned by the local landholder, in exchange for food and other small items (Schmink and Wood 1992, 43). The local post would be linked to a supplier and would also be part of the debt/patronage system. The rubber eventually landed in the hands of the rubber barons, who exported the goods to foreign centers of commerce (Hecht and Cockburn 1990, 73). Migrants moved into the Amazon region from the northeast and other parts of the country to take part in the boom. The population in Amazonia increased by 400 percent (Barnham and Coomes 1994, 73; Schmink and Wood 1992, 45). This, of course, was a lavish period in the Amazon's history, during which excessive and decadent wealth flowed through centers like Manaus, which was dubbed the "Paris of the Tropics"; indeed, per capita wealth increased by 800 percent during the first rubber boom, followed by a dramatic collapse when the rubber trade was shifted to an Asian rubber plantation system after 1910 (Barham and Coomes 1994, 73).

Settlements and excursions into the Amazon intensified during the rubber boom. Not coincidentally, at the same time, given the increase of population in the interior, indigenous pacification efforts across the country became systematized by Cândido Mariano da Silva Rondon. Rondon played a major role in developing a federal policy on indigenous/outsider affairs in Brazil, including the development of the Service for the Protection of Indians (SPI) (Ramos 1984, 90). Rondon was a military officer who, at the turn of the twentieth century, opened up the interior from 1890–1919. Rondon's politically motivated excursions had the purpose of pacifying and integrating indigenous peoples into the national agenda in order to strengthen the "collective individual" of the

Brazilian nation (Ramos 1998, 155). The SPI was founded in 1910 and in 1936 formally took over the guardianship of the indigenous population in Brazil.[11] In this model, the attitude toward indigenous groups was paternalistic and driven by Colonel Rondon's motto, "Die if you must, but never kill," which stood for his policy that "pacification" could be met with attraction methods. Rondon's campaign differed from earlier treatments of indigenous groups as slaves or as enemies in war (Ramos 1998). Rondon's methods were considered progressive and more humane; however, those methods often had devastating consequences (Ramos 1984, 97). The most severe was death, but social and cultural upheaval also ensued. In addition, Rondon's efforts at pacification often intersected with other interests in the interior. As previously noted, other economies and missionaries that had slowly been expanding from key spots along the Amazon River began to penetrate the hinterlands.

With the establishment of SPI, later FUNAI, indigenous groups were asked to walk the slippery slope of being "internal outsiders," as they were neither considered proper citizens of the Brazilian nation nor external to it. This Catch-22 was outlined in the 1916 Civil Code, which established indigenous peoples as objects of guardianship. Indigenous peoples in Brazil are subject to these national laws, and, unlike some Native American peoples, they never had a history of treaty formation with the Portuguese or other colonists. Thus, national law is the only legal system and precedent within which indigenous peoples operate. The 1934, 1937, and 1946 Indian Statutes continued to define indigenous peoples as requiring federal guardianship, and, at the same time, noted some rights-based provisions about land occupation and use, albeit with the federal government ultimately having authority over of the land and subsoil rights.

During the period from 1862 to 1906, roughly overlapping with Rondon's exploits and the rubber boom, some Kayapó peoples were decimated by disease, while others sustained fissions to grapple with the shifting world around them. The SPI-directed Kayapó "pacification" efforts for the Gorotíre Kayapó (the group A'Ukre villagers came from) began around 1937 when the Kayapó peoples began to have more systematic contact with settlers in nearby towns. Tense relations took the form of ongoing repeated battles with rubber tappers, varying levels of integration to SPI posts, and exposure to different missionary groups. Communities and individuals moved in and out of attraction and missionary centers, finding that prolonged periods of contact often caused disease and death. Some groups, like the Xikrin Kayapó, joined the rubber tappers in the forest, and other villages, like Gorotíre, became places of resettlement for the increasingly fragmented population of Kayapó groups leaving the attraction posts (Fisher 2000). In an effort to solidify their relationship with the fragmented groups, the SPI started trading with certain Kayapó villages that had products, such as Brazil nuts, to sell them in Belém, the largest urban center in Pará.

As Schmink and Wood (1992) tell it, the second rubber boom started a two-decade-long conflict among rubber extractors, SPI agents, government officials, the federal police, the rubber bank, and many indigenous groups (including the Gorotíre Kayapó) in Pará. They note, for example, the rubber tappers, backed by the *Banco do Borracha* (Rubber Bank), accused SPI agents of facilitating systematic Kayapó raids by giving them firearms. A publicized media battle and a behind-the-scenes political battle followed in which these competing groups were pitted against one another. These events escalated to the extent that an anthropological team spearheaded by the now-famous Brazilian anthropologist Darcy Ribeiro—who was working for the SPI at the time—was brought in.[12] The team recommended that landing strips should be developed at indigenous posts, radio/telegraph services should be provided in the area, and indigenous lands divided. Based on these suggestions, the government of Pará decreed in 1952 that a reserve be established for the Kayapó. Although this decree was never upheld according to Schmink and Wood (1992), it was one of the first efforts, but not the only one, among the Kayapó to demarcate a homeland using the state's legal mechanisms. Nonetheless, relations with Brazilian society remained a mixture of persistence aimed at retaining territorial boundaries, developing alternatives to an unstable economy, and countering dominant narratives that marginalized their peoples.

We can see that several legacies from the first rubber boom persist: the concentration of propertied land estates in the hands of a few, the expansion of trade networks in the Amazon Basin that linked the interior to foreign markets, the system of social relations developed to support the increased trade networks, a persistent encroachment on Indigenous Lands as rural and urban settlements became more established, and the development of federal policies directed at indigenous peoples (Barham and Coomes 1994, 103–4). Even with the long history of export markets in the region, the state still considered the Amazon as peripheral to other developed economies in the country in the aftermath of the first rubber boom, despite the increase in trade networks, the development of new settlements, and continued dependence on a foreign export economy. At that time, the focus of Brazil's wealth was still in the southern regions (Cardoso 2002, 52). Other changes, such as the abolishment of the slave trade (1888) and subsequent establishment of the new republic, continued to drive the proven economies in the southeast of the country (Cardoso 2002). This was soon to change. The Kayapó peoples' defense of, and claims to, their territory and their rights would be challenged further when ranchers, miners, and loggers became part of the Amazonian landscape after the end of the second rubber boom, the time in Brazilian history when the military generals took center stage. In the 1940s, the Amazon region was flooded with *seringueiros*. The rubber from Asian plantations was inaccessible to the allied powers in World War II, and the United States turned to the Amazon, once more, as its source of latex. This time, the second rubber boom was the precursor to a series of events that would subsequently mark Kayapó peoples and their environment for centuries to come.

Development and Democratization

Development

In 1940, in the Amazonian city of Manaus, then-president Getúlio Vargas stood in front of a crowd of onlookers and gave a speech to encourage development of the Amazon. He remarked, "The Amazon, under the impact of our will and our labor, will cease to be a simple chapter in the history of civilization. . . . Everything which has been up to now done in the Amazon, whether in agriculture or extractive industry . . . must be transformed into rational exploitation" (quoted in Hall 1989, 3). In his speech, Vargas argued for economic activities in the Amazon that moved beyond the chaotic landholdings, small-scale agriculture, and extractive economies that followed the collapse of the rubber boom, toward "rational exploitation."

Part of Vargas's plan was a march to the west that, like that led by Rondon, summoned Brazil's indigenous groups to augment the national Brazilian character. Inspired by Raúl Prebisch's concept of national developmentalism, Vargas promoted a "nationalist authoritarian regime: the long arm of the state extending into the backwoods to spearhead economic development while ensuring social justice" (Garfield 2001, 25). His plan was realized when he formed the Superintendência do Plano de Valorização Econômica da Amazônia ([SPVEA], Superintendency for Economic Valorization of the Amazon), which focused on road construction and other economic incentives. Vargas' speech and subsequent plan could not have anticipated the dramatic land changes or the nationalistic flavor they would take in the following half-century. At that time, it was merely an inspirational call to define an urban and potentially industrialized vision of center/west regions and the Amazon.

In 1964 the military took political control of Brazil and set upon a development project that prioritized the Amazon region as critical for nation building and economic sovereignty (Fisher 1994). The dictatorship successfully mobilized the largest migration to the Amazon since it had first been colonized, and substantially complicated and altered the historical patterns of land use and land rights. The objective was to transform the Amazonian landscape, characterized by low population density, weak social organization, river-based travel, chaotic landholdings, and decentralized power, to road-based societies (Schmink and Wood 1992). The programs also sought to streamline the property regime structures and to intensify agriculture, mining, and ranching activities.[13] The government, initially under General Médici, initially implemented several systematized, large-scale development projects under the Programa da Integração

Nacional ([PIN] National Integration Program) (Fisher 2000; Wood and Wilson 1984, 146). There were several projects other than PIN, such as Operation Amazônia (Operation Amazon), and Programa Integrado de Desenvolvimento do Noroeste do Brasil (Polonoroeste, Northwest Integrated Development Program). Some of the main goals of the grandiose plans were to build a network of Trans-Amazonian highways (some of which were worked on by Payakan), create dams for hydroelectric power, speculate on mineral wealth, and sponsor migration to environs around newly built roads for agricultural development. These plans were organized by newly created national development agencies—Superintendência do Desenvolvimento da Amazônia ([SUDAM] Superintendency for the Development of the Amazon), the Instituto Nacional de Colonização e Reforma Agrária ([INCRA] National Institute for Colonization and Agrarian Reform), and the Amazon Bank—although these were often backed by multilateral lending institutions like the World Bank ([SUDAM replaced SPVEA] Fisher 1994; Martins 1984, 468). The state of Pará received many of the benefits promoted by SUDAM, and, as a consequence, ranching, mining, and logging developed in the state.

Like many nation-building projects, PIN programs severely underestimated the complexity of the diverse livelihoods already present in the region, dismissed the historical precedent for land and riverine use of the biophysical environment, fueled social tensions already in place, and ascribed to conceptualizations of place radically different from those of indigenous peoples (Martins 1984, 470; Santos 1984; Sawyer 1984, 189). These programs also overlooked the long-standing presence of indigenous groups that relied on large tracts of land for settlement relocation, long seasonal treks, and more immediate resource procurement activities. Agrarian reform, by means of INCRA, rested heavily on expropriation measures that left many rural producers unhappy, and a mess of land transactions from previous rubber-tapping regimes and de facto possession rights that the Instituto de Terras do Pará (Land Institute of Pará) tried to sort out first, after which future governors of Pará attempted to resolve (Schmink and Wood 1992, 62–63). Nevertheless, the colonization of the Amazon also offered migrants an "alternate space," for peasants moving away from other forms of exploitation (Sawyer 1984, 192). In the wake of these programs, the Kayapó peoples reinvigorated their fight for territorial demarcation, especially with the widespread deforestation that accompanied these programs.

The Kayapó peoples had a small victory in 1961, when one subgroup joined several other indigenous groups as the first inhabitants of the Xingu National Park, located in Mato Grosso, Brazil. The park was under the jurisdiction of FUNAI. While some hailed the creation of the park as a major success for indigenous rights, its creation was overshadowed by what anthropologist Alcida Ramos (1998, 149) calls "benevolent paternalism." The success of the Xingu Park's demarcation as the first indigenous territory was eclipsed by the military regime's promise of developmental projects in the Amazon region and their ability to concentrate "problem" indigenous groups in one area. Moreover, even though the park was federally recognized, the enforcement and protection of these lands was never ensured, a story that continues today. Despite outlining provisions for land occupation and rights of use, land demarcations and decrees were rarely enforced and were under constant pressure from new roads being developed in the region.

Government-sponsored colonist programs began alongside newly constructed highways (such as the Trans-Amazonian Highway, BR-230, PA-150, and PA-279). State-sponsored rural/rural and urban/rural migrations begun under the leadership of INCRA were followed by spontaneous migrations. Thus, the colonist plan had a dual purpose: (1) bringing "people with no land to a land with no people," and (2) building up agricultural capital and private property (Little 2001, 105). The military regime's policies had immediate and considerable impacts on the environmental degradation and social organization of the Amazon region in general, and the state of Pará in particular. Large-scale development and infrastructural projects (such as mining and ranching enterprises), and even those projects focused on small-scale farming and road construction, transformed the Amazonian environment and greatly impacted its peoples. Property rights remained unclear and unprotected, and those with private property titles were mostly large landholders (Cardoso 2002; Fearnside 2001). Policies such as the Land Statute (1964), the Forest Code (1965), the Mining Code (1967), and the renovation of the SPI to FUNAI (1968) that followed federal, state, private, and spontaneous development sought to update and restructure regulations governing the unwieldy "Wild West" atmosphere that characterized the region (Hecht 2012, 4). Even with attempts at streamlining regulations, high levels of deforestation, the urbanization of the Amazon, and the continued displacement of indigenous groups and landless peasants persisted.[14]

These "neo-natures," or the combination of logging activities, metallurgical extraction, silvo-industrial, and agro-industrial activities, also contributed to a dramatic change in land cover (Hecht 2012, 4). The rate of forest loss from 1978 to 1989 was 1.98 million hectares per year, from 1990 to 1994, 1.38 million hectares per year, and from 1995 to 2000, 1.90 million hectares per year (Laurance, Albernaz, and Da Costa 2001). Approximately 75 percent of the deforested lands, and 11 percent of the area forested in 2002, are now cattle pasture (Barreto et al. 2005, 2; Fearnside 2001). However, since 2004, deforestation rates have somewhat declined, leveling off with subsequent heightened attention paid to conservation, which will be discussed later. Gold was found on the reserve as early as the late 1970s, but extraction escalated in the 1980s (Hecht 2012, 4). Land conflicts around the Kayapó lands have been characterized as "explosive," and deforestation rates are particularly high (Fearnside 2001).

Economies of Extraction and Infrastructural Politics

While the Kayapó peoples attempted to define minor portions of their current territorial homeland in the 1950s, the consolidation and fragmentation of the region in southern Pará and northern Mato Grosso from the 1970s onward only heightened interests. Beginning in the 1970s, following initial pacification efforts and the second rubber boom, the urban centers surrounding the Kayapó Lands mushroomed, as newly built roads resulted in mining operations (i.e., gold and cassiterite), timber extraction, small farms, and ranching activities (Merkens et al. 2002; Schmink and Wood 1992). Frontier towns deeply troubled Kayapó communities, which had only recently established sustained contact and connections with a long-term settler presence in the area. In one decade alone, from 1970 to 1980, the state of Pará experienced a population growth as high as six percent (Sawyer 1984, 195). Municipalities split, creating new sources of revenue for governments and towns soon to populate the areas (Schmink and Wood 1992, 50). The frontier towns, which today define the areas surrounding the Kayapó Lands, became spots on the map, seemingly built out of nowhere. Large-scale mining operations like the Serra dos Carajás—the largest iron ore project in the world—began the landscape of conservation and extraction we see today.

Mineral wealth identified by the 1971 to 1975 radar satellite mapping surveys of the Amazon, which are commonly referred to as RADAM and RADAM-BRASIL, only solidified ongoing mining interests in the area, which were subject to the 1967 Mining Code (Momsen 1979). Large-scale hydroelectric dams were set up to power mining operations, some of which were centerpieces of nationally driven export-oriented development policies. Hydroelectric dams were soon slotted under a regional power company, Electronorte. Years later, Electronorte was the same company that backed two proposals for hydroelectric dams on the Xingu, one in the late 1980s, and that of Belo Monte Dam, which the Kayapó are continuing to fight today (Schmink and Wood 1992, 67). Alongside large-scale, more infamous mining operations, small-scale gold mining drew *gamipeiros* (miners) to the area, disfiguring a rapidly expanding and changing landscape. Although logging in Pará had begun as early as the 1960s, it intensified in the 1970s with newly built sawmills and roads.

Within the milieu of gold, ranching, and farming enterprises in southern Pará, timber markets swallowed the area surrounding the Kayapó Lands at the same time that Tucumã and Ourilândia do Norte were battling out their niches in the region. As Schmink and Wood (1992) have argued in one of the first political ecology works, the towns of Tucumã and Ourilândia do Norte, currently important urban centers on PA-279 for the northeastern villages in the Kayapó Lands including A'Ukre, aptly serve to illustrate some of the false starts, best intentions, and rapid transformations of frontier zones. Tucumã was one of the contested private colonization programs—as opposed to public programs—in the Amazon region, backed by a private company. The company sponsored migrations mainly from the south of Brazil to Tucumã, a zone identified with nutrient-rich soils (*terra roxa* or "red land"), to three thousand lots being proposed for agriculture and cattle ranching (Schmink and Wood 1992, 200). The company designed the town, built up the infrastructure (schools, roads, and post offices), and provided different forms of assistance (credit) for the newly migrated population.

According to Schmink and Wood (1992) although the project got off to a rough start, it was able to eventually get underway around the same time that gold was found not far off in what was to become Ourilândia do Norte, spurring spontaneous migrations to the edges of the Tucumã project. Tucumã was soon infused with access to an unplanned economy—gold—that, not surprisingly, was initially important to the economies of the newly migrated and struggling farmers and ranchers. The gold economy cemented the linkages between Ourilândia and Tucumã that continue today and in recent years has surged again as a centerpiece of the local economies. The private project ended in 1985, and by 1988 the lands of the Tucumã project had become part of the local municipal government (Schmink and Wood 1992). Tucumã and Ourilândia remain important centers of commerce on PA-279. The once-majestic Hotel D'Oro (Gold Hotel), which sits just off the palm-lined main street in Tucumã, remains a powerful reminder of this recent chapter in Tucumã's history and its ongoing interconnections with Ourilândia do Norte through different mining enterprises in the region.

While logging had also nominally been part of the area, by the 1970s the timber industry was rampant, and Pará had become one of the more important timber-producing parts of the country, churning out wood from more than 140 species (Uhl and Vieira 1989, 98; Veríssimo et al. 1998). Not more than thirty years later, timber production in Pará constituted 13 percent of its gross product, and 65 percent of the total roundwood in Brazil (Veríssimo et al. 1998, 128). Migration projects, road building, and government incentives for sawmill construction supported Pará's shift from an insignificant to an established player in timber production (Uhl and Vieira 1989). With infrastructure in place, logging was able to flourish. Of all targeted species for logging surrounding the Kayapó area, the one most fixated on was broadleaf mahogany (*Swietenia macrophylla*), one of the most profitable timber species in the world.

The Kayapó and their then-occupied lands became potential partners for loggers as their villages were located in an area where legal enforcement of environmental laws was difficult, and where there were plenty of mahogany stands (Merkens et al. 2002). Moreover, villagers were interested in generating badly needed revenue for their communities, as federal agency budgets often could not meet local demands for different services and basic needs, such as health and education services (Turner 1995b; Zimmerman 2010). Broadleaf mahogany is distributed sparsely throughout the forest, making timber-extractive activities more of a scouting venture than a clear-cutting activity, thus, ostensibly, making both the presence of loggers and the impact of the selective logging practices minimal intrusions on village life. However, logging roads, the sloppy extraction of young and dead trees, and the depletion of genetic information (e.g., mahogany and other species) hindered mahogany regeneration (Zimmerman 2010). This process also impacted villages in ways that were unexpected and spurred intense intra- and intercommunity fighting. Road building and contact with settlers increased the prevalence of disease in those villages engaging in logging, increased intra and intervillage fighting over common pool resources, and resulted in social differentiation that was marked by monetary revenues. Logging had been halted by 1999 when international watchdog organizations, such as Greenpeace, encouraged the Brazilian government to stop illegal activities in the area and local communities decided the social, ecological, and health tradeoffs were not worth the needed revenue stream (Zimmerman et al. 2001).

As conflict over logging heated up, small-scale mining ventures were founded in the Kayapó Lands. Certainly, gold mining in southern Pará already had well-established centers near the Kayapó Lands, such as those close to Ourilândia do Norte. Miners were eager to find new sites, especially in areas like Indigenous Lands that had previously been unexplored (Schmink and Wood 1992). Placer mining techniques commenced in the 1980s, outside Gorotíre and other villages. Many Kayapó villages established contractual relationships with miners, despite governmental legislation prohibiting such activities. The chiefs, young Kayapó leaders, and villagers argued that, much like the logging, this income generated the much-needed cash flow for health and other services the government had not been providing since it downsized federal Indian agencies (Turner 1995a). Increased monetary wealth coming into the community also resulted in young leaders spending their money extravagantly on cars, urban residences, prostitutes, and alcohol—a moment in the Gorotíre Kayapó's history well documented by anthropologist Terence Turner (1995a; also see Noronha Inglez de Sousa 2000). A *Los Angeles Times* story that ran at the time with the title "How Gold Led Tribe Astray" argued that "Brazil's Kayapó are an example of how a good relationship with Mother Nature can turn bad" (Long 1995). The environmental community, especially NGOs, criticized these activities that had been undertaken by the Kayapó—curiously, not two decades later, some of those same organizations shifted their mission statement to advocate working alongside corporations, like mining enterprises, to promote sustainable development and conservation efforts among indigenous communities through corporate, socially responsible initiatives (Turner 1995a).

At the same time, other villagers challenged these new leaders' spending patterns, and contested the uneven distribution of the monetary benefits of mining within the community (Turner 1995a). Villagers also had firsthand experience with the adverse social and environmental effects of these large-scale extraction activities, whether it was from mining or logging. For example, one elder I spoke with reflected that "when the loggers enter with machines they leave the forest the same. With the gold miners it is different. There is poison in the water. But with logging after one or two years it returns to exactly how it was . . . Yet what did it do for us? All we did was fight. The loggers appeared to be our friends and now where are they? They are gone." Another elder echoed a similar sentiment reflecting on the past: "My grandfather used to be a fierce warrior. . . . But now there are no longer wars. Now everyone who is family is a friend. Except for during the time of logging when the Kayapó started to fight with one another over the boundaries of their lands. But now the logging has stopped and there are no longer any more fights. Now it is prohibited to fight with a friend." By 1999, the villagers' discontent, health concerns associated with malaria and mercury contamination—a direct result of placer mining techniques—and increased governmental enforcement of policies concerning extractive activities within Indigenous Lands had halted mining activities.[15]

Mining and logging activities were not the only exchanges Kayapó communities had with outsiders in the latter half of the twentieth century. In the 1970s, at the same time logging and mining interests were intensifying in Pará, the military regime also made some administrative changes, that had already been hinted at, that directly affected indigenous populations. In 1967, the SPI, which had declined as a functional body, was revamped and renamed FUNAI. And FUNAI, like the SPI, was arguably a governmental body through which the "federal government under military rule sought to extend its control of the economy of the interior" (Fisher 1994, 224). Anthropologist David Maybury-Lewis (1979, 2) suggested that the purpose of FUNAI was more to assure the security and development of the Brazilian economy than to protect indigenous rights. With legal backing to do just that, FUNAI continued to oversee and advocate for indigenous groups.[16] For the Kayapó this meant that FUNAI oversaw all activities that went on near, in, and around the Kayapó-occupied lands. As a result, FUNAI also became the main entity that brokered relations between loggers, miners, chiefs, and communities. A mixture of hostility and cooperation characterized Kayapó interactions with these governmental agencies.

The restructuring of FUNAI at the moment in Brazil's history when the Amazon region was quickly changing was not unexpected. The Kayapó and other indigenous groups have historically held inconsistent positions within the nation-state, but certainly as distinctive peoples within the country; federal interests and policies toward indigenous peoples intensified in order to fit the "Indian question" within state-making responses to development initiatives. As noted above, federal policies toward indigenous peoples were far from consistent;

however, despite the changing rights associated with indigenous peoples, over the years federal policy did tend to assume that a divisive civil society was a threat to the emerging nation-state. However, removing this divisiveness meant to undermine cultural distinctiveness, both legally and ideologically.

European scientific ideas about race and racial correlations with "advanced" civilizations had begun to influence Brazilian politics in the 1900s. At the turn of the twentieth century, Brazilian elites felt that the inferior aspects of indigeneity and other minority populations could be erased through biological means. While influenced by European biological-based scientific ideas about race and advancement, Brazilians did not uphold the continental thought that racial mixing produced "barbarous" populations. Instead, Brazilian elites found common ground with theorists, such as Joseph Arthur Bogineau, then head of the French diplomatic mission, who envisioned mixing as way to "whiten" the population. Whitening in this context was considered imperative for the "sparkling future of Brazil" and to rid the nation of Afro-Brazilian and indigenous minorities, which would be achieved in part by easing the immigration process for European migrants and supporting racial mixing (dos Santos and Hallewell 2002, 72–73; Warren 2001, 70).

Popular representations of indigenous peoples, colonial and state policies toward indigenous peoples, missionary tactics to civilize indigenous peoples, and legal measures were all directed toward subsuming indigenous identities within the hegemonic discourse of the larger geopolitical entity. However, all this changed in the mid-1980s. New social movements and global trends paved the way for a postauthoritarian state, and the shift to democratization and multiethnic platforms. The military rule and mega-development policies characteristic of the Vargas dictatorship (1930–1945 and 1951–1954) and the military era (1964–1985) were diffused in the latter half of the 1980s. In that same decade, the development of an international environmental agenda, what is now referred to as global environmental governance, and a growing transnational indigenous movement altered the political and economic landscape, and the ways in which Kayapó communities could resist, negotiate, and confront (figure 4).

Neodevelopmental Futures

In the 1980s and 1990s, the Kayapó received considerable attention in the media as they launched themselves, with political organization and leadership, into the international arena. Their mobilization efforts capitalized on distinct new regional and international social movements, as well as on the reforms that were outlined in the 1988 Brazilian constitution. As outlined in the introduction, the constitution defined a new, liberal, democratic state that moved away from the centralization of authoritarian regimes toward privatization measures and more municipal control of governmental resources (Schiffer 2002, 212;

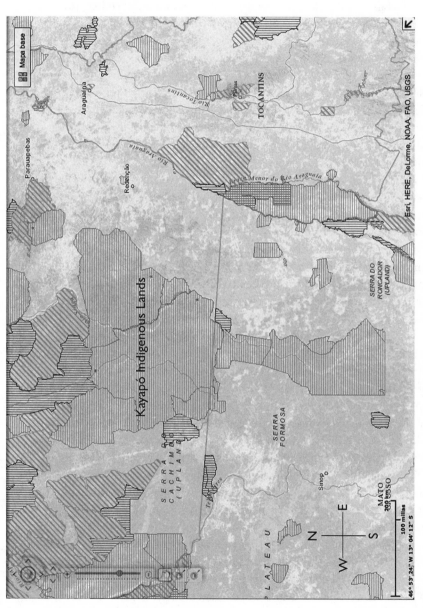

Figure 4. Deforestation around the Kayapó Lands. Layers show Indigenous Territories, protected areas, and deforestation since 2000. Made with RAISG (http://raisg.socioambiental.org/mapa-online/index.html).

Toni 2003). It also spurred the adoption of a series of environmental measures that were initially envisioned in a policy that had been put forth a couple years earlier by then-president Sarney called Nossa Natura (Our Nature). Article 68 described the protection of the country's natural resources for conservation purposes, and was the first to explicitly grant land rights to indigenous peoples through land acquisition and demarcation.[17] The Amazon was envisaged as an "inhabited forest and mosaic countryside," dominated by green markets alongside other recognized economies (Hecht 2012, 4–5). A period of reorganization followed after 1988, in which old national networks of power were transfigured to accommodate the new transnational nodes of people, places, and goods, based on ideas about conservation, trade liberalization, and privatized industry (Schiffer 2002). For indigenous peoples, including Kayapó communities, the process had mixed results.

The 1988 constitutional backing of indigenous rights and conservation programs was soon linked to the financial concerns of the country's development plans. High-profile social movements, backed by regional and international networks, like the indigenous movement combined with the environmentalist movement, began to draw international attention to the loss of traditional forms of productive practices, loss of worldwide forest cover, and climate change. Established in 1982, the United Nations' Working Group on Indigenous Populations was set up as a forum where indigenous leaders could address some of these rights-based concerns (Muehlebach 2001). Just prior, the 1987 Brundtland Commission Report was a benchmark document that outlined a program for development that incorporated social and cultural needs within economic and environmental concerns across different generations. Multilateral organizations, such as the World Bank and the Inter-American Development Bank, reorganized their lending policies to reflect concerns about social equity and the environment, when activist groups began to pressure them for accountability (Goldman 2005; Lawson 2007). New policies rewarded countries that embraced state-sanctioned multiculturalism, communal rights for indigenous territories, and sustainable development policies (Horton 2006, 840). For example, Brazil's World Bank loans in the 1970s and 1980s focused on building the Amazon's infrastructure to attract migration to the region and support large-scale mining and iron-smelting operations in the central-eastern part of the region.[18] However, from the 1990s onward, grant funding (as opposed to loans) was used to fund conservation projects and social development concerns like the Rain Forest Pilot Program ([commonly known as PP-G7] Redwood 2002). Similarly, the first debt-for-nature swaps were made at this time, pioneered by the Nature Conservancy to demarcate the Grande Sertão Veredas National Park.

Up until the mid-2000s, Brazil has been a frontrunner in second and third wave conservation efforts to demarcate sustainable-use protected areas (Rylands and Brandon 2005, 613). In 1970, only 0.36 percent of Brazil's land area was protected (Toni 2003). By 2005, Brazil's protected areas jumped to 584,407 km², or 6.86 percent of its landmass (Toni 2003). Extractive reserves, like the Chico Mendes Rubber Reserve in Acre, are examples of this type of protected area, where local forest dwellers govern their own common pool resources through individual and communal property land rights to tap rubber, gather Brazil nuts, and practice subsistence agriculture (Cardoso 2002; Hecht 2007).

Democratization and neodevelopmental reforms had several implications for indigenous peoples in Brazil, such as the Kayapó. Federal policies and privatization measures began to move away from centralized government activities, to attract foreign capital and connect Brazil to the new North-South and South-South networks. While metropolitan cores like that of São Paulo became deeply entrenched in neoliberal projects, in the Amazon this only accelerated growth in already established industries (Schiffer 2002). If anything, the opening up of capital for foreign investment only attracted companies to develop agricultural projects or to conduct further exploration for mineral wealth in the region and promote conservation–corporate alliances surrounding the pricing of nature. Other changes in governmental departments impact indigenous groups and their relationship to their lands. The creation of the Instituto Brasileiro do Meio Ambiente e dos Recursos Naturais Renováveis ([IBAMA] Brazilian Institute for the Environment and Renewable Natural Resources), the national environmental body responsible for coordinating and implementing environmental policy, and the restructuring of FUNAI's internal organization are two major changes that affect the Kayapó. In 1989, four federal departments merged to create IBAMA. Theoretically, IBAMA was also responsible for the administration of conservation areas—a job that now sits with the Instituto Chico Mendes de Conservação da Biodiversidade (Chico Mendes Institute for Biodiversity Conservation [also known as ICMBio])—and regulation of illegal logging, although "charges of fraud and corruption in the forest exploitation inspection system are [thus] made constantly" (Toni 2003, 153).

Terras Indígenas, or "Indigenous Lands," are the federal responsibility of FUNAI and they are, regardless of national law, for the Kayapó, their sovereign mandate. Originally, FUNAI was a centralized government agency overseeing different aspects of indigenous administration including health and education. The decentralization processes that began after the 1988 constitution also restructured FUNAI. Starting in 1999, indigenous health issues were slotted under FUNASA and later with the Special Secretariat on Indigenous Health; educational programs became the responsibility of local municipal governments. The budget of FUNAI was also cut drastically. Despite the budgetary issues, Indigenous Lands continued to be cast in a conservationist light, and indigenous groups were increasingly envisioned as environmental stewards or protectors of national patrimony. Indigenous leaders, began to use environmentalist scripts as mechanisms by which to reach concerned audiences and potential supporters of their cause, and, importantly, create new alliances and partnerships. These scripts were attempts to make cultural difference legible and palatable, as leaders and their communities had intimately experienced and continued to experience a hegemonic construction of their bodies, lands, and livelihoods as inferior. The partnerships ushered in a new era of political networking and governance that relied on cross-scale and multi-scale linkages across peoples, nations, and lands. As with Subramanian (2009, 22), I contend that indigenous politics "can be informed by notions of sovereignty, equality, and rights, even as it uses idioms and forms of negotiation that appear antithetical to a politics of self-determination."

For example, consider Payakan Kayapó's statement in the mid-1980s about the Kayapó lands.

> The forest is one big thing; it has people, animals, and plants. There is no point saving the animals if the forest is burned down; there is no point saving the forest if the people and animals who live in it are killed or driven away. The groups trying to save the race of animals cannot win if the people trying to save the forest lose; the people trying to save the Indians cannot win if either of the others lose; the Indians cannot win without the support of these groups, but the groups cannot win without the help of the Indians, who know the forest and the animals and can tell what is happening to them. No one of us is strong enough to win alone; together, we can be strong enough to win. (Payakan quoted in Hecht and Cockburn 1990, 193)

With the help of Payakan and other Kayapó leaders, the Kayapó peoples led one of the best-known indigenous activist campaigns during this time. As a result of their efforts, Kayapó leaders succeeded in establishing a moratorium on the first energy-driven loan the World Bank had considered granting to Brazil to halt a hydroelectric project near their territory. In 1988, two Kayapó leaders traveled to Washington, DC, to discuss the social and ecological consequences of building a hydroelectric facility near their territory with the World Bank. In a much written about meeting that took place in 1989, the Kayapó organized a Meeting of Indigenous Peoples of the Xingu in Altamira who opposed a development project (by the company Electronorte) to install the dam. This demonstration embodied the first "concerted political and social actions of a new alliance of indigenous nations of central Amazonia: the charter events, as it were, for future, united action in defense of their imperiled world" (*Kayapó* 1989, 18). During the 1989 meeting, Tuira Kayapó made a powerful statement to the energy company representative present that reverberates today. One version of her comments translate her quote to, "You are a liar—We do not need electricity. Electricity is not going to give us our food. We need our rivers to flow freely: our future depends on it. We need our jungles for hunting and gathering. We do not need your dam" (International Rivers 2008, np). The demonstrations at Altamira were certainly not the first time the Kayapó had experienced threats to their lands, yet it was the Altamira demonstration that firmly emplaced Kayapó communities in the international spotlight as peoples who will take on global environmental governance, sustainability, and indigenous sovereignty.

The 1989 Altamira efforts demonstrate several important developments in the organizational and institutional networks available to the Kayapó at this time. First, FUNAI and missionary activists were no longer the only avenues through which communities and individuals could address issues of social well-being, market availability, and land rights. The indigenous and environmentalist movement opened a discursive, performative, and legal space where indigenous groups could protest development policies, and advocate for other rights-based issues. Kayapó leaders effectively created new performative discourses that drew upon Western rhetoric regarding biodiversity and sustainability to garner support for their specific cause, even though these terms were not necessarily part of their customary rhetoric (Turner 2003a). Additionally, NGOs working for social and/or environmental issues, international celebrities, and private companies attempting ecologically conscious marketing schemes became part of the Kayapó repertoire for garnering support to demarcate and enforce their territory, and to open up alternative economic markets. Kayapó peoples capitalized on these new potential alliances with international organizations and figures to help defend their territory and explore new ways of making a living.

The burst of activity both before and after the 1989 conference is quite remarkable, and it demonstrates not only the breadth of activities the Kayapó were involved in but also the somewhat conflicting character of those decisions. A'Ukre, founded in 1979, has been deeply embroiled in this history. During the 1990s, A'Ukre forged cutting-edge partnerships and programs that reflected several conservation and indigenous rights trends that had taken hold worldwide, and engaged in three main activities during this time period: illegal timber extraction, a fair-trade Brazil nut oil project, and a conservation–community alliance that brought external researchers and revenue into the area. When briefly tabulated, these achievements are remarkable. As noted in the introduction, Anita Roddick, founder of the Body Shop, selected two communities to start a Brazil nut oil project, and A'Ukre was one of the villages selected to be part of the Body Shop's now-defunct Brazil nut oil project (Turner 1993). Leaders of A'Ukre also helped to establish an ecological research station near the village called (Pinkaití). This eventually resulted in a Kayapó program funded by CI. While that program no longer exists in the same form as it did in the early 1990s, it persisted for almost two decades and resulted in a series of projects in the Kayapó Lands meant to benefit communities and conservation alike.

In addition to CI, Instituto Raoni ([IR] Raoni Institute) also established programs in the western and eastern parts of the reserve, respectively, to help with territorial monitoring and sustainable development projects. Finally, major portions of the Kayapó Lands were demarcated, including lands that contained the village of A'Ukre (Zimmerman et al. 2001). Even more noteworthy is the observation that these programs were set up when the village was in the middle of a maelstrom. During those same decades, as already noted above, A'Ukre and many other villages were illegally engaged in the sale of mahogany, which brought a substantial and unprecedented amount of wealth to the community before it was stopped at the turn of the century (Zimmerman 2010).

The Altamira conference also reflects the effectiveness of the "scaling up" of Kayapó leadership and the creation of new forms of political action, which had been growing since the 1980s. During the decades of the 1980s and the 1990s, magnetic Kayapó leaders had stirred the public's imagination and demonstrated remarkable abilities for political organization, cultural mobilization, and persuading Western and non-Western audiences with their oratory skills. According to Laura Rabben, Raoni (also called Ropni), Pykatire, Kube-i, Megaron, Tuira, and Payakan, among others, mobilized "their followers for rituals of protest that have provided an alternative to raiding, international violence, and communal schisms" (Rabben 2004, 55). For example, Raoni helped to obtain federal recognition for Kayapó Lands and, in that process, toured with the pop star Sting, who subsequently set up the Rainforest Foundation to help with territorial demarcation. As already noted, Tuira made international headlines at the Altamira conference. Payakan, then a young leader from A'Ukre, had similar success with the fight for indigenous rights (Rabben 2004). Along with other leaders in the community, he was instrumental in coordinating the resistance march on Altamira, traveled to the United States to battle against the hydroelectric dam backed by the World Bank, negotiated logging contracts, carried out timber extraction activities in the reserve, and forged partnerships with external institutions.

Moreover, Kayapó leaders and warriors are experts in making counterspaces for indigenous authority in public and political spheres. Political expression has taken the form of song, dance, and visual aesthetics drawn from powerful ritual and ceremonial practice and has capitalized on visual technologies to advance both this expressive form and its political weight. These political tactics are in marked contrast to the behavior of Kayapó communities in the 1960s after pacification, when many Kayapó were made to feel ashamed of their traditional attire, such as body paint and lip plugs, and made efforts to conceal these cultural intimacies when interacting with nonindigenous Brazilians (Turner 1991a). Bodily aesthetics and presentation became a visual representation of the dependency, struggle, and tension that confronted the Kayapó peoples as they continued to encounter politics that racialized their bodies and lifeways. Many Kayapó individuals, eventually started to emplace Brazilian clothing and goods into different styles of ceremonial and daily dress, incorporating new modes of corporeality into their lifeworlds (Turner 1991a, 229). Soon, Kayapó leaders began to employ videography and photography to document their own cultural activities, to record their political activities—especially with exogenous groups—and to use videography and photography as representational weapons for mobilization efforts as well as for individual and collective expressive cultures.

In the 1990s, several Kayapó leaders (mostly men) were trained in documentary filmmaking, and today villages still enjoy making movies and exchanging films of ceremonies and other events (Turner 2003a; author's interviews). Yet, as Graham (2014, 306) notes, "identity-based assertions and claims to difference that are articulated against dominant social orders almost inevitably erase or flatten social distinctions, power differentials, and hierarchies, including those based on gender." In the Kayapó case, this has meant that with few exceptions male leaders have obtained high visibility within identity politic struggles, masking community-led or other gender-inflected practices that have also been central to resistance strategies and transformative discourses, with few exceptions, such as the notoriety of Tuira in the 1989 protest. Yet, where other groups, like those that came together in the Lacandón area of Chiapas, Mexico, to form the Zapatistas, have been able to effectively deploy "radio fields" and digital fields to promote their cause, more geographically isolated, but globally interconnected, groups like the Kayapó who are without easy access to regular communication technologies have relied more heavily on territorializing radio frequencies and distributing videos and photography to get their message out, although these digital landscapes are now rapidly changing (Bessire and Fisher 2012).

The 1989 Altamira conference is now overshadowed by a 2008 Altamira rally that had a similar goal of resisting large-scale hydroelectric development, in this case it was the Belo Monte Dam, near or on Kayapó Lands. In this way, Kayapó activism and other legal maneuvers (court battles, environmental impact processes) surrounding their territory remains a necessary part of daily and political life. Federally sponsored policies postdemocratization have continued to promote the expansion and development of areas in Pará and Mato Grosso by attracting private investment in the region, even though new federal policies have embraced many conservation measures. *Avança Brasil* (Advance Brazil), a governmental initiative designed in 2000, spanned "large expanses of the basin" to "accelerate economic development in the industrial agriculture, timber, and mining sectors of the economy" (Fearnside 2006a; Laurance et al. 2001, 438). This has been followed by programs, such as the Action Plan to Prevent and Control Deforestation in the Legal Amazon (2004–2009) that had positive results in the short term (Hall 2013). Additionally, some state-administered funds continue to reflect federal priorities for economic expansion. In Pará, where the Kayapó lands mostly sit, state-led interests lie in agricultural modernization, and especially in the development and exploitation of soybean production (Hecht 2012; Toni 2003). Pará and Mato Grosso have become two of the largest producers of soybeans in Brazil, with Brazil being the second largest soybean exporter in the world (Fearnside 2007; Barrionuevo 2007). Mining in the region also continues to threaten indigenous territories, since Congress has the final say over subsoil rights and concessions to their lands (Chernela 2006). Thus, conservation measures compete with other federal and state policies that attract foreign capital for the expansion, urbanization, and deforestation.

Conclusion

Heckenberger (2006, 312) concisely states, "In Amazonia, it has been diffi-cult to address questions of cultural variability and the diversity of landscape because little is known about the long-term history of the region; and, as often the case, an absence of robust historical knowledge is often taken as a lack of history at all." Perhaps it is because of the absence of "data," in the Western sense of the term, one might conjecture, that Amazonia and its imaginaries still have a powerful hold on the current readings of the region. The history presented here is one that demonstrates spatial processes that have been racially motivated, ontologically marked, and economically driven over time to disrupt and deterritorialize indigenous lifeways. The Kayapó peoples have met these challenges with an "adaptive, creative force," continuing to make a radically different vision of place that accommodates for multiple, contrasting agendas despite violent histories of change (Larson 1998, 14).

The strand of political ecology and feminist political ecology that is particu-larly pertinent to this chapter is research that examines indigenous livelihoods as linked to a wider and historically produced landscape of global environmental governance that includes protected areas, indigenous territories, conservation issues, infrastructural politics, state-making policies, and political and economic global trends that are marked by cultural difference and different geographies of belonging. I began by stitching together different sources of knowledge, including those from the community of A'Ukre, to explore mythical events, and another from archaeological and other historical evidence in regard to the patterning of pre-Columbian landscapes. In combining these diverse perspec-tives of Amazonian history, I cast a wide net and offer thick brushstrokes on precontact history as well as offer different ways of reckoning time and place. I stress that Kayapó oral histories emphasize an approach to territorialities that is markedly different from Western notions of history and landscape. These histories reflect long occupation in the area, one that is defined by a relation-ality between human and nonhuman beings that have co-produced place over time and marked by movement among different planes of being, urban cen-ters, and neotropical environments. In this way, Kayapó histories represent the affective, cosmological, and temporally entrenched connections to territory and its ongoing formations—landscapes that are not contained solely within legal boundaries, but is marked and made life-giving through stories, practices, and being in place.

Pointing to the complex interactions and human impacts on Amazonian pre-Columbian landscapes, I also emphasized the moments of contact and exploration, and their role in transforming Kayapó livelihoods and creating dominate narratives that have striated the region since colonial times. This is the period for which European imaginaries of the Americas generated fabled histories (Erikson 2008). These are the "Ür natures," that continue to seep into discourses about Amazonia today of green hells and pristine natures, and, in doing so, shape relationships to and policies about the region (Hecht 2012; Slater 2002). Regional interests drove the political economy of Amazonia during this epoch when Brazil became a colonial territory, a new republic, and eventually a nation-state. Colonial policies were not favorable to indigenous peoples, and through different forms of contact and pacification as well as hegemonic discursive positionings, many groups were devastated and forced into slave labor, or fled to the interior. Kayapó groups were not unaffected by these transformations, and had direct and indirect contact with settlers during this period. Contact with settler communities for the Kayapó was marked by migration, travel, warfare, and death. Yet, even with the centuries of change and transformation from 1500 to the 1900s, the intense territorial conflicts present in the Amazon today arguably began in the 1940s, when a new chapter of the Brazilian Amazon's history was written.

Kayapó efforts at territorial demarcation intensified during the mega-development and agro-industrial phase, as they faced new obstacles surrounding their now fiercely defended homeland. During this era, new settler communities, small-scale and large-scale farmers, ranchers, loggers, miners, rubber tappers, and extractivists became well embedded in a modernist vision of a productive landscape alongside, but also often in conflict with, indigenous territorial needs and histories of occupation, use, and production (Fisher 1994; Hecht 2012; Little 2001; Schmink and Wood 1992). After ratification of the Brazilian constitution in 1988, the subsequent Amazonian "mosaic countryside" was one of multiple socio-natures, where conservation and development were regarded as necessarily linked, and indigenous and other local economies valued vis-à-vis land demarcation policies. Nonetheless, deforestation continued alongside innovative and long-standing strategies for agribusiness, reforestation, and conservation, as well as the greening of corporate economies.

Moreover, in the 1970s and 1980s, the rise of high-profile movements like those of the environmentalists and indigenous peoples encouraged the emergence of new networks among external actors and indigenous groups. During this period, Kayapó peoples continued to experiment with market integration, were actively involved in exogenous politics at the local and national level, and persisted in forging what were hoped to be long-standing partnerships with external groups, despite negative media attention. Initial efforts at mobilization were defined by arguing for the integrity of their land; as for example in the 1989 Altamira protest. These social performances and protests were often defensive measures against the state, and were organized with the help of international NGOs and celebrity activists. Protests and governance strategies were rooted in the Kayapó peoples strength and expressive forms, documented visually and embodied in performances in place, which asserted the distinctiveness of their peoples, while at the same time deployed commonly used scripts for a legible politics of representation. Kayapó peoples' mobilization efforts remained and still remain focused on territorial retention, integrity, and demarcation, which they argue are critical for an effective politics of representational justice.

By the 1980s and 1990s, it seemed that Kayapó villagers and leaders had effectively sidestepped the economic constraints imposed on them by the frontier region that surrounded them and state-controlled ideas of indigenous citizenship. One leader reflected on this strength and said, "For now, we have partnerships, and it is certain that we have everything under control. Because the Kayapó are still using their traditions and customs, we will be okay. There are no roads to the village. . . . The way we are now is good." Kayapó leaders also built on old state-defined pathways of resistance to capitalize on international and transnational networks of power. These new alliances, economic activities, and forms of leadership and organization seemed to promise a different type of territorial security and autonomy despite limitations in pathways for procedural, distributional, and recognitional justice in regional and national forums.

However, this scenario did not last. In 2001, the Body Shop ceased working with A'Ukre and other villages, moved its operations elsewhere, and severed its relationship with the Kayapó. The large hydroelectric dam proposed in the 1980s was revised and put back on the drawing board, erasing any confidence in its cancellation (Chernela 2006). In addition, only a few of the NGOs that had expressed interest in the early 1990s remained, thereby indicating the ephemerality of forging certain partnerships. Notably, conservation NGOs continued to work within the area, although today their relationship to the Kayapó peoples has already shifted. The decentralization of FUNAI left the organization with minimal resources and more bureaucratic procedures and waypoints for indigenous groups to navigate in order to create an effective administration of health, education, and other concerns within their territory. At the turn of the twenty-first century, the seemingly well-formulated avenues for the Kayapó peoples to combat state-led agendas had deteriorated, and a new, more complicated picture emerged wherein partnerships and alliances were not so tidily defined.

The next phase in the Kayapó's history is already underway. When President Dilma Rousseff, the favored successor of the Worker's Party, and then-president

Lula (Luiz Inácio Lula da Silva) was elected in 2011, and again in 2014, a new energy-driven discourse began to leach into the identity of the country's '*socio-ambientalismo*' (socioenvironmentalism) for future decades. There has been a resurrection of some of the development policies that defined the 1960s and 1970s with a combined interest in using green economies and markets for the reduction of greenhouse gas emissions, a "backtracking" on many of the land-mark environmental policies in Brazil (particularly the Forest Code), and an uphill struggle to define the country's future economies, as its current wealth and success is built on economies of deforestation from previous decades (Zaks et al. 2009). Brazil's major exports remain centered on iron ore, soybeans, and cattle (Hecht 2012). Moreover, new legislation, such as that of PEC 215, which "would effectively halt the process of recognizing and demarcating indigenous territories throughout Brazil" amplifies the land question, indigenous rights, and ongoing projects to reterritorialize and map the Amazon in a way that meaningfully addresses indigenous futures and lifeways (Campbell 2015, 80).

It is important to read the subsequent chapters with these histories in mind, as they undergird and shape current territorial conflicts in highly politicized ways. They also point to the multiple ideological and material factors that underpin current territorial struggles in the Amazon and reveal the drastically different but tangled conceptualizations of making territory, people, and place. Subsequent chapters explore the layered aspects of these territorialities in more depth by showcasing how the Kayapó efforts at territorial retention and coun-termapping projects necessarily rely on maneuvering across these varied land-scapes and histories. Diverse claims to space and ties to place are relevant in considering different actors' perspectives about landscapes and their use. The discourse of environmental politics and construction of nature are of interest, as these powerful narratives and imaginaries shape ideas about what improvement and landscapes "should look like" (Neumann 1998, 15).

2

Performing Ceremony, Making Beauty

> All that we are is a story.
> —Richard Wagamese, *One Story, One Song*

Introduction

Koko urged me to sit next to her to watch the ceremony. I kicked off my flip-flops, and as I was preparing to sit down on the blanket, she grabbed the long-sleeved shirt tied loosely around my waist and asked, "Can I wear this?" "Sure," I said, as she pulled it over her sleeveless dress. I nudged in closer to Koko in the chilled night air and drew my legs up to get comfortable. As I watched the dancers who were performing the finale of the naming ceremony called Bemp, I knew I would probably be here for a while. They danced in a circle under the purple-black evening sky. We, like many other villagers, were sitting at the edge of the circle, set back a little, and the dust, being kicked up by the slow, pounding feet, settled over us before hitting our lungs. I could see the silhouettes of tents, as flashlights and ember-tipped sticks of wood swirled around in the darkness. Kids ran around, sometimes startling me as they came up from behind, their small feet moving so very quietly. Families were getting comfortable on blankets, like the one I sat on—it was a store-bought cotton item that barely softened the hardness of the central plaza. Paper-thin, the blanket did not stop the chill of the evening from creeping up from the ground. Still, it served as a thin layer, protecting us from the orange-red dirt that stained clothes, hands, and feet, and had a way of getting between toes and scattering around ankles.

Koko had made camp for the night, and she and her husband were one of the naming ceremony sponsors (*mekraremetch,* alternative spelling *mekrareremej*). Tall, deep green, palm fronds hung near our heads, and their tips made a silhouette in the lean-to that had been made especially for the name recipients. I had been told that being a festival sponsor for a naming ceremony was a lot of work, and Koko and her husband were obligated to give the dancers food and drink during the course of the night. If I tilted my head back, I could see two tall trees (*awry*) standing like goalposts on either side of the men's house (figure 5). Earlier, two men's groups, one from the elder and one from the younger age grades, had raced each other to see what group could raise a tree first—this was

Figure 5. Close up of the plaza area where ceremonies take place. Village houses are shown in the background.

a dangerous but important act during Bemp. The carefully crafted scaffolding, which was used to support the trees, was barely perceptible. Koko's young son, who was a name recipient this year, sleepily sat near us. His body was covered with geometric designs that had been lovingly painted in genipapo. These paintings were overlaid with matching *mẽ pa djê* (upper armbands) and wristbands, from which bright red *mòt* (macaw) feathers dangled. Fluffy yellow-white tufts of *kwỳi* (parakeet) stuck to his body. His oil-slicked hair was shaved in a deep "v." Bright red *pỳ* (urucum) had been placed around his mouth, below his nose, and around his cheeks.

Koko and I had a budding friendship at the time the festival was taking place. Over the past month, together with other women, I had helped her fulfill her festival sponsor duties. We had traveled across the river to collect banana leaves that we carried back in large sturdy bundles that hung from the *banhóró* tumpline straps, which we balanced across water-submersed logs when traveling to her house. I had walked alongside other women with my *kay* (or *ká*, an open-weave basket) to carve out the stones (*kẽn*) from the ground that would be used for the festival fire pits. I had helped by chopping *pingrã* (firewood) that was piled high into those same baskets. Women worked with each other to collect the wood as they lifted their share onto their heads and then piled on more firewood until it sturdily sat carefully balanced on top. These items (banana leaves, firewood, and rocks) formed the base for the ceremonial hearths used to make the manioc and fishcakes for the festival. While the women sponsors of the festival and their teams of women workers cultivated the requisite items for ceremonial hearths in the village, the men of the community fished for *krwytire*—the fish prized for naming festivals. After two weeks of being away, the fish came back smoked and tightly wrapped in large bundles. At the moment of their arrival *menóronùre* (young men without kids) ceremonially brought the bundles up from the river after the hunting and fishing expedition as they carried the weight of the festival food on their heads and backs.

Ceremonies were always accompanied by singing, and the songs tended to merge into dreams during the sleep-deprived nights of the finale. Going to sleep I smelled the urucum on my face and the smoke-filled fire pits. I remembered the way the metal basins caught the light as they were filled with the dark, roasted, yellowed kernels of manioc flour and the white, fleshy interior of the fresh fish catch. Glossy green banana leaves looked like flower petals as women laid them down to wrap the fish cakes. Still in the night, I recalled the resonance of the almost-silent chop of the genipapo fruit as it was sliced in half with a machete, the scraping on the side of bowls as women's fingernails clicked when they squished the seeds, water, and charcoal. The different sized *palitos* (Portuguese stylus) were fashioned as women prepared to spend hours body painting their husbands, children, ceremonial friends, and sometimes brothers (figure 6). There was also the rhythmic sound of shaking nut, hoof, and teeth-studded belts and anklets as men walked through the plaza or danced in the night. Everyone was both full of energy and bone weary during this time, as the dancers continued to go around and around.

I knew how hard Koko had worked to prepare for this ceremony and was happy that she had invited me to sit next to her that evening. Everyone I had spoken to in the village over the past couple months was also eager for me to "see" the ceremony. As Gaston Gordillo reminds us, it is Lefebvre that said, "it is by means of the body that space is perceived, lived, and produced" (1992, 162 quoted in Gordillo 2014, 11). I was still trying to grasp what that meant as I settled in for the finale that evening. I watched as Kaite, one of the lead dancers, went by. Three "troupes" were out on the line, circling around. Koko said they would continue doing this all night. I followed the dancers and their macaw song. "Ak ak ak" they sang, with their hands outstretched in the shape of a "T," tilting up and down as if in flight. "Ak ak ak" they sang again, while repeating dance steps, around and around, all night long.

While watching, I suddenly caught sight of Fabio, a visiting photographer who had also been circling the plaza, but in his own camera, shutter-stop, photographic step. He had joined the village weeks earlier to record the ceremony. He seemed to be everywhere during the dance. He was inside the circle, close to Kaite at one point, and then behind the dancers. Fabio's visit seemed to

Figure 6. Young women readying to paint a visitor's arm in the village. She is using a fresh batch of genipapo paint.

be perfect timing. The Bemp finale, for which preparations had been started months before, was finally taking place. Fabio's arrival in the village only exacerbated the electric atmosphere that had taken hold of A'Ukre. In addition to the Bemp, which Fabio would be photographing, the chiefs were going to arrange other shorter rituals that typically accompanied other naming festivals so they could highlight the range of dances and songs that the Kayapó performed during their ceremonial cycle. This was all because Fabio was present. Otherwise, the Bemp sequence and its shorter rituals and longer finale would have taken place without these additional accompaniments. Fabio was lucky, I was told by several of my Kayapó friends, as A'Ukre still practiced many ceremonies and have "not forgotten their culture."

The complex intersections between indigenous identities and their connections with performance gripped me that evening. It was as if Laura Graham and Glenn Penny's (2014, 2) words came alive: "Performance and performativity are fundamental to understanding the emergent, processual, and contextual nature of Indigeneity." Bemp was the first naming ceremony I attended with the Kayapó, and the analytical attention given to it in this chapter reflects my encounter with the celebration as much as it illuminates what matters for villagers in A'Ukre. Rituals, especially naming ceremonies, among the Kayapó have been described as occasions of transformation, continuity, and change. For example, David Maybury-Lewis's (1979) Harvard Gê Project argued that the Central Gê and Bororo were known for their complex ceremonial processes that were marked by kin and nonkin solidarities, a repertoire of songs and choreographed dances, and ritual objects that were often linked to prescriptive inheritances or gendered use—all of which reflected dialectical tensions between self/other, nature/culture, and public/private. From William Fisher (2003, 117) we learned about Kayapó worldviews and the way in which naming ceremonies are a "temporal and spatial coordination of exchanges." Vanessa Lea (1986) carefully outlined the inheritance principles of households in the community and the vital role of *nekrêtch* (specific ritual objects, alternative spelling *nekrej*) that circulate through lineages and community life that, like Ewart (2014, 22) with her work with the Panará, counters the dual organization of Central Gê and non-Gê peoples. In this way, Lea (2012, 410) shows that "people are a composite of their relationships," which are cemented through different formative and transformative activity-based and spatially oriented practices activated during ceremony.

In this chapter, I explore the pivotal role of ceremony and song in the *mejkumrei* or "good" life in Kayapó communities and later suggest their centrality in making claims to land and rights to life in neodevelopmental, democratic Brazil. I show that justice efforts enacted in different spaces and ceremonial practices carried out within communities are evocative of several processes that comprise the politics of making indigenous territorialities today. In this chapter I emphasize ceremonies that take place in villages to show the ways in which ceremony and song have long mediated the borderlands between self and Other, as well as village and exterior; I further stress that identity politics are just one manifestation of a longer history of engagement and performativity with human and nonhuman Others. Santos-Granero (2009a, 478) emphasizes, as I do here, that "society and people can exist only through the incorporation of dangerous foreign entities and forces. The Self is only possible through the incorporation of the Other." In this way, ceremonies are the life blood of the villages, the composite of what makes Kayapó peoples beautiful and strong, and the source from which they have always drawn to secure their lifeways.

In this way, ceremonies are not "a shared system of meaning devoid of situated struggles" (Moore 2005, 19). Ceremonies are active sites of the production and reproduction of personhood, community life, and increasing resistance strategies wrought during this latest wave of identity politics and territorial control. In this vein villagers actively produce spaces of resistance, contestation, and expressive politics through ceremony and song—spaces derived from indigenous cosmologies of place-making and ceremonial practice. Fritz Roth (2008) makes a similar observation in his work with Tsimshian communities and their potlatching ceremonies, which are likewise vital events that support and nurture life. Fritz Roth (2008, 3) notes that "in ceremonial life, as in the oral histories that stand behind and validate it, names and lineages are agents that cocreate events in response to political and social realities. Potlatches are real-world, risky events—rather than staged and scripted performances—and in the same way the oral histories that describe the origins and careers of names and clans are linear chronicles to which names, through their deeds, are constantly adding new chapters." While not identical to Fritz Roth's reflections, the naming ceremonies that the Kayapó peoples perform also are at once prescriptive and creative, circular rather than linear, and constantly adding new chapters to the worlds that they navigate. It is these new chapters I am interested in this part of the book, and their intersection with self-determination efforts and efforts to forge a good life.

Kayapó feelings about ceremonies also are echoed in Howe's (2002) description; although employed in a different context, that they "are nothing without the families and communities, the stories and the histories, and the jokes and shared grief that hold [them] together" (quoted in Byrd 2014, 55). Kayapó sentiments about ceremonies also reverberate in Royce's (2011, 72) description of Isthmus Zapotec mortuary practices in that "it is the work by family and community that restores and maintains family and community." While Kayapó notions of "family" and "community" do not necessarily correlate with Zapotec ones, it is the impulse of the statement that resonates in the Kayapó context. Ceremonies are a relational and collective process, but they are also far from homogenized. Rather, in ceremony, we see distinctive aspects of individuals and their relationships to each other and nonhuman others amplified as they perform acts that are necessary for its completion, as well as for their own growth and transformation. These activities, far from mundane tasks, are considered skilled and creative processes that make place and people, in this case the community of A'Ukre and life over time (Overing 2003). One consultant nicely summed up what ceremonies meant to the peoples of A'Ukre: "Ceremonies contain the happiness of the village."

At the same time, much analytical attention over the past several decades has certainly given weight to what Conklin (1997, 711) describes as "indigenous body images, high technology, and Western notions of cultural authenticity" in the production of indigeneity. Certainly, I evoke this same trilogy of concepts when describing Bemp above, and in this chapter I wish to highlight the polysemous nature of *metôrô* (or ceremonies). Drawing upon Goeman's (2013, 23) argument that "native-made spaces . . . are too often disavowed, appropriated, or coopted by the settler state through writing, imagining, law, politics, and the terrains of culture," this chapter details the way in which Kayapó communities, leaders, and individuals practice and carry out ceremony. Based on villagers' explanations of the foundational importance of ceremonial practice, I offer several arguments about how sociality, body painting, and feathers are part of local sensibilities and expressive performances that offer distinct ways of conceptualizing socioecological interactions. The relational context that ceremonies produce are grounded in Kayapó ontologies and at same time remain esconced to the broader geopolitical and socioecological scales in which making indigenous territorialities occur.[1]

Performing ceremonies, for the Kayapó, are enmeshed in larger projects of resignification and signification. Kayapó villagers, chiefs, and song leaders marshal and carry out ceremonial forms within political and quotidian contexts to incrementally create enduring, albeit sometimes spontaneous, counterspaces of resistance and contestation. The visiting photographer and my own presence in the village during Bemp are testaments to this compound layering and the complexities of visual signification that occurs during performative events. I suggest that in unpacking the diverse worlds that ceremonies bridge, we can see the pioneering efforts the Kayapó have made to make these worlds intelligible to nonindigenous viewers while at the same time blurring the boundaries between self and Other to make strategic claims to land and territory.

Moreover, ceremonial performances are complicated by widely circulated Kayapó-produced or non-Kayapó-produced photographs and filmography of such events that represent a growing international visual vocabulary of indigenousness that serves to complicate and index authenticity, exoticism, essentialism, and nationally produced imaginaries. Collectively these are what Ramos (2003) has called the "Pulp Fictions" of indigenism and indigenous groups; the Kayapó "often respond to the structural and symbolic marginalization of indigenous peoples, places and practices, usually by showcasing cultural resilience, territorial integrity, political determination, and economic necessity" within different visual, digital, and performative mediums (Smith 2013, 329). Since the rise of Kayapó interethnic politics, the panindigenous movement, and a regionally situated Amazonian indigenous movement across Latin America in the 1970s, indigenous leaders' struggles for different rights-based and justice claims have been accompanied by an associated visual politics, where ceremonial regalia, distinct dress, and body modifications are employed strategically, instrumentally, and most importantly, as embodied and representational practices that reflect shared notions of personhood and identity. Kayapó leaders and warriors are noted as experts in the performance of indigeneity while organizing protests, writing up statements of dissent, and participating in conferences (Conklin and Graham 1995). For example, Donna Haraway (1992) cites Kayapó videographers in her seminal piece on *The Promise of Monsters*, and Alcida Ramos (2003), in the same chapter referenced above, uses the Kayapó as a case to consider essentialism and exoticism in Brazil. Some of the more famous media coverage of Kayapó activist efforts have been the already mentioned 1989 and 2008 Altamira protests where Kayapó participants employed both *mrôti* (black) and *py* (red) body painting, and ceremonial regalia including headdresses, armbands, and beaded sashes (figure 7). Kayapó leaders, such as

Figure 7. Silver basin full of urucum, the base of the red paint.

Raoni, Megaron, and Tuira, gained fame for their speeches and practices at these high-profile meetings. These large-scale events are now complemented by Facebook posts, tweets, blogs, and other digital forms of activism, resistance, and storytelling. In chapter 1, I discussed how the devastating effects of pacification efforts on Kayapó peoples politicized certain body practices in which missionaries and others, including state officials, made communities question their bodily presentations (e.g., length of hair and use of body paint). However, in the aftermath of the more intense change, communities began self-reflexively using body painting and other symbols of their identity as a Kayapó nation, knowing the complicated histories these had in national laws and imaginaries and forcefully asserting a cultural politics of difference that celebrated their distinctive position as citizens of Brazil and members of a tribal nation.

Take, for instance, Chief Raoni's participation in the 2012 film *Belo Monte: Anuncia de uma Guerra* (*Belo Monte: Announcement of a War*) that was quoted in the introduction of chapter 1. In addition to depicting scenes of Native and non-Native inhabitants' lives on the river, the core of the film centers on interviews with a wide range of experts, stakeholders, and local resource users who are in various ways deeply invested in the outcome of the dam project. Raoni appears frequently, as the Belo Monte Dam will affect Kayapó communities socially, culturally, politically, ecologically, spiritually, and economically. In fact, the film begins with Raoni describing how when he had been a child, his father had impressed upon him that he had a responsibility to be a voice for the Kayapó in times of trouble. Raoni looms in front of the screen in the first clip. His torso is painted black, and he wears his much-photographed yellow headdress. In other parts of the film, viewers see Raoni shaking hands with James Cameron and Arnold Schwarzenegger, meeting diplomats and leaders in France, and talking to a wide range of audiences at home and abroad.

In another example, Mayalú Txucarramãe, a young Kayapó woman, launched a campaign called the Mebêngôkrê Nyre Movement, in 2012. This movement emerged from Mayalú's involvement in educational programs in Kayapó communities where she helped train indigenous teachers and created culturally appropriate materials for Kayapó schoolchildren. As an outgrowth of this work, the focus of Mebêngôkrê Nyre is on youth involvement in self-determination efforts (Amazon Watch 2013). This is the first movement within the Kayapó nation that specifically focuses on youth, although for decades seasoned Kayapó leaders have noted that their activist efforts have been for future generations. Mebêngôkrê Nyre is also one of the first Kayapó movements born in the digital age. The daughter of Chief Megaron, and also relative of Chief Raoni, Mayalú is part of a long lineage of powerful Kayapó and other indigenous leaders who have eagerly embraced film, photography, and other digital mediums as integral to activist and political projects. Mayalú's campaign points to a new chapter of recognitional politics among the Kayapó and is supported by historical activist efforts in the area, but it is also invigorated by political strategies that will increasingly be shaped by youth involvement and digital media.

Alcida Ramos (1994) comments that these techniques for indexing authenticity as part of the politics of indigeneity, which have served many groups, have also resulted in negative consequences by creating expectations of "indigenousness" being tied to culturally encoded visual cues.[2] What has taken place, Ramos contends, is the production of the "hyperreal" Indian, where highly decorated indigenous leaders have conditioned the world to read indigeneity as being something that is intimately linked to certain hairstyles, dress, and body decoration practices. As a result, when indigenous individuals do not conform to the developed international visual vocabulary of indigenousness, they are discriminated against, and considered less "authentic," or worse, not "genuine" (Fine-Dare and Rubenstein 2009).[3] At the same time, government officials use these signs of "authentic" indigeneity to classify certain groups as not "real," and subsequently deny these groups their rights. The advent of the expectation of a hyperreal Indian, as Ramos notes, is a problematic one—which Graham and Penny (2014, 1) suggest is often tied to "blood and soil."

As Graham and Penny (2014, 2) hold, however, indigeneity and its performance is a product of the post–Cold War era, one that indigenous peoples use actively to "produce identities through performances that often entail deeply contextualized and historically contingent creative acts," and that is part of a process of "emergence," rather than one of calcification. Ginsburg, Abu-Lughod, and Larkin (2002) call attention to "media worlds" and the freight that these "worlds" carry in a globalized, postcolonial context. Pushing for a more "capacious" framework, they suggest that "through grounded analyses of the practices, cultural worlds, and even fantasies of social actors as they interact with media in a variety of social spaces, we have begun to unbundle assumptions regarding the political economy and social relations shaping media production, circulation, and reception, and the impacts of media technologies themselves" (Ginsburg, Abu-Lughod, and Larkin 2002, 3).[4] What Prins (2004) has referred to as "indigenizing visual media" and Banks and Ruby (2011) have highlighted in their title of the edited volume *Made to be Seen*, both exemplify the constellation of practices that are caught up in image-making, whether it is in the intimate aesthetics of daily life, a semipublic ritual event in a village, or a large-scale protest. Naming ceremonies invite us to consider these strangely textured histories in real, virtual, and imagined worlds.

The sensuous and textured aspects of local conceptualizations of space, place, and personhood, which are enlivened in ceremonial practice, cross different ideological and material borderlands as they move in and out of territorialities of transformation and activism. In this way, ceremonies like Bemp inevitably take place on multiple registers and in plural landscapes of action and representation. As villagers employ dances, songs, and ceremonial performances in public spaces, they use them as a complex assemblage of practices to index personhood, agency, indigeneity, and political activism. These layered approaches to performance and performativity show the many worlds that the Kayapó border-cross as part of their ongoing struggles to retain their lifeways and the fluidity with which they maneuver through the territorialities that produce and are produced by them.

What is in a Name?

Names carry many meanings for the Kayapó, but beautiful names are one of the greatest honors that people are given. Sometimes when I close my eyes to remember A'Ukre, I see elder women, their gray-black hair loosely framing their faces as they count their children and grandchildren on their fingers, pressing the tips of each finger one by one onto their lips after they have spoken each name. Or I hear the voices of my close Kayapó friends and their insistence that I write down the names of their family members. It is the women who remembered these things, who would ask me to remember details in a way that made sense to me. I look at the lists of names in my jottings. I try to remember. Names are part of being. They are also part of becoming.[5]

Naming ceremonies capture all of this. Kayapó individuals are given several different types of names and distinctions over the course of their lifetimes

(Bamberger 1974; Fisher 2003; Lea 2012). Once a child is born, an elderly family member (not the child's mother or father) will give the child several names. These are typically nicknames, but can be unofficial beautiful names. One might have five or more names but will commonly go by just one or two of them.[6]

As close interlocutors taught me, it is often the mother who remembers all of the child's names.[7] Before children become adolescents, their parents can choose to sponsor a naming ceremony in order to formally recognize their children's beautiful names. If naming ceremonies are performed, the children will formally own their beautiful names or sometimes be given new ones. The names that are bestowed upon the youth carry with them naming lineages and histories from within the community. There are other benefits that come with the names. Some are associated with certain privileges—like wearing particular ceremonial decorations in future festivals—or with restrictions—like adhering to food taboos. Furthermore, if you are given a beautiful name, you are connected, in a way, to the other individuals who received their names at the same ceremony. In this manner, names are both personal and ultimately social, and contain within them coded information about daily life and proper relations between human and non-human beings (Vom Bruck and Bodenhorn 2006, 25).

It was early August when I began to work with Koko in preparation for the upcoming Bemp (naming) ceremony. The photographer Fabio's arrival marked not only the onset of final preparations for Bemp, but also meant that others would soon be visiting the village too. Although I had only lived in A'Ukre for a couple of months at this point, I was not surprised by Fabio's visit. Despite the fact that A'Ukre was mostly a fly-in community (a forty-five minute charter air flight from the nearest town or several day boat ride), I soon found out that travel to and from the village was a frequent aspect of village life—and so too was the employment of video and photography in ceremonial contexts, as Terence Turner (1991a) has noted. Villagers moved constantly and came and went for a variety of reasons: to visit friends and family in other villages and local towns, to look for temporary wage work, pursue educational opportunities, purchase goods, attend meetings, or get medical help. Flights routinely brought in health personnel, such as doctors, nurses, and dentists. River travel became much more common during the wet season, despite the many day journeys to and from the cities. Officials from FUNAI, employees from a local mining company, health personnel, and filmmakers all visited after I moved to A'Ukre. However, Fabio was the first professional non-Kayapó photographer to visit, and given that Bemp was about to take place, I was quite excited. The path that ran alongside the project house, which connected the village to the river, was full of activity. Everyone seemed to be busy.

Diego, a middle-aged leader, and Marcio, a friend of mine who lived in the village, stopped by to chat with Fabio and me one afternoon prior to the start of Bemp. Marcio and Diego both supported Fabio's work. Diego said, when Fabio arrived, that he considered Fabio's photo project as one of *saúde* (health), because Fabio was not destroying the forest, but was instead bringing health to the community through a revenue-generating project that did not disturb their lifeways. Marcio suggested that if I were not already considering it, I should join the women with their ceremonial preparations. He noted that the men in the village would leave soon to fish for the ceremonial food. Fishing during Bemp required the men of the community to camp out for weeks, although they would try to get fish more quickly this year given the photographer's timeline. There were no assurances, however, that the men would be able to get enough fish in a shorter time frame. "Tep kuté mari" (only the fish would know), Marcio concluded. An anticipated euphoria was building.

When the time came, I got up in the mornings and joined Koko. She, like the other festival sponsors, was responsible for overseeing a small group of women. Part of Koko's job for the past several months had been working with the women in her network to prepare for the ceremonial-related tasks. After someone had offered to pass down beautiful names to a child, the parents, like Koko, had to seriously consider accepting the proposal. Of all the ceremonies the Kayapó perform, naming ceremonies are the most elaborate and time-consuming, and for this reason, a proposal to pass down names is not taken lightly. Planning and preparations for the main ceremonial events, which take place over three to four days, start months earlier. Food has to be harvested and caught, ceremonial dresses must be prepared and cleaned, songs have to be learned and relearned, and dances have to be practiced; all so that when the final days of the ceremony arrive, the dance sequences unfurl in a series of events that honor naming ceremonies and the weight they carry in the community.

While it requires community-wide involvement to orchestrate a naming ceremony, a large portion of the labor, planning, and provisioning for the event lies in the hands of the parents or sponsors of the name recipient or recipients. By August, Koko and her husband, Luis, had been in charge of a variety of activities, such as organizing different age groups and kin to harvest manioc to make farinha and planning fishing expeditions. I remember Luis, bent over in his canoe and his bright green shorts contrasting with the muddied river, handing out fish to the villagers after a particularly bountiful harvest. "It is for the festival, anyone can go ask for a fish," a young man explained to me as we arrived near the river's edge. I watched—knowing that ceremony was not limited to songs and dances but also meant sharing food and labor—as villagers grabbed silver-black fish by the eyes or threaded several together with a vine to carry them back to their homes. Ceremony was the taste of fire-smoked fish that families would enjoy that evening, and, for Luis, as a proud sponsor, it was his recollection of the weighted feel of the thin fishing line on his index finger, as he pulled up catch after catch.

Ceremonial sponsors had to ask different ceremonial friends to dance for their son (or daughter) in the finale. This was an honor, but it also represented danger. Since the dancing continues all night long, dancers say they are vulnerable to the presence of evil spirits, who wish to do them harm. For the Bemp ceremony, the dancers are macaws in the final performance. Koko and Luis also adhered to taboos, such as not eating certain foods or abstaining from body painting, for the duration of their sponsorship. Their work was hard and constant, but achieving the goal to have their child, or in this case children, as name recipients, would be worth the effort. Their children would retain this achieved status within the community forever and for the rest of their lives know that their names embodied one of the most cherished aspects of being Kayapó.

It is difficult to imagine life in a Kayapó village without naming ceremonies. The hard red dirt in A'Ukre's plaza is intended primarily for ceremonial and ritual activities, and mainly for the long, elaborate name-giving ones. In a consensual decision-making process, the entire community decides when these naming ceremonies will take place. William Fisher (2003, 118) explains: "Great names are transmitted from senior members to their junior protégés of the same sex in eligible kinship categories, along with ceremonial wealth, known as *nekrêtch* or *nekrêx*. Most transmission is from relations closely associated with the recipient's parents, that is, *ingêt* (MF, FF, MB, MBS) or *kwatyi* (MM, FM, FZ) to *tabdjwy* (CS, ZS—for males; CD, BD—for females), but parents themselves are forbidden to pass their own names to their offspring."

Bemp, the ceremony performed that August, is described as a male-naming ceremony, and thus a name reserved for men. There are names for women too, but they are given at other naming ceremonies, and although it is described as a male-naming ceremony does not mean that only men participate or dance. Oftentimes Bemp is accompanied by *mëintykre*, a promissory marriage ceremony, and followed by the ceremony that marks a young man's transition into adulthood. *Mëintykre* was not being carried out the year I attended Bemp, a topic that spurred much discussion in the community about how ceremonies could properly be carried out.

Beautiful names are composed of two parts. One part is the great or beautiful prefix, and the other is the common part (Bamberger 1974). Both elements of the name are important, but the prefix acts as a verbal road map. It is a word that immediately cues the listener that this name is a great name and that it was formally recognized during a ceremony. The individual with this name will be distinguished in future ceremonies by wearing the ritual objects that are associated with that beautiful name, by practicing certain ritual observances, or by embodying certain valued characteristics associated with the name.

A relative of the name recipient gives the child his or her names at the end of the ceremony. The only rule is that the name givers cannot be the child's parents and are preferably not the same-sex siblings of either parent, for example, a mother's sister, or a father's brother. Ideally, those who pass down their names are the mother's brother or father's sister, as noted by Fisher, to cross-sex nieces, nephews, or grandchildren.[8] To initiate a ceremony like Bemp, a relative of the child expresses a desire to give his or her name to the child and then nominates the parents as sponsors at a community meeting; the relative has to get final approval for this intention from the community. If approved, the parents have to accept *mekraremetch* (sponsorship), as Koko and Luis did. Several parents can provide sponsorship in one naming ceremony. Normally no more than four sponsors participate in a single festival, but that too can change. Over the years, small differences in Bemp may occur and lead to lengthy discussions within the community about the "right" way to enact the ceremony.

That which binds ceremonies or ritual actions together is not readily visible to outsiders but is meaningful to the Kayapó, for the conviviality it ignites, the transformations it entails, the relationality it embodies, and the ancestral practices it animates. Widely viewing non-indigenous publics have now become familiar with Kayapó activists, like Raoni, who joined the fight for justice and indigenous rights through ceremony, dance, and song. Yet, familial, ceremonial, and personal relationships, critical to ceremonial performances and vital for successful ritual acts, are not always intelligible to non-Kayapó viewers. Instead, the media often makes generalized comments about the coordination and repetition of ceremonial regalia and body painting across large groups of protesters. Take, for example, the opening lines of Alan Clendenning's news coverage of the 2008 Altamira protest that begins with "Painted and feathered Amazon Indians waving machetes and clubs." New stories such as these reduce ritual and ceremony to mere performance and ignore the semiotic weight of the use of certain objects (war clubs and machetes), the care that is taken in the application of body-painting techniques, the rules that are affixed to objects and name transmissions, the practice that goes into collective demonstrations, or the cosmological force behind all of it. A social and historical life to rituals grounds Kayapó worlds and relationships, and it is these very same practices that are the *tycht* (strength) and *mêtch* or *metire* (beauty) that sustain Kayapó activists and protesters (figure 8).

The Social Life of Naming

An elder warrior named Tonti once told me, when he, his wife, and I returned from visiting a garden, "Some indigenous peoples let their heritage spoil. We do not. A'Ukre is a living culture. We are strong." I would come to respect Tonti like a father by the time I left A'Ukre. His constant fight for the Kayapó's future always presses on the horizon of my thoughts. His words stick. The great political prowess the Kayapó have displayed in the public sphere is tightly connected

Figure 8. Men dancing during a ceremony. Note the use of feathers, beads, and body work.

to the organizational skills, multiple social networks, cultural forms that celebrate individual distinctiveness and collective strength, and leadership necessary for naming rituals. Indeed, ethnographers have been keen to note that Kayapó's social and cultural life is defined by different types of social cooperation (i.e., kin relationships, age grades, ceremonial friendships, and male associations) and by their high level of social ties and effective hierarchical political organization, which are all tied to shared notions of well-being (Diniz 2005; Fisher 2003). Villagers spoke of how naming ceremonies are arenas in which social ties are mobilized, highlighted, and reified. As a consequence, the physical space (men's house, plaza, households) around the village is expressive of different social networks, experiential practices, and duties. All these social ties have spatial implications when considering the interplay between everyday place-making practice (e.g., naming ceremonies) that cut across time, space, and territorial politics. Elizabeth Ewart (2003, 276) suggests in understanding Gê spatialities scholars should consider gradations as villages are generated by the lived actions of people; it is these gradations of lived experience that are central to my discussion of ceremonial practices, indigenous politics, and personhood.

Social relationships include *tchêt* (men's societies), age grades, ceremonial friends (also called great friends), matriuxorilocal household clusters, informal friendships, and other kin identifiers. During ceremonies like Bemp, these relationships are visibly accentuated. For example, Koko turns to the women in her household—her sisters (biological and classificatory), her mother, and her grandmother—during naming ceremonies and formal friends to help with ceremonial duties. The community will map out ceremonial dances and events with regard to the spatial location of Koko's and the other *donos'* (owners or sponsors) house in the village. In this way, matriuxorilocal households play a central role in naming rituals. As described in the introduction, Kayapó villages are arranged so that domestic households encircle a central men's house in a manner that creates a semi-enclosed village space containing a purposefully cleared plaza area.

Lea (1995, 2001) contends that Kayapó households are also "Houses."[9] A House is a concept developed by Claude Lévi-Strauss, who suggested that households are physical structures, as well as a type of social unit. Lea (2001, 172) argues that Kayapó households are Houses because they "occupy a specific space," where the "heritage of names and prerogatives" links household members to "a founding ancestor." Particular "heritage and prerogatives" are what the Kayapó call *nekrêtch*.[10] *Nekrêtch* can be the ceremonial names, objects, songs, food restrictions, and other prescriptive forms of action or ceremonial knowledge that are passed down from generation to generation (Lea 1995, 2001; Turner 1980, 1995c). This relationship has been described in other Amazonian groups as an owner-master category that involves "control and/or protection, engendering and/or possession, and that applies to relations between persons (human or nonhuman) and between persons and things (tangible or intangible)" (Fausto 2008). According to Lea, matriuxorilocal dwellings serve an important function as symbolic repositories and transmitters of nekrêtch. Lea describes the richness of Kayapó communities in relation to the concept of the House, showing how inherited wealth through the matriline, including songs, dances and other objects, serves as the grounding point from which ceremonial life radiates outward.

One the other hand, Turner (1965) argued that there is a pronounced public/private domain in communities where politically active men's societies govern economic, public, and ceremonial life visibly in the centrally located men's house. Turner (2009b, 158), also drawing attention to *nekrêtch* in naming ceremonies, counters that "names and *nekrêtch* are the properties of the individuals who give and receive them, not of any communal society or household." Turner (1965) further suggests that a political economy of control is operative in ceremonial life, whereby men's ceremonial roles are visible and critical to the production of personhood (see also Gordon 2006). Where Turner's materialist approach counters Lea's, they agree that ceremonies coalesce and reinforce different networks, both at the intra- and intervillage level.

Gordon (2006) argues that neither Turner's theory nor Lea's approach reflects Kayapó life. Gordon (2006) adds an analysis to this discussion that emerges from the theory of the economy of predation. Gordon (2006, 95) builds on Turner's and Lea's work, emphasizing the point that *nekrêtch* emerges from an indigenous, not Marxist, "consumptive" practice where objectives are transformed (economy of predation) by individual lineages and practices over time. This argument counters a corporate group or a "House" based reading to ceremonial practices and emphasizes individual and community agency over guiding transformative practices that subsume external goods, ideas, and items into Kayapó sensibilities. Arguably, however, I align this analysis most closely with Lea's (2012) approach to the House and feminist and decolonizing analyses of space, which I suggest also is attentive to multiple scales—the individual, the House, and the community—challenging Gordon's argument that the economy of predation is a useful, but not the only, lens from which to understand the production and reproduction of Kayapó life as it dialogically interpellates between self and Other.

Moreover, Turner (2009b, 158) suggests ceremonies "constitute the social community as a totality." Coelho de Souza (2002, 580) affirms that "ordinary social action corresponds to the fabrication of kinship and thus of human beings, but ritual metamorphosis is an essential" in this process. Naming ceremonies illuminate other ties beyond the House that extend into different and layered territorialities relationally bounded together. The emphasis on the transformation of individuals over time, the circulation of goods, and the creation of beauty and strength is not only limited to *nekrêtch* but also encompasses other practices that are in constant dialogue: the production and reproduction of life that is undergirded by powerful top–down processes (such as coercive neodevelopmental policies that instigate and reinforce injustices) and Kayapó quotidian and ceremonial practices of domesticating "alterity." If we consider place-making as central to this agenda, then we see how *iñho pyka* (our land), which both indexes Kayapó notions of territoriality and a federally recognized homeland, is a space from which the Kayapó perform ceremonies that reinforce their ancestral place in the world across time and space. This life is supported by relational processes that constitute community, place-making activities that form sociospatial ties to the land, ceremonial practices that affirm and amplify temporal and spatial connections, and territorial governance strategies rooted in Kayapó ways of negotiating with outside people and substances.

Life, in this way, is relational. One main feature of social ties is captured in the age-grade system. The age-grade system is a nonkin relationship that identifies village residents in distinct age sets based on their gender, biological development, and, later, their development as part of family units that share different substances. Age grades have specific ceremonial functions, body-painting designs, and body ornaments associated with them. For example, the Bemp ceremony that I watched with Koko included women and men whose children all had a similarly painted fish (*tep*) design for a portion of the Bemp ritual. Moreover, age grades are the main nonkin relationship that is used as an organizing principle behind subsistence activities, recreational activities, and, more recently, educational services. Age grades are significant markers in individuals' lifespans, defining different stages of personal development over time, as well as shaping their cooperative activities with others. Age grades might determine with whom you play soccer, go fishing, watch films, or harvest manioc. These are part of what Overing (2003, 294) has called care-based practices, which includes trusting and other relationships that are ascribed to the "domain of the intimate." While not the only social relationship that defines how one carries out caring and quotidian activities, it certainly patterns daily life in profound ways.

In naming ceremonies, age grades also guide activities. Men organize their ceremonial fishing or hunting expeditions, for example, by age grades. Festival sponsors like Koko rally multiple women in different age grades to gather wood, banana leaves, and rocks, as mentioned above, the building blocks of the ceremonial fire pits. These coordinated activities of age grades and other kin enable intra- and intervillage coordination and cooperation, which have helped immensely with orchestrating extrapolitical protests and other political events as well as retaining ties in less visible moments of coordination and contestation.

Ceremonies also benefit from strong political and ceremonial leadership in villages, which follows a hierarchical system similar to other Gê societies. Each village typically has at least two chiefs (*benyajure* [Kayapó] or *cacique* [Portuguese]) who are responsible for political, economic, and ritual decision-making in the community. Chiefs, elected by politically active men in the village and by community consensus, hold the office until they deem themselves too weak to continue. A good chief, whether a man or woman, has extensive knowledge of the mythic and historical landscape and orchestration of ceremonies, excellent skills as an orator and warrior, takes care of community, and is generous with time, work, and goods the community needs to flourish (Turner 1965; Verswijver 1992b). The chiefs I spoke with are also concerned about how Kayapó futures can thrive, while still engaging with *kuben* lifeways—and how prospering in the future means working within systems in place without sacrificing Kayapó ways of being.

I recall one afternoon in particular, sitting on bench in an open area where dried mango leaves had recently fallen, when the elder chief Teodoro talked with me about the future of A'Ukre. He was optimistic about the possibilities: "Things are going well now . . . the community listens to us [the leaders]. We protect our culture. I tell my grandson that we have to continue with our culture. We have to paint, dance, and have to think in Kayapó. We cannot leave these things aside." While Teodoro used the Portuguese word for culture here, in other contexts, he and other Kayapó consultants I spoke with used the Kayapó term *kukradjà* which referenced cultural practices or Kayapó knowledge systems, in order to discuss Kayapó traditions, customs, songs, rituals, ceremonies, and the material aspects of their life that they associate with being Kayapó.[11] Other chiefs talked about living in Kayapó and kuben worlds and the necessity to maneuver between the two ways of living—all the while strengthening Kayapó lifeways. Chiefs were focused on the care of the community, resolving different disputes, and making sure that their—both villagers in A'Ukre, as well the Kayapó as a whole—concerns were heard.

Chiefs felt supported by a series of other leadership positions that helped to govern life in A'Ukre. *Chefes*, or lower-level age grade chiefs—also called leaders—who are elected yearly to help the main chiefs of the village, support the *caciques*. The number of *chefes* varies, but normally one *chefe* is elected per age grade and per chief. Therefore, for example, the *mebenget* (warrior class) age grade will have two (or more) *chefes* who organize the age grade based on chiefly alliances, although this system has changed over the past five years in A'Ukre and chiefs now organize different age grades rather than men's societies. Women leaders often achieve leadership by association, that is, they are the wives of elected male chiefs and *chefes*, but sometimes they are in stand-alone leadership positions based on qualities similar to those exhibited by men. In this way, women hold important leadership positions in the community and coordinate the tasks carried out by women to care for and govern the village. Women also are sometimes elected to more prominent governance positions in the community, such as recent elections that have identified women caciques, similar to those of men, including in A'Ukre. Other types of leadership within the village include local healers or shamans, as well as men and women who hold esteemed positions by working with the school, health clinic, or NGO projects.

The political societies associated with chiefs that I just described, are called *tchêt*. Men officially join the men's house during adolescence when they are initiated into a political society. In addition, young men go through several, but at this time not all, initiation rituals to prove their manhood, including rituals involving wasps, venomous caterpillars that sting their chests, and the scraping of their arms and thighs with sharp fish teeth. Paolo, a resident of A'Ukre, took me to one of these wasp-nest ritual sites one afternoon. I had been talking with villagers about landscapes and their meanings, and Paolo wanted to show me and talk to me about spaces important to his life history. Paolo was around twenty-six years of age and already had three young children. He was easy to talk with, calm, and patient, as well as very knowledgeable. He was part of the *mekrare* age grade (adolescent males or men with young families), yet was still learning how to master hunting in the forest and already working on clearing new gardens for himself and his father-in-law. He described the wasp-nest ritual to me as we neared the spot in the forest.

"It is terrible, Laura," he said. "We will find a wasps' nest, and when they are sleeping, we will build a ladder that will reach the nest's height. We (the men) will then wait until morning when the wasps are just waking up, to go and hit the nest. There is a long line of us, and the first one up gets stung the most. The women cry and cry the whole time. They help their brothers and husbands afterwards. It hurts a lot."

"Do you have [anything] to help with the sting?" I asked.

"Yes, but it only helps a little."

"What is it for, then?"

"To be strong," he said. "It shows that you are strong."

Reminded of being stung by a wasp several weeks earlier, and how my hand had swollen to twice its size, I could only imagine the pain the young men would feel. Standing below the now abandoned site, I looked at the scaffolding that led to the place where the wasp nest would have been. The wasp nest must have been thrown somewhere or had already decayed; it was nowhere to be seen. I would return to this place many times in the months to come, as other young men showed me where they had undergone this important but painful ritual. A couple of years later, a Kayapó friend played a film he had made of a wasp ritual for me. The film showed the dances that had taken place prior to the ritual, and then, on the day of the event, you could see the quick climb up the scaffolding, followed by the men holding their heads and bodies as they walked away. Mothers and sisters were wailing, in a performative keen but also emotionally raw way, and swatting the wasps with bundles of leaves as the men walked away from the scene.[12]

The wasp-nest ritual was one of the many tasks men were required to carry out as they started a family and gained status in the community. Many consultants described other tasks that men had to perform before they could marry: clear and plant a garden, hunt and fish on their own, and make *farinha*. Fulfilling every one of these requirements, many said, was no longer common, or at least not necessary. Finding wage work, or a way to earn cash income, Portuguese fluency, knowledge of new digital worlds, and experience in towns and cities were also cited as necessary skills. Men like Paolo and those in his political society may join together for communal group work, such as helping the chief build a new house, clearing and planting the chief's garden, and supporting the chief in factional disputes. Later in life this might mean that, as an elder he might become a health aide or be selected for diplomatic trips to Brasília or participation in international conventions. The women I worked with also talked about multidimensional strategies of community governance and the now common mixed economies of daily life. Days might be patterned by employment at the school, periodic work as field assistants to researchers in the area, or organizing bead projects to sell bracelets and other objects in urban areas alongside subsistence harvests.

Many of the elder men I interviewed also noted that a young man no longer symbolically makes the transition to active political membership by sleeping in the men's house. Previously, a young man initiated into the men's house would move out of his mother's house and into the men's house prior to marriage. This custom is not common in A'Ukre today, and a man now moves directly into his wife's house.[13] The new husband, however, still has restricted social interactions as a newcomer to the home. He might eat food alone in his new residence, eat at his former home, and have relatively little interaction with his wife's family members until he and his wife have their first child. Husbands still observe social taboos concerning activities that show respect, such as avoiding talking directly to their sisters-in-law or their fathers- and mothers-in-law. These practices, however, may change over time, as the family grows and as the wife and husband share substances (food, bodily substances, shelter) and generative activities that fortify the couple and make new family members (see Overing 2003; Santos-Granero 2009a, 483).

Finally, the ceremonial or formal friend relationship is another important facet of social life for the Kayapó that is distinct in that it is passed through the patriline. These relationships are associated with specific requirements, such as being assigned dancing or painting roles during ceremonies or rituals, and are visible during ceremonial and ritual activities. One shows the utmost respect of ceremonial friends and the activities that they carry out for you and your family in ceremonial cycles by, for example, not talking with them directly. Formal or ceremonial friendship is complemented by a joking relationship with the spouses or other kin of ceremonial friends, a conviviality that makes daily life full of joy and levity that builds a good life.

Daily interactions among age grades, gender groups, men's societies, ceremonial friends, joking relationships, and kin groups change constantly depending on the seasonal round, subsistence cycle, and ceremonial obligations, as well as other events going on in the community. In addition, these social relationships are enacted within different identities marked by leadership positions, gender, age grades, political societies, and ceremonial obligations. The village's spatial organization, in other words, dynamically maps out ever-changing social codes and proper relationships between peoples and their lands by correlating different social relationships to the layered world of generative activities, such as subsistence, wage work, media, recreation, and ceremony, that form the corpus of community life. In this way, the village is home, and their land is made meaningful by the carefully cultivated practices of the community, which is at the center of Kayapó conviviality. A'Ukre is made strong by various social networks and the lived experiential practice of different livelihood activities. The social relationships of daily life in a community are fortified during ceremonies, other activities, and the symbolic weight they hold.

On Being

The dancers had been preparing all afternoon, and Fabio was arduously documenting the steps leading up to the performance on his camera. The men and women who were the dancers this year were the ceremonial friends of the ritual sponsors. I had watched earlier that afternoon, as monochromatic beads were wound tightly around the ceremonial friends' wrists and forearms, and patterned, multicolored, beaded armbands were fit snuggly over their upper arms where bunches of long, red macaw feathers and slightly smaller yellow feathers hung. Heavy rounds of similarly colored beads were wrapped around their torsos as sashes. The men wore bright, loose-fitting shorts, and the women wore tight, spandex pants. Thick, red paint, a pigment made from the urucum plant, covered their mouths, and solid, vibrant black geometrical designs covered their bodies, arms, legs, and chests.

A friend of mine, Nhakti, one of the dancers, glossed her hair with oil as she readied for the event. She, like the other dancers, had white cotton leg bands fitted tightly around her calves and dangling white tassels that inched down toward the beaded bands on her ankles. More objects hung from her side, including a woven sling. Her ears were pierced with shiny, round metal disks, a testament to one of her beautiful names, Nhak, and the earrings were also embellished with a couple of small macaw feathers. She wore a white necklace and a thin headband adorned with one long red macaw feather. Her cheeks were elaborately painted with genipapo, and her torso was covered with small white and yellow parakeet feathers. Most of the dancers looked similar to Nhakti but with small variations in their ceremonial adornments—either *nekrêtch* or other objects given to them.

Earlier in the day villagers had traced a circular pathway for the dancers, which was carved out in the plaza area right outside the men's house. This is where they would spend their evening, in what has been described as a type of bird's nest (Turner 1991b, 139). As it neared the time of the performance, and before I sat down next to Koko, one of the middle-aged dancers, Kaite, approached me, and we talked for a moment. He would lead the group, Kaite said, as he already knew how to perform the macaw dance very well. I moved away from the crowd where the dancers stood and got a comfortable spot from which to watch. As the performance started, the dancers arranged themselves in three groups spaced apart in the circle. I spotted Kaite in the front and Nhakti a little further back. In the light that flooded the plaza that late afternoon, Fabio was still making the rounds with his camera, clicking away. I lamented that the community no longer had the film camera gifted to them several years ago for local filmmakers to use. Kaite led the dancers. They raised their arms in such a way that their feathers dangled and hung just so, imitating flight. At some point, later in the night, I heard Koko calling my name to come join her. We continued to watch together.

The dancers covered part of the circle, stopped, and then started again. During this dance, they might reach an "elevated state," because of lack of sleep and the constant, rhythmic chant of the macaw song (Posey 2002b, 38). Later, Marcio stopped by and explained to me that the dancers would move in this way all night—taking breaks only when they were too tired to continue, while others stepped in for them. Sometime in the middle of the night, many of the onlookers had their faces painted and their hair ritually cut. During Bemp, the macaw dancers are visual reminders of the relationships villagers have with animals, plants, and other aspects of the biophysical environment. In this dance, the Kayapó "become" macaws, and the word for ceremony means to fly (Turner 1991b, 139). As Turner (2008) has explained, "they try to present themselves as animals, or rather as hybrid animal-human beings, analogous to the ancestral human and animal forms of the mythical age before the differentiation of animals and human society."

Ceremonies could not occur without ongoing access to the animals, plants, and other beings provided by the lands and waters that support their livelihoods. On innumerable occasions walking through the forests, an elder would turn to me and explain, "Women love this tree because of its nut that they use in ceremonies" or point to bark, birds, vines, and other resources that they rely upon that are found not more than a day's walk from the village. Community members made ceremonial objects fashioned out of feathers from forest and savannah birds, woven out of grown or store-bought cotton, harvested ceremonial food from gardens and rivers, and beaded together with store-bought, Czech-made glass seed beads on fishing line. It also could not have taken place if there had not been a long history of passing down ceremonial songs and performances from generation to generation or the creativity of new generations to innovate as time went on. The interface between residents and the other goods, animals, plants, and otherworldly communities in their lands are integral facets of naming ritual performances. It is these relationships that are often not understood by a wide-ranging viewing public that may not appreciate that public performances that the Kayapó carry out have travelled from a culturally rich local context to an entirely different, but equally charged, political context.

In an often-cited 1998 article and many subsequent works, anthropologist Eduardo Viveiros de Castro suggests that Amerindian groups have an ontological relationship to the environment that does not divide the world into a nature/culture binary.[14] He proposes that the term multinatural perspectivism more accurately describes indigenous conceptualizations of human and nonhuman interactions.[15] The strength in multinatural perspectivism, Viveiros de Castro (1998, 476) suggests, is that it focuses on the "position of the subject" to describe indigenous perspectives and worldviews. A focus on the subject redirects the anthropological gaze toward subjectivity and identity rather than pigeonholes explanations into a dualistic nature versus culture patterning. For example if one explores Amerindian ethnolinguistics, identity categories that classify different beings (human and nonhuman) are not fixed, but "contextual" and "variable." Viveiros de Castro (1998, 478) asserts: "Thus self-references such as 'people' mean 'person,' not 'member of the human species' to register the point of view of the subject. To say, then, that animals and spirits are people is to say that they are persons, and to attribute to nonhumans the capacities of conscious intentionality and agency that define the position of the subject."

Placing emphasis on the subject's perspective rather than on defined categorical placement moves the emphasis from set categories of humanity or animality, or of nature and culture, to one of subject position. Here, human and nonhuman entities alike are capable of intentionality and agency. It is this proposition, that the "point of view creates the subject," which renders multinatural perspectivism an attractive theory to draw on when talking about indigenous modes of knowing. Furthermore, multinatural perspectivism neither seeks to reify romantic ideas about indigenous ways of knowing, nor relegates indigenous thought to something that is "primitive" in character. Instead, it builds awareness about the complexities of subject positions in the world—human and nonhuman.[16]

Relatedly, many South American indigenous myths recognize the social and relational capacity of all beings (e.g., animals). Stories tend to acknowledge the anthropocentric characteristics of animals, and also the intentional aspects of their livelihoods. Animals express different human traits, Viveiros de Castro (1998) argues, because according to most Amerindian thought, all beings (human and nonhuman) have a soul. Multinatural perspectivism, then, suggests that the bodily expression of identity makes animals and humans similar beings, since they have "formally identical" souls (Viveiros de Castro 1998, 471). The difference is their bodies, which are a compilation of "affects and capacities" that mediate between spirit and material form, and which are constantly in the process of becoming. In this way, Viveiros de Castro further stresses that personhood is *made*. Multinatural perspectivism thus asserts that all beings occupy diverse subject positions, which are fluid and changeable over time.

Terence Turner, who has long worked with the Kayapó, counters this reading of indigenous ontologies. In Turner's (2009a, 20–21) close reading of Gê and Bororo myths, he suggests that, "the myth tells how the contemporary forms of each [animals and humans] became differentiated through a process in which the ancestral humans transformed themselves into modern humans through their invention of culture, while the ancestral forms of animals became less like humans, losing their protocultural possessions, and thereby became totally natural beings like modern animals, completely lacking cultural traits. The perspectivist interpretation of the myth, in short, gets it exactly wrong at least as far as this set of myths is concerned." Or in another work, Turner (2008) expounds, "The whole point of Kayapo ceremonial activity as I have described it is precisely the dramatization of a shift in perspectives, from one of relative identity between protohumans and protoanimals to differentiation between their respective contemporary descendants, fully socialized humans in contrast to dehumanized animals."

The problem with multinatural perspectivism, for Turner, is that it fails to take into account the differentiation that made humans into "modern humans," and animals "less like humans" and instead relegates contemporary indigenous thought to the protohistorical past in which animals and humans remained indistinguishable. He also argues that the "shift in perspectives," rather than "perspectivism," is what is dramatized in Kayapó naming ceremonies. He intimates that the power of myths and ceremonies is the power of transformation and of making humans and animals over time. While the present represents a shared past, it does not mean that the "shared subjective conscious" persists (Bessire and Bond 2014, 443).

Bessire and Bond (2014, 442) also make a pointed critique of perspectivism, based on the political and historical realities it seems to deny. They posit that, "because Indigenous peoples do exist, we cannot take ontological anthropology solely on its own terms. Under what conditions, we wonder, are such multinaturalist ontologies created, enacted, and made amenable to ethnographic analysis or capture?" In a similar vein, feminist indigenous scholar Zoe Todd (2014) takes issue with this reading of indigenous ontologies, but here she draws attention to the long-unrecognized indigenous contributions to discussions of the "more than human," and the problems with accrediting the "revelations" of nonindigenous scholars with these same ideas:

> Discourses of how to organize ourselves around and communicate with the constituents of complex and contested world(s) (or multiverses, if you are into the whole brevity thing), was spinning itself on the backs of non-European thinkers. And, again, the ones we credited for these incredible insights into the "more-than-human," and sentience and agency, and the ways through which to imagine our "common cosmopolitical concerns" were not the people who built and maintained the knowledge systems that European and North American anthropologists and philosophers have been studying for well over a hundred years, and predicating their current "aha" ontological moments (or re-imaginings of the discipline) upon.

Todd, like Bessire and Bond, highlights the stark political economies and histories of violence that are not acknowledged when considering indigenous ontologies in multinatural perspectivism. In trying to take indigenous ontologies seriously, as Viveiros de Castro and other scholars do, the very project that they seek to resist has the potential consequence of ending up reifying the categories they set up to unbind (Bessire and Bond 2014). Yet, in other works, Holbraad, Pedersen, and Viveiros de Castro (2014) have posited ways in which to conjoin the politics of ontology with the political. They clarify that "it means giving the ontological back to 'the people,' not the people back to 'the ontology,'" and further, the mission is one of striving for "permanent decolonization of thought" (Viveiros de Castro 2009 quoted in Holbraad, Pedersen and Viveiros de Castro 2014). Providing indigenous understandings of these same questions, as Todd requests, or sharing epistemological space with "disruptive thing beings and things that travel between ontologies" is part of sharing performance and activism (Bessire and Bond 2014, 446).

Several points are relevant here. The Kayapó I worked with were intimately familiar with the razor sharp borderlands that they crossed continually, and the racially charged landscape in which they were still embedded. For example, one afternoon, a governmental representative traveled to the village to talk about a recent event that impacted Kayapó communities, and in a pause during the discussion pulled out a magazine with an article about monkeys. He pointed to the article, which commented on violence and sexual behavior, laughed, and audibly said something about indigenous peoples, suggesting that the Kayapó were similar to monkeys. Alternatively, as astute followers of the news and the political tenor of Brazil, villagers noted that an official had said that the Kayapó were no better than pigs and only wanted to "devalue" the Kayapó. In another example, Pablo overheard something a non-Kayapó Brazilian health aide said in the village and pulled me aside and said, "You must talk with the indigenous health aides. Sometimes these people think we are no better than animals."

Villagers were aware of ongoing constructions of their identity that were derogatively aligned with animality, otherness, and marginalized subject positions. These were *perigroso* or "dangerous"—as the consultants would say—narratives, as they continued to rob communities of their dignity and rights. It was important to Kaite and Koko to explain ceremonies to me in a way that did not align Kayapó notions of personhood with animality, but with community and transformations in life stages over time. It was, as Viveiros de Castro (1998, 480) suggested, in the performances in which dancers mimic or become other beings, or as Turner wrote and was referenced above, "become macaws," that villagers emphasize their humanity and their ability to maneuver between these worlds. In other words, the Kayapó are sensitive to frames that highlight indigenous ontologies as alterity. These very narratives have the possibility, as Bessire and Bond (2014) point out, of becoming misinterpreted in ways that deny the political realities in which they circulate and the long histories of indigeneity and animality as correlates, yet at the same time ceremonies are powerful precisely because they serve as lived experiences that mediate between different transformative ways of being in the world.

Kaite's words still resound. "Soon you will know because you will see." It was critical to the men and women I worked with to highlight the sensorial and collective aspects of the ceremonial experience that linked villagers together across time and space. This created personhood, through the caring expression of different embodied worlds, as I will explain below. Certainly, the material, design, and emotional attributes of village ceremonies are summoned in activist efforts and other forms of expression of Kayapó identity politics in regional, national, and international political contexts. It is exactly the "constructional and relational perspective" that carries the weight of ceremonies and is mobilized to penetrate cities, towns, courtrooms, and televisions (Santos-Granero 2009b, 7).

Given the fact that anthropologists and other scholars have developed "thick" ways to talk about different subject positions, relational networks, and nature–culture encounters, these theoretical frameworks illuminate the dense layers at work during Kayapó ceremonial performances and, in turn, political protests. Returning to Bemp and the macaw dancers, then, these approaches tell us much about ceremonial performances, and how networks comprised of people, animals, and objects reverberate through Kayapó daily life and into political life as well. This type of inquiry exposes how local ways of knowing and being are expressed in naming ceremonies, how they are enacted in the quotidian aspects of Kayapó lifeworlds, and how these meanings are mobilized in ways that are at once quite visible but at the same time illegible to non-indigenous publics.

Macaws

The heavily adorned macaw dancers in the Bemp ceremony demonstrate in multiple ways how animals, plants, and people coincide in Kayapó ceremonies. In a seminal article on anthropology and the body, Terence Turner (1995c) suggests that the body is a site for individual and social manipulation, where bodily development and change correspond to changing social relations and positions. Many times, these bodily changes and changing subject positions are solidified through ritual and ceremony, and are ensured through daily habituation and practice. Turner (1995c, 148) posits as follows: "Cultural treatment of the body remains in contemporary societies an index of fundamental cultural notions of personal identity, agency, and subjectivity. These notions in turn proceed from the schemas or processes through which the cultural actor is formed to the social appropriation of the living body and its interaction with the ambient object world."[17]

Here, Turner stresses expressions of cultural identity tied to bodily modification and embodied actions, as well as the way in which modification and internalization of different practices, behaviors, and norms denote different relationships with human and nonhuman beings and worlds. The "ambient object world" plays a formative role in individual and collective social identities.

Among Kayapó peoples, the various relationships that individuals have with animals, plants, and other nonhuman objects are visibly expressed during naming rituals. For example, many of the ceremonial items and regalia that I described as part of the macaw dancers' dress are fabricated from goods that have been harvested, collected, hunted, or bought by mothers, fathers, brothers, sisters, and other relatives and friends. Objects made out of macaw feathers, cotton (which was previously grown in gardens, although it is now more frequently bought in stores), shelled earrings, headbands made out of palm fibers, beaded armbands, leg bands, sashes, belts, anklets, earrings, and other items comprise several of the objects with which dancers adorn their bodies. Object use during performances determine how human and nonhuman forms are mediated in ceremonial dances. As Turner (1991b, 150) noted, for the Kayapó "to 'become araras' [macaws] is to become fully human, in the sense of a social being capable of transcending and creating the structure and meaning of social life."

According to Kayapó beliefs, the body's core and inner organs are the "source of its natural, infrasocial appetites, powers, and energies," and the body's extremities (hair, hands, feet, and so on) are the parts of the body that have the most direct contact with the biophysical world and, thus, social interactions (Turner 1995c, 152). If bodily presentation in ceremonies works to organize and express different social relationships within the community, as well as those with plants, animals, and otherworldly facets of human-nature entanglements, then assignment and incorporation of these objects into ritual performance has particular symbolic, generative, subjective, constitutive, and substantive significance. The use of feathers on the crown of the head, dangling from armbands, and affixed to earrings, are all patterned after the idea that they serve as the physical objects which mediate between the Kayapó and their relationships with varied beings over time, such as the macaws. As Turner (2009a) notes, certain name recipients have the inheritable ability to wear particular feathers at particular ritual moments. The same is true for women's and men's work that goes into the creation of armbands, legbands, earrings, sashes, headdresses, necklaces, body-painting designs, and everything else the dancers wear that displays the traces of their makers and those who may have worn them before.

The macaw feathers are particularly significant, as they come from semidomesticated macaws that are kept as pets. Macaws are highly sought-after pets, dangerous to harvest, and raised for their feathers. Residents go to the forested area to find macaws to keep as their own.[18] For the rest of their lives (which average about 30–50 years), the macaws spend their time in shaded areas behind houses. The sound of these birds, repeated in the song of the Bemp finale, is one of the familiar sounds of village life.[19] Macaw feathers also have important implications for dancing in ceremonies, which is described as "flying" among the Kayapó, since many of the finales for naming rituals ask dancers to *become* birds, as in the case of the macaw dancers for Bemp (Turner [1980] 2012,

498). In addition, many of the songs sung during the finale, and other ritual objects, are used to embody or "become" bird forms, by mimicking their dress or their song.

The ceremonial objects used in Bemp are not merely decoration; they support, reflect, and nurture different relationships within the community. Rosengren (2015, 84, 94) shows that those objects that compose indigenous dresses are often "intimately linked" to the maker where the "producer leaves a part of him—or herself—in the product fabricated." The social and subjective lives of the objects link different individuals and generations within communities to new ceremonial performances. They can represent a long lineage of ceremonial items and skilled practices that have been passed down during naming and other rituals. This "historical" life gathers communities, friends, and families together over time (Santos-Granero 2009b, 3). In addition, the materials the objects are made from require labor and sourcing from the surrounding forest, savannah, or town. For example, as explained, macaw feathers are part of a double process of first harvesting and then relocating macaws to the village as pets, and require ongoing care and attention from their owners. Feathers are then used in the production of ceremonial objects for ritual performances and subsequently aid in transformations of personhood through dance, domestication, and ritual inheritance. Macaw dancers (objects, body paint, song, and dance) enact and embody these relationships and their makings in an emotion-filled and affect-laden performative context.

Ritual performances locate the dancers in a semiotic field of representation, whereby personhood is understood and shaped. Thus, the physical production of individuals are interwoven in the social production of people and life over time (Seeger, da Matta, and Viveiros de Castro 1979). As noted, naming rituals bestow ceremonial names, a very prestigious honor in Kayapó communities, on children. The dancers, who are ceremonial friends of the name recipients, have a very specific responsibility to the honored children. Kaite, Nhakti, and the other dancers who were charged with being macaws are part of the ongoing mediated process of constructing personhood—both their own as well as that of the name recipient. Within ceremonies the "inherent transformability of physical bodies" is a grounding point by which the "body services as a locus of sociality" (Rosengren 2015, 80). Kayapó notions of personhood change over an individual's life cycle, as he or she moves into different age grades, ceremonial friendship responsibilities, familial obligations, and honorific roles based on ceremonial names and other specialized skill sets. Taking a cue from Rosengren (2015, 82) again, I suggest that ceremonies then serve as space in which the "intimate social circle and personhood" result in a "transformative process that is cumulative and encompassing."

Finally, the dancers are visual and auditory reminders of the human–animal–nonhuman interface, as well as a reminder of the ongoing processes that are involved in being and becoming over time. Personhood, in other words, is not static; rather, it relies on a variety of activities and transformations that are part of the quotidian, the relational, and the ceremonial. In this case, the macaw dancers are representative of the work required to give beautiful names to children, the mediation of socionatural worlds, and the dancers' own changing responsibilities in the village.

Body Painting

Photos of Kayapó individuals circulating on the internet and in the media have become commonplace in the landscape of indigenous rights, and Kayapó women draw on body-painting traditions that dominate everyday life, ceremonies, and celebrations to make sure the results represent the strength of being Kayapó. It is the women who are the expert artists who, more often than not, are also the ones that have presented the aesthetics that concerned citizens now recognize as being inevitably intertwined with Kayapó lifeways. From birth to death, body-painting is stitched into the daily fabric of village life. Mothers wait until their small children are sleeping to paint their bodies, almost in their entirety, in the black genipapo ink. Young girls dot each other's cheeks with the red oily paint of urucum, experimenting with body-painting designs and skills early. In the rare moment that urucum is applied beyond the face, hands, and feet, first-time mothers will ask the young women in their families to be painted from head to toe in urucum, to honor the birth of their first child. Daughters lay their heads on their mother's warm laps to have intricate geometric designs painted on their faces with the more enduring genipapo ink.

Women in the same life stages will paint each other, chatting while they press their fingers across each other's skin. Wives paint husbands. Sisters paint brothers. When leaders (women and men) prepare for travel, paint applied in the village will stay with them in cities and towns, reminding them of home and the task ahead. As community members get ready for different meetings or protests, body painting becomes part of the landscape of resistance. Lux Vidal (1977) and Gutstaaf Verswijver (1992a) argue that painting is continuous, deeply rooted, and fundamentally tied to Kayapó conceptions of being whole, human, and beautiful in this world. Terence Turner (1995a) points out that body painting is an activity representative of local cosmologies, social relationships, and ceremonial practices. Turner calls this the social skin.

Body painting is also a key element in ceremonial performance and, like the example of the macaw feathers, is part of making Bemp. It is difficult to miss the ubiquity of body painting in ceremonies. Women, like Koko, are skilled artists and train from a very early age to master body painting for daily and ceremonial activities, although are not allowed to used genipapo until after adolescence. Women grow genipapo trees in their backyards and plant urucum in their fields for this purpose. I have talked with women and watched as they send genipapo fruits to relatives in newly founded villages. I have also spent countless hours watching Kayapó women cut the round, mossy-green fruit of the genipapo in half, scoop out the flesh, and mix it with charcoal sourced and cured especially for this purpose, along with a little bit of liquid to make a black paint. This paint is used for body art, and once applied can last up to a week, sometimes even longer. The newer the paint, the deeper the black pigment will be. Sisters, mothers, and friends paint genipapo on their faces, arms (above mid-forearm), legs (above mid-calf), and torsos (below the collarbone). The paint is watery and slightly lumpy, and I learned from friends that a variety of techniques exist to make sure that the design is strong. As Vidal (1981, 170, italics in original) notes, "Among the Kayapo, *to be*, or better to make sense, is in a large measure *to appear* in a culturally appropriate manner. Body painting and body ornamentation as a whole, must be seen as a code itself internally patterned and itself a part of a larger patterned universe."

Body painting is an intimate activity. The smell of the paint, the cool or oily touch on the skin, and the hours spent as either a wearer or painter mark life in profound ways. According to the women I worked with, genipapo designs are geometric, with a base of vertical and horizontal lines that are broken by patterned motifs (see also Vidal and Giannini 1995). These motifs are associated with the flora and fauna of the environment, representing, for example, *rop-krôre* (jaguars), *kapran* (tortoises) or *tep* (fish). Particular designs can invoke myths and stories in which Kayapó turned into animals and fish. Other designs are stamped on the body from shapes carved out of the genipapo fruit. If working on intricate designs, women prefer to use a thin, flat stick, about the size of a small coffee straw. On journeys to collect firewood, banana leaves, or Brazil nuts, friends would often stop in front of the particular species that could be used to make these kinds of applicators, use their machetes to cut off small slivers of its bark, and pack the material away to refine at home.

To begin, women would dip their hands into the genipapo mixture, and then, steadying the palito between their teeth, slide their thumb and forefinger down the stylus to coat it with genipapo. Since the desired design is a dark black color, constant reapplication is necessary, as when my friends would scrape the palito between the crevices in their palms, picking up the pooling ink that gathered there. Women sometimes paint their bodies with fine designs similar to those applied to their faces. It takes several hours to paint a child's body, or, of course, much longer to paint a grown man. Often, Nhak and Iredja would wait for their younger children to become sleepy before they started the painting process. Since women are the main body-painting artists in the village, adult women almost never have the fine designs applied to their bodies that are customary for men on ceremonial occasions; instead, they are covered with thicker, less intricate patterns.

As my instructor, Nhak showed me that the thick, bold, flat lines are painted with both the right and left index fingers. Using the same technique to coat her right hand with the genipapo, Nhak used a kneading motion to slough off any excess charcoal and get a relatively uniform application of genipapo on her palm and finger. Similar to painting faces, the desired design has a rich black color, and in order to create this, Nhak tells me that you have to press your finger firmly, and drag it down or across the body. To show me, she pressed her finger on my arm and pushed down with solid force. Then, to illustrate the difference, she lightly traced her finger down my arm and admonished that this would not work. This technique was bad. Light applications that trickle across the surface of the skin inevitably appear weaker. Finally, for children, a special black design is applied to the top of the head with a charcoal mix; some explained this was to deter malevolent spirits.

To make a bright red paint, the seeds of the urucum plant are mixed with oil. This paint does not last as long and is slippery and thick to the touch. It transfers onto clothes easily, has a way of getting into your eyes when you are trying to wash it off, and in this way becomes an inevitable sensorial and relational aspect of ceremony. Urucum is applied to the face in thick lines, as a band across the eyes, around the mouth, or liberally rubbed on the lower arms, calves, and feet (Turner 1995c). Sometimes young women and children dot their cheeks with the urucum or make other designs on their faces, or women might use it for protection before going gardening. In certain rituals, the urucum is applied all over the body. In addition to its use for body painting, the red paint is used to dye white cotton tassels affixed to baby slings, mats, baskets, and war clubs. Unlike genipapo, the urucum washes off with a good scrubbing after its initial application but often stains the skin a faint orange-red. Villagers warn of its sting when it gets into your eyes but also laud its vitality and richness.

Nhak prides herself on knowing designs for different age grades, rituals, and representatives of various animals. Individual creativity is valued, all the while several design motifs are continuously circulated: "symmetry, fine regular parallel lines, close texture, correct proportions" (Vidal 1981, 172). Many women in the community are known for their exceptional painting abilities. The process of painting is cherished, solidifying family bonds and friendship, as designs show social relationships and symbolic meaning through display (Turner 1995c; Vidal and Giannini 1995). Like ceremonies, body painting is an important social event in the community, and not being able to participate in it affects individual and community morale.

Body painting is a critical part of any Kayapó ceremony. Macaw dancers, name recipients, other dancers, onlookers, and children are painted for the festivities. Chiefs and other ritual leaders help to decide the appropriate designs that everyone will use for the different stages of the ritual process. As a marker of their sponsorship, festival sponsors like Koko and Luis forego being painted throughout the preparatory phases of Bemp. There are also rules about painting prior to, during, and after the ceremonial fishing and hunting expedition. In the end, however, men and women of different age sets are painted similarly, as are the macaw dancers, to create visual uniformity during the final phases of the festival. Like the crafting and passing down of ritual objects, painting is also a highly social process, fortifying different ceremonial relationships, kinship relationships, and other nonkin relations.

Body-painting designs are part of the life of the community. They reflect intergenerational knowledge, acquired skill sets, individual histories of practice, personal identities, and myths. They are also used to indicate different and ever-changing social relationships, as well as relationships and interfaces between people and nonhuman worlds—representing mythic moments, embodying shared past histories, and reflecting different affective characteristics of charismatic animals. Body painting makes people beautiful. When painting or being painted, Nhak always admired how *metire* (beautiful) it looked. Also when gossiping with my other women friends, they pointed out particularly nice designs on children or on other individuals. Whenever I prepared to leave the village, Nhak asked if she could paint me, so that I would remember them as I traveled away from A'Ukre she said. During ceremonies, body-painting designs mean all of these things.

Conclusion

Toward the end of his stay, Fabio showed me a photo of Kaite and the other dancers taken at the beginning of the finale dance. It is a close-up of the dancers, and Fabio must have been right beside them when he took the photo. Kaite is looking slightly down, his mouth, covered in urucum paint, is open, and he is presumably singing the macaw song. Nhakti is not in the frame, but seven similarly adorned dancers follow behind him. You can see their beads and designs, as well as make out some of the intricate patterns painted on their bodies. Bright macaw feathers point backward and stand out sharply against the busy background. In the lower left-hand corner of the photo, one gets a glimpse the legs of the name recipients, who are sitting in front of a makeshift lean-to. The lean-to's green palm walls poke up, and provide a contrast against the red-brown clay on the ground.

In addition to the work that Koko, Luis, and the other festival sponsors completed in preparation for the finale, Fabio's photo aptly demonstrates how multiple agendas and meanings converge today in the Kayapó Lands. Kayapó ceremonial regalia have become widely recognized as part of Brazil's indigenous rights movements, and it shows up in films like *Belo Monte: Anuncia de uma Guerra* or Mayalú's fight posted on Twitter and other social media pages. The same care and attention that goes into how chiefs and leaders present themselves on the world stage is derived from ceremonial and relational practices that are necessary for the Kayapó nation to thrive. The strength and beauty of ceremonial regalia and the power of collectively performed dances and rituals have been deeply felt around the world during public protests. However, the local circulation of these meanings, as described in this chapter, figures differently into villagers' lives during the performance of naming rituals and other ritual events as they mediate between plural worlds, not just Kayapó and Westerner but those of other human and nonhuman forces.

Ceremonies like Bemp are inescapably intertwined with Kayapó lifeways and at the same time are inscribed with meanings often unknown to an international, or sometimes even a national, audience. Naming ceremonies like Bemp requires the cooperation of many interlocking relationships in order to bestow beautiful names on the honored children. These names are weighty and carry with them many meanings. Beautiful names are prestigious, and according to the residents, they make Kayapó individuals beautiful and whole. Names also give the name recipients certain honors, prescriptive actions, and responsibilities. Bestowing these names is a community-wide affair in which multiple social relationships and networks are mobilized. The particular activities that individuals carry out highlight, at that moment, their roles in the naming process. As future ceremonies unfold, ties are reconfigured for different name recipients, parent sponsors, and ceremonial friends. Not surprisingly, this tangled web of social and political relationships suggests a notion of personhood based on interconnected but distinct positionalities that pattern individual experience over time. Ceremonies also connect the current villagers to their ancestors (through performance of the same ceremonies and bestowal of names), memory (the more recent past), and disparate places (repetitive ceremonial performances in different villages connect people across time and space). These social relationships have a spatial component to them, and the performance of naming ceremonies in the village reifies the importance of that space and its expressive territorialities as villagers make place home.

Secondly, naming ceremonies are not only events in which social relationships are fortified between past, present, and future generations, but they also reflect the complex relationships the Kayapó have with nonhuman worlds. I have suggested that ceremonial practice and objects are all aspects of how Kayapó individuals express their own identities, and the transformations required over a lifetime, as individuals transition between states (important life events, ceremonial obligations, and rites of passage). Many scholars have also been concerned with nature–culture dualism and have striven to develop a vocabulary that discusses human–environment interfaces without reifying the dualistic tendencies of the already deeply sedimented terms of nature and culture (see Descola and Pálsson 1996). Viveiros de Castro's (1998) suggestion that all beings have the capacity to be agents in this world, Santos-Granero's (2009a) argument that the identity politics should encompass indigenous ontologies of the relationship between the self and the other, and Lea's (2012) demonstration of the importance of Houses within Kayapó life are all useful frames to understand the complexities of Kayapó naming ceremonies and hint at why they are so powerful but also may fall short of highlighting the broader historical, political, and economic fields in which they are enacted.

By highlighting the social life of and transformative possibilities inherent in ceremonial objects and body-painting designs, I show the substantive processes that make relations possible in Kayapó worlds—relationships that are vital components of the ritual process. Objects, like macaw feathers, are part of household *nekrêtch*, individual inheritance, and performance. Body-painting designs represent multiple meanings of practice and performance, both as symbols of individual identity and traditional skill sets. Moreover, these activities do not take place in isolation but require coordinated activities on the part of the dancers and the whole community during the ceremonial round, and, to this end, the community can transfer the practices that make ceremonies work to other festival or performative engagements for political or expressive purposes.

Bemp is many things to Kayapó villagers, and naming ceremonies are weighty events that define Kayapó livelihoods. Far from being fixed and timeless performances they are momentary but cosmologically grounded expressions of Kayapó life. It is the prescriptive but organized "instaneity of contact" that is a fundamental component of distinguishing and blurring boundaries between humanity and other nonhuman forces (Schuler Zea 2010, 3). The local meaning emplaced, embodied, and lived within naming ceremonies and other rituals is tied up with the Kayapó's most honored characteristics: beauty, strength, and power. In addition, the ability of ceremonies to bring people together across time and space, as well as to solidify relationships between communities and nonhuman worlds, makes these activities integral to the fabric of daily and political life. These facets of naming ceremonies are seldom legible in the public sphere during political protests, global environmental governance arenas, or national contexts. At a fundamental level, naming ceremonies are meant to serve as a rite of passage, where child name recipients are changed from being common to being beautiful by receiving names that should always be circulating within Kayapó communities and across generations. This transformation requires the cooperation of the entire community as part of which different social relationships are activated—namely the same type of cooperation and organization that the Kayapó have drawn on in external politics.

If Kayapó lifeworlds are fortified by relationships produced, maintained, and mediated within the borderlands of ceremonies enacted in the village space and the resources provided by their lands, then territorial claims are not just about territory but are about nurturing life projects of communities that give them sustenance within plural territorialities over time. The inability to perform ceremonies would be destructive to villagers in ways that are hard to describe. However, the ability to continue with naming rituals over time relies on secure land tenure, as well as ongoing access to the plants, animals, and landscapes needed for the enactment of those rituals. It is no wonder that chiefs and leaders use their ceremonial regalia as they border-cross into a different public sphere. Not only are they a marked visual presence, but for the Kayapó wearers, these objects also carry meanings that are strong reminders of the lineages, people, places, and beings they hold dear. In charting the various meanings of a Bemp ceremony, we see the transformative possibilities of ceremonies, both within community life and with relationships with outsiders, and how ceremonial making is not only a place-making but also a space-making activity. In this way ceremony, and its constitutive elements, are a form of activism and advocacy that ushers in new possibilities for political authority and indigenous justice based not on legal codes, bureaucratic structures, and contracts but relationships sustained through song, dance, and community. In this way, making indigenous territorialities maps onto place and personhood in ways that are supportive of territorial retention but that can never be captured through bounded notions of a people or place.

3

One is Capable of Eating Money"

> Agroecology is not just a collection of practices. Agroecology is a way of life.
>
> —Nelda Sánchez, in *Agriculture and Food in Crisis: Conflict, Resistance, and Renewal*

Introduction

During the first weeks of September, 2012, the Kayapó NGO Associação Floresta Protegida ([AFP] Forest Protection Association) organized the first seed fair, *Feira Mebengokré de Sementes Tradicionais* (Mêbêngokre [Kayapó] Traditional Seed Fair), in the Kayapó village of Moikarakó. The fair brought together Kayapó communities from across their lands in addition to sixteen other indigenous peoples to share knowledge, songs, art, and, of course, seeds. The coverage of the fair, which includes blog posts, new stories, images, and interviews, highlights the different types of exchanges the fair fostered. In some of the interviews, which are now posted online, indigenous participants Boakire Kayapó, Iban Huin Kuin, Maria Ribeira Apynajé, Kumaré Waiãpi, Kunhankatu Kaiabi, and Irety Apinajé all speak about the importance of the seed fair for them and their communities. For instance, Boakire Kayapó, who is from the Kayapó village of Kremaiti, commented, "I came here to participate in the first traditional seed fair here in the village of Moikarakó. It is good because it is a pleasure to get to know our relatives that came from afar and learn about the traditions and knowledge of other customs" (available at http://sementeskayapo.blogspot.com.br). Exchanging corn, watermelon, manioc, fava beans, Brazil nuts, and many other foods, people at the seed fair celebrated the varied expressions of indigenous foodways and provided a political and cultural space for indigenous communities to gather together to talk about these practices. As anthropologist David Sutton (2010, 121) has written, "the tastes and smells of homeland frequently accompany people in their travels," and the many traveled leaders and community members that participated in this event were excited to sustain food practices that had long histories in supporting the peoples and landscapes of the region.

Innovative events like the seed fair draw attention to the ongoing struggle for food sovereignty and food justice that indigenous peoples and rural communities, such as farmers, the landless, and the small-scale producers around the globe face as they struggle to maintain control over their livelihoods and the production of foods and practices that nourish them. It also is evocative of the growing farmer-to-farmer (indigenous and otherwise) networks that aim to support smallholders and agroecological principles in the face of neoliberal reforms. *Via Campesina*, the international organization that started in 1993 and in 1996 launched its mission for food sovereignty, is backed by an alliance of indigenous peoples, farmers, and agricultural workers (migrant and otherwise), and it offers one example of this phenomenon. From the antiglobalization messages of Indian activist Vandana Shiva, to the advocacy efforts of writer and Kentucky agrarian Wendell Berry, to the powerful messages of American Indian activist Winona LaDuke, and to seed fair participants like Boakire Kayapó, these efforts point to larger landscapes of struggle, contentious politics, and the social movements that are building alternative visions for rural and urban development. Altieri and Toledo (2011, 594, 606) remind us that smallholders are far from disappearing: "In Brazil alone, there are about 4.8 million family farmers (about 85 percent of the total number of agricultural producers) that occupy 30 percent of the total agricultural land of the country," and across Latin America, "small farmers increased by 220 million between 1990 and 1999." The "repeasantization" of rural spaces around the globe has challenged large-scale, corporate investment in seed technologies, agro-industrial landscapes, and their adverse impacts on access, use, and management of agricultural landscapes, as well as the attendant social and cultural milieus in which they operate. Slow food movements, school gardens, urban farms, farm-to-plate restaurants, and the growing interest in foraging practices by celebrity chefs like René Redzepi offer other examples of counternarratives to neoliberalized visions of the food system. Yet, whereas practices of chefs like Redzepi are lauded in *New York Times* articles with attractive titles like "Nordic Chef explores Backyard," the harvesting practices of Kayapó individuals, like Boakire, continue to be marginalized (Bruni 2010). This is where food sovereignty and food justice movements have been the most vocal.

Together food sovereignty and food justice emphasize the political and economic conditions that produce foods, draw attention to the diversity of food regimes, including how cultural difference operates within different tastes and cuisines, and point to the privileging of certain foodways over others, as well as comment on the inaccessibility and inequality of particular food landscapes. In other words, they highlight territorial projects that produce injustices and reflect on place-making activities that can recuperate, revive, or reinforce local foodways.

Within this literature, food justice and food sovereignty movements have emerged as sites from which to address the landscapes of power at work; they have an explicit focus on identity, rights, and recognition (Alkon and Agyeman

2011). Food sovereignty and food justice movements may have similar goals, which have shaped their cultures of resistance and practices on the ground, but they also have different histories of activism (Alkon and Mares 2012). Food sovereignty was defined in 1996 by Via Campesina and further described in the 2007 *Declaration of Nyéléni* as "the right of peoples to healthy and culturally appropriate food produced through ecologically sound and sustainable methods, and their right to define their own food and agriculture systems" (Nyéléni 2007). Deriving from the Global South, food sovereignty movements seek to restore or maintain local control over the production, distribution, marketing, and consumption of different food items and honor the cultural difference within varied foodways. These practices are envisioned not just as alternative but as explicitly counter-neoliberal approaches to food systems in order to change the current hegemonic norms of high-intensity inputs, reliance on chemical fertilizers, and monocropping (Cadieux and Slocum 2015). Moreover, food sovereignty movements challenge other dominant extractivist economies, including mining, hydroelectric development, and other large-scale, land-use changes that erode local foodways and ways of being.

In Brazil, food sovereignty movements have largely had their origins in rural areas, for example, with landless peoples and small-scale harvesters being some of the most visible. These movements have not only struggled to retain particular types of foodways but are also caught up in struggles for de jure and de facto rights to land, water, and seeds (Alkon and Mares 2011, 347). For instance, the MST and other rural organizations in Brazil seek to redistribute land from the hands of the few to the hands of many (Holt-Giménez 2009). Other movements across Latin America, including in Cuba, Mexico, Peru, Ecuador, and Bolivia, also address agrarian injustice and promote local foodways and livelihoods (Altieri and Toledo 2011). The aims of these agrarian and mostly nonindigenous groups have both shared and diverged from the platforms of indigenous peoples in Brazil.

Food justice, like food sovereignty, takes a comprehensive approach to food security, or adequate access to food, and argues for more equitable and fair food systems. Largely derived from community-driven projects in urban, impoverished areas in the Global North, food justice platforms are founded upon environmental justice principles that acknowledge the heterogeneity of urban populations, the racial, gendered and ethnic disparities in the food system, and forging community-based and culturally meaningful alternatives to industrialized food options (Alkon and Mares 2012). Food justice movements are also attentive to structural issues and community-based solutions, which acknowledge individual contributions to change but also advocate for a holistic, system-wide, multi-scale, approach to this change. Alkon and Mares (2012) contend that food justice movements, however, falter in their ability to counter neoliberal logics despite their advances in addressing racialized landscapes and the uneven burden of agro-intensive food systems on marginalized communities. Skeptical of the government's ability to attend to marginal populations, food justice adherents turn to developing markets for food and food-related products, community-supported agriculture, and other market-based venues to develop democratically based, robust local, and regional economies. What Alkon and Mares (2012) argue, however, is that these markets open up alternative spaces for development yet do not directly challenge the larger food system, failing then to dismantle the very neoliberal logics they seek to counter. However, as food justice and sovereignty both advocate for different facets of justice and power at the grassroots level. In this chapter I show how the platforms of these movements have served as a critical base from which Kayapó peoples draw attention to their foodways and advocate for valuing the landscapes and peoples that are responsible for the production of diverse tastes in the Amazon region. Moreover, as powerfully argued by Mares and Peña (2011, 201), most alternative food movements "apparently forget that these practices are already fully 'alterNative'—in the sense of the deeply rooted practices of Native peoples that alter and challenge the dominant food systems" and further argue that working with historically marginalized populations, or those that are not necessarily adequately represented by these movements, is part of a deeper project of justice. What is more, is a growing "decolonization of the diet" movement, seeded, in part, among First Nations people in Canada, but with worldwide reach, seeks to recuperate and honor indigenous foodways in the wake of colonial and neoliberal projects that have systematically eroded the health and well-being of indigenous peoples (Bodirsky and Johnson 2008). The Kayapó peoples I work with could not agree more.

For the Kayapó, their foodways are tied to large expanses of lands and waters to forage, hunt, garden, and harvest for the foods that give them life. In their struggle for recognition, retention of their territory, and promotion of indigenous lifeways, the Kayapó peoples articulate their subsistence practices as part of cultural continuity, and their ability to continue these practices as a pathway to self-determination and sustainable futures. With a large territorial base of their own, the Kayapó peoples diverge from other disenfranchised landless peasants, small farmers, and migrants struggling for land or place-based recognition. What they share, though, is a history of dislocation and political and economic marginalization. For villagers in A'Ukre, it has been difficult and painful to watch the wholesale transformation of the landscapes they call home and the simultaneous persistent construction of these places by settlers as "wild," "unproductive," or in the way of "development." As outlined in chapter 1, this history has been one of fragmentation, displacement, and violence, as landscapes have been destroyed for mining operations, cut for timber economies, deforested for agricultural and ranching businesses, and sited for hydroelectric development. In addition to these powerful players in the landscape, landless peoples, displaced peasants, and small-scale extractivists are also attempting to carve out a livelihood. For community members I spoke with, retaining their lands also means fighting for the maintenance of a living terrain that is ultimately interwoven with cultural identities and proper relationships with plants, animals, and other beings. Interlocutors expressed that making gardens and harvesting resources were integral to making a community and a life. A'Ukre community members also talked about local foods as critical for the Kayapó's well-being and for their cultural identities. These conversations and the declarations that have been issued by Kayapó leaders continue to support a vision of the Kayapó Lands as one that is congenial to their lifeways and critical for their livelihood practices. For example, in a 2010 statement made by sixty-two indigenous leaders, including three Kayapó chiefs, they emphasized, "The forest is our butcher shop, the river is our market" and concluded with a quote from an American Indian activist who wrote, "No one is capable of eating money" (*Declaration* 2010). Teodoro, a Kayapó leader in A'Ukre, explained it to me this way: "We have gardens to plant things like manioc, yams, and other foods. Sometimes people hunt and fish. Because feeding the village is good. Because when you have food you are strong. So we continue to work in the village and continue to plant things."

The seed fair is representative of a suite of different events, practices, and forums the Kayapó are engaging with to promote their livelihoods. In A'Ukre, a recently established program with the AFP supports local foods by employing Kayapó women from the village to provide meals for students at the A'Ukre school, rather than having to rely on store-bought foodstuffs. Villagers also talk about food as a way to retain their connections to conservation organizations and build sustainable development projects, as I will discuss in chapter 4. They describe subsistence practices in opposition to the "toxins" in industrially produced food, the "weakness" that comes from eating too much city foods, and the strength derived from good food from the forest. For example, Nhak and Iredja's cooking continued to be evocative of different foods that traveled from forests, savannahs, rivers, gardens, and sometimes city stores to "plates." I recall taking thick, purpled gulps of *kamêrê káák* (açai) freshly made in *kawas* (large mortar and pestles), peeling rinds off with our teeth to eat ripe mangos, the sweetness of Brazil nut milk and banana drinks, the graininess of bright yellow corn (*baú*) cakes, and the hot broth of meat (*mry*) soup. I remember the smell of fried manioc cakes in the morning and, if the family still had coffee, the thermos of weak brew; I remember sharing a green plastic tub full of rice, beans, village-made manioc, and roasted fish with families. We ate cold roasted *angrô* (peccary) before going out for a long day in the garden, packed *tyryti* (bananas) in our baskets for all-day treks in the forest, and folded pinches of salt in discarded pieces of plastic bags for long fishing trips. We carried small pails of freshly roasted *yàt* (sweet potatoes) down to the river to wash our bodies and eat after working in the fields. I talked with women about the seedlings growing on their porches and the dried corn hung up in their houses for future gardens.

This chapter analyzes the Kayapó peoples' struggle for food sovereignty by honing in on swidden practices as a powerful way in which the Kayapó fight for recognition of their foodways as embodied and skilled practices that sustain the territorialities that support the peoples and lands they call home. I show that the villagers increasingly emplace these subsistence practices and long-held harvests that nourish families and feed communities in broader conversations about justice. The effects of large-scale, land-use transformations, such as the predominance of intensive ranching and agro-industrial practices, unpredictable climate patterns, and policies that have often favored large landholders, have resulted in undermining small-scale agricultural practices and disadvantaging indigenous communities. In this chapter, work with women and men in A'Ukre in their fields provides the basis for highlighting the creative and productive strategies Kayapó communities are using to retain their food sovereignty.

Swidden cultivation, alongside hunting, fishing, foraging, and cash-income, defines the mixed economies of contemporary Kayapó life. However, despite several decades of research on the value of swidden cultivation, outsiders and the scientific community do not always acknowledge the value of these practices (see Dove 1993). Moreover, while an increased access to store-bought foodstuffs in the village has provided different food options for families, the residents of A'Ukre express a strong preference for local foodways over imported ones. Moreover, strength or being *tycht* (strong) continues to be something community members talk about when they talk about food. As João Kayapó said to me one morning, "Seeds are like the Kayapó. You have to care for them and water them for them to grow and be well. For kids, you have to take care of them as well, and give them food to grow strong." Continuing local foodways has not only become relevant and important to maintaining food sovereignty and security for the Kayapó peoples, it is also a key locus of making one's place and personhood. Creating fields and food, then, is not just about nutrition but also about making indigenous territorialities.

Swidden, Shifting, and Slash-and-Burn Cultivation

Villagers in A'Ukre practice swidden agriculture. They plant manioc, sweet potatoes, papaya, yams, beans, bananas, plantains, urucum, cotton, watermelon, sugar cane, pineapple, squash, rice, and other foods in their fields. Women take pride in their fields and grow many different types of plants. The women I worked with complimented one another on their manioc varieties, talked about growing sweet potato varieties that their families loved, raised alarm about agoutis and other animals eating their crops, and were concerned about the early and erratic rains they were seeing. Their identification of varieties was multisensorial; women talked about the color of the stems, the way different plants smelled, and their relationships with other species. I recall the assuredness of Ireti's step as she, slightly bow-kneed, walked through her fields while she pointed to different plants and gestured with the tip of her machete. I can still smell the smoked tobacco from her *waricoco* (pipe), indicating she was an elder, and the glint of the green plastic liter bottle full of water in her basket as we walked around.

"This is all mine," Ireti said as she walked around her field. She showed me the tall stocks of corn plants, and she gestured to the different manioc varieties that she grew (these are the bitter ones, these are the sweet ones) and the abundance of sweet potatoes. This was just one of Ireti's gardens, she explained, as she had many and that this was "*âpeii tycht*" (hard work). On our way out to the garden that morning, she showed me *puru tum* or "old fields" that were filled with manioc or banana trees that were still productive, which edged fields that were no longer in use. To many first-time visitors to swidden fields like Ireti's, the field–forest mosaics seem chaotic and messy, but there is a patterning based on sophisticated polycropping techniques, burning strategies, and long-term engagement with the landscape.

Swidden agriculture is also called—arguably somewhat derogatorily—slash-and-burn agriculture. Swidden agriculture is practiced by approximately 300 million people in tropical environments across Latin America, Africa, and Southeast Asia (Montagnini and Mendelsohn 1997, 118). A form of shifting cultivation, swidden agriculture is a low-intensity productive practice that often involves the application of agroecology principles and fire ecology to clear (slash) and burn forests for farming purposes. In A'Ukre, leadership in the community determines the timing of the burns, which correspond to the dry and wet seasons. Forests (primary or secondary) are cut during the dry season, and ideally the completion of cutting and chopping takes place well before the rains begin. In June and July, I often saw men returning from the field–forest mosaic with their axes and sweat soaked shirts after a long day working on their gardens. "It is us [the men] that prepare the fields, cut the wood, and set fire. We plant corn, potato, banana, manioc, beans. We plant everything," Tonti explained. The burning of the dried brush, leaves, and woody materials enrich and prepare the soil for planting. Fire, as Hecht and Cockburn (1990, 39) point out is vital for the management of the tropics and neotropics, and swidden systems reflect this long history of indigenous groups using fire to prepare new fertile beds for the year. Tropical forest soils are notoriously poor and acidic—even though recent research has offered examples of anthropogenic modification where this is not the case—and all the nutrients within tropical forest environments are contained in the vegetative and other living matter above, not below, ground (German 2004; Heckenberger, Peterson, and Neves 1999; Woods 1995; Woods and McCann 1999). "We set fire, we plant, and we weed," was a common description of the process of field preparation. Or, as one community member put it, "If you don't set fire, the plants don't grow well, mix well." Crops are planted, and, shortly thereafter, the soon-to-follow rains water the recently formed fields. Fields are productive from one to five years and often follow a succession of different harvests and cropping techniques as soil fertility declines and weeds are increasingly difficult to manage. Once no longer productive, fields are left to grow fallow and new fields are created or old ones reworked.

Swidden agriculture relies on seasonal fluxes, fire, labor, and attentiveness to all of these processes for making fields. As opposed to intensive, industrialized agriculture, swidden is also a low-intensity method that does not require mechanized machinery, herbicides, pesticides, or fertilizers. Many swidden plots are also polycropped and intercropped with a variety of species, although this is not always the case (Weinstock 1983). Harold Conklin, Clifford Geertz, David Harris, Roy Rappaport, and others argue that swidden plots, especially those found in Indonesia, Venezuela, and Papua New Guinea, mimic tropical forest succession and are excellent examples of polycropping and intercropping techniques that rival the biodiversity of the forested environment (Beckerman 1983a, 2). Other researchers have suggested that polycropping is variable and not always present. For example, among the Bari, Candoshi, Yanomamö, Ye'kwana, Piaroa, Buahibo, and the Kayapó peoples, intercropping is either avoided, especially with year-round crops like manioc or plantains, or practiced only in specific patterns within targeted zones (Beckerman 1983a, 2; also see Beckerman 1983b). Moreover, anthropologists have documented that some groups employ a combination of several different polycropping and monocropping methods in forest and savannah zones, such as those found in Papua New Guinea. Here, Bine-speaking groups diversify their agricultural practices with polycropping in the forested zones and more monocropping techniques in the savannah areas (Eden 1993).

Yet, despite these arguments, many fields (intercropped, polycropped, or monocropped) often exhibit selected multiple varieties or cultivars of a particular species (polyvarieties), increasing the diversity of the field composition and thereby reducing pests and exhibiting a planting pattern of nested, concentric circles, the latter of which are especially found in Amazonia.[1]

It would be remiss to discuss swidden agriculture or plant varieties without invoking the now-famous work of anthropologist Harold Conklin, already mentioned in passing above. Swidden agricultural practices were immortalized in Conklin's ethnoecological research in the 1950s that painstakingly detailed the productive practices among the Hanunóo of the Mindoro Islands in the Philippines (Conklin 1954, 1957, 1969). Conklin is attributed as the first researcher to distinguish between swidden and shifting cultivation and provide a detailed case study of the swidden techniques of the Hanunóo (Harris 1971, 475–76). Based on his research, Conklin provided a "conservationist" appeal to Hanunóo techniques in order to counter arguments premised on the notion that local communities do not know how to effectively manage agricultural production (Padoch, Harwell, and Susanto 1998, 5). In a nuanced linguistic and taxonomic analysis, Conklin both describes the diversity of crops (species and varieties) and emplaces those taxonomies within an ethnoecological framework of polycropping techniques (Beckerman 1983a). For instance, Conklin cataloged more than 1,600 plant varieties and species (400 cultivated plant species and varieties) alongside Hanunóo knowledge about slopes, erosion, and mulching (Russell 1988, 81).[2]

Conklin provided ample support to argue *against* the belief that swidden agricultural practices degrade and disturb biophysical processes and *against* the contention that swidden is one of the main causes of widespread tropical deforestation (Rosaldo 1989, 184–86; Russell 1988; Schmidt-Vogt 1998). Indeed, in the introductory pages of his 1957 publication, he notes this negative bias toward shifting cultivation by outlining its common usage; "frequently, it implies an aimless, unplanned nomadic movement or an abrupt change in location, either of which may refer to the cropping area, the agriculturalist, or both" (Conklin 1957, 1). Conklin's study was and still is considered one of the first examples of an ethnoecological approach to local agricultural practices and is less well known but equally valuable as a document decrying popular and governmental environmental racism directed at indigenous or local swidden techniques.[3]

Conklin's work in the 1950s and 1960s was a seminal contribution to ethnobiological and ethnoecological work, which are still vibrant fields of study today (table 1). Historically, the term "ethnoecology" has been attributed to Conklin, while the term "ethnobiology" was attributed to Harshberger starting in 1986 (Cotton 1996).[4] Ethnoecology is often discussed in tandem with the more popular area of interest, ethnobiology. Ethnobiology focuses its inquiries on relationships among local groups, plants, and animals, and ethnoecology is a much broader consideration of local and place-based knowledge and practices within ecosystem processes (Anderson et al. 2011).[5] As Gragson and Blount (1999, vii, xviii) note, ethnoecology is "the study of relationships between organisms and the totality of the physical, biological, and social factors they come into contact with" in order to develop "an anthropologically informed concept of ecosystem."

Conklin's research, by mere publication, forayed into the world of politics by presenting a rigorous scientific work on the complexity of local agricultural techniques and management, a clear deviation from economic botany or salvage ethnography. Conklin's studies were also a precursor to research in the 1970s and 1980s that were concerned with the limitations of focusing simply on taxonomic systems and, instead, began to apply what was newly branded as traditional ecological knowledge (as opposed to local folk knowledge) to broader contexts and frames of inquiry, which supported indigenous knowledge systems as holistic approaches to human-environmental interactions.

Table 1. Major fields and subareas of study associated with understanding human–environmental relationships.

Field	Definition
Ethnoscience	"Ethnoscience is the ethnography and/or ethnology of knowledge, or ethno-epistemology, or descriptive epistemology" (O. Werner 1969, 329).
	Altieri (1993, 257) define it as "complex system of indigenous technical knowledge."
Ethnobiology	"Today, ethnobiology is, first and foremost, the study of how people of all, and of any, cultural tradition interpret, conceptualize, represent, cope with, utilize, and generally manage their knowledge of those domains of environmental experience which encompass living organisms, and whose scientific study we demarcate as botany, zoology, and ecology" (Ellen 2006, S1).
	"Ethnobiology is the scientific and humanistic study of the complex set of relationships of the biota to present and past human societies . . . The field can be divided into three major domains of inquiry: economic (how people use plants and animals), cognitive (how people know and conceptualize plants and animals), and ecological (how people interact with plants and animals, especially in an evolutionary and coevolutionary framework" (Stepp 2005, 211).
Ethnoecology	Gragson and Blount (1999, vii) describe it as "the study of relationships between organisms and the totality of the physical, biological, and social factors they come into contact with."
	"Ethnoecology may be defined as indigenous perceptions of 'natural' divisions in the biological world and plant/animal/ human relationships within each division. These cognitively defined ecological categories do not exist in isolation; thus ethnoecology must also deal with the perceptions of inter-relatedness between natural divisions" (Posey et al. 1984, 97).
Agroecology	Altieri (1989, 38) sees agroecology as "a new scientific discipline that defines, classifies and studies agricultural systems from an ecological and socioeconomic perspective" (also see Altieri 1987).

These new approaches mixed interpretative and material considerations and outlined a more expansive understanding of landscapes as multidimensional spaces where affective, spiritual, and other geographies of belonging and being coalesced (Nazarea 2006). Finally, Conklin's work is evocative of later research practices that became prevalent in the 1990s, which stressed not only indigenous resource management techniques and their associated embodied practices and knowledge systems but also advocacy issues associated with intellectual property and indigenous rights (Brush 1993). Interestingly, Darrell Posey, who worked with the Kayapó, became one of the more vociferous advocates for indigenous rights and indigenous land-use practices and published widely on the issue before his death.

Posey is well-known for his Museu Goeldi "Kayapó Science" research project that generated several publications about and with the Kayapó peoples.[6] By the time the project was complete, nearly twenty scientists and technicians had worked primarily but not only in the village of Gorotíre where they analyzed different aspects of Kayapó ethnoecology and ethnobiology. The studies produced several research papers that detailed the Kayapó peoples' use, classification, and management of their environment. In particular, Posey's many publications from this project emphasize the different classificatory principles and practices that the Kayapó use to manage and guide their practices within the forested and savannah environments. For example, in his better known pieces, Posey argued that the Gorotíre Kayapó peoples actively modify and enrich their agricultural soils, have an extensive knowledge of medicinal plants, are knowledgeable about astronomical events, and practice different agricultural techniques that complicate our understanding of swidden agricultural systems, including nomadic agriculture, planting in forest openings, trail plantings, *apêtê* (forest-island) systems, and swidden dispersal (Posey 1979, 1983, 1986, 1992, 1999). Overall, Posey's work attempted to demonstrate the value of indigenous approaches to making a living and, in the spirit of Conklin, extended an analysis of swidden or slash-and-burn agriculture beyond Western scientific agricultural paradigms (Posey 1985, 139). However, some researchers fiercely criticized and questioned Posey's results, specifically his discussion of the *apêtê*, which Posey argued was a landscape domestication system practiced by the Kayapó in Gorotíre (Parker 1992, 1993). Posey described *apêtê* as a technique used by the Kayapó to actively produce forest-islands of useful species within the forest–savannah mosaic.[7]

More publications have surfaced since the original Posey debate, including work by Susanna Hecht (2009), also part of the original project, who continues to support Posey's original claims.[8] While debates about *apêtê* continue to persist, Posey's contributions to indigenous rights and intellectual property rights cannot be overlooked. As one of the founders of the International Society of Ethnobiology and critical to the Declaration of Belém (available at http://

ethnobiology.net/global-coalition/declaration-of-belem/) generated at the 1988 conference on the International Congress of Ethnobiology, Posey was one of the academic frontrunners in creating an international forum to discuss indigenous rights, informed consent, and benefit-sharing regarding local knowledge systems (Hunn 2007, 4). Posey's research program consistently interwove ethnoecological and ethnobiological approaches into the injustices indigenous groups face as well as drew attention to the value of local practices for sustainable futures, such as those very practices that the seed exchange in 2012 were meant to highlight.

Fields, Forests, and Food

The swidden cycle in A'Ukre is a significant, but not the only, chronological, ancestral, and ceremonial marker that temporally organizes spatial, economic, and social activities. Several Kayapó myths relay stories that are grounded human–plant–animal–weather relationships concerning planting, caring for, and learning different foodways. One tells the story of how the Kayapó were liberated from eating bad food, such as bark, vines, mushrooms, and insects when a rodent introduced them to corn. In another mythic event, a woman came down from the sky (Sky Woman). After marrying a man from an Earth village, the Sky Woman saw that the people were facing hardship and did not know how to grow good food. Seeing that they were hungry, she convinced her husband that she needed to return to her sky people to collect seeds and plants to bring back to the village. Together, she and her husband went to a large tree where she ascended back to her sky community, and after much waiting, she finally came down bearing the seeds and other materials necessary to grow gardens in the villages. *Baú añho metôrô* (the corn harvest) is one of the main agricultural ceremonies in the community, for which the Kayapó gained international notoriety when they organized their 1989 Altamira protests around this festival (Turner 1995b). The manioc ceremony (*kwôrô kangô*) is another important agriculturally associated festival, although this event is not specific to a particular season, as manioc can be harvested throughout the year. Many songs from the manioc festival were adopted from the Juruna (non-Kayapó) group, and the festival is prized because it invites the entire community to participate (Turner 1965).

Fields are created in the red clay soils immediately outside the village plaza area, in the sandy, dark soils found beyond the inland streams, and sometimes in plots downriver set just far enough from the river's edge to avoid flood damage during the wet season. Connected to households by a vast network of garden and forest trails that radiate out from the village, swidden fields are easy to stumble upon, even with an untrained eye (figure 9). Trails to the fields also serve as collection spots for different forest species that grow alongside paths and routes to other places within the landscape: temporary fishing camps,

Figure 9. Example of a swidden field in process. Sweet potatoes are in the foreground and rice behind.

hunting paths, and longer trekking trails to other villages or historic areas.[9] The river and the uncut forested areas define the loose boundaries of the swidden zone. Indeed, the primary forest area that contains trees over a certain diameter is normally avoided by villagers, who prefer secondary forests with smaller trees that are easier to clear for field production.

Ethnographic records indicate that, in the 1960s, Kayapó planting practices in the village of Gorotíre consisted of a polycropping and intercropping system arranged in a series of concentric circles, as the circle is an important "glyph" in Kayapó cosmology (Posey 1979; Turner 1965). Some individuals in A'Ukre still use this circular pattern, and planting techniques are similar to what is described as historical planting patterns. Within A'Ukre, each household has at least one productive field and can have up to eleven or more fields with varying levels of productivity and crop availability. This changes to accommodate how many generations are living in the household. Fields are left to grow fallow for five to ten years before they are cleared again, and they usually retain initial ownership (Hecht and Posey 1989; Posey and Hecht 1990). Ownership here means that certain households or family groups retain the ability to work and gather harvests from that plot, while others are often allowed only with permission. Normally, the eldest woman of the household oversees the use of the suite of fields, but her married daughters and their husbands also may have established fields of their own.

When asked, villagers reported that they choose new fields based on different ecological and social factors that include proximity to the village, soil type, initial vegetation cover, placement of older fields, location based on other kin-based relationships, and if clearing an old field, length of time that a field has remained fallow. Fields normally follow a succession of stages before they are left to grow fallow or are abandoned altogether. The first two years of a field are the most productive, and during this period, individuals will spend most of their time planting, weeding, mulching, burning, and harvesting. In the following years, long-lived species, such as manioc (bitter and sweet), sweet potatoes, yams, and bananas are harvested when needed, although weeding might stop. In the final years of productivity, only the banana trees continue to yield fruit. The size of fields varies proportionally to family size or political leadership. Chiefs normally have the largest fields. Fields are also organized along matriuxorilocal residence patterns, men's societies, ecological zones, and seasonal weather patterns. In this manner, the swidden zone in A'Ukre is populated by a series of loosely connected, highly productive fields, fallow areas, and secondary forest growth, all of which are distributed along family lines, soil types, and historical occupation of the area.

In the fields, villagers plant and grow bitter manioc, sweet manioc, sweet potatoes, and yams alongside banana and plantain plants and papaya trees. Tonti explained the process this way. "First we plant watermelon and corn. And then yams and then manioc. One day and then the next day. And after that we plant bananas. Our old field has everything—it has manioc; it has bananas. We collect the seeds from our squash and other seeds from the old field. Everything is then ready. We plant rice and after potatoes and after manioc and after bananas. And papaya, we throw the seeds around in the field and the seeds are born."

Beans, sugar cane, pineapple, cotton, and urucum are also planted in some fields. Cotton is the least common, with urucum very commonly found near or around fields. As noted in chapter 2, urucum is a routine part of body painting practices as it is the source of an oily red paint. Papaya, rice, watermelon, sugarcane, and pineapple were not initially part of the Kayapó food crops but were introduced by FUNAI and other outsiders postcontact. Some reports indicate that the introduction of these crops occurred as late as the 1960s (Flowers et al. 1982, 206). Rice is another crop introduced by FUNAI, and it is grown along field edges or monocropped in fields dedicated entirely to a cash-based market. A handful of villagers grow rice as a subsistence or cash crop.

Interestingly, according to most consultants bitter manioc was not processed into farinha until postcontact, although some elder women in the community insist that this history is inaccurate and they always planted and processed bitter manioc into farinha. Most agreed that in the past bitter manioc was peeled, grated, strained, and dried for several days. Both ethnographic reports and interviewees acknowledged that FUNAI, then SPI, taught the Kayapó how to make farinha and donated large roasting pans to the villages to begin production (Werner et al. 1979).[10] When I was living in A'Ukre, there were three farinha roasting pans that villagers coordinated the use of during heavy processing, but the villagers hoped that more will arrive.

In a typical field, tubers, such as sweet potatoes, are located in the center and surrounded by taller crops, such as manioc, bananas, and plantains (Posey 1979) (table 2). Villagers reported that planting sweet potatoes in the middle helps keep pests away, although this is not always successful. Varieties of banana trees neatly line the edge of the fields, demarcating one plot from another. Within this general organization, patterned intercropping and monocropping normally occurs (see Werner et al. 1979 for a comparison). In the center of the field, where the sweet potatoes are concentrated, it is common to find papaya trees, even though sweet potatoes are normally tolerant of the hot sun (Hecht and Posey 1989, 175). Yams and corn are planted alongside one another or interdigitated with bitter and sweet manioc varieties. Corn, squash, rice, and beans occupy a peripheral-central area with corn stalks dominating the vegetative cover during the first few months in the life of a field.

Individual field design techniques vary as fields exhibit villagers' preference for, knowledge of, and access to different varieties of crops. For example, more commonly planted crops were most prevalent (sweet potatoes, manioc, bananas, corn, papaya), but only some villagers wanted to grow or had access to "city" or store-bought crops, and others were knowledgeable about plants grown for medicinal purposes. As an example, one interviewee reported only having *yàt aka* in her field because that is the variety of sweet potatoes she and her husband preferred. On the other hand, most villagers reported practicing patterned intercropping, a continuous rotating of fields and field size to deter blights, plant disease, leaching, and erosion, which are common in monocropping techniques (see also Hames 1983, 22; Hammond, Dolman, and Watkinson 1995, 336). Villagers noted that those who decide to plant rice and corn, but especially rice, have to be vigilant about birds destroying their crops. In the first twelve months in the life of a field, and sometimes into the second year, the plot is consistently monitored. This is when weeding, deterring of game, mulching, and burning take place. Mulching materials are a combination of organic debris and fire ants (Hecht and Posey 1989, 173; 1990). Depending on the owner of the field, a certain amount of weeds may be allowed to proliferate, as several medicinal species naturally grow in disturbed garden areas.

Birds can be especially pesky during planting at the onset of the rainy season. On a cloud-covered morning in October, I joined a *mebenget* couple to plant rice in their field. The field was a short fifteen-to-twenty-minute walk from the village on easy-to-find and well-worn paths. The series of fields I

Table 2. Garden harvest: species reported by households for cultivation.

English	Kayapó	Portuguese	Scientific Name
Banana	Tyryti	Banana	*Heliconia* sp.
Beans	Mát krwát'ý	Feijão	*Phaseolus*
Corn	Baú	Milho	*Zea mays*
Cotton	Kadjatnhi	Algodão	*Gossypium* sp.
Manioc	Kwôrô	Mandioca	*Manihot utilissima*
Papaya	Kátembaré	Mamão	*Carica papaya*
Pineapple	Akrañiti	Abacaxi	*Ananas sativus*
Rice	Baúgogo	Arroz	*Oryza satiya*
Squash	Katem	Abobora	*Cucurbita maxima*
Sugar cane	Kadjwati	Cana de açúcar	*Saccharum officinarum*
Sweet potato	Yàt	Batata doce	*Ipomoea batatas*
Tobacco	Kariñho	Fumo	*Nicotiana tabacum*
Urucum, Annatto	Pý	Urucum	*Bixa orellana*
Watermelon	Katetypkrwy	Melancia	*Citrullus vulgaris*
Yam	Môp	Inhame	*Dioscorea* sp.

visited that morning were impressive, in that the fields were a series of inter-connected plots worked simultaneously by several families that belonged to the same matriuxorilocal household complex. The wife of the couple that I was with, Prytupi, was the daughter of one of the village leaders, and she was well known and oft commented about within the village because of her strength and work ethic. Later, when I would discuss fields with other women in the village, Prytupi and her family's fields were often mentioned as being large and of high quality. Prytupi and her family were also known to spend entire days in their fields, going out with their families, and resting, processing, and cooking food in the structures built on the edge of the agricultural plots during periodic breaks. The small structure stored firewood, too, and also had things like pans, oil for hair, lighters, gardening equipment, and extra baskets available for use.

Prytupi and her husband were planting rice the day I joined them, being one of the few couples I had worked with that season who were doing so. The couple had sectioned off a corner of their field complex to plant outside of the patterned inter- and monocropping zones dominated by sweet potatoes, yams, manioc, corn, sugar cane, and other food crops. They were planting rice a little bit later than expected. The couple had already burned their field in the previous month, but they had been travelling in the Kayapó Lands and visiting relatives in another village to attend a naming festival. They arrived in A'Ukre a little later than expected, which delayed their rice planting. The delay meant that they had to keep constant vigilance over the fields to protect them from pests during the planting season. They often stayed in their fields from dawn to dusk to ward off birds and other unwelcome intruders.

The rice area was sectioned off as a monocrop (with some watermelon inter-mixed at the fringes). Prytupi's husband mentioned that he got his rice seeds from FUNAI. I never learned if these particular seeds were part of FUNAI's project that community members had discussed and through which villagers could sell bags of rice to local buyers at competitive prices, or if the seeds came from FUNAI for another reason. Nevertheless, Amaral, Prytupi's husband, had brought with him a newly bought tool that looked something akin to a dibble bar. He planned on using it to plant the rice. With only one dibble bar, Prytupi and I commenced planting with the more customary planting "toolkit" (hands, feet, and machete) while Amaral planted separately on the other side of the rice area. Prytupi made small divots with her machete in the slightly moist, black-ened red soil, and I followed behind sprinkling a pinch of pale rice seeds in the newly made impression and loosely covering the seeds with my foot to lightly spread the soil over them.

We worked like this all morning. In the midst of it, a handful of children arrived, two of whom were Prytupi's and Amaral's sons; the other two were their nephews.[11] No more than seven or eight years of age, the boys picked up some sticks and eagerly ran around the field noisily batting them together to scare away some birds. After hours of planting, I left mid-afternoon for a break and returned not more than an hour later—rain seemed imminent. Prytupi was chopping firewood and throwing it in piles, preparing to build a small fire to roast a handful of recently harvested sweet potatoes. I joined her. A strong wind began to blow and the rain began. We scrambled to put all the firewood in a dry place in their field house, and we did the same with the already collected banana leaves and the sweet potatoes while waiting the rain out.

Because fields demand a lot of time, villagers build temporary homes and camps to accommodate the long hours spent away from home. These struc-tures, like the one Prytupi and I took shelter in when the rain started, often con-tain fire pits, open clearings needed for food production and firewood storage, and provide a well-shaded spot for childcare. Sometimes these structures are small, though, and only have space to store firewood. Open clearings are used to dry bitter manioc, which is the base for *djwyngrà*, a dried manioc cake used for meat and fish dishes and sometimes combined with forest fruits. Covered structures are critical for shading young children that are brought to the fields from the sun, and smaller structures are important for *ex situ* firewood storage. If a group is planning to stay several hours in a field, the original sweet potato collection and other harvested foods are roasted in fire pits for a postharvest snack. Snacks often are the excuse for a much-needed rest from hauling heavy loads and are eaten in well-shaded forest oxbows and streams en route to the village or in the field itself.

Forest streams also serve as sites for bathing, as well as midway production sites for cleaning the harvest or the initial soaking and subsequent pressing of bitter manioc. The cool water of these streams is delicious after a morning under the burning warmth of the sun. No irrigation or water system is needed, since fields are timed with the rainy season. However, fields located near water sources are considered well situated for initial preparations of farinha and a postharvest resting point.

Where agricultural field maintenance, plantings, and harvests are often the responsibility of women, men like Amaral also play a role in swidden field preparation and management. Husbands semifrequently go to the households' agricultural plots to help women plant, weed, or harvest, but variations to the norm exist. For instance, some men spend days in the fields, whereas others spend only minimal time after clearing takes place. I regularly, and more often, saw men in fields in the initial stages of preparation—clearing the dense under-brush and chopping down trees—which was described to me as men's work. Villagers noted that each year men of the *mekrare* age grade and above (elder age grades) are responsible for clearing new fields for their families. Typically, a man in the *mekrare* age grade will help his father-in-law (*mebenget* age grade) clear a field until he is able to handle the work on his own or ask others to help him with the task of clearing.

Often, but not always, men from the same household will plant fields in the same area so they can help each other with the clearing. For example, a father may ask his son-in-law to work with him to clear a field. This was the case with Nhak's husband. Fields that belong to the same household that are placed near each other make it so women from within that household can mutually assist one another in planting and harvesting. Because of the abundance of land near the village, there very rarely is a problem with members of different house-holds choosing the same field site. If a household member is gone during key moments in the agricultural cycle, his or her family is able to use and work in fields of other household members. Very rarely do households find themselves in a situation where they are not associated with the production or maintenance of a new field, regardless of whether it is owned by the head of the family, the head of the household, or another relative. New fields, additionally, have a certain honor for young men of the *mekrare* age grade, because they indicate a key passage in a young man's social development and familial responsibility.

Women are responsible for most other field duties, such as weeding, plant-ing, burning, and harvesting. Within a household all women over a certain age share the labor requirements for doing so (although this is not always the case), such as with Nhak and Iredja. However, the eldest women or woman in the house often spend/s the most time in the field(s) monitoring, weeding, and harvesting. Women often ask other friends and family members to harvest with them if they want company or to help with harvesting manioc for ceremonies or farinha preparation. "See, this is what women do. They ask their friends to go with them to the fields. The Kayapó are like that," Marcos didactically and succinctly noted when I was going to harvest manioc with his wife and daughter for the first time.

Field visits with elder women in the community or with the female heads of the household demonstrated their long-term knowledge of landscape domestication and swidden management as well as the conviviality that often accompanies work. One morning in November, I visited the field belonging to Marcia, an elder and veteran of the village, who was Prytupi's mother. Marcia, Marcia's sister, and I walked along the path that radiates out from the land strip to her new field, which had been planted a couple of months before and, I was told, needed some weeding. Marcia pointed out three of her old fields to our left: one with only bitter manioc, one with bitter manioc and bananas (there had been sweet manioc there, but as Marcia mentioned, "agoutis eat everything"), and one with bananas. She also has two older fields in the sandy soils on the far side of the landing strip, one of which I recognized, as it was one that I was frequently shown by different villagers when I asked about agricultural fields in the village.

Marcia's field is particularly productive and, as with Prytupi's fields, noted because of its variety of crops: bitter and sweet manioc, watermelon, corn, beans, squash, sweet potatoes, yams, bananas, sugar cane, urucum, rice, and cotton. Her new field that year had sugar cane, watermelon, corn, sweet manioc, bitter manioc, yams, bananas, urucum, and rice. In the shade of some of the sweet manioc plants, her husband was also growing plants used as medicinal remedies—remedies that I was instructed not to "weed" out. For half an hour we took a tour of her new field as she pointed out different crop varieties and her strategy for field composition. Like the other fields, she planted varieties of sweet potatoes in the middle surrounded by manioc (sweet and bitter) interspersed with corn. On one edge, watermelon, rice, urucum, and bananas were patterned and interspersed among one another with the banana plants at the very edge. This particular field was connected to her sister's and her eldest daughter's, and it was one of the larger field complexes made that year (2007).

After the tour, we spent the morning weeding and collecting thick piles of cut vegetation to eventually burn. Marcia had already started two burn piles and was continually smoking while we weeded. We worked for two hours until her daughter, who had arrived and had started weeding as well, called out that she was heading home. At this time her sister also decided to start back for the village, and I joined them. Making observations about the village, as well as the old fields we passed, Marcia and her sister gossiped on the way home.

Figure 10. Women roasting sweet potatoes on an open fire.

Digging

In the middle of working with community members in A'Ukre, Teodoro said to me, "When you go back to the United States and someone is saying something about indigenous peoples, you can say no, I have lived with indigenous peoples, and this is what they do. They harvest potatoes and roast them in their field, and when they are carrying them back they stop to eat and bathe so they do not arrive hungry. You can tell them that this is how we are." In this way, sweet potatoes became much more than work to me but a way to understand how harvesting practices were caught up in larger projects of signification and at the same time critical to an individual's life cycle and expression of personhood (figure 10). Digging for sweet potatoes, or what the Kayapó refer to as *yàt*, is hard work and takes place almost year round. Under smoldering bright green banana leaves and on top of smoky, hot rocks, the burnt pink-brown, yellowed, and white-cream colored sweet potatoes are the celebrated harvests of both the dry and wet seasons. Kneeling in the dark soil, I was digging for sweet potatoes one morning. I loosely clutched the flat side of my machete as I repeatedly plunged the tip of the blade into the dirt. Once glistening new with a flat sheen, the machete now was slightly tarnished, the blade a bit dull, with tufts of dirt clinging to various parts of it. Soon my blade tip snagged on something, and I bent over and began excavating. In moments I saw what I had hit. It was only a root. No sweet potato. I sat back on my haunches, wiped my hands on my banana sap-stained pants, and surveyed the field. Senna and Iara were not far from me, digging too, moving from one spot in the field to another with seeming ease and throwing the sweet potatoes in nearby piles. We were all crouched in an open, sunny area, surrounded by the low-lying, heart-shaped leaves of sweet potato vines. In this area, shade was hard to come by even though a few papaya trees were scattered about. Immediately beyond us, rows of sweet and bitter manioc marked an uneven border between the sweet potato area and the rest of the field. Only standing three to six feet tall, the deep green palmate leaves and knobby branches of the manioc plants edged the sweet potatoes and poked out from underneath the banana trees, which lined the border of the field. I looked up beyond the manioc, beyond the glossy banana leaves and to the forest seemingly steaming in the mid-morning sunny haze. A bird circled high overhead.

Prior to the field visit that day, I did not know Senna and Iara that well. A'Ukre, although not the biggest village in the Kayapó Lands, was sizable. I had chatted with Senna and Iara before and bumped into them quite frequently during different daily routines, going to and from swidden plots, sitting outside of houses conducting interviews, attending ceremonial events, chatting on the radio, bathing in the river, sitting on the pharmacy bench, and hanging out by the soccer field, but beyond my structured field visits, we had not exchanged many words. However, when asked, Senna was more than happy to show me her field that season, demonstrate to me how she harvests different crops, and point out her other plots to me. Similar to my other conversations with women, I asked what she planted and why, where the seeds came from, how many swidden fields she worked, what types of soil she preferred, and where she had learned it all. That day, she had invited her neighbor, Iara, to come with us. Visits to fields with women like Senna and Iara and talks with women like Ireti soon emphasized the creative aspects of women's and men's work and their knowledge associated with swidden fields, field spatial location and composition, and field management and practices. It is also another way to understand the making of different territorialities, as swidden practices are critical to the production of personhood, through skilled action, generative practices that provide life-giving substances to families and friends, and place-making activities that transform landscapes over time.

Senna caught my eye and stood up.

"Nhana yàt? Nhana?" (Where are the potatoes? Where?), she asked as she moved toward me.

"Mari kit" (I do not know).

We had been in the field for most of the morning. Senna knelt down near me and began searching for potatoes.

"Yàt, yàt, yàt," she said as she pointed to where I could find them.

"Ba nhe ba mari kit (I do not know)," I repeated.

"Omu (Look)," she said as she again pointed to the places where she had located potatoes. "Añho prova" (your test), she said and laughed.

"Iñho prova" (my test), I said and sighed, repeating the mixture of Kayapó and Portuguese.

Senna stood up and moved back to the area of the plot in which she had been working. I returned my gaze to the ground, fixing on the spots that Senna had pointed out, and went back to digging. I spent many of my mornings with women like Senna and Iara in their swidden fields. Senna and Iara were both in the *mekrabdjire* age grade. This meant that they worked on their own or their mother's established swidden plots and were consistent visitors who planted, weeded, maintained, and harvested those plots. I, too, became a common fixture in the swidden field mosaic because I was interested in the daily routines and the productive and substantive, embodied practices that formulated the domesticated landscape surrounding Kayapó villages like A'Ukre. By domesticated landscape I am evoking Clement's (2006) term of a similar name, "landscape domestication," which refers to the practices and processes by which humans intentionally manipulate and shape the biophysical environment in order to meet their needs but also to mediate human and nonhuman actions. Domesticated landscapes are called a more "productive" and "congenial" environment by Clement, and in A'Ukre, swidden fields can be described as both.

Senna and Iara are competent and expert horticulturalists. They are also, admirably, expert sweet potato harvesters. I learned from the various women that I interviewed that part of the tasks *mekrabdjire* women and older had to master was the maintenance and harvesting of swidden fields. Successfully carrying out swidden tasks, like sweet potato harvesting, was only part of the list of characteristics of an ideal, skilled *mekrabdjire* woman that I collected, but it was a critical one. Women learned from an early age the various tasks required to maintain a successful plot, but their ownership of these activities was not embodied until they had kids. Experience often came from direct observation and practice in their mothers' and grandmothers' fields, but also could come from other field visits. Digging for sweet potatoes is something that most women of the *mekrabdjire* age grade and above did frequently. Sweet potatoes are a crop harvested almost all year round. It is only rivaled by manioc, which *is* available year round.[12] Moreover, rarely do women harvest only sweet potatoes. The women I worked with piled on top of baskets filled with sweet potatoes a variety of other crops, like corn, bananas, manioc, or sugar cane. The way in which women filled their baskets depended on the season and the size of the *kay*, but typically they hauled in around 15 k per field visit (figure 11).[13] On the day I worked with Senna and Iara, they did not bring any of their children with them, but other women that I worked with would and did.

Sweet potato harvesting requires specific types of knowledge that are observed, embodied, passed down, and learned. By learning and knowing well (*mari mêtch*), I am referring to the experiential, observational, embodied, and creative processes of learning and knowing valued by the Kayapó individuals. I often

Figure 11. Sweet potato, corn, manioc, and watermelon harvests.

heard consultants say, each Kayapó has to find their own *pry* or "way." Inflecting the "transference of creative powers" is a relational process where the individual is an active agent over their life course and where a "healthy sense of self . . . is constituted intersubjectively" (Allard 2013, 557; Overing 2003, 308). Similarly, learning is the "act of endowing knowledge [and] is a reproductory act: it is a work that gives life" (Overing 2003, 307). Kayapó ideas about learning *kukradjà*, broadly speaking, are deeply contextual, as well as cosmologically rooted—based on experience, in situ practice, and learner initiatives. Learning can also involve a type of mutualistic mentor–apprentice relationship when an individual seeks to acquire a particular skill, such as weaving baskets, hunting game, or knowing medicinal remedies, although both learner and mentor need to prepare themselves in different ways for this exchange. Learning is not pre-programmed but is cumulative and built on a multitude of experiences with the human and non-human, such as listening to or retelling myths, songs, and stories; enacting and mimicking different skills; and systematic and episodic personal and interpersonal interactions. For example, a girl's visit from a young age to the fields with her mother or grandmother turns into an embodied and transformative experience that becomes key to harvesting potatoes with women of a similar age grade and gives life to her family and peoples.

Learning is also an affect-laden and memory-filled experience that reflects the sensorial and corporeal knowledge acquired by doing tasks over time. In Gilsi Pálsson's (1994) analysis of fishermen in Iceland, she describes the fishermen's knowledge as a holistic enterprise, a combination of cognition, emotion, mind, and body. Similarly many scholars have described local knowledge systems, indigenous and other place-based types of knowledge, as rooted in cumulative engagement and practice, which is akin to Kayapó notions of education, learning, and knowing. This embodied type of knowing is also constitutive, as Kayapó peoples emphasize the transformative properties of sharing substances and conviviality as critical to both the production of self and community over time. These practices, or the "fabrication of consubstantiality of bodies" are "part of a wider process, which established relations" between humans and non-humans over time (Vilaça 2002, 354). Also, recent scholarship has highlighted the role that personal biography, historical events, unexpected changes, and situational factors play in indigenous knowledge systems (Lauer 2012; Lauer and Aswani 2009; Spoon 2011). This is all part of what the Kayapó mean when they refer to knowing well.

McGregor (2004, 390) holds that "indigenous knowledge cannot be separated from the people who hold and practice it, nor can it be separated from the land/environment/Creation." Non-Western knowledge is often discussed as a "knowledge-practice-belief complex" that intertwines spiritual and moral codes in regard to human-animal-plant–spirit relationships, technical skill sets, and other ways of knowing (Berkes 1999). Citing McGregor, Zanotti and

Palomino-Schalscha (2015, 2) write, "In this sense, IK is embodied and lived, passed down through oral transmission from one generation to the next, gained by mimicry, observation and experiential practice, shaped from dreams and other-worldly experiences, and learned through elder–youth apprenticeships." These ideas are condensed in the terms, *traditional ecological knowledge* (TEK), *traditional environmental knowledge* (TEK), *traditional ecological knowledge and wisdom* (TEKW), and *indigenous knowledge* (IK), although all of these terms are not without their critics. Several scholars take issue with the coupling of "traditional ecological" and "environmental knowledge" for many reasons. "Traditional" can infer and often implies static, long-term, ahistorical change, when in reality proponents of traditional environmental or ecological knowledge argue for conceptualizing knowledge as dynamic, changing, and lived. "Traditional" is also a designation of knowledge systems often associated with indigenous peoples when local, nonindigenous populations, who have occupied their environment for many generations, also have their own specific place-based knowledge linked with livelihood strategies; hence, many scholars prefer *local ecological knowledge* to traditional environmental or ecological knowledge, to capture all place-based peoples. "Ecology" and the "environment" have raised further problems, as they can be reductive, non-Native notions rooted in Western approaches to science and conservation; and they fail to capture indigenous worldviews (Cajete 2000). Many indigenous groups have social and moral codes on how humans should interact with other living and nonliving entities, but these prescriptions for practice are not necessarily discussed or conceptualized as "environmental" or "ecological" (Berkes 1999, 6). The potential dissonance between Western semantics and indigenous cosmologies and ontologies is why some scholars prefer to use the general term IK over TEK (Agrawal 1995). However, "indigenous" is also a loaded appellation with twentieth-century origins that usually carries multiple meanings and does not capture knowledge specific to particular peoples and tribal nations. At the same time, the term *knowledge* can often be used to simply refer to technical knowledge of particular species or land management techniques rather than the holistic, experiential knowledge associated with other aspects of human–environment relationships, such as the spiritual, ritual, and ethical elements of indigenous practices (Nadasdy 1999). For some TEKW resolves the reductionism of traditional environmental or ecological knowledge (Turner, Ignace, and Ignace 2000). For others, this does not resolve the question at all.

As Blaser et al. (2010, 9) argue, "indigenous knowledges take account of and care for the multiplicity of relations that exist between the elements of creation, all of which are endowed with life and agency." Or as Davi Kopenawa (2013, 300) notes, "when you are young, you don't know anything yet. You have a thought full of oblivion. It is only much later, once you've truly become an adult, that you can take the elder's words inside yourself." As I argue here and elsewhere in the book, the Kayapó ways of knowing and being are intimately tied to making a place and personhood over time. Yet, despite the issues with the terms, I employ IK here. I use it to draw attention to indigenous knowledge as just as relevant to "managing" landscapes as "Western" scientific knowledge. I also use IK to marshal rights-based discussions about the ownership, commodification, and circulation of IK in external contexts.

Senna's comment to me about my "test" is indicative of both the content of the knowledge and the way that knowledge is acquired. Senna knew that I wanted to "know" (*mari*) about agricultural fields in general and, at this particular moment, harvesting sweet potatoes, in particular. Using the Portuguese term for test, *prova*, Senna jokingly but rightly compared my attempt at acquiring a particular skill set from a domain of knowledge I knew nothing about to something that she thought I, as a foreign, Western woman would know, namely, a test. She laughed, too, not only because she thought it was humorous that I, as an adult woman, was having a hard time carrying out a task every Kayapó woman my age knew, but also as a playful joke, as humor often served as way to encourage understanding and the enjoyment of difficult tasks in life. Later, in other interviews, I asked women about how they "knew" where to locate sweet potatoes. The responses included the small rise in the soil, the way that the vines bunched together or plunged into the soil in a particular way, and the "feel" of the potato on their machete blades. The seemingly effortless way in which Senna and Iara were throwing endless potatoes in piles demonstrated their skill and knowledge of sweet potato harvesting, but it also belied the hard work required to do so. Later, while chatting with some *mebengete* (elder) women who were somewhere between forty and fifty years of age, they asked about my field visits and if I liked harvesting sweet potatoes. I responded enthusiastically, "Yes, I do." I then queried, "Do you?" One woman, Ireti, said that sweet potato harvesting is hard work, the sun is hot, her back hurts, and the potatoes are heavy. "*Oti*" (heavy), Ireti concluded, emphasizing the "i" sound to stress the weight. It was hard work.

Furthermore, practitioners and users of such knowledge are a heterogeneous group, and their skill set and lived experiences vary by age, gender, class, and other markers of difference. For instance, tasks like harvesting potatoes are generative and embodied skill sets acquired by and required of women, especially women of the *mekrabdjire* age grade and above, in order to maintain fields and transform the land to provide for their families. Tasks are often age specific and gender specific (among other distinctions) and have various levels of flexibility and plasticity affixed to who can perform what tasks and when. In A'Ukre, women that I spoke with would often refer to *menire añho âpeii* (women's work) or *menire añho kukradjà* (women's knowledge). This constituted various life-generating tasks like household activities (food preparation, butchery, cooking, cleaning, firewood, and water collection), ceremonial honors (body painting, beaded objects, woven cotton bands, and preparation for dances), subsistence practices (swidden fields, foraging, and fishing in nearby rivers), and other "care" giving activities (visits to pharmacies, walking children to school or attending school, bathing, watching films with their families, and beading). Men also carry out ceremonial honors (knowledge of ceremonial dances and songs, preparation of nonbeaded ceremonial regalia and objects, and ceremonial hunting and fishing expeditions), perform subsistence tasks (hunting, fishing, foraging, preparation, and weeding of swidden fields), attend political events (intracommunity, intercommunity, and village-outsider events), make handicrafts and tools for sale or personal use, and other similarly situated care giving activities (wage labor, attending school, and visiting the pharmacy).

But within this generalized frame comes contextual and personal variability. As discussed by interlocutors, this means that in the routines of everyday practice men might find themselves harvesting manioc, or women might be in local cities side-by-side with men who are leaders vociferously attending political rallies. Nevertheless, repeated and routinized differentiated tasks bring with them gender and age-grade specific knowledge and embodied experiences. Moreover, far from rote or mundane tasks, these activities and practices are part of "substance production—from felling the forest for gardening to preparing ritual substances and foodstuffs for consumption" (Londoño-Sulkin 2012, 69). In other words, these are transformative events that include a "number of factors, acts, and events contributing to the ongoing creation or transformation of the life forces of a person" while at the same time fortifying social processes (Overing 2003, 307).

Soils

My days going to the swidden fields patterned my time in A'Ukre as I explored the relationships among horticulture, landscapes, knowledge, and practice. The day I joined Senna and Iara, we had trekked quite a ways from the village, spending thirty minutes on the trails at a quick but not laborious clip. Senna's field was beyond the grotto, which was a forested, stream-filled area that was a border zone between the red clay soils near the village and the sandy soils beyond. This meant that I was digging up sweet potatoes with Senna and Iara through sandy soil, which loosened easily. The clay soils near the village were not as forgiving, and it took more endurance, patience, and skill to harvest those areas—something I would later find out about.

Pyka kamrêk, pyka ti, pyka tyk, and *pyka kajaka* are the four main, but not the only, different types of soil found around A'Ukre, according to the villagers. During a household survey, interviewees noted that they also prefer to have at least one field in two of the four major soil types: *pyka kamrêk* (dense, red, clay soil with lateritic gravel), *pyka ti* (sandy soil near seasonal streams), *pyka tyk* (dark soils), and *pyka kajaka* (more yellowish/whitish soils). Red clay soils are found in closer proximity to the village and used because of location and shortened travel time from fields to households. "You see, Laura, *pyka kamrêk* is good for crops," Marcos said to me. Fields planted in this soil type at a minimum can be a five-to-ten-minute walk from the village. The men and women who were interviewed reported that *pyka tyk*, or dark soil, is more fertile and prized despite its distance. "All women like *pyka tyk*," an elder woman said to me when I asked about the different soil types. "It is good for sweet potatoes and for everything," she concluded.

The dark soil found in A'Ukre places villagers and their homes at the center of debates about the fertility and sustainability of agricultural practices in the Amazon. Indeed, researchers who previously worked with the Kayapó have earmarked Kayapó swidden techniques as something to pay attention to—Kayapó soil and fire management practices could "contribute to development" of the fertile ADE and provide us with clues about past use (Hecht 2003, 368; also see Hecht and Posey 1989). *Terra preta do índio* ([ADE] also known as *Indian Dark Earth*) is a type of fertile and resilient dark black soil found in upland and lowland parts of the Amazon region.[14] This type of soil has been noted for centuries, but interest has intensified since the 1980s among a multidisciplinary group of Amazonian scholars: geographers, geologists, archaeologists, historians, anthropologists, soil scientists, and others (Woods and Denevan 2009, 1). *Terra preta* soils are found in the archeo-anthropogenic horizon of former settlement sites—frequently in the managed and manipulated areas in the landscape—and contain high concentrations of ceramics, compost, bones, lithics, shell fragments, refuse, kitchen waste, and other organic matter intermixed with a buildup of ash, charcoal, and chemical elements (Denevan 2006, 156; Novotny et al. 2009, 1004).

Decidedly anthropogenic, *terra preta* soils are the result of past—most likely pre-Columbian—indigenous activity (Smith 1980). While dating has varied, radiocarbon dates from the *terra preta* site places the formation of the soils most likely in the Christian era, but other sites have radiocarbon dating as early as 450 BCE (Rebellato, Woods, and Neves 2009, 20; Woods and Denevan 2009, 1). *Terra preta* is similar to *terra mulata*, another anthropogenic soil. *Terra mulata* does not have the deep black coloring of *terra preta* but rather is a lighter, brownish color and contains less debris (for example, little to no ceramics). *Terra mulata* is found more extensively in areas where swidden agriculture was practiced over long periods of time (Woods and Denevan 2009, 1). To get the fertility levels and deep coloring of *terra preta* soils requires the input of organic matter and slow-burning techniques, such as "charcoal from cooking and processing fires and settlement refuse burning" (Woods and Denevan 2009, 1). The carbon in *terra mulata* "probably comes from infield burning or organic debris" (Woods and Denevan 2009, 1).

Terra preta and *terra mulata* soils have caused a recent stir in Amazonian research, as their presence is firmly embedded in debates about soil fertility, anthropogenic modification, and age-old disputes about carrying capacity as epitomized by earlier and vibrant disputes among Betty Meggars, Anna Roosevelt, Donald Lathrap, and Robert Carneiro. *Terra preta do índio* also tugs at unraveling Amazonian imaginaries of a pristine wilderness by resolutely situating a pre-Columbian indigenous presence in what are often rendered as "wild" environments untouched by human groups. Moreover, *terra preta* presents possibilities for a sustainable agricultural future in the Amazon, a topic of great interest, especially among swidden farmers (indigenous and nonindigenous), who often are blamed for forest destruction (Glaser et al. 2001).

Kayapó practices are important to this discussion for two reasons. Researchers, such as Susanna Hecht and William Denevan, argue that Kayapó swidden practices might offer a present-day example of strategies and techniques that closely resemble the aboriginal (pre-Columbian) agriculture in the Amazon that formed the *terra preta* sites (Denevan 1992, 2006; Hecht 2009). As noted in earlier chapters, the Kayapó are formerly a group that lived primarily in the savannah and within savannah-forest ecotones and have, over the course of two centuries, relocated primarily to mixed forest and savannah zones, and they have changed their subsistence practices in the process. This could account for why Kayapó swidden techniques are distinct. Most Amazonian indigenous groups practice a version of swidden agriculture that follows a short cropping and long fallow technique (Denevan 2006). However, Kayapó peoples practice a version of swidden agriculture that is a semipermanent cultivation model of more semi-intensive and intensive fields (Denevan 2006, 155). Fire is also an important method for maintaining fields among the Kayapó, and these "soft" burning techniques are another reason that Hecht (2009) and Denevan (2006) are interested in exploring Kayapó practices further.

After the initial burning of the field, which releases nutrients into the soil and prepares the field for agricultural use, fields are burned throughout the year. Sweet potato vines quickly form a thick, knotty ground cover that is cut and piled at the height of the dry season harvest and sometimes clumped during the wet season harvest. Women wait to set fire to the vines in interspersed piles. Harvested corn stalks and cut weeds are also piled and burned, both to clean the garden and to provide a smoke screen from insects during the wet season. The women I interviewed report that these burnings ensure field fertility, future growth of crops, and deter snakes and other venomous animals. Moreover, harvested rotten sweet potatoes are reburied in the same location to guarantee a continual sweet potato harvest.

Manioc roots are either entirely cut or selectively cut, and cuttings are replanted in the same field area or saved for new fields. Banana trees, with their sticky sap, are cut down for harvesting. Hearths are built and rebuilt to cook tubers, manioc/meat bundles, and other items. Other applications of fire include managed-savannah areas that are burned at opportunistic moments throughout the year and village areas containing leaf litter and trash that is gathered and burned.[15] Where researchers point out that charcoal content is one of the main reasons for *terra preta* fertility, Kayapó swidden practices certainly provide many examples to support Hecht's argument for proto-*terra preta* development in Kayapó fields (Mann 2002). However, it is important to keep in mind that while Kayapó practices may help us improve our understanding of pre-Columbian agricultural practices and sustainable agricultural alternatives for the present-day, their agricultural techniques should not be considered static or ahistorical; their history is also marked by violent exploration, colonization, pacification, and territorialization.

Kayapó swidden techniques figure into the *terra preta* scholarship in another way. As already noted, the villagers praise the dark soils near A'Ukre. This suggests that the fertile soils surrounding A'Ukre could have been anthropogenically modified prior to the Kayapó's occupation of the site (*terra preta* or *terra mulata* soils). In interviews with women, there is a consensus among them that they are continually finding "artifacts" while gardening, both in A'Ukre and potentially in other villages as well. Indeed, during interviews with chiefs, when I queried about how to scout for founding a new village, one of the things they noted as important was the soils. Also, numerous interviews with women in A'Ukre point to strong evidence that their fields in *pyka tyk* sit atop or partially atop old middens, as women digging for sweet potatoes often find ceramics and stone tools from previous occupants.

Without a proper analysis of the soils from A'Ukre, the presence of previous anthropogenic modifications remains unanswered.[16] Whether or not the dark soils present in A'Ukre are anthropogenically modified by past occupants, these soils are recognized by community members as more fertile based on experiential knowledge of planting more fickle crops, like rice and corn, which are well suited to these soil types rather than red clay soils. Root crops and tubers, such as sweet potatoes and manioc, are noticeably more abundant and easier to harvest in *pyka tyk*. Fields with this soil type can be up to a two-hour roundtrip from the village, which makes transport an important issue. As research on *terra preta do índio* and *terra mulata do índio* continues to expand and develop, further inquiries into the relationship between Kayapó swidden practices and village formation should provide additional fruitful arenas from which to explore issues of soil fertility and sustainability in the Amazon.

Space and Time

So far I have discussed the practice of swidden agriculture in the village of A'Ukre and have situated it within the context of debates about swidden that have corresponded with and sometimes fueled different theoretical dispositions within ethnoecology, ethnobiology, and ethnobotany. I have also described the embodied and generative skill sets required for field harvest (sweet potatoes), crop transportation techniques, layout of agricultural fields, field architecture, crop species, planting techniques, field life, and the fertility of soils. Throughout this discussion, I have attempted to impress that swidden work should not be characterized simply as a utilitarian impulse to feed one's belly or attend to "vulgar needs," but should be characterized as a social and place-making process part of foodways and lifeways. Digging, mulching, burning, harvesting, roasting, and processing intersect the realms of work, knowledge, and sociality. Visits to fields with friends, sisters, daughters, husbands, and others are not only a subsistence-based task but also a place where conviviality, knowledge transmission and acquisition, and storytelling gather together. As such, many women and men from A'Ukre spend a lot of their time in fields, old ones and new ones, with friends and other family members. In addition, the questions of whether and when to visit fields next—which field and with whom—often guide women's daily agendas, as many of the women I spent time with broke up their days and weeks among field visits, life-giving activities, ceremonial obligations, and other tasks.

For instance, a common early morning scenario in Nhak's household as I visited the porch was the smoky smell of an early morning fire, water boiling for a soon-to-be-made carafe of coffee, and leftover smoked fish or meat on the small iron grill. Nhak and Iredja would be tending to various duties, such as feeding children, fixing beaded objects, combing hair, and piling firewood. And their grandmother in a nearby hammock often would be giving out orders or tending to small infants. Their husbands would move in and out of the porch area, the main house, and the men's house. Wondering if a field visit was necessary or if other tasks associated with ceremonial obligations, like painting children, husbands, or each other, needed to be carried out, Nhak might ask her children or younger sisters to go find out if anything was going on that day, or if maybe they would need to harvest firewood or manioc in a group for a festival preparation. Most women, including Nhak, would leave their houses early in the morning (the average hour was 8:00 to 9:30 a.m., but women and men noted in interviews that *amrebe*, or "in the past," women would leave not long after first light) and work up until mid-to-late afternoon, depending on the demand.

Upon hearing the news from the age-grade leaders or women chiefs, Nhak would make her decision on what to spend the morning hours doing. Nhak's daily routine was not that different from other women's in the village. When going to the swidden area, I would often see women setting out in small groups. While going in these large groups was explained in terms of the critical mass necessary for harvesting a substantial amount of manioc for farinha, women talked about going to fields together for a variety of reasons, including spending time with friends and family. As such, the swidden practices, in terms of acquisition of different types of knowledge and performativity of different place-attachments, are a critical sphere where women maintain relationships and skill sets. In addition to a social space, several of the women I interviewed reported that *menire* (women) have gender-specific, human–animal relationships that are related to swidden tasks, such as using fish teeth for planting manioc, collecting seed varieties, or listening to the call of a particular bird species for warnings of danger in their garden. Women, especially of the elder age grade, still smoke in fields, spit to ward off evil spirits, or paint urucum on their faces as a form of protection and strength. Interviewees repeatedly described certain aspects of swidden knowledge as *menire añho kukradjà* (women's knowledge) and often described women as having the knowledge necessary to harvest sweet potatoes, manioc, and other food crops in their gardens. In other Amazonian contexts, scholars have documented the importance of women's knowledge about manioc varieties, trading and exchange patterns, and diverse planting techniques (Boster 1985; Chernela 1986; Emperaire and Peroni 2007; Rival 2002). Kayapó women are also charged with retaining the vast repertoire of manioc, sweet potatoes, bananas, and other varieties in their fields, and are involved in a generational trade network of varieties.

Interestingly, anthropologists Gustaaf Verswijver (1992a) and Joan Bamberger (1967) both report a significant amount of magico-religious tradition, symbolism, and songs associated with Kayapó swidden traditions. For example, Verswijver noted that women sing songs while clearing, planting, or harvesting fields. These and other practices noted by Verswijver no longer were part of the daily routines in A'Ukre, according to villagers and based on observation in practice. In addition, one of the ceremonies that involves the clearing and planting of fields has never been performed in A'Ukre. Villagers reported that many traditions associated with gardening are no longer practiced as frequently as before. "This is something my grandfather would know, but we no longer know this now," Marcos said to me many times when I asked about techniques noted by earlier ethnographers. Where many interviewees remembered other Kayapó in the past who knew different songs, rituals, and other practices and could vaguely recall some, more often than not they reported that they did not know some of the traditions that were practiced *amrebe*, or in the distant past. With that said, some consultants could have been politely refusing to talk about practices, as they may have been something that only specific learners should know. Regardless of their alignment, or not, with previous ethnographic observations in the region, fields do play an important part in naming ceremonies and still remain vital in storytelling traditions and generative, place-making practices. Furthermore, farinha production, firewood harvests, and other activities contribute to small-scale rituals and the large, elaborate naming festivals. To prepare for many ceremonies, I spent my time working with *mekrabdjire* women in the fields and forests, as they, along with *mebengete* women, were responsible for the majority of food production for most major festivals, including the manioc and corn festivals.

With that said, swidden plots are also arguably an integral part of the political organization of the village. In addition to household fields, village leaders (husband and wife teams) are the caretakers and owners of fields that are prepared and maintained in their early stages by different political societies. When young adult men pass from the age grade of *meboktire* to *menóronùre*, they are considered members of the political system and take an active role in the men's house. Part of this transition requires young men to join one of the men's societies, which are headed by village chiefs. New memberships to a men's society are solidified in part by helping a chief clear and maintain his agricultural fields. Hunting, construction, and fishing activities may also be required. The chiefs' agricultural fields are distinct in that the fields are normally larger than those for a household and often have a more diverse array of species planted than does the average field. For example, a chief's field might include beans, cotton, and rice, which are common species, but normally not abundant in an average field. Large plots, especially a chief's plot, are politically charged and can require substantial time commitments that households may otherwise be dedicating to their own plots (also see Fisher 2000, 118).

A'Ukre villagers also had experimented with a type of commonly managed field as a result of a FUNAI-driven agricultural project. In 2005, FUNAI reportedly gave the community rice seeds to plant, and according to the organization principles of the community, each chief was responsible for selecting an optimal field site for planting and mobilizing his associated society to grow the rice. These fields, which in 2006 were referred to simply as "community" fields, failed when flooding ruined the plots. Extra fields for mono- or cash cropping, such as these, are not usual. Consultants indicated that they had no intention of planting fields like these in the future because of their negative experience and their inability to attain new seeds easily. These rice fields stand out, as well, in that the customary patterned polycropping techniques were not employed as they were with Amaral and Prytupi's field.

Finally, swidden practices connect kinship networks and ecological spaces across the Kayapó Lands. The gifting of seeds, cuttings, and harvests are common throughout the year. The cuttings are especially popular to exchange prior to and during the planting seasons in August and September. Fields, in a way, become seasonal representations of different types of social ties and labor inputs. As already noted, multiple relationships are forged during field management, such as the friendly excursions of Senna and Iara. For example, household ownership of fields and gendered human–environmental and political connections to fields create a social and spatial patterning within field production. Fields are also sites of experimentation, as community members plant new seeds from extralocal sources, and they are sites where seeds from within A'Ukre and from across their lands can circulate. In this way, fields are plural landscapes (social, ideological, and material) within the community and cultivate Kayapó territorial belongings based on foodways and cuisines that fortify their people and lifeways.

Conclusion

As early as the 1970s, Eugene Anderson (1972, 265) called for anthropologists working with small-scale societies to have a more integrated and explicit focus on "modern food problems." As discussions of global food security intensify, researchers have scrutinized the productivity and sustainability of swidden agriculture, especially when subsistence crops are combined with cash crops (Brush 1975; Carneiro 1960). For instance, in Kalimantan, Indonesia, Michael Dove explored the combination of subsistence- and market-driven swidden systems where farmers plant customary crops alongside the cultivation of rubber and pepper for monetary income. In this case, the combination of subsistence and cash crops offered the local community a successful mixed agricultural strategy (Dove 1993).[17] Yet, in other areas, the viability of swidden as a source of economic return instead of just subsistence goods has been questioned (Montagnini and Mendelsohn 1997; Weinstock 1983). Other topics of research address not only the mixed swidden systems, but also the complications involved in transitioning from swidden to other forms of supposedly more efficient cultivation techniques (Padoch, Harwell, and Susanto 1998). In A'Ukre, villagers were experimenting with new types of crops for consumption, as well as some that were destined for the market, such as rice. While the rice experimentation was carried out on a more ad hoc basis than systematically among many villagers, its presence, and the growth of projects related to indigenous health and well-being spear-headed by FUNAI, FUNASA, and conservation-related NGOs means that similar types of projects will probably be marketed or crafted in the future with the residents of A'Ukre.

As conversations about food systems abound in literature concerning the loss of traditional forms of agriculture, interlocutors from A'Ukre report they have retained a certain consistency in recycling seeds and cuttings from previous gardens, families, and villages, customary swidden practices, and in sustaining a genetically diverse crop base while incorporating new crop varieties (see also Nazarea 1999; Thrupp 2000). Furthermore, previous researchers working with the Kayapó have noted that their patterns of semi-intensive cultivation are evidence of the positive impacts of local anthropogenic disturbance regimes on biodiversity, such as agro-forestry systems, trail plantings, and seed exchanges, while at the same time new research into ADE has presented intriguing lines of inquiry into Kayapó swidden practices (Hecht and Posey 2002 [1989]; Posey 1985). For villagers in A'Ukre, as with many others in Kayapó villages, secure land tenure in the form of a federally demarcated territory has been beneficial for retaining and experimenting with swidden practices. Moreover, the transmission of knowledge through practice contributes to the robustness of the local knowledge systems, as well as for continuing to make territory and home. These practices are articulated not only as key to community life but as part of larger conversations about food sovereignty and justice in the region.

Not only critical to retaining food systems, swidden practices are inherently tied to senses of belonging and place in A'Ukre, as residents make fields to sustain their lifeways. Daily activities related to and within fields serve as constant reminders of different human, animal, and plant relationships. As community members advance through their life stages, they are associated with different subsistence roles, skills, and knowledge sets that revolve around productive and transformative practices and ties to the village landscape. Several key moments in a man's or woman's development as an individual, part of a family unit, or a community member depend upon subsistence practices and their understanding of their homeland. For example, a man's ability to clear a field for his household or his men's society indicates a key stage in his social development. Similarly, a woman's knowledge of planting gardens, gathering cuttings, and locating foraged foods is highly desirable.

Food has a way of "provid[ing] a medium through which stories and histories are told and remembered, places described, identities formed, and community imagined" (Choo 2004, 206 quoted in Komarinsky 2009, 42). Practical, applied experience is important for daily activities and for the accumulation and transmission of knowledge. "Knowing" is closely associated with listening and hearing, as well as observing and practicing, in this case, different subsistence activities. *Kukradjà*, or "knowledge," is only obtained over time and through constant practice (Murphy 2004). The villagers value their different kinds of knowledge about a variety of skills associated with subsistence activities, consubstantiality, or ceremonies. Beyond honors accumulated on a ceremonial level, which distinguishes "common" names from "beautiful" names, working hard and knowing how to perform a task skillfully and adeptly is a highly prized social attribute. Those that do not work hard or perform their associated subsistence roles are considered lazy and weak. Consequently, the foodways provide a way to examine social and spatial patterns of behavior and territorialization practices. These patterns, although routinized, are complimentary to other activities, like political and ritual ones. Furthermore, subsistence activities have an impact on how the landscape and the territory is ordered and organized. Through practice and acquisition of knowledge and skills, villagers perform daily tasks that are necessary and important for maintaining a complex set of social relations while, at the same time, providing life-giving needs for their households. Grown food in the community was constantly referred to as "healthy" and distinguished from store-bought foods. Many consultants saw that making fields and continuing foodways was a source of strength for the community and a distinctive Kayapó way of supporting livelihoods, one that diverged from an agro-industrial system based on capital accumulation. As Santos-Granero (2009a, 485) has observed with his work, "the making of beautiful, skillful, and moral Yanesha men and women requires the ingestion of certain foods and the avoidance of others at different stages of a person's life." Similarly the making of beautiful, skillful, and moral Kayapó men and women is wrought from horticultural practices that make place in a way that aligns with indigenous ontologies rather than hegemonic territorial acts.

Yet, these comments should be tempered with knowledge of the pressing issues related to the larger political economy of Amazonia and broader international developments. Although the Kayapó inhabit a federally demarcated region, persistent threats to both the borders and integrity of their lands threaten to alter, perhaps dramatically, Kayapó lifeways. As emphasized in earlier chapters, over the past several decades developmental and neodevelopmental regimes, including, but not limited to, rubber, logging, mining, ranching, agriculture, and roads, have been the greatest threats to the Kayapó lands. Large-scale hydroelectric projects like the Belo Monte Dam are the most insidious threat so far, and although A'Ukre is not on the Xingu River proper, other villages are, and the reverberations will be felt throughout the area. Finally, the changing climate and other adverse environmental changes associated with and independent of Belo Monte Dam might negatively impact swidden systems, as mentioned previously, since they are timed to coincide with the dry and wet seasons. Variable or unpredictable climate patterns, such as a pronounced drought, would have dramatic consequences for villages like A'Ukre. Thus, while Senna and Iara can still depend upon harvesting their fields, they are now potentially facing a new suite of unprecedented obstacles. These uncertainties are exactly the kind of challenges that villagers confront as they maneuver among their territories' multiple mandates while at the same time fight to retain the foodways that define their livelihoods.

Moreover, the global consumption patterns that currently drive our food and energy systems are unsustainable and have produced inequalities that have social and spatial consequences. Proponents of a degrowth society emphasize formal and informal exchange networks, or nonmonetized economies, that promote just and sustainable futures. Robust local and regional food networks can help to generate "transitional" practices and narratives that combat inequitable food systems. Leff (2012, 6) proposes that "political ecology emerges in the South from a politics of difference rooted in the ecological and cultural conditions of its peoples, from their emancipation strategies for decolonization of knowledge, reinvention of territories, and reappropriation of nature." In this way political ecology and feminist political ecology joins transitional discourses to support movements that recognize different knowledges, experiences, and ways of being in the world. The Kayapó's fight for territorial retention allows communities to persist in practices that sustain the convivial and critical exchanges that produce and maintain life. These practices are also increasingly politicized, as seen in the Seed Fair, and woven into grassroots struggles that are now characterized as part of "alternative food networks" (Sage 2014, 255).

In this way, swidden for the Kayapó is part of a larger food sovereignty movement in Latin America and across the Amazon. Countering the agro-industrial and extractive landscape in the region, supporting the limited and controlled incorporation of imported food stuffs, and developing sustainable alternatives to intensive extractive economies compose a vision that is shared with the Via Campesina and other regional movements in the area. *Radical Territories* is then about shifting the conversation to support practices, such as swidden, that are generative for indigenous lifeways and part of a new territorial and place-making politics. As Bodirsky and Johnson (2008) emphasize, "traditional indigenous foodways remain important for the ongoing health and well-being of contemporary Indigenous North American peoples." Extending this to practices in A'Ukre, I show that swidden is part of knowledge networks, social relationships, and individual identity. Rather than a destructive force to lands and peoples, swidden is about nourishing current lifeways and creating strong networks and alliances that allow these foodscapes to persevere in the future. Food then becomes a mechanism to counter the spatial and economic effects of neoliberal logics, develop a robust political presence in quotidian lifeways, and maintain community and cultural identity in the face of widespread change.

4

Valuing Nature

> Many words walk in the world. Many worlds are made. Many worlds
> make us. There are words and worlds that are lies and injustices. . . .
> We want a world in which many worlds fit. The nation that we con-
> struct is one where all communities and languages fit, where all steps
> may walk, where all may have laughter, where all may live the dawn.
>
> —Subcomandante Marcos, *Our Word is Our Weapon: Some Writings*

Introduction

The fruiting season was hot and wet. Even in the early morning when I visited
Nhak's house and drank sugary coffee, the hard sun dripped heat.[1] When I
gazed across A'Ukre's pale, red plaza, it was pockmarked with deep rivets from
the heavy rain and dotted with clumps of unkempt weeds soon to be cleared for
the next ceremony or festival. From where I sat on the porch, I could see beyond
the houses where the forests and fields begin. It would be cooler there, I thought
one day, while I tried to finish my coffee before Elisa, an elder woman who lived
across the village, arrived. When she shadowed the porch entry moments later,
I could see that she had brought her youngest child with her. Held in a brightly
woven cotton sling, her daughter, who was nine months old or so, was perched
on her hip while clinging to her yellow dress. Elisa was a friend of the family
with whom I was spending time, and I welcomed the opportunity to learn from
her. She was taking me to harvest *krem* (*Endopleura uchi*), one of the forest fruits
ripening at this time of year. In addition to being good to eat, the fruit was also
processed into an oil that was much loved for ceremonial preparations.

I picked up my *kay* and machete and followed Elisa out across the plaza and
then to a patchwork area of fields and forest. The path was narrow—a thin dirt
strip that began in the village and jutted out crookedly to the fields and beyond.
Elisa pushed across fallen logs and branches that had been broken back to clear
the path. We stepped over debris as we made our way into the forest past the
fragmented variable landscape of the swidden area. The limp crunch of the slippery leaf litter sounded like the cold wetness familiar to me as the sound of a
temperate autumn. Leaves squished and flattened as we sought out a *krem* tree. It
was warm and cool at the same time under the shaded canopy. I was reminded of
the succinct statement that Marcio, one of my ongoing interlocutors in A'Ukre,
had once made while trekking not far from where I stood: "It is nice here."

Finding a tree, Elisa picked up *krem*—a green-yellow fruit. With its mottled, smudged colors, *krem* was difficult to see on the forest floor. Oval in shape, *krem* looks like an egg, but to the touch it is firm and sturdy with a bit of a give. While Elisa systematically moved around the tree, I began slowly walking forward, scanning the ground for the fruit. Finding two, I heard Elisa's voice behind me saying that we should move on. Another tree was nearby that was likely to have more *krem*. Elisa returned after a while and handed me a fruit. She invited me to take a break from harvesting and try one. "Kukren" (eat), she urged me. I watched her peel the leathery skin off with her teeth and sink them into the fruit. I did the same, rubbing the fruit on my shirt and then peeling off the skin with the tips of my front teeth. The fruit was mealy, like an apple gone bad, but thick and starchy. I rolled the grainy interior around in my mouth, peeled and spit out more rind, and finished eating it as we collected our full and heaving baskets in order to head back home where we would eventually turn the fruit into aromatic oil ready to be passed along the body or through hair.

For the next couple of months, wild forest foods became ready for harvest. During the wet and dry season, I spent a great deal of time with women, men, and families on harvesting outings for fruits, nuts, fibers, and plants that served as food for families, resources for artisanal or ceremonial objects, materials for body painting or bow-making, or firewood for starting a *ki*. Filling up baskets with *krem*, pinching back leaves as we walked down paths, slinging long poles of *buriti* palms over our shoulders, cautiously observing honey harvesting areas, or stopping to slice thin slivers of bark off of a tree for body paint applicators patterned the rhythms of walking on forested paths (*pry*).

In the 1980s, scholars began referring to these resources—the fruits, nuts, fibers, mushrooms, honey, insects, medicines, and other foraged items, including bushmeat, birds, and insects—as NTFPs.[2] Worldwide, more than 200 to 300 million people, like the Kayapó peoples, depend on forested and other surrounding environments (gardens, grasslands, and fields) for food, fuel, fibers, and oils for daily life (Pimentel et al. 1997, 91). Mongongo tree nuts, babassu palms, breadfruit, sago palms, gums, and legume seeds produce an "enormous" amount of food for communities (Pimentel et al. 1997, 93). In the post-Brundtland era, NTFPs have become a centerpiece for community-based sustainable development programs and form a significant portion of global environmental and forestry governance interventions that emphasize joining conservation with poverty alleviation measures.

In this chapter, I connect and expand on several bodies of literature regarding NTFP work, including foraging practices, forest ecosystems, and indigenous foodways, in order to analyze the extent to which NTFPs form part the transformative politics that the Kayapó support. As Kayapó peoples shape and relationally coconstruct landscapes congenial to their well-being or a *mejkumrei* life over time, these practices increasingly accommodate new transactional orders, such as NTFP markets. The NTFP projects rely on new relational norms (e.g., alliance building with NGOs), which are necessarily mediated by historically situated exchange patterns of Kayapó communities that over the past several decades have endured and accommodated other market opportunities and outsider engagement (e.g., trade with FUNAI and illegal logging in the 1990s). As much anthropological work on this topic has shown, the material and nonmaterial impacts of NTFPs, the gendered dimensions of harvesting and labor, the symbolic and spiritual facets of NTFPs, the multispecies encounters that NTFPs ultimately interface with, the complexities of community–conservation relationships and the politics involved in the pricing of nature—are all part of the fabric of NTFP programs (Agarwal 1992; Charnley and Poe 2007; Choy et al. 2009; Lyon and Moberg 2010; Tsing 2015).

Moreover, similar to swidden activities, foraging, such as the trek or *pry* that Elisa and I took to the forest that afternoon, simultaneously affirms place-making practices and social continuity through relational interaction with the landscape all the while remaining positioned within multi-scale conversations about global environmental governance. In this way, generative everyday practices, such as foraging, are interconnected with international, national, and regional political ecologies that are driving unsettling neodevelopmental agendas in the region (hydroelectric development and soy expansion) and simultaneously spurring new regional grassroots alliances premised on sustainable rural livelihoods and the landscapes they inhabit (Turner and Fajans-Turner 2006). A critical approach to NTFPs emphasizes the diverse outcomes of NTFP engagement, where the environment, justice goals, indigenous cosmovisions, "plural value-articulation institutions," and processes of commodification are taken into consideration (Kallis, Gómez-Baggethun, and Zografos 2013, 97). Rather than envisioning new market opportunities as incremental adaptation to change or a conflict between the "incommensurability of values," I show the process in which community members in A'Ukre emplace, subsume, resist, or are stressed by, both ideologically and materially, mixed market economies (see Martinez-Alier, Munda, and O'Neill 1997). Where a Marxian view of commodification would hold that neoliberalism is "absolute in character—either uniformly good or bad"—a locally situated perspective reveals that NTFP projects are emplaced within particular historical trajectories, as well as transactional economies (Dressler and Roth 2011, 852).

Arguably, Kayapó notions of exchange have always been guided by a set of transformative practices that substantively incorporate foreign things, objects, peoples, and ideas within their lifeways (Gordon 2006; Lea 2012). Yet, as Nadasdy (2007, 218) urges, "it is precisely the relations of capitalist resource extraction and agro-industry that are the most responsible for the marginalization of indigenous peoples and the dispossession of their lands and resources." Overwhelming and disruptive policies and practices, such as continued agro-industrial development and energy infrastructures in the Amazon, have the potential to devastate and erode Kayapó projects for self-determination. Where neodevelopmentalism programs in the region based on pro-poor platforms and state-based extractive and energy economies emphasize market-based and capacity building interventions, communities orient their engagement with or resistance to broader-scale changes with short-term goals and intergenerational gains in mind.

In this chapter, I am especially interested in the tensions between village-level projects for well-being and their intersection with successive waves of extractivism, developmentalism, and conservation in the region. In doing so, I concentrate on those harvests related to fruit and nut gathering, and how Kayapó peoples incorporated these set of practices into projects of place-making, territorial retention, and identity politics at different scales. The focus of the literature discussed includes political ecological and feminist political ecological considerations of NTFPs, particularly questions surrounding the governance and pricing of nature; historical ecology work illustrating anthropogenic notions of landscape; approaches to place and space that emphasize the embeddedness of multisensorial modes in place-based practices; and foodways research that highlights the various sites of production to sites of consumption within different systems. Just as food sovereignty and food justice have become powerful calls to action and frameworks from which local communities seek to retain control of their food systems and counter neoliberal and neodevelopmental logics, sustainable forestry management and multi-use forestry systems have become prevalent approaches to addressing neo-extractivism, global conservation agendas, and local livelihoods (Guariguata et al. 2010). In continuing livelihood practices integral to *kukradjà*, or Kayapó ways of knowing and being in the world, foraging is ultimately linked to projects for self-determination and strength.

I begin by offering a discussion of NTFPs and then expand on their predominance in community-based practices that support Kayapó livelihoods. I show how the NTFP marketplace, since its intensified development in the 1980s, has persisted as a proposed alternative development strategy for rural and land-based resource-dependent communities. Renewed interest in NTFPs also has prompted a reevaluation of historically situated informal and formal economies that have always existed in the region based on these same products. A historical ecology approach considers this long record of trade and exchange, providing a deep temporal perspective of the harvest of forest products. In the following section, I also locate NTFPs as part of the landscape of foodways, showing the diverse locations—backyard gardens, agricultural fields, field-forest mosaics, forests, and savannahs—in which NTFPs are fixed. Finally, in exploring Brazil nuts, a NTFP that has been particularly dominant in the region and for the residents of A'Ukre, I tease apart several of the complexities of mixed economies, the partnerships market development fosters, and the gendered dimensions of practice. I demonstrate through a discussion of different approaches to NTFPs and their relevance to Kayapó livelihoods, their connections to practices that are constituted of making home and place and the important implications that use and access have for territorial conceptualizations and imaginings. As a final note, although I make use of the term NTFPs in this chapter, this designation was not widespread in A'Ukre. More commonly, NTFPs were referred to by their Kayapó common names, such as *krem*, or were described as *pidjô* (fruit) or *ba añho* (from the forest) to distinguish gathered products from store-bought or city goods.[3]

To NTFP or To Not NTFP

Over the past several decades, NTFP markets have been available in A'Ukre through informal exchanges, commercial venues, individual sales, and community–NGO partnerships (Zanotti 2009). These different modes of NTFP engagement reflect popular policy and environmentalist stances on NTFPs, where NTFP projects were envisioned as income for resource-dependent and small-scale communities in order to meet the goals of conservation and livelihood needs without engaging in highly extractive economies (timber, ranching, mining), corporate agribusiness, or intense deforestation. The rationale for the generation of these market economies is that community-based, customary use of forested environments for already available and harvested resources could be viably integrated within conservation and development programs, offering sound use of forestry systems within global economies but also providing moral alternatives to neoliberal production (Godoy and Bawa 1993; Moberg 2014; Nepstad and Schwartzman 1992). By working with local communities through different collaborative means, such as in comanagement regimes or cooperative alliances, NTFP development projects often intended to support local knowledge systems, democratic decision-making, customary harvesting practices, and already in place governance structures (Charnley and Poe 2007).

NTFPs were also believed to have the potential to increase the value of forested environments through more intense production, potentially generating more income than timber economies or agricultural products (Arnold and Pérez 2001, 438). Through an emphasis on capacity building, NTFP programs could offer communities opportunities to generate income within certain sectors of society that may not have had access to the market or cash. Today, many communities rely on NTFPs to provide income and to fill in gaps during lean harvest times (reduce vulnerability), diversify the diet, and sometimes offer farm inputs ([e.g., trees for shade or land for swidden cultivation] Arnold and Pérez 2001, 441; Shackleton and Pandey 2014).

NTFP markets today are reinforced by local and alternative food movements that emphasize single-source, artisanal, certified, and other goods that provide moral, ethical, and justice-seeking alternatives to the "impersonal logic" of industrial commodities (Moberg 2014, 8). Likewise, a heightened awareness of the plight of the "rainforest" has resulted in an economic environment in which socially and environmentally concerned consumers have the option to buy groceries, cosmetics, or luxury items with a conscious.[4] For example, from the Body Shop to Aveda to the Brazilian Chamma da Amazônica, cosmetic companies have incorporated NTFPs into a range of beauty products and associated items.[5] American and European consumers frequently encounter supermarket aisles packed with such products as rainforest dark chocolate and cereals touting names associated with the tropics and neotropics. For example, açaí (*Euteurpe oleracea*), a fruit also found in the Kayapó area, is now popular in U.S. health food stores. Marketed as a super-antioxidant, weight-loss remedy, and all around miracle elixir, açaí can be bought in the form of pills or, more popularly, in fruit smoothies, in which it is mixed with pomegranate and blueberry juice, among other ingredients. At the same time that the greening and green-washing of certain strategically placed market items has raised a consumer-based awareness, deforestation in the Amazon and many social justice issues are unresolved. Critics of the NTFP marketplace remain skeptical of equitable relationships and partnerships in these commodity chains, raising alarm about the commodification of "the environment and social relationships," as well as continued unfavorable labor conditions (Besky 2008; Guthman 2004; West 2006, 184). Moreover, Sidney Mintz and Christine Du Bois (2002) do well to remind us that diverse transactional economies (moral economies and subsistence economies) exist at sites of collection, production, and harvest to sites of distribution and consumption.

Despite the widespread use of NTFPs by rural communities and interest in NTFPs since the 1980s, evidence of the benefits and stresses of NTFP markets has produced mixed reactions to NTFP programs. These programs have been unevenly integrated into and remain marginal to sustainable forestry initiatives (Morsello et al. 2014). NTFPs can also have varying ecological and social consequences. The increased demand for and collection of a subsistence-based item may give rise to overuse of the resource, exacerbate harvesting pressures, and take away from other subsistence-based activities upon which communities customarily rely. Moreover, if NTFP projects are developed without taking the heterogeneity of local communities and the expertise within these communities into consideration, they can stress social institutions in place or upset access to, use of, or availability of a resource or wage-earning activity. For example, in a review of different case studies, Chernela and Zanotti (2014, 308) emphasize the distinctions between local economies that might be operating alongside market-based mechanisms. They highlight the stress that markets can place on customary exchange networks and problems linked to monetizing a subsistence good. As scholars have been critical of the pricing and privatization of nature as a solution to livelihood needs, NTFPs can also encourage new and not always locally relevant institutional, financial, and technical capacity building required for such projects; the reproduction of top–down development models; environmental stresses, risks, and uncertainties that projects are not equipped to accommodate; and unanticipated impacts on local livelihoods, including changing household and inter- and intracommunity dynamics (Büscher et al. 2012; Pokorny et al. 2012).

These arguments are complimented by other studies that find a troubling notion of "community" that has risen in development, justice, and environmental work, which suggests that the heterogeneous, overlapping, and historically situated composition of local identities need to be taken into consideration when examining natural resource governance and sustainable development (Nagar et al. 2002; Paulson and Gezon 2005). Feminist political ecologists have been especially vocal in arguing for an intersectional approach to identity, complimented by an analysis of asymmetrical power relationships and an examination of the discourses and narratives produced within these marketplaces. Intersectionality, in particular, points to the "material and emotional dimensions" of subjectivities that are "wrought through the intersection of gender, 'race,' ethnicity, age, sexuality and so on through spatial practice," which becomes particularly salient when considering the enactment of NTFPs programs on the ground (Elmhirst 2011, 131).

The implicit linkages that have been created between notions of indigeneity and small-scale markets also pose problems when indigenous groups invest in other types of markets or create corporations of their own. Part of the complication with NTFPs is that while they may seem like innocuous solutions to market problems, the premise behind NTFPs remains quite political. The heavy reliance on NTFPs and other interventions subsumes efforts for recognitional justice as they weakly offer distributional solutions to justice through market-based mechanisms (see Scholsberg 2007). The positioning of certain resources within the category of NTFPs and others outside of this definition (e.g., mineral resources) suggests that "NTFPs are resources that local people may be allowed to exploit" and that "NTFPs are resources that *no one* but local people would want to exploit" (Dove 2011, 211). In other words, ascribing small-scale market development to NTFP product markets and simultaneously failing to designate large-scale extractive economies as NTFPs, even if they are also based on a nontimber good, results in a valuation regime that continues to privilege intense extractivism. Dove's concern is that these rhetorical ambiguities make it easy for communities to advocate for rights, access, inclusion, and compensation based on certain NTFPs but not others. An overarching critique is that ultimately the valuation of the natural world is incompatible with indigenous cosmovisions and justice claims.

Nearly all NTFP projects in A'Ukre have been based on Brazil nut markets, which has been historically important to the region and locally important to community members in A'Ukre. As mentioned previously, the Body Shop, the international cosmetic chain, began a fair-trade project with the community of A'Ukre in the 1990s. They provided the infrastructure for community members to process Brazil nut oil, which the Body Shop bought to sell in a Brazil nut line in their stores. While the project ultimately failed, the project itself, which I outline in greater detail below, is a powerful example of the growing interest of consumers, conservation organizations, companies, and local communities in developing high-value, niche product markets that link consumers with producers in a way that meets social and ecological goals. This type of community–corporate alliance is also indicative of a private sector trend to adopt corporate social responsibility principles, especially in relationship to sustainable development initiatives that focus on NTFPs.

Although the Body Shop project was short lived, villagers in A'Ukre also created a long-term partnership with CI that lasted over twenty years. I discuss this partnership in the next chapter, but what is notable here is that this partnership and the alliances that it subsequently proffered focused on creating alternative markets in the region to counter different waves of agro-industrial expansion, mining (particularly gold mining), and timber economies. The NTFPs were an obvious initial choice for conservation organizations to create development programs within different communities, and NTFPs became a centerpiece for several of the programs initiated by CI. As with the Body Shop, Brazil nuts also played a significant role in these programs, especially in A'Ukre. Nevertheless, other products, ranging from honey to jamborandi (*Pilocarpus jaborandi*) leaves to cumaru (*Dipteryx odorata*) seeds, across the Kayapó Lands have been part of these economies. Despite mixed experiences with markets and different degrees of willingness to participate in diverse types of economic activities, part of what I wish to explain is that community members in A'Ukre insist that NTFP projects continue to develop and sustain desirable cash-income flows for villagers and should be part of livelihood strategies (Zanotti 2009). As the pricing of nature has become more complex, it is also worth noting that NTFP programs are now part of a larger portfolio of markets in the region, including payment for ecosystem services and burgeoning carbon markets, both of which Kayapó communities are exploring as well (Chernela and Zanotti 2014).

In A'Ukre, several harvested products are part of sustainable development programs and retain multiple identities as they shift between being food items or commodities, Brazil nuts being the most visible example. Moreover, the Kayapó interlocutors I worked with rarely spoke of going into the forest in a way that characterizes their harvests as commoditized wage labor. Foraging as an activity serves to sustain social relationships and human–plant–animal communities as much as the collection of a good for food or market. Consultants often reflected on the hard work required (*âpeii tycht*) and the conviviality spurred by such practices. These practices also were affect- and emotion-laden, as outings in the forest with friends and family were seen both as dangerous but life-giving.

As an example, my heart sank when, after visiting A'Ukre in the rainy season, I left before having the opportunity to gather açaí. "We had planned to search for açaí together," Nhak said. "We were going to take you to harvest," she said, noting how much she loved looking for açaí in the forest and how the food sustained her and her family. Or as Paolo commented to me one day when we were talking about family life, "Little kids are so wonderful. When they say father please bring this food for me, it makes you feel good to go out and harvest it for them." So while the literature designates these harvested items as NTFPs, to residents in A'Ukre, they function as more than a forest good.

Despite the criticisms of NTFPs, community-based resource management schemes that incorporate NTFPs have the possibility of coupling local users and market activities in a way that supports, rather than fractures, the local community through their market participation (Anderson and Ioris 1992). At the same time, it is important to keep Dove's (2011) wariness in mind, as concerns about NTFP designation, implementation, and consumption define the larger political ecologies at work, which shape people in landscapes often in unjust and inequitable ways. For A'Ukre, community members also critically reflected on NTFP markets; they see their participation as a possible pathway to generate revenue but were also frustrated with the short-term bursts of cash income that typically accompanied them, their difficulties with moving products from the community to the exterior, their ability to participate in projects, the unequal financial returns projects proffered, and their acknowledgement that NTFP program creation also was a relational process, whereby they had to forge ongoing productive alliances with those entities who became partners along the way. Nevertheless, ideas for new NTFP programs in the community were always many, and oftentimes when I asked about these projects, they talked about it in a way that distinguished A'Ukre's lifeways from other predatory practices that currently dominated the area.

A closer examination of NTFP projects also draws attention to the temporal facets of dynamic socioecological interactions, especially the ideological, cosmological, and ecological entanglements within landscapes. In this vein, historical ecologists have adopted a unique lens to analyze the long-term coproduction of landscapes that are produced from the diverse interactions between human and nonhuman entities over time (Balée 1994; Crumley 1994; Rival 2006).[6] Within historical ecological approaches, landscapes are considered relational, plural, and "multidimensional entities" that exhibit both intentional and unintentional human modifications over space and time. Historical ecologists provide empirical data to counter isolationist and static narratives of people and place by showing that landscapes are in fact "multidimensional" (Balée 2006, 1).[7] While the Amazon continues to be marketed and fueled by international imaginaries as an uninhabited wilderness, a green hell, a fecund Eden, or occupied by "isolated" indigenous peoples, historical ecologists counter that the

Amazon that we see today represents centuries of coevolution between social and environmental factors and, more recently, decades of deforestation, development, and conservation measures (Balée 2006; Slater 2002).

If we further conceptualize Kayapó harvesting practices as activities carried out in anthropogenic environments and "multidimensional" landscapes, gathering fruits and collecting nuts in the forest or savannah become storied activities that tell us about how previous indigenous peoples in the region dwelled in place, as well as how previous and current Kayapó livelihoods intersect with taking care of the land, rivers, and other spaces and beings. Cultural geographer Jay Johnson relays (2012, 829), "Our landscapes are the storied histories, cosmogonies, philosophies, and sciences of those Indigenous knowledges that are increasingly being pushed aside by the 'gray uniformity' of globalization and its progenitor, European colonization." In this way, trees, lianas, vines, and soils stand as rich volumes about the past use of landscapes and reveal many of the ways in which people make their livelihoods in opposition to or despite hegemonic logics that seek to erase or deny them.

For instance, the manipulated soils of ADE, as discussed in chapter 3, are indicative of past, possibly intentional, human labor to make the earth good and offer spaces from which communities like A'Ukre can engage in swidden farming—current life-giving practices for their peoples. Similarly, the dispersion of fruit and nut trees across different parts of Amazonia, including the state of Pará, reveal the complex anthropogenic landscapes that have been cocreated across space and time, offering glimpses of distinct ways of being that are generative for human, plant, and animal communities. Finally, historical ecology's long, temporal (diachronic) lens lends itself to inferences about cultural attitudes and beliefs associated with landscape composition. In A'Ukre, a historical ecological perspective supports oral histories that speak of vast movements across the landscape, previous occupants in the area who have left soils that nurture current lifeways, and former foodway strategies that relied on semi-domesticated or found forest products.[8]

Meanwhile, for villagers in A'Ukre, moving, climbing, standing, laughing, joking within and through the landscape—whether in the forest, savannah, or a transitional zone in between—are acts that evoke the social ecologies of local imaginaries, interspecies and interindividual relations, and cosmological orientations.[9] Feld and Basso (1996, 11) got it right when they described the layered aspects of place: "The terrain covered . . . includes the relation of sensation to emplacement; the experimental and expressive ways places are known, imagined, yearned for, held, remembered, voiced, lived, contested, and struggled over; and the multiple ways places are metonymically and metaphorically tied to identities."

In addition, the Kayapó peoples with whom I worked spoke about NTFPs in ways that evoked the sociability of being in the forest, the complexities of mixed economies, the histories of being in a particular place, and the contrast between Kayapó *kukradjà* and *kuben* lifeways. Seasonal gathering is reflective for the Kayapó of the different relationships that people have with one another and landscapes that contrast with settlers' (ranchers, farmers, loggers, and miners) socioecological goals. Moreover, as with swidden practices, harvesting is marked by expertise gained as individuals move through different age grades and acquire differential knowledge and access to resources, as well as gender-inflected practices. For example, although harvesting *krem* has traditionally been marked as "women's work," it is more common for women, men, and families to take part in harvesting Brazil nuts. Everyday practices of collecting, processing, using, and eating fruits constitute local cosmologies and notions of proper relationships. Harvesting enhances and affirms gendered and age-classed sociospatial interactions, reflecting a dynamic, lived space mediated by Kayapó villagers. Moreover, harvesting is as much an economic activity as it is a place-making practice during which villagers keep each other company and spend time together in the forested landscape.

Mapping the material and nonmaterial meanings associated with harvesting practices reveals that territory, for the Kayapó peoples, is more than a conservation unit, federal land, or an "unproductive" or "biodiverse" vast, marketable landscape. The Kayapó peoples make territory, or more importantly place, with daily and seasonal movements in the landscape, time spent with friends and family in the fields and forest, mediation between human and nonhuman forces, and recollection of the memories of ancestral places and historical events, ceremonial events, and forest goods sold. A venture into oily, grainy, stringy, and richly colored Amazonian fruits, such as *krem*, shows the ways in which NTFPs are simultaneously part of multiple transactional orders at once: subsistence, market, social, and cosmological, which place different emphases on individual actions, collective interests, ownership regimes, and knowledge production (see Dove 2011, 139).

In this way, local harvesting practices challenge Anglo-European notions of territory, where for most of history, ownership of land and land claims have been based on the enclosure and revaluation of the commons, transforming land cover for agricultural production, or putting a price on resources "of the land rather than the land itself" (Cardoso 2002, 51). For example, in the twentieth century, smallholders in Amazonia had to show "occupancy" in order to apply for property titles, which meant that land had to have a structure on it or be used for ranching, agricultural, or similar activities, although land conflict and land scarcity has been a common issue in Brazil since colonization (Pacheco 2009; Simmons et al. 2002).

In teaching us to regard landscapes as integral to local livelihoods, Kayapó peoples offer a different vision of territory and territorialities. This vision of territory is one in which forest products can enter markets but are also part of a complex mosaic of local economies that are substantive for supporting life: harvested forested areas, swidden gardens, and interconnected villages, rivers, and pathways. Current villages are often sited in "congenial" spots in which Brazil nut trees are abundant, soils are fertile, and villagers can connect their homes to longstanding trails and locales in the region. Activities associated with Brazil nuts fortify social relationships and relationships to land-based resources in a way that is not structured by property rights or ownership based on compartmentalization, exclusion, individual "occupancy" as defined by the state, or valorization as expressed by conservation organizations, but rather by places structured by local sensibilities regarding the landscape, proper human–animal–plant relationships, and subsistence activities—in other words, ongoing activities that sustain a good or *mejkumrei* life.[10]

Fruits in a Wet Land

If we consider NTFPs as the nonwood flora and fauna in the environment, then in A'Ukre, these are found in a complex mosaic: beyond the forests, beyond the community, household gardens, field–forest mosaics, and forest–savannah ecotones. I take these areas to be lived spaces, places that villagers travel through on a routine, seasonal, and sometimes unpredictable basis following, among other things, ripening fruits. This pattern produces what Ingold (1993) refers to as taskscapes, which are landscapes populated by activity-based undertakings that define daily life. Here, taskscapes are produced by villagers and as villagers respond to the movements and nonmovement of other species in the landscape. Landscapes are a confluence of several different lived realities—biophysical, historical, ideological, moral, and cosmological; in tracking down fruits and people in A'Ukre, we are offered a lens with which to examine place-making practices and their role in the transition into and out of different life stages and phases of expertise.

There is no singular NTFP landscape in A'Ukre; NTFPs can be found in household gardens, which are composed of fruit trees planted by chiefs and leaders during the founding of A'Ukre and other trees and plants that come from seeds or seedlings from the forest or savannah, exchanges with relatives, purchases in stores, or from governmental or NGO projects in the community. In A'Ukre the ring of mango trees encompasses the most visible fruiting trees in the village, and it embraces the circle of households in the central village plaza space. The long, feathery green leaves dominate, providing a comfortable and well-shaded space for lounging, preparing food, and cooking behind houses. I spent much time with friends processing bitter manioc by slipping the buttery yellow but pungent smelling interior out of its hairy, brown shell, beading different handicrafts, or participating in body painting sessions. Genipapo trees, a mainstay of any woman's repertoire of fruits in her household, are also found here. The seeded interior of the dusty green genipapo fruit is the source of the black body paint that is part of being Kayapó, beautiful, and strong. Several other trees had also been planted in these backyard gardens— either imported from other villages; from seedlings found in the forest; or those bought in Brazilian cities and towns through projects organized by FUNAI, the health organization, or environmental and indigenous NGOs. The result was a mix of mango trees interspersed with coconut palms and açaí, cacao, acerola, and genipapo trees. Owners would care for trees and share their foods, children would harvest fruits, and friends and family would ask permission to harvest. I often found Nhak's daughter and her friends climbing the trunks of the trees to pick the fruits or, if out of reach, harvesting the fruits with a long forked pole. Backyard activities of Nhak's children and their friends, such as climbing trees, looking for chicken eggs in the mango leaf litter, fetching water from the spigots, and playing around, will prepare them for more laborious and weighty subsistence tasks. In this way, these activities emphasize embodied way of know-ing from an early age; life-giving practices that formulate the skilled dimensions of the intimate spaces of everyday life.

In addition to household gardens, fruits figure into other NTFP mosaics in village life. As discussed in the previous chapter, bananas and plantains often demarcate the borders of fields. Papaya trees populate the center of gardens and are interspersed among sweet potatoes. In some fields, watermelon and pine-apple are planted as well. During river travel, nonedible fruits become import-ant indicators of potential fishing spots, as certain fish species, such as pacu, are attracted to fruits that suspend from low-hanging branches at the banks of the river (see Posey 2002c, 56). While hunting, certain fruit trees are known harvest spots for particular animals and key sites at which to harvest meat that can be brought home. Men and women are knowledgeable about fruits and trees that they do not eat but that are favorites of tortoises, birds, and other game that make for a good meal. In this way, the NTFP mosaic links together species cultivated in gardens, cared for in backyards, found along river routes, and identified along hunting trails. While all of these items could potentially be sourced for NTFP markets, most of the attention on market-based possibilities for NTFP projects has been on foraged fruits, nuts, and seeds found in the forest and savannah areas.

It is hard not to notice the welcome ripening of different fruit species during the rainy season in A'Ukre, which takes place from September to May. Along-side fruits like *krem*, forest fruits mean the thick, purple broth of açaí, roasting pequi with manioc flour, and peeling the sweet, white film off of the deep purple inga seeds. Açaí (*Euteurpe oleracea*), pequi (*Caryocar brasiliense*), bacaba (*Oenocarpus bacaba*), cacao (*Theobroma cacao*), inga (*Inga* spp.), and uxi (*Endo-pleura uchi*) comprise the edible fruits that are gathered (see table 3 for a list of gathered fruit and nut species). Most fruits are available only in the wet season

Table 3. Gathered fruits reported by households.

English	Kayapó	Portuguese	Scientific Name
Açaí (Variety 1)	Kamêrê káák	Açai	*Euteurpe oleracea*
Açaí (Variety 2)	Kamêrê káákti	Açai	*Euteurpe oleracea*
Bacaba	Kamêrê	Bacaba	*Oenocarpus distichus*
Brazil nut	Pi ý	Castanha do Para	*Bertholettia excelso*
Cacao	Kubenkrãti	Cacau	*Theobroma cacao*
Inaja Palm	Rikre	Inajá	*Maximilliana* sp.
Inga	Kônhõkô	Ingá	*Inga* spp.
No common name	Krem	Uxi	*Endopleura uchi*
Pequi (Variety 1)	Prin	Piqui	*Caryocar brasiliense*
Pequi (Variety 2)	Prin kákti	Piqui	*Caryocar brasiliense*
Wild banana fruit	Tyryti djô	Banana Bravo	*Musa* sp.

with some exceptions, such as certain *Inga* spp. trees in the village that ripen in the dry season. Two varieties of pequi are the only fruits reported as available in both the forest and savannah. The majority of fruits and nuts gathered by villagers in A'Ukre are harvested in a similar manner—by groups of women, families, or, in the case of Brazil nuts, in small groups, in pairs, or individually. Because the species vary in terms of their height, location, and fruiting season, different skill sets are required to harvest.

For instance, take the harvest of inga fruits. Inga is the generic name of a tree with more than 180 species represented in the neotropics. It is a leguminous, nitrogen-fixing tree with pinnate and oblong leaves (Calvacante 1996). Harvesting inga was hard work. Reaching a tree one morning not far from the village, Panh, who helped to lead the harvest with several other women, explained that we cut the tree at the base so that we could reach the high hanging fruits. Looking up, I saw the long, green, stringy seed pods that were ridged with shallow furrows; they visibly hung down. The branches were well above our reach. With a taste akin to a forest-grown version of cotton candy from the thin film of fluffy white sweet fruit that covers deep eggplant-colored seeds, inga is well worth the work. Crouching on the edge of the tree once it had been felled, I grabbed the easy-to-reach, long thin pods and shoved handfuls into my basket. "This is how you harvest," Nhak, who was also with us, told me, and she showed me what she meant as we filled up our baskets with the fruit.

Villagers also loved pequi when the rains came. Combined with manioc flour and bundled in banana leaves, roasted pequi was delicious. The buttery yellow pequi fruit is located in the forest or savannah, although many interviewees preferred the savannah variety. Pequi evoked memories of different landscapes and travels, and its hardened nut sometimes used as adornments to ceremonial belts, anklets, and handicrafts (See González-Perez, de Robert, and Coelho-Ferreira 2013). Many elders were fond of pequi and the memories it evoked of shared labor, providing for families, and trekking with friends and loved ones. At the beginning of the gathering season, I sat down with an elder woman who talked with me for a bit about pequi, of which she told me, "I know that pequi is ripe right now in the savannah, and I am sad that I am too weak to go there. I wish the women would walk there this year and harvest the fruit so I can taste it. It is the season for pequi right now, and I miss it." Pequi, like other fruits, was a taste that reminded her not just of home but also of shared moments trekking through the lands that sustained her and her people. Trekking to the savannah could be an arduous task. It was a daylong undertaking that took you to the end of the landing strip and through the forest–field mosaic to forested paths that forked to different destinations—for instance, a trail to an old village or to a waterfall. The savannah trek also requires climbing up a steep hill, which signals the transition from forest to savannah ecotones. At the top of the hill, numerous paths crisscross the savannah landscape, connecting villagers to old village sites, routes to other villages, and rivers full of fish (see Zanotti 2014b). Residents told me that they burn the savannah seasonally in order to clear the land and see it better. Men will often make treks there to gather fibers, medicines, and fish. Families catch parakeet clutches to raise back home; their feathers play an important role in naming ceremonies. In the village, one household had planted a pequi tree near the family's yard. Its fallen flowers with white whiskers were favorite playthings of young children. In this way, gathering pequi animates the landscape as part of the same seasonal fabric that encompasses other fruits gathered in forested areas, structuring relationships between fruits, forests, and savannah landscapes. It is a cocreation of place that is relational and substantive, that endures through repeated, careful activities across space and time.

Similar to pequi, açaí patterns life in the wet season. The two varieties of açaí found around A'Ukre have a green-purplish blueberry-like fruit (drupe) and have long, slender boles topped with pinnate leaves. When açaí was ripe, I would set off to the forest with Nhak and other women, sometimes joined by their dogs. Once several meters down the path, we would pair off as we spotted trees with ripe fruit. The fruit sits nestled at the top of the palm, hanging in what looks like fruit-studded chandeliers. The branchless boles make the trees easy targets for a particular kind of climbing that is probably familiar to most who spend time in the Amazon area. The women that I joined all harvested these fruits in a similar manner. Nhak, always my teacher, reached the top of the palm by affixing a fibrous strap around her feet and rapidly climbing up. On arriving at the hanging clusters on top, Nhak would quickly and force-fully tap the joint at which the fruit is affixed to the tree with her machete.

She would then throw down her machete, grab the cluster, and slide down. Throughout the collection phase, Nhak and the other women with us would stay in touch with one another as they climbed up and down trees by calling out one another's names, a simple phrase, or a joke, or would sometimes merely make signature whooping calls to inform the others of their location. The search for another tree to harvest commenced shortly after finishing in one area, and they tried to harvest before the sun got too high in the sky, as the tops of the trunks would get hot to climb. The trip could thus take as long as four to six hours in the forest, including travel time, to gather enough. In the middle of the harvesting, there was often a quick break to enjoy roasted manioc or bananas, after which we returned to the task. Climbing trees was tough afternoon work in which the women physically moved both horizontally and vertically within the forested landscape in their interactions with fruits, trees, and everything else in the area. They tried to harvest in the morning—so the boles of the trees were not too hot—and avoid harvesting after too much rain, which made the trees slick to climb. The work, though, was worth the wait. Not long after anyone arrived in the village with açaí, it was processed so that everyone could enjoy the thick, mealy juice.

The Kayapó men and women with whom I worked spoke about açaí in a variety of ways. Interviewees noted that when they built A'Ukre, açaí already existed in patches in the forest, which often—but not always—flooded in the wet season. Some women reported that when residents made A'Ukre their home, they planted açaí seedlings in forested areas around their swidden plots. A few had even attempted to grow açaí seedlings in their backyards. While other fruit trees were also planted in fields or yards, no one who was interviewed suggested that they created clusters of fruit trees in the interior forested areas; instead, they relied on açaí that they found on their major fruit collecting expeditions. Thus, the landscape around A'Ukre at that time was populated by a small number of planted açaí saplings in the yard and forest area and clusters found in the forest. Açaí harvesting took place in the forest where clusters were located, which meant that the women and sometimes the men who harvested had to be knowledgeable about cluster location and harvesting norms.

Some of the açaí patches around could be potentially indicative of past human inhabitants in the area, given the evidence that former groups had lived around A'Ukre (Brondízio 2009). However, the dominance of açaí in certain locales around A'Ukre may also reflect the palm's tendency to grow abundantly in flooded areas. Nevertheless, the skinny boles of the trees, collecting practices, and rich purple juice have marked it as a powerful imaginary in the Amazonian landscape, as well as a signature tree that reflects past and present human modifications to the landscape.

Fruit trees, like inga, pequi, and açaí formulate a key part of contemporary livelihood strategies of villagers, as the fruits offer tastes and practices that navigate market and subsistence economies, symbolic and social meanings ascribed to forest goods, and NTFP market possibilities. Over the past several decades, meanings affixed to NTFPs have changed A'Ukre's local economy and global transactional orders, which has influenced the cultural, economic, ecological, institutional, and infrastructural contexts that shape the life of the producer, harvester, and product (Brondízio 2008, 12–14). Fruits, nuts, seeds, and other foraged products around A'Ukre are illustrative of the mosaic of generative practices carried out in congenial landscapes coproduced over time. Forest fruits are planted in backyard gardens; bananas, papayas, and other fruits are harvested in agricultural fields; pequi is a much-desired forest/savannah fruit; and açaí has a long history as a seasonal food. As a collection, the fruit trees featured here underscore the social and material life of harvesting practices, which, in turn, "reflects demands of mixed market economies, offers a way to continue to make place in a charged region where land and territory are often in question, and serves as a stimulus to knowledge creation and transmission" (Zanotti 2014b, 112).[11] Villagers pass down oral histories regarding the collection and identification of resources, which, in turn, influences stories about the landscape, village formation, and harvesting. The collection of each resource requires specific skillsets that are fostered at a young age through experiential learning, knowing the land (*iñho pyka mari mêtch*), embodied knowledge, and youth–elder interactions. At the same time, harvesting is as much a social and symbolic practice as it is a physical one, as the relations fortified in forested spaces and then back at home structure life in the community. This structuring has always been part of a symbolic economy of transformation where resources are made meaningful and "good to eat" through harvesting, processing, and distributional practices (see Gordon 2006).

Such insights into the place-making practices that compose the mosaic of NTFP landscapes in A'Ukre demonstrates that NTFPs and, in this regard fruits that are grown, cultivated, and cared for, are part of the daily fabric of the intimate, life-generating and life-giving practices within the community. These practices are ultimately linked with ways in which communities transform both landscapes and plants into congenial and substantive spaces. Yet, as this short description shows, while these fruits and their associated practices figure largely in daily life through processes, such as cultivation, domestication, and harvesting, they have not been the main focus of sustainable development programs in A'Ukre but a space in which to affirm alternative futures divorced from intensive extractivism. In the next section, I turn to Brazil nuts, a longtime player in the Amazonian economy and one of the most important gathered foods that villagers in A'Ukre harvest.[12] Called *castanha do para* (Portuguese) or *pi ý* (Kayapó), at least twenty-five Brazil nut groves are located near or around the village (Ribeiro et al. 2014). Brazil nuts, which have been part of informal and formal economies, serve as an interesting entry point to explore the vagaries of market-based mechanisms within communities, as well as the contingencies of neoliberal conservation and a neodevelopmental and neo-extractivist state.

Brazil Nuts

Brazil nuts figure prominently in "rhizomatic transnational" flows that have pulsed through A'Ukre's history (Choy et al. 2009). Villagers in A'Ukre remember exchanging NTFPs with FUNAI beginning in the 1960s (when they were living elsewhere), but such exchanges probably took place much earlier. In those years, Kayapó communities traded Brazil nuts, animal pelts, and other products for such desired Western goods as beads, machetes, and sandals (Fisher 1991). Kayapó consultants also mentioned founding villages in areas that already had Brazil nut groves and other forest fruits (see also Ribeiro et al. 2014). Interviewees recalled that certain Brazil nut groves accessed from the river are the same groves that the group visited to collect for FUNAI when they were still located at Kubenkranken. Some even said that this is why they knew the area around A'Ukre and why this spot may have been selected for A'Ukre. In a conversation with a leader in the village, he described the founding of one village to me (italics added).

> I was living in a village, and my mother and father moved to [another village], and I was studying there with missionaries. I was in a FUNAI plane in the past and saw . . . [a place] . . . and thought it was pretty and thought to remember the place. *Then one year, I was looking for Brazil nuts, and I saw it nearby, and I thought that I liked the place a lot.* At the time I was living in [another village], and it didn't have many white people. It only had one white man from SPI. . . . I . . . then moved to the Xingu Park and then moved back to the [first village]. A FUNAI representative asked me to help the chief of the village to help us because a lot of people were dying at the post. Then a fire was set, and we called for all [of our friends] and had a reunion. Who is going to help us? I was selected to talk to the three chiefs because they didn't know the way of the white man, and I was the only one with contact. I moved there and lived in [yet another village]. [This village] was sort of close to the [spot], and I saw it again and founded the village then. [This village] is a quiet, tranquil village.

Similarly, Posey (1985) observed that the Kayapó (Gorotíre village) planted Brazil nut trees in swidden fields to increase the availability of key resources. A'Ukre was founded in 1979, and even though some villagers planted Brazil nut trees in their backyards, the field area does not contain many nut-bearing Brazil nut trees. Instead, villagers relied on the Brazil nut trees found in the forested area, and they had many spots to choose from when considering a Brazil nut harvest for either subsistence or commercial purposes. These trees are part of the forested landscape beyond the fields, and may possibly be the result of plantings by previous inhabitants of the area (Balée 1989, 1992). Their previous use in trade networks in the early twentieth century and harvesting practices that date even earlier point to a longstanding relationship with the Brazil nut trees.

Brazil nut collection takes place in the forest at the site of the groves. Brazil nuts grow in *ouriços* or "hard mesocarps," which fall down to the ground during the rainy season. Interviewees say it is dangerous to be around Brazil nut trees at this time. The *ouriços* are thick, and agoutis and possibly other animals, which operate as the primary dispersers of Brazil nut seeds, break open the mature Brazil nut casings with their teeth (Jorge and Peres 2005). The grapefruit-sized casing is heavy and cumbersome and does not pack well or efficiently in Kayapó baskets, the major means for transporting the harvest back to the community. For this reason, villagers prefer to break the casing open near the tree. This practice allows harvesters to assess the quality of the nuts before throwing them in their baskets, as well as reduce the amount of weight in their baskets.

As it takes time to gather all the ouriços together and to break them open, harvesting becomes a social activity. When I joined some of my friends to harvest, we often gossiped about village affairs as we broke open the ouriço with a sharp machete. Sitting on the forest floor on top of plastic store-bought sacks or flip-flops, we harvested the nuts for hours. Broken ouriços piled up around us as baskets slowly filled to be taken back to the village, where the seeds were stored for household consumption or for sustainable development projects. Sometimes, my friends would carry whole ouriços back with them in order to decorate them and sell them as handicrafts. Generously applying urucum to the casing, women added beads and other decorations to the top. In this way, from handicraft to trade item to food source, Brazil nuts are a mainstay of the social, economic, and dietary life of villagers. Like the fruits featured above, collecting Brazil nuts reflects an intimate knowledge of the landscape connected to collection and practice (figure 12).

Brazil nut collection is a village-wide activity that happens frequently. Collection has intensified postcontact primarily because the consistent demand for Brazil nuts has made it a viable, marketable item in regional and international contexts. Today, regional FUNAI offices no longer only trade for Brazil nuts and sometimes pledge to allocate some of their budget to the harvest and transportation costs of the nuts. The growth of urban towns in the Amazon region and migration to the area has increased the demand for regional food products in the Amazon, such as Brazil nuts, offering different possibilities for villages to create markets (Brondízio, Safar, and Siqueira 2002; Browder and Godfrey 1997). However, moving the product from the site of collection to the buyer is often the most difficult portion of the transaction. For example, a consultant reflected, "We need to find a way to sell Brazil nuts. . . . Now we can't sell them when we want because we don't have a way to transport them." The sale of these

Figure 12. Close up of shelled Brazil nut from a nearby grove.

products without a formal project infrastructure remains sporadic, as money for transport is difficult to find. Still, villagers in A'Ukre have found buyers in local or regional urban areas who are willing to purchase sacks that weigh 60 kg at competitive prices. Thus, at least for A'Ukre, individual and village-organized sales of Brazil nuts in nearby markets have been a seasonal option when sustainable development programs have not been in place.

Villagers, however, perceive this informal type of Brazil nut sale as inferior to sustainable development projects, which, they argue, offer the most viable long-term source of income. For example, my first meeting with one of the young leaders, Diego, revolved around this topic. Diego said that he had been thinking of a cacao project for the community, as he thought that such a project would benefit the village. He wanted to find a way to help the community earn cash, something that would be good for them, and sought to establish a sustainable development project, as other villages had been successful with such projects. Also, Marcio frequently mentioned that the village used to have a Body Shop project that helped the village, but "the [Brazil nut] oil stopped, and now we have nothing." These comments point to the variable role that NTFP markets have played in A'Ukre. While Diego hoped to start a project in the village now that others were defunct, Marcio highlighted the income lost now that the Body Shop project was no longer functioning. Despite several uneven experiences with markets and community members' willingness to participate in what would be identified as sustainable and unsustainable economies of extraction, villagers insist that NTFPs provide viable options for long-term sustainable development in the village. As previously mentioned, nearly all of these projects have been based on Brazil nut markets.

The most iconic project with A'Ukre has probably been the Body Shop program in the village. In the 1990s, the Body Shop, the international cosmetic chain, began a project with Kayapó villages to produce Brazil nut oil for body-care products. The Body Shop project is an evocative example of how Brazil nuts, açaí, and other NTFPs became a dominant norm in sustainable development projects across the globe from small-scale marketplaces to community–corporate alliances. The Body Shop project was particularly interesting, not only because of a controversy surrounding the use of a Kayapó's image in an advertising campaign, but also because of the village outcomes. The Body Shop project provided several unique opportunities for market involvement. During the project, adults who had relatively little or no income could earn up to US$227 per year, with households averaging US$1441 per year (Morsello 2006). While men in the community were eligible for positions with FUNAI, the clinic, or the local NGO, the Body Shop project provided women an opportunity beyond handicraft production to systematically and steadily participate in markets. The Body Shop, alongside CI, was one of the few international partnerships that the village had that would offer possibilities for international niche market development of "ecofriendly" products like Brazil nut oil. Although the Body Shop project ended, it was an interesting experience for villagers, one which they often referenced when considering new sustainable development options in the area.

In addition, CI's former presence in the area, which resulted in the decade-long CI–Kayapó program, created several cash-income opportunities centered on sustainable development initiatives, one of which has been based on Brazil nuts. Beginning as early as 2007, the AFP, a local Kayapó NGO, began to investigate the possibilities of Brazil nut sales within the community. This action resulted in research that showed sales of Brazil nuts into already established regional economies was the best option for Kayapó villages like A'Ukre, in which transportation and communication are real barriers to market development (Camargo and Mekaru 2006). Since 2007, A'Ukre and other villages are now selling dried, unmodified Brazil nuts in this marketplace. The AFP formed several other projects—first in conjunction with CI and subsequently in alliance with the newly formed partnership with the Wild Foundation and International Conservation Fund of Canada (ICFC) once the CI partnership ended. These include programs that support: Kayapó foodways by selling local foods to the village school for afternoon snacks or hosting seed fairs (as noted in the previous chapter), a newly formed project to sell cumaru seeds, and ongoing research into projects that may, for example, work within REDD (Reducing Emissions from Deforestation and Forest Degradation) marketplaces or within the framework of payment for ecosystem services.

The AFP has also built upon longstanding projects and programs with A'Ukre that CI began as part of a sustainable development and capacity-building portfolio. The longest-standing part of CI's collaboration with A'Ukre took place together with Pinkaití, which will be discussed further in the next chapter. Although currently semiactive, ongoing maintenance of the research station provides semiannual jobs to community members, who clean the area, fix trails, and identify the status of different structures. Furthermore, since 2004, CI, the University of Maryland, and the Kayapó have codesigned and run a short study-abroad course at Pinkaití and the village of A'Ukre. The course provides the community with several different types of income: a community entrance fee, salaries for Kayapó guides/experts for the duration of the course, and the sale of handicrafts to the students at the end of visit (see Zanotti and Chernela 2008). This partnership is now administered by a series of international and local NGOs; one of the premises of these programs is that Kayapó villages can achieve "economic autonomy" through the "sustainable management of nontimber forest resources" (available at: http://www.wild.org/where-we-work/kayapo/). Critiques of community–conservation partnerships note that the sustainable development initiatives created between Kayapó villages and NGOs are built on the same assumption that commodity production is the answer to changing socioecological and economic dynamics in the area (see also West 2006, 43). That is, the programs described here ascribe to the rationale outlined above, namely, that the development of sustainable markets is a solution to conservation and livelihood issues. Yet as I will describe below, and I have already emphasized, villagers consistently told me that they "liked" the projects, that they brought the communities strength, and were critical for present and future cash-income opportunities; their NGO alliances were not based solely on sustainable development markets but rather on a range of activities that supported local livelihoods.

A'Ukre villagers find the potential for a Brazil nut project coordinated with local NGOs desirable for several reasons. While NTFP markets make up only one part of this commodity-based landscape of conservation, these markets, according to consultants, serve as one of many interesting new entry points of exchange with outsiders. Examining NTFPs from multiple perspectives and spending time in the forest with women collecting fruits and nuts made it easy to understand why different villagers found Brazil nuts and other, similarly designed projects so desirable. As previously mentioned, the sale of Brazil nuts fits into the village's existing social institutions and the subsistence patterns. Elisa or Nhak could spend time with friends, family members, or children while gathering the nuts. Furthermore, as a foraging task with a high level of participation among men and women of all ages, collecting Brazil nuts is an activity in which anyone who wishes can engage. A market-based activity that provides everyone with the opportunity to participate avoids inducing stress and anxieties among villagers about cash-income sources and uneven access to markets. We have seen in the case of mining and timber that cash in the

hands of a few young male leaders had negative consequences for several villages (Turner 1995a; Zimmerman 2010). On a smaller scale, the few salaried
positions (which were mostly held by men) present in A'Ukre during the time
in which I was there created tensions among different individuals who were
not employed in these positions and who had relatively few options for earning
cash. Economic activities that tend to concentrate cash in the hands of a few
individuals or households lend themselves easily to misused funds or a failure to
redistribute goods within the many different social networks and social ties that
these households have (Zanotti and Chernela 2008). Consequently, activities
like NTFP projects that center on such activities as Brazil nut collection enable
villagers to continue with their subsistence activities, provide the maximum
level of participation within the community, and draw upon local land use and
subsistence practices. These characteristics contribute to making this project
one that Elisa, Marcio, Diego, and others regarded as a good project to pursue.

Another positive aspect of NTFPs, like the Brazil nut projects in the village, is that their harvest does not highly alter the forested environment and
does not require intensive training on the part of villagers. Interviewees prefer
NTFPs projects not to amend local resource management strategies, to require
minimal-to-no training or to provide training on-site, and to allow villagers
to carry out their subsistence and ceremonial activities with relative ease. As a
collection, these practices pointed to a general goal that villagers talked about
in terms of retaining *tycht* (strong) communities that are fortified by knowledge
systems and practices built not exclusively but predominately from experiential
learning in the landscapes they call home. As an example, Marcio repeatedly told
me that he wanted to keep mahogany in the forest here so that he could pass
along his knowledge to his children. He queried: "If there is no mahogany in
the forest, how are they [his children] going to know what it is?" While directly
referencing the mahogany extraction that took place in the village in the 1990s,
comments like this made by Marcio and other villagers demonstrated, through
discussions on "knowing" the forest, the value of access to intact resources for
their children. The NTFPs projects are regarded as one way of retaining intact
resources, as they do not require villagers to engage in extractive activities that
might have adverse impacts on their home life.

Moreover, women and men that I spoke with in A'Ukre not only talked
about the importance of going to the forest and savannah, but also the dangers that it carried with it. Younger women with families discussed how they
preferred to go in groups or with their families, as there were possible run-ins
with evil spirits, other supernatural elements, or chance encounters with charismatic wildlife or invaders to their land. All of these might cause them harm or
deter them from their *pry*. Elder women, who had grown up during the more
intense period of movement and contact sometimes went alone to gardens or
in pairs to the forest. They talked about moving through the forest with ease

and little fear, aided by decades of embodied practice and strengthened by the smoke their *waricoco* (pipe) produced, which helped deter spirit encounters. Elder men also were confident in their ability to navigate different terrains, both the physical and the supernatural, out on forest walks. Yet, women and men both impressed that knowing and navigating encounters in the forest was necessary for adult women and men. Forest outings allowed them to gather the resources needed for their families and community, as well as participate in the transformative practices that make place and people over time (e.g., harvesting resources for ceremonial, market-based, or daily activities). Going to the forest was never a predetermined journey, as the women and men I spoke with might have a destination in mind, but their path was coconstructed by the plants, animals, and other beings they saw along the way. In this way, there was always the possibility of different encounters; encounters that are guided by moral, ethical, and prescriptive codes. For example, those with beautiful names might practice hunting taboos (such as when or how to harvest a macaw), or those individuals coming from particular lineages or with certain shamanic abilities could deter or avoid precarious meetings with snakes or other spirits.

In this way, pro-and-con arguments for NTFPs are not just about incorporating locally relevant valuations of nature into broader economic regimes, but rather different ways of conceptualizing "naturecultures" that are divorced from Western dualism and affirm orientations that shape and guide human environmental relationships across moral, ethical, and spiritual dimensions (Haraway 2003). This includes those activities and skill sets required through the life course that makes it possible for individuals to contribute to the production and reproduction of life. However, the stance of community members in A'Ukre to NTFPs has been both what Muraca (2012) defines as a "creative imaginary" for possible futures based on indigenous cosmovisions and a pragmatic to the constraints that community members battle against. For example, these include access to and use of regular public services, such as education, health, and sanitation, in their village. Chiefs repeatedly talked about working with external agents, both within and exterior to their village, to make the services necessary to their community available in culturally appropriate and desired ways. This also means that there are differing opinions within the village, which cut across age, gender, and other distinctions, about the exposure to and incorporation of non-Kayapó practices and beliefs in their community, such as NTFP markets. But this also includes contested ideas over the incorporation of non-Western songs and dance and community life as well as new youth styles derived from fashion popular in local towns. So while A'Ukre's approach is at once aligned with models of degrowth that counter neoliberal projects as an indicator of progress and the good life, community members were also interested in and navigating possible opportunities for cash-income and market opportunities that can provide for the community.

To untangle the different dimensions of the NTFP marketplace and their reception in the community further, it is also critical to emplace these programs within other cash-income opportunities in the village. A typical household or family relies on a blend of governmental aid, salaried work, seasonal work, and opportunistic sales to generate cash. Six year-long, much-desired salaried jobs in the village existed in 2007, including one position of employment as a FUNAI agent, three school teacher positions, two other positions affiliated with the school, and three health aids employed by a local health NGO. However, this number has expanded over time to include two cooks at the school, and additional opportunities to work for or at local NGOs; there are currently other prospects with growing sustainable development programs in the village as well. Another source of steady income for approximately 30 percent of the households in the village (as of 2007) comes from government pensions provided to elders. All elders are eligible for these pensions, but the process that must be undergone in order to receive a pension requires villagers to overcome numerous bureaucratic hurdles that several families do not have the resources to carry out. Finally, some women are enrolled in federal child welfare programs that are conditional cash transfer programs that provide financial assistance to mothers with children under the age of three who fall within certain income brackets.

Seasonal work is an additional option. Eight men with whom I spoke in the community reported leaving to engage in seasonal work in other Kayapó villages during ceremonial lulls or in the wet months when travel is easier. Some of the men in the village often temporarily relocate to Xikrin villages, which have financial resources from mining concessions from Vale, the mining company.[13] Xikrin chiefs offer employment to other villagers to clear agricultural fields or patrol the borders of their reserve. A typical stay does not exceed one or two months, and the men then return to A'Ukre. As seasonal work is not stable or secure, men often seek out a variety of wage work activities in order to satisfy their household's economic needs. Villagers also engage in the sale of handicrafts, some of which are made from timber and nontimber forest resources, while others are made from glass beads. These handicrafts are currently part of co-op sales in major cities, sales to particular galleries or shops, or informal sales directly to individuals.

It is worth noting that even though projects based on Brazil nut collection are attractive to the community, Morsello (2006) observed that when the Body Shop program was in place, villagers sacrificed certain ceremonial and subsistence tasks in favor of participating in the Brazil nut oil project. A potential consequence of NTFPs is that community members will have to make difficult decisions between customary resource-use activities and market-based activities. In addition, a long-term project based on a single NTFP could stress that resource and create incentives for overharvesting (Arnold and Pérez 2001; Guariguata et al. 2010; Wollenberg 1998). Villagers face many challenges, however, to implementing and maintaining these types of initiatives. As with any experimentation with the market, projects can also have unintentional consequences, positive or negative, when different transactional economies are placed alongside one another.

Conclusion

Doreen Massey (1994, 121) opines that places "are not so much bounded areas as open and porous networks of social relations." The NTFP projects and their practices are social and physical activities that structure relationships and practices in the landscape. Daily and seasonal life are driven by these harvesting practices, as well as multidimensional strategies for maintaining sovereignty over livelihood practices that align with Kayapó cosmologies and ways of being. Time spent in the forested and savannah landscapes gathering fruit makes place, fortifies social ties, and amplifies relationships between humans and nonhuman beings. "Knowing" is closely associated with listening, hearing, and other sensorial modalities, as well as observing and practicing, in this case, different subsistence activities. *Kukradjà* or "knowledge," is embodied over time and through constant practice that is at once substantive and generative. Careful acts, though, are not only restricted to subsistence activities but also extend to NTFP marketplaces. Working with Kayapó peoples about their management of, and use of, fruit and nut trees helps discern anthropogenic Amazonian landscapes, potential modifications by previous inhabitants, and the ongoing coproduction of places over time. It also gives us a sense of the continued impact of the historical composition of landscapes on contemporary livelihoods and the way in which the Kayapó interact with and actively shape socioecological relationships.

Growing NTFP markets have rendered fruit and nut trees as part of new transactional economies and exchange patterns within the community. For indigenous producers like the Kayapó, these market opportunities offer new venues for cash-income and potential sustainable alternatives to the highly extractive economies that dominate the region. Interviewees have stressed their preference for these types of markets, as they enable villagers to carry out lifeways and activities that sustain them while earning cash-income. In A'Ukre, markets for Brazil nut products have dominated the different opportunities available to the villagers. Sustainable development projects in the form of community–company and community–conservation relationships alongside village-organized and FUNAI-administered trade and sales have marked the economic life of the community over the past several decades. Despite the positive feedback about NTFP product markets, it is important to remember that these product markets are part of a broader economic shift and of an emphasis on conservation and development enterprises across the world that put a price tag on socioecological relationships. Local producers experience the challenges and opportunities of markets and the commoditization of different products in unequal and power-laden contexts. As the Kayapó continue to struggle to retain their lands, their relationships to local resources and landscapes persist while they creatively apply these same practices to changing market-based contexts.

Despite many challenges to implementing and maintaining NTFP projects, community members cite several reasons for their preference for NTFP projects, and they spoke about a series of factors that constitute a valuable market endeavor for them to pursue. These include projects that generate a long-term source of income, enable villagers to continue with their subsistence livelihoods, provide the maximum level of participation within the community, capitalize on local land use and subsistence practices, coordinate with social institutions and cosmologies already in place, promote intervillage collaboration and cooperation, build upon or further solidify community–outsider partnerships, minimally alter the village landscape, train community members in ways that align with local governance structures, and do not involve environmental impacts that interfere with subsistence and ceremonial needs. These factors, when examined as a collection, indicate that community members are invested in cash-income opportunities that maintain the production and reproduction of ceremonial, subsistence, and political life (see Gordon 2006).

Muraca (2012) shows that proponents of neoliberal and global economic orders assign value to economic growth as linked to distributive justice, which fails to address recognitional justice and alternative economic models that are supportive of a good life rooted in indigenous perspectives. Communities like A'Ukre did not see NTFPs as peripheral to their daily activities but rather centrally located in a suite of actions that strengthened their projects for making indigenous territorialities. The NTFP projects were discussed as critical to both short-term gains, such as for filling cash-income needs of communities, members, and longer-term, intergenerational goals of growing communities in a way that fortified partnerships already in place, as well as current territorial goals. Regardless of the shortcomings of NTFPs, villagers repeatedly noted that these products offer them various opportunities to engage with markets, collaborative partnerships, and other villages in meaningful ways. It will be interesting to see future developments in the area, which will be especially important surrounding carbon markets and ecosystem services, given new considerations emerging related to climate change and the potential changing composition of the ecologies of the region based on the development of the Belo Monte Dam complex. As placer-based gold mining has resurged in the region, as well as other extractive economies, communities will have to make difficult decisions, once again, regarding engagement—or not—with these trespassers on their lands. Future developments will necessarily involve conversations over individual versus collective rights as markets are developed and intellectual property concerns are addressed (see Soares da Silveira 2012).

5

Communities and Conservation Redux

> There are no rules of place and space.
> —Massey, *For Space*

Introduction

It was during the rainy season in January of 2007 when I visited Pinkaití with three Kayapó guides: Bento, Marcio, and Pátricio.[1] Pinkaití was the result of a community–conservation partnership between the villagers of A'Ukre and CI. Launched in 1992, Pinkaití started what is now a more than two-decade-long relationship between villagers, conservation NGOs, and eventually indigenous NGOs as well. Since then, the partnership has changed and mushroomed to include more than twenty villages in the Kayapó Indigenous Lands and a five-part program that integrates research, local capacity building, territorial enforcement, and a suite of sustainable development programs. I had fond memories of Pinkaití from a short stay there several years before when I worked as part of a group of conservation biologists, students, and anthropologists participating in a field-based study abroad course. On this hot afternoon, years later, I was interested in examining what Pinkaití looked like in the off-season. I was also curious to understand how residents of A'Ukre, the Kayapó village I was working with, related to Pinkaití when no research activity was taking place at the site as a way to examine notions of territory, land, and place. In the weeks leading up to the trip, I had watched many men in the village return from daylong fishing expeditions with baskets brimming with citrus fruits, which they had reportedly collected at Pinkaití. Never having imagined Pinkaití as a seasonal collection spot for these fruits, the time seemed right to visit. I had recently purchased gasoline, the swollen river meant that travel would be straightforward, and a lull in ceremonies at the village meant I could ask several men to serve as guides for the trip.

Pinkaití is a little more than 10 km upriver from its host community, A'Ukre. In 2007, the station had remained more or less inactive for years after having been heavily used by a variety of researchers in the 1990s. The base camp consists of an open, weedy, plaza-like area, a handful of buildings, a network of research trails, and an agreed-upon reserve area that covers 8,000 ha of protected forest adjacent to the station. The project's defining landmark is a large blue concrete building, what the residents of A'Ukre refer to as a "big house." This house was built during the logging years (also in the 1990s) out of city-bought construction materials. The sparsely furnished house stores books, equipment, and other project items. In another corner, an open-air, palm-thatched roof structure serves as a kitchen that has a homemade oven and several tables and benches. Four or five residential structures, or open-air huts covered with plastic tarps, are set slightly back in the forest and ring the kitchen-project area. When the area is in use hammocks or tents are placed underneath the tarps as a dry place to sleep. Over the years, project participants (researchers, NGO staff, and Kayapó field guides) have planted various fruit trees in the main plaza area, as well as some herbal teas common to Brazil. An entrance to the forest leads to an outhouse and the network of project trails just beyond (figures 13–14).

All of my guides had been to Pinkaití before. Bento, for example, assisted in creating the project trails during the formation of the Pinkaití area and was later sporadically employed by project members to help with various initiatives in the area. As an elder and senior to the other two men joining me that day, Bento remarked that his declining physical health prevented him from being as active as he had been in previous decades. In addition, since researchers had not stayed there for some time, his consistent involvement with the project had ended years earlier. Bento would be my guide at Pinkaití, explained Marcio, a respected younger leader in the community with a family and grown kids of his own.

Marcio had initially played a prominent role in the early years of the project and helped coordinate Pinkaití researchers and field assistants. Over decades, his collaboration with Pinkaití researchers had decreased as the project waned. He also had been involved in other initiatives in A'Ukre in the 1990s, mainly a Brazil nut project (now no longer active), which, among other things, took him away from working with Pinkaití. When I conversed with Marcio in the village, he had positive things to say about the overall goals of the ecological research station. "Researchers here helped A'Ukre a lot. We are the only village in Pará that has a project like this"; he mentioned this several days before we went on our trip. Marcio retains close relationships with the researchers who had started Pinkaití, and he continues to choose to work on project-related initiatives.

Pátricio differed from the other two men joining me that day. A member of a younger age grade, at the time of the trip he had never been employed by the project but had visited Pinkaití several times on fishing expeditions. Before traveling that day, Pátricio noted his consternation about his work history at Pinkaití. "I have never worked for the project. I would like to work for the project, but I am never asked." Not knowing Pátricio that well, I was not sure of the reason why other villagers and chiefs in A'Ukre would not have selected him as a field assistant. The selection process for who worked at Pinkaití was aligned with the customary way political and economic decisions were made

Figure 13. Pinkaití Project House at Pinkaití Research Station.

Figure 14. Group walking down forest trails, not far from Pinkaití.

in A'Ukre. Village leaders and politically active adults identified those residents who would be ideal to work with researchers, and decisions were made during meetings in the men's house.

Given my estimate of Pátricio's age, however, it was more than likely that he was a young teenager when Pinkaití started and potentially too inexperienced to join the researchers or other project members in the forest. Many of the project participants selected during community meetings, at least in the initial years, were at least in an age grade where they had children, and more often than not, they were already grandfathers. As part of the elder male age grades, the men selected would have proved their competence as hunters and horticulturalists, and with their political involvement in the village. Pátricio would potentially have been only in the *menóronùre* age grade when the project started (an adult but childless man), which might have been a reason he was not sought after by the chiefs. In any case, he was eager to take me to the project area that day and, even if he was not directly involved in project affairs, felt it a worthwhile trip.

Part of the reason Pátricio and Marcio mentioned they were joining the trip that day was to help with navigating the motorized canoe and to take advantage of the abundant fishing site near the station. They also advised that they should accompany Bento and me, if we needed any help, since I was inexperienced from their perspective in walking the forest alone, and Bento's eyesight was declining. When we arrived at the station, Pátricio said that he and Marcio would collect fruits from one of the trees and see me back at the canoe. Bento, who had helped build the project trails, would lead me around so that "I could see something." Bento lit his tobacco pipe and gestured for me to take one of the overgrown pathways. We did not make it through the entire trail system established by non-Kayapó researchers and Kayapó field assistants, as many were not easily passable, but we were able to walk some of the main trails. I had already traversed the paths as a participant in a course years before, and was not really concerned with "knowing" the entire network. I was, however, interested in Bento's discussion about his relationship to the project.

Bento talked proudly about his role in creating the trail system as we slowly made our way through the forested area. "This is my work. I made a lot of these trails," he remarked as we walked several overgrown paths. "This trail goes to the savannah. This one goes to monkey's head mountain." He pointed out several other trails, each time, noting where they went and what they were used for—whether they were transect trails or if they connected to a Brazil nut grove or other village paths. When asked how the spot was picked for Pinkaití, Bento relayed that villagers already knew this place. In the past the site of Pinkaití had been a rubber tapper encampment, now long gone. When the village was looking for a spot to start the station, this site came to mind; it was not far from A'Ukre, the previously habitable spot would make clearing easier, and the villagers already knew of the area.

Bento interrupted his narrative to point out several plant species used for medicines, fiber, or construction. Bento also stopped our "tour" to make sure I heard the rustle of capuchin monkeys in nearby treetops, the distinct sound of howler monkeys off in the distance, and the flurry of the red-beaked curassow (or what we took to be a curassow) fleeing our intrusion. I had the distinct feeling that Bento had done this several times before, working with foreign researchers and acting as a guide to point out culturally relevant aspects of Pinkaití and patiently stopping to answer when I asked questions. He was keen on demonstrating his knowledge of how the forested environment provided for villagers in A'Ukre, his role in helping to create this particular project area, and his ongoing relationships with researchers. On our return we collected fruit in the base area before wandering back to the canoe. Shortly after our descent to the river, we met the other guides, who had been fishing in our absence. They asked if I had learned what I wanted to know, and satisfied with my answer, we started back for the village.

Lowe (2006, 2) reflects, "Natures are 'made' at the intersection of humans with their particular social histories, and plants and animals with their unique evolutionary and ecological histories. Neither 'science' nor 'society' will tell us all the interesting things one might want to know about these natures." In this chapter I explore how natures are "made," spaces "produced," and relationships sustained within "particular social histories" as they relate to community–conservation partnerships, specifically, the Kayapó–CI partnership.

When A'Ukre's young chief Payakan invited Barbara Zimmerman, a Canadian tropical forest biologist, to Brazil in the 1980s, neither would know that their budding relationship would result in one of the more lasting community–conservation relationships that emerged in the 1990s. Perhaps at the time they began the relationship, they could foresee the critical importance this partnership would take on as persistent development threatened the Kayapó Lands. Anthropologist Terence Turner (quoted in McCarthy 2008, np) has described the rampant development and deforestation in the region darkly this way as, "a Dracula movie. Every twenty years or so, it surges up out of the coffin. You have to drive the stake back through the thing and make it go away again. But it never really goes away. It keeps coming back" (available at http://www.npr.org/templates/story/story.php?storyId=91007395).

Kayapó efforts have benefited from a string of strategic alliances and partnerships with celebrities, companies, and NGOs. The goal, in many of these environmentally oriented, rights-based and social justice efforts, has been, and still is, focused on the demarcation, protection, and enforcement of the Kayapó Indigenous Lands. Moreover, the politics of territorial management today have rendered community partnerships critical alliances. The Kayapó peoples of A'Ukre have excelled in maintaining some of the more successful partnerships over the past three decades. It also should be noted that, although the

Kayapó–CI program endured for almost twenty years, the program was restructured in 2009, and is now supported by the Wild Foundation, ICFC, and the Environmental Defense Fund. Moreover, in 2007 AFP ramped up its programs in the area, and today this indigenous, Kayapó NGO also plays a critical role in fashioning projects in the area. As this chapter presents research that took place before the restructuring and growth of AFP, I discuss the partnership as the Kayapó–CI relationship, since these were the terms the Kayapó community members used to talk about their interaction with the organization and the researchers associated with it. This alliance would become indicative of the increasing number of NGOs in the Amazon region during democratization and neodevelopmental reforms in the Amazon. It also is evocative of the possible pathways for political, social, and economic action through partnerships forged between state institutions and civil society organizations. At the same time this partnership is also reflective of linkages between conservation programs and different types of enclosures (protected areas, indigenous lands, and forest reserves) and global environmental discourses.

Communities and Conservation

Some of the most dramatic land changes in Brazil in the past three decades are linked to the demarcation of different types of protected areas and indigenous reserves. The International Union for Conservation of Nature (IUCN 1994, 3) defines a protected area as "'an area of land and/or sea especially dedicated to the protection and maintenance of biological diversity, and of natural and associated cultural resources, and managed through legal or other effective means." In 1970, global protected area coverage amounted to 1,000,000 km^2, and it took a little more than two decades for it to swell to 15,100,000 km^2 (Zimmerer 2006, 8; Zimmerer, Galt, and Buck 2004, 520). Currently 12 percent of the earth's surface is under some sort of protection (West, Igoe, and Brockington 2006). The increase in protected areas across the globe, heightened attention to the conservation of culturally and biologically diverse landscapes, and ramped up strategies related to environmental governance in international and national contexts are evidence of what geographer Karl Zimmerer (2006, 1–2) labels environmental globalization. Environmental globalization is a form of global territoriality that is defined by the increased coordination among different institutions, knowledge systems, and efforts positioned to influence and govern nature.

Though protected areas are relatively new phenomena, diverse peoples around the globe have always marked, in many ways, distinctive locales in their surroundings. However, the recent increase in protected areas is rooted in a fortress model of conservation that began in the late nineteenth century. This model was first presented in the United States during the formation of Yosemite and Yellowstone parks, which were envisioned as crucial to national patrimony and critical to the protection of wildlife and habitats. Since the formation of what is now called the Yellowstone approach, protected areas have flourished. At the same time, concerned stakeholders have also heavily criticized protected areas for their exclusionary attitude toward land management (Vaccaro, Beltran, and Paquet 2013). Many protected areas, like Yellowstone, were defined to the detriment of local populations, whose subsistence lifeways were often criminalized and undermined in the wake of demarcation, which reflects early state-led projects that militarized different landscapes in the name of conservation. In the late 1980s, a growing concern about a strict preservationist approach to protected area demarcation paved the way for a new model where local communities were considered copartners in the fight rather than obstacles to environmentalist concerns. Now a centerpiece and preferred conservation strategy for regulating human–environment relationships, protected areas have expanded into transboundary and multinational corridors, areas that have defined, multi-use zones that are sometimes designated to include rural, indigenous, and place-based communities within their boundaries (West, Igoe, and Brockington 2006). In Brazil, this has taken the form of extractive reserves, state parks, national forests, sustainable development reserves, and Indigenous Lands, to name a few (Fearnside 2003).

Community involvement with conservation projects is a well-researched topic, and the results on this issue are mixed, controversial, and ongoing. While I do not want to repeat the entirety of this more than three-decade-long conversation here, some of the findings as they relate to the Kayapó–CI partnership are noteworthy. Scholars, who have been at the frontlines examining successes and failures, have highlighted the difficulties between such programs, especially the resulting conflicts between Western scientific approaches to management strategies that rely on rational, bureaucratic procedures, and local ways of knowing (Fairhead and Leach 1996; Shepherd 2010; Vaccaro and Beltran 2010). Diverse stakeholders comanaging resources also pose unique problems, in that with this plurality of perspectives comes competing perceptions of proper, moral, and ethical human–environment relationships (Escobar 1999; Tsing 2005). Moreover, comanagement regimes and partner-based conservation strategies are inevitably enacted out in uneven landscapes of power and agency, where defined local "communities" may not meaningfully be involved in decision-making processes (Berkes 2004, 2007; Fairhead, Leach, and Scoones 2012; Himley 2008). The notion of community is also problematic, as discussed in the previous chapter, since it seems to present a homogenous entity without considerations of existing hierarchies and differentiation that impact access to, management of, and perceptions about natural resources (Brosius, Tsing, and Zerner 1998; Rocheleau and Edmonds 1997). What these findings suggest is that community–conservation partnerships have distinct relational and interactive components where multiple knowledges, practices, governance strategies, and nature/culture interface, often in politically and environmentally charged arenas (Escobar 1998, 1999; Goldman, Nadasdy, and Turner 2011; Latour 2004; West 2006). In recent years we have witnessed resurgence in strict preservationist models in the wake of messy community–conservation partnerships, as well as a move away from enclosures to environmental services (Dowie 2009; Robbins et al. 2005).

Given the complexities of community–conservation initiatives, hybridity has emerged as a way to frame and discuss these rich and varied interactions, and it is a concept that will be relevant here to examine the Kayapó peoples' experiences of their homeland and conservation partnerships in the landscape of global environmental governance (Ballinger 2004; Haraway 2008; Latour 1993; Rosaldo 1989). Hybridity, in general, often describes the confluence of distinct practices or ontological frames into emergent performative spaces, everyday practices, and routine discourse (Orlove 2007).[2] Goldman, Nadasdy, and Turner (2011, 13) note that science and technology studies scholars have been particularly astute at developing a vocabulary for describing and analyzing hybridities: Callon and Law's (1995) "hybrid collectifs," Latour's (1993) naturesociety hybrids and hybrid forms (e.g., quasi objects), and Haraway's (2003) now seminal notion of "cyborgs," as well as "naturecultures." In thinking about these hybrid forms, Escobar (2001, 155) elaborates, "hybridization is another attempt at making visible the dynamic encounter of practices originating in many cultural and temporal matrices, and the extent to which local groups, far from being passive receivers of transnational conditions, actively shape the process of constructing identities, social relations, and economic practice."

In this chapter I expand our understandings of territorialities by exploring the applicability of hybridity to the Kayapó community–conservation partnership. The relationship between the Kayapó village of A'Ukre and CI presents an interesting case study for this type of inquiry. Because of this ongoing partnership, Kayapó villagers negotiate non-Kayapó worldviews, like those of conservation biologists, on how to best use, manage, and protect their lands. In addition, the on-the-ground enactment of the partnership required daily interactions between researchers, NGO staff members, employed Kayapó field guides, and intermittent interactions with other villagers. This interactive aspect of the partnership produced a series of practices and interpersonal relationships that, years later, contour the way in which villagers view the partnership.

Using several examples from research with A'Ukre residents, I explore whether the resulting interaction is indeed a form of hybridity. Given that hybridity is constituted by and produced from "many cultural and temporal matrices," it would appear to be a particularly productive metaphor from which to explore the collaboration between the Kayapó and other actors. In doing so, a focus on hybridities has the possibility of upending the naturalization of nature–culture binaries and local–global distinctions, and of providing scholars with a new vocabulary to discuss socioecological systems and their attendant territorialities (Whatmore and Thorne 1997, 289). The notion of hybridity also has the potential to reflect the complex interactions that take place during the production, practice, and performance of partnerships in everyday contexts, as well as the spatial and relational networks that ensue. As many scholars have noted, indigenous knowledges and, I would add, naturecultures are intimately and "fundamentally tied [to] contingency and habitus" (Raffles 2002, 326). Remembering that "Western scientific" knowledge is also situated, the performative spaces of encounters and the residual memories they leave behind are ripe arenas in which to explore hybridity (Brosius and Hitchner 2010, 143; Haraway 2008; Latour 1993).

Acknowledging the situatedness of scientific practice and the relationality of partnerships, however, does not obviate the asymmetrical power dynamics involved in knowledge production, incorporation, and spatial application. As discussed in chapter 2, where indigenous knowledges may be valued, in practice those same knowledges are often placed within a Western framework and disembodied from spiritual or cosmological frames for managerial and policy use (Agrawal 1995; Berkes 1999). Thus although we can call attention to the situatedness of both local and scientific knowledge, we must not forget that they are enacted in webs of power relations that define the relationships between and among users, scientists, policy makers, government officials, and other interested stakeholders. Haraway's (2003) proposition of naturecultures also captures this by elaborating on the how the commonly presented binary of nature/culture is a construct of modernity. Furthermore, Gupta (1998, 20) stresses that hybridity does not have to result in the dilution or erasure of local identities but should render visible "a set of locations that are formed by structural violence and stratified by different kinds of inequalities." Gupta's acknowledgement of the structural constraints and limitations in which hybrid knowledge and natures are formed also strongly points to a political ecology (and postcolonial) framework, which demands attention of the nested, multiscalar networks of meaning-making and resource use, access, and governance (Biersack 2006).

Results demonstrate that although hybridity seems an apt descriptor for characterizing this relationship, especially in the context of Escobar's discussion of the two-way interface of uneven power relationships and Gupta's consolation that it is not necessarily born out of lack of agency, I argue that emphasizing hybridity does not accurately portray these interactions or their territorialities and overlooks critical junctures or inflection points within community–conservation relationships. A reliance on the term hybridity sets up the assumption that there is something "emergent" or "new" taking place, when in practice, ethnographic evidence indicates that the Kayapó have always incorporated, borrowed, and exchanged goods and ideas into their lifeways (Gordon 2006; Lea 2012). It also suggests Kayapó peoples have all agreed that something hybrid or new is taking place, when community members may have different experiences with or opinions about the partnership. In other words, hybridity as a term seems to elide the historical and ongoing facets of Kayapó livelihoods that have often incorporated other, not specifically Western, practices, through trade, exchange, warfare, and other practices of sharing as well as the heterogeneity of individual and collective practice. This advances our understanding of how Kayapó communities continue to navigate different expressions of territory and territoriality within the same setting, especially in the context of community–conservation partnerships, and in doing so make non-Kayapó conceptualizations of the Kayapó lands legible to communities and stakeholders in the region in different ways: through political action, community–conservation partnerships, or shared claims to expert knowledge. Making these practices legible within the confines of community–conservation relationships, however, does not make Kayapó peoples into environmental subjects nor are Kayapó peoples operating solely within state-based norms of decentralized natural resource management approaches (Agrawal 2005). Rather Kayapó peoples navigate this partnership in multiple ways: through adopting different environmental scripts that are accessible to non-Kayapó partners, emplacing community–conservation relationships within the broader fabric of social life within the community, and by carrying out the partnership with the understanding that its spatio-temporal dimensions will change over time and so too will different community members have varying dispositions and ideas about what the partnership may mean for the community and their life.

In this way, residents of A'Ukre place their time spent with researchers in A'Ukre and Pinkaití in culturally relevant frames of meaning, value, and experience. This is similar to what Vanessa Lea (1986, 2012) has proposed regarding Kayapó relationships to material and nonmaterial goods. Lea describes the way in which the Kayapó domesticate objects from non-Kayapó sources, rendering the material aspects of alterity legible. It is also aligned with Els Lagrou's (2009) observations about other Amazonian groups incorporating nonlocal objects, in this case beads, into meaningful ceremonial acts. Lagrou (2009, 56) suggests that the inclusion of nonlocal objects into ritual contexts "should not therefore be analyzed as hybridism, but as legitimate demonstrations of specific modes of producing and using substances, raw materials and objects according to logics of classification and specific transformations." I extend Lea and Lagrou's understanding of the incorporation of material objects in everyday practice to nonmaterial and also economic aspects of making community–conservation partnerships. I emphasize that interpersonal relationships, storied events, and the practice and production of knowledge are key elements to consider when examining the resulting encounters and entanglements from the community–conservation interaction and their associated spatial politics. I argue that these nonmaterial aspects, as well as the economic benefits from the partnership, are similarly transformed into Kayapó understandings of and interactions with people and place, knowledge acquisition practices, and notions of conviviality. Thus, it is these social facets of community–conservation partnerships that served, for the residents of A'Ukre, as the salient experiences that bridged different ontological and epistemological divides, created a relationship, and sustained a territorial boundary and a space for making indigenous territorialities for more than three decades.

Pinkaití

Pinkaití was one of the first manifestations of the Kayapó–CI relationship. As the only research station in the Kayapó Indigenous Lands and the longest standing project developed between A'Ukre and CI, Pinkaití is a testament to the ingenuity of Kayapó leaders, as well as current environmentalist concerns. For some villagers, Pinkaití is indicative of the past three decades of tough work with NGOs, reflecting hard-won battles for territorial recognition. For others, Pinkaití demonstrates the ongoing importance of understanding the uncertain political economy of the current Amazonian landscape and cash-income opportunities in Indigenous Lands. And for others, the relationships made between researchers and Kayapó field assistants at Pinkaití point to a different kind of exchange where ideas, life experiences, and friendships are forged. Given ongoing efforts at political strategizing and territorial governance in the face of new challenges, I have no doubt that this partnership and its subsequent iterations also will serve as a launching pad from which to address emergent concerns regarding climate change, fire, droughts, and hydraulic futures as well.

The Kayapó–CI partnership evolved from a relationship between Barbara Zimmerman, and the then chief of A'Ukre, Payakan, that began in the 1980s. This interaction led to a brainstorming event where Payakan, the community of A'Ukre, and Zimmerman decided on an ecological research station, later known as Pinkaití, as the first initiative of the partnership between Zimmerman and the community. The community of A'Ukre scouted for and decided upon a site for the station upriver from the village. It was nestled near a small hillock, with a waterfall, Brazil nut groves, and mud lick nearby. Villagers decided that the location was perfect for an ecological station that would host a series of researchers. As already noted above, this site was already known within the community as an encampment where rubber tappers formerly resided.

In 1992, after two years of working to establish and build the research station, Zimmerman and the community secured funding from the Gordon and Betty Moore Foundation, which established a Global Conservation Fund Grant with CI. This funding allowed for the creation of some new CI programs. The Kayapó Program has been in existence since that time and is active today in different form, as the partnership and partners have changed and developed over time, as I explained above. The initial support for the Kayapó Project helped to fund scientific research at Pinkaití where Kayapó guides and non-Kayapó field researchers generated a body of ecological data about the Kayapó Lands that was simultaneously meant to benefit Kayapó activist efforts and conservationist platforms. Over the course of the 1990s, Pinkaití funded several graduate students from European, North American, and South American higher education institutions and produced several publications and master's theses and doctoral dissertations.[3] Villagers in A'Ukre often nostalgically remember this period of the most intense research, from the 1990s to 2003–2004, as the golden era of Pinkaití in the village. They note that this is the era when Pinkaití was "strong."

To better understand this period in A'Ukre, one needs to consider the political economy of the village during those same decades. The era of Pinkaití's "strength" took place while other types of cash economies were accessible to the community. As explained in the previous chapter, The Body Shop had started a project in A'Ukre based on the production of Brazil nut oil. During its tenure in the village, the now-defunct Body Shop project provided short-term revenue for community members and employed both men and women. Income differed between community members and varied by age and gender, and the project was not without controversy or difficulties. Despite these outcomes, the project did offer an example to community members that sustainable development initiatives within the villages were possible (Morsello 2002, 2006).

More importantly, at the same time, illegal logging was also rampant in the region, and it provided a huge influx of cash income for participating villages that made deals with loggers to enter their village lands (Zimmerman 2010; Zimmerman et al. 2001). Thus, Pinkaití's "golden era" was a period when A'Ukre had several cash-income sources, some of which were directly linked to extractive activities that resulted in the destruction of various parts of the forested areas. For this reason, CI's goals for the partnership were partly based on the mutual understanding that no logging or hunting would occur in the 8,000-ha protected reserve surrounding Pinkaití. After much deliberation and contestation, villagers agreed. Drawing upon an environmental script one chief thought would be legible to me, a *kuben kayaka*, he framed the partnership this way, "CI is helping us to take care of our earth. We are protecting our land. It is a good thing for us."

Moreover, the Pinkaití program was set up to offer villagers opportunities for wage work and to raise international awareness about the conservation potential of Kayapó Lands. The project, many villagers noted, was also an experiment with generating cash income without participating in highly extractive economic practices. According to interviewees, researchers contributed to or could contribute to the village's cash flow in several ways. First, researchers were required to pay a monthly entrance fee to the village or negotiate an equivalent activity that would benefit the village. In consensus-oriented village meetings, chiefs and men decided how to distribute the money or goods to the village. Ideally, each researcher was also in charge of presenting their research and asking the chiefs to select the best possible field assistants for the particular task at hand. Many men were selected for these tasks, especially those of the more senior age grades. In addition, in the later years a trail maintenance crew began, who were Kayapó assistants paid to clean and clear the paths so that the trail system would not get too overgrown over time. Finally, some researchers started informal projects for selling handicrafts in their home cities or in regional towns and cities near the Kayapó Lands. In this way, the project started with twin goals in mind: conservation and sustainable development initiatives. However this landscape has become increasingly complicated, as communities have received financial compensations from legal mining going on in the region.[4] In many cases, the lines that are drawn between these different governance and market strategies are not rigid, but blurry and confusing.

The sustainable development project portion of the Kayapó–CI partnership, with the exception of Pinkaití, was not the only priority for the area. Surveillance programs that supported the retention of territorial borders and initiatives to support local political institutions and governance quickly became part of the program. The surveillance program has helped over the years to work with governmental entities, like FUNAI and the federal police, to fortify the borders of the lands in an area where governmental enforcement and presence has always been difficult or poorly funded (Chernela and Zanotti 2014). From addressing waves of gold mining in the region to identifying illegal fishing in the resource-rich rivers to maintaining connections to local and regional FUNAI offices, territorial surveillance has been vital for maintaining the 1,200-km^2 border of the Kayapó Lands.

From the beginning, CI made administrative and program decisions to secure a long-term presence in the region and also to build the partnership to comply with the Brazilian government's evolving regulations concerning permits and access to Indigenous Lands. On the recommendation of FUNAI and based on other interests, CI, along with villagers, started the AFP, mentioned above, to help run the day-to-day aspects of the Kayapó program. The AFP was originally stationed in Redenção but then moved to Tucumã, Pará. In 2005, the Kayapó–CI program reached out to the IR, the Belgian-funded NGO that the leader Raoni began when he was touring in Belgium. The IR had worked on the western side of the reserve, but in 2005 the Belgian funding stopped, and CI stepped in to take over. The main regional NGOs that work with the Kayapó, such as IR and AFP, were initially primarily funded by CI and overseen by the CI–Brazil program, although for particular projects, these organizations might receive grants or support from other environmental NGOs.[5] Instituto Socio-ambiental ([ISA] The Socioenvironmental Institute), a São Paulo-based NGO, has been active in the Xikrin Kayapó territories to the north and the Xingu

National Park to the south (Schwartzman and Zimmerman 2005). The Instituto Kabu, similar to AFP and IR, also now works with Kayapó communities in the western half of the reserve. Due to permitting and funding constraints, Pinkaití is no longer as active a functioning research station as it used to be, and the last researcher from the initial project funds reportedly left around 2004. Since then, a handful of researchers have worked at the station, although interest still remains, and a regular summer field course carried out by the community and project partners happens in A'Ukre and at Pinkaití as well. The Kayapó program has moved on with other projects in the interim.

The Kayapó–CI program, along with AFP, actively supported and promoted intervillage cooperation through funding community meetings that join chiefs together from the various parts of the reserve. The relationships among CI, local indigenous NGOs, and the villages are mostly mediated through meetings as part of this pluralistic governance strategy between and among villages and NGO actors. In meetings, the Kayapó–CI program joins chiefs and leaders together in ways that are difficult for most village members to coordinate on a yearly basis because of the cost involved in transportation. Whether related to a community event, health issues, administrative concerns, governance problems, or a potential partnership with an outside organization, meetings were the preferred forums for community members to discuss and deliberate about a range of affairs. In A'Ukre, meetings regularly took place in the men's house. Outside the village, A'Ukre residents told me they held meetings in a varied assortment of formal and informal settings: administrative buildings, schools, backyards, and courtyards. At these meetings, leaders strategize about enforcing their territorial borders, discuss recent political events, consider options to build their economic portfolio, and also talked about other topics relevant to the concerns of the Kayapó peoples. The then CI project in the Kayapó Indigenous Lands reflects what are considered pressing concerns: a need for more accurate data on forestry governance, the role of market integration and deforestation on the sustainability of livelihood practices of Kayapó peoples, documentation and meaningful recognition of indigenous knowledges in conservation contexts, and multiscalar governance strategies to address "wicked problems" in the region.

Partnering

Residents of A'Ukre now refer to the ecological research station simply as Pinkaití, or "the project," which could signify Pinkaití or any type of development program within their village, depending on the context. Most commonly the "project" was invoked in interviews and in more casual conversations to relay everyday activities that took place at Pinkaití. It was not "CI's" presence that was remembered by Kayapó field assistants but particular researchers, stories, and events. This is not surprising, as I came to learn that Kayapó field assistants spent long hours in the forested and riverine landscape with researchers at the station. During nonwork hours at Pinkaití, Kayapó research assistants reported that they would perform different subsistence-related tasks (i.e., fishing and handicraft production) or socialize with the other researchers and Kayapó field assistants during time off. At Pinkaití and in A'Ukre, multiple interchanges took place; researchers and Kayapó community members shared beliefs, aesthetic values, ideas, and attitudes about the landscape. In this way, the research station served as a living place where people, animals, plants, paths, and stories converged (Adey 2010, xvii).

Time spent at the research station, and the time spent by researchers in the village, have created a body of stories and experiential knowledge about the people, flora, and fauna within this locale. Stories that still circulate within the village include the researchers' fears of jaguars, of forest spirits encountered, lost but then found researchers and Kayapó field assistants, landmark treks, and eventful fishing episodes. Stories were not always jovial and sometimes were cautionary tales when Kayapó field assistants realized that the researcher may not be physically able to handle nonresearch related requests to go on lengthy treks. In the dry season it is customary for villagers to trek to the savannah to harvest different palm fibers, medicines, or search for clutches of eggs of a savannah bird. During my research, after some conversation with Kayapó friends and advisors, we decided it would be good for me to see the savannah and to look for someone who may be going soon to join.

Days later I was sitting outside of an elder couple's house having a long discussion about whether I would be able to complete the walk or not. My ability to climb up hills was in question precisely because a previous researcher had a similar request years ago. This researcher had much difficulty, according to Paolo, my potential Kayapó guide, which concerned him. The savannah, which is a several hours trek from A'Ukre is at the top of a steep hill, and Paolo noted that when the researcher arrived at the top he was panting, weak, and needed a lot of water. I assured Paolo and my other Kayapó friends that I had lived in a place with tall mountains, was able to trek for long periods of time, and would make sure to bring enough water. After multiple assurances and testaments from myself and other villagers that I was fit enough to go, Paolo set a date for the trek for me to join him and his wife. When we finally made it to the top of the hill and saw the savannah before us, the thread of that conversation continued. Paolo commented, "Here is where the researcher had to stop. He was very weak," and then added he was pleased I was okay as we pushed forward.

These storied histories of Kayapó–researcher interactions resound with the way in which residents of A'Ukre interact with each other, new researchers in the area (including myself), and the landscape over time. Many Kayapó place-names and place-attachments are not only based on mythical stories and events, but also on individual and community experience and on the repeated and routine enactment of different activities within particular locales (see also Verswijver 1992b; Zanotti 2014a). Accordingly, Pinkaití and other areas in the landscape (e.g., the savannah) have become a common reference point when discussing fishing plans, ceremonial treks, events that took place with researchers, either in Pinkaití or beyond, and familiar stories that are told and retold among village residents. Pinkaití is also near, and on the route to, seasonal ceremonial encampments and hunting treks that are used periodically throughout the year. Pinkaití is also sometimes a place for young men to camp on overnight hunting expeditions in the dry season, as well as a place to visit for seasonal sources of fruit—what the example at the beginning of the chapter describes. As Tsing (2003b, 37) relates in her research among the Meratus, "Everyday travels through familiar forests remind people of their past experience. And people tell stories of their past by recalling their movements across the forested landscape." Certainly, Bento, Marcio, and Pátricio evoked their own storied past associated with Pinkaití (or lack of) while visiting the research station that hot January in 2007, but other events were also repeated to me, as in the examples above, during interviews over the course of my research highlighting the ways in which Kayapó and conservation actors coproduced place over time. These stories were constantly reinforced through casual conversations with villagers when they discussed river travel, fishing spots, and the CI presence in the area. Storied histories were not merely a recollection of past events, but events that formulate what Paige West (2006, 7), drawing upon Lefebvre, calls "rich site[s] of spatial production."

Furthermore, the sociability of Pinkaití was a vital component of the partnership discussed by villagers years later. Former Kayapó field assistants reported that the jobs at the research station, in addition to serving as field assistants, included trail maintenance, trail blazing, canoe trips, fishing, bathing, meals, and visits to A'Ukre during field breaks. While at the station, field assistants could stay in touch with relatives downriver sometimes through radio communication. The activities at the station offered the Kayapó and researchers opportunities to exchange knowledge, jokes, and amity that fit into Kayapó norms of different social relationships. Kayapó understandings of knowledge acquisition and practice are fundamentally relational, experiential, and multisensorial. Mentor–apprenticeship interactions, elder–youth storytelling, men's house gatherings, age-grade subsistence-based activities, and key familial and other relationships that activate during ceremonial preparations and rituals all are ways in which knowledges are acquired and transmitted (Murphy 2004; Turner 1995c). In other words, activities that take place in and knowledge about place is not only centered on human–animal–plant interactions but is also a way in which social relationships between villagers of A'Ukre are forged, sustained, and carried out. This happened as well with researchers at Pinkaití.

Some villagers who worked at Pinkaití reported that they developed camaraderie with certain researchers. Others expressed loss over these researchers
leaving and their inability to keep in touch with them over time given the
remoteness of the village and limited-to-no access to phones, computers, or
other methods of communication. I often was asked, "Have you heard news of
Raquel?" or "Teresa sent us a message and gifts. Can you send something to her
when you are in the city?" These demonstrated the frustration at the limitations
of communication networks in the region and the restrictions this placed on the
researchers' and the community members' ability to continue to connect and
share, materially and socially, in ways that align with notions of exchange. Key
moments in building camaraderie or friendship that former Kayapó research
assistants noted normally took place in instances when villagers could share
events, food, and ceremonies. Also, if the researcher spent time in A'Ukre, rather
than Pinkaití, during field breaks, households would often adopt researchers
into their families and then would apply their Kayapó extensive kin network
to researcher responsibilities while staying in A'Ukre (see also Chernela 2005).

Oftentimes, the brunt of the researchers' "fictive" kin-based responsibilities
took place during Kayapó nomination ceremonies or other, smaller rituals. As
discussed in chapter 2, naming ceremonies are the longest, most elaborate, and
complex ceremonies performed in Kayapó communities. The acquisition of
beautiful names is an important honor for the recipient and distinguishes those
individuals from common, nonbeautiful community members (Fisher 2003).
Both men and women when talking about their relationships with Pinkaití
researchers would highlight the way in which researchers participated in seasonal ceremonies, short rituals, or certain Kayapó bodily practices when they
(the researchers) were on field breaks. Not coincidentally, field breaks often corresponded with important ceremonial events, so that the Kayapó field assistants
could take time off. Villagers reported that researchers were often adopted into
matriuxorilocal households, were painted with genipapo and urucum while in
A'Ukre, and had a diverse array of experiences with ceremonies and community events. Some of the most vivid stories about researchers were unprompted,
retold to me during ceremonies or when villagers recalled past ones. Villagers
would focus on how the researcher participated in community life and would
complement those who could expertly perform daily Kayapó tasks or ceremonial obligations (e.g., climbing açaí trees, fishing, or carrying firewood). Interviewees would comment if the researcher had or had not participated in a ceremony, or if the researcher had modified their bodily presentation in accordance
with Kayapó customs.

Through bodily participation vis-à-vis body painting or by dancing during
ceremonies, researchers were included into a socially mediated structure of
"semiotic codes," to use Turner's (1995c, 148) term. In explaining the cultural
saliency of embodied practices among the Kayapó, Turner elaborates: "In the

case of circulating tokens of personal identity and value, such display typically involves specialized forms of bodily appearance. Where these forms of bodily appearance carry the main load of communicating the nature and value of personal identity, they frequently involve the direct modification of the body itself and/or the elaboration of complex semiotic codes of bodily adornment fraught with social messages about the content and value of personal identity and status."

Here, Turner (1995c, 148) draws attention to the relational, social values attributed to bodily appearance and the way in which bodily appearance and visual display relate to "personal identity and status." Returning to researcher stays in A'Ukre, whether they participated in ceremonies or body-painting events, the researchers momentarily embodied a performative and symbolic space that the Kayapó peoples highly valued and actively mediated, even if they could not display the same indicators of personal identity with these modifications. While it is speculation to consider whether the researchers were aware of the meaning associated with their particular performance, the experience was meaningful to Kayapó villagers interviewed years later. Consultants often remembered specific researchers on account of their participation in these ceremonies and approvingly noted when researchers valued "beautiful" practices by participating in them (e.g., body painting, shaving of the head, and dancing).

Closely linked to bodily modification and participation in village events is the related discussion interviewees had of a researcher's short- or long-term presence at Pinkaití or A'Ukre. Residents noted that an enduring presence in the village, repeated visits to A'Ukre, and action-oriented goals and research that benefited the village were major factors considered when evaluating the project, and they constituted a powerful relationship in the production of place over time. Villagers recognized that their experience of the partnership was mostly mediated through interactions with researchers at Pinkaití during the nascent years of the relationship. Although the umbrella organization to a certain extent stayed the same over the years, the people who were employed by, involved in, or affiliated with CI or Pinkaití were evaluated separately and individually. For example, the long-term connections some researchers maintained with the village was often remarked upon: "This researcher has been with us for a long time; she is real kin (*inobkwy djwy*)" or "that researcher is good because he speaks the truth. He does not lie to us." For those who have continued their ties with the village since their first visit, an ongoing dialogue exists. Not many villagers remembered researchers who stayed only a short time in the area or ones that they did not cultivate strong relationships with, but they did recall individuals who spent time in the village, worked with the Kayapó for long periods, and participated in Kayapó customs and ceremonies. In these cases, adopted families would persist.

Lowe (2006) encountered a similar situation while harvesting sea cucumbers with Togean people in Indonesia. In thinking about her encounters, she looks to Rabinow's (1996, 6) concept of *philia*, or the geography of friendship. In Lowe's (2006) work, she finds it useful to distinguish between sharing thought and collecting knowledge when looking at encounters that are driven or shaped by conservation efforts to examine how friendship plays a role in this process. In the Pinkaití example, the sociability of the partnership also enabled a different kind of relationship, with researchers and residents involved in many different forms of exchange that went beyond the sharing of or conflict between "Western" and "indigenous" knowledges.

Just as place-attachments, place-based meanings, and sociability are part of the ongoing way in which villagers engaged with the Kayapó–CI partnership, language also emerged as an important characteristic of the relationship. Oratory, or the ability to present speech acts in a persuasive manner, is a valued form of learning, speaking, and being in the world for the Kayapó, especially for men, but women leaders also have their own prized speech acts. Turner (1995c, 154) observes, "Oratory, called 'teaching' is [also] an important Kayapó genre of communicating cultural lore and wisdom." While scholars have typically ascribed beautiful oratory to political speeches, mostly carried out by elder men, other scholars, such as Lea (2004), have noted complimentary forms of expression by women, such as wailing. For this reason, most Kayapó individuals place value on the ability to properly and eloquently execute political speech acts, both within Kayapó communities and in external arenas, as well as communicate Kayapó perspectives in ways that are legible to non-Kayapó individuals. Furthermore, bilingualism (Portuguese and Kayapó), and increasingly English, is desirable or critical for Kayapó leaders and community members to know as they navigate national and international political, economic, and legal landscapes (Schwartzman and Zimmerman 2005). In A'Ukre, Kayapó men who achieve Portuguese fluency are frequently appointed to various political leadership positions within their village and selected as representatives to serve in extralocal political contexts, as in the case of Marcio. Women's inclusion in these types of leadership positions has been uneven, although there are some women leaders who have gained similar recognition. In early 2015 A'Ukre ceremonially recognized a woman leader in the community, marking her status as a strong woman chief in the community.

Villagers interviewed noted the importance of gaining access to experts, scientists, and researchers who could help them learn or practice Portuguese as it relates to conservation science. When pressed as to why, consultants mentioned, in different ways, that they need to speak in a way that is convincing and legible to *kuben* in order to help their village and protect their land. Many Kayapó field assistants and others involved in the project reported that Pinkaití was a place where they could share and learn Portuguese with researchers and not just practice their conversational Portuguese but also acquire the technical language of conservationists and researchers, acknowledging that the Western frame of science was considered legitimate in governmental and academic arenas. Given that many villagers have limited exposure to Western approaches to conservation biology, ecology, and other fields while living in A'Ukre, Pinkaití built on local expertise in what leaders thought was a key skill. Other consultants discussed their wish to learn non-Kayapó names of species to "know" more about the world that they lived in and to acquire different types of knowledge, even if it was from non-Kayapó sources. One interviewee, Bepkoko reported, "When I worked with [one of the CI researchers] I learned the names of many different animals. I like to learn these names and know more about the animals. When you are here you should teach us the names too so we know more." Like Bepkoko, other villagers expressed a keen interest in knowing the scientific or common names of species or following up on the species they already had learned about in order to increase their vocabulary for potential future use. They poured over the mammal and bird guides that I had brought with me to A'Ukre, and some recognized them as the same guides Pinkaití researchers had in years past.

Finally, the project, as a conservation-development initiative, had a strong economic component to it and was initially started as a joint venture between CI and A'Ukre to explore various sustainable development alternatives in the area. An overwhelming majority of consultants when asked what they thought about the project noted that the village was excited to have the project in the area and enjoyed the revenue-generating component. Villagers liked, and continue to like, the project because they were able to earn cash while helping outsiders understand the landscape better at a minimal cost to the community. For example, no serious landscape alterations needed to take place (e.g., roads), the researchers were removed from daily village life but worked closely with select residents, and the researchers did not use the forest for subsistence purposes so were not stressing the village's resources.

The partnership with CI and then with AFP increased awareness of outsider appreciation of "biodiversity" or at least Brazilian and European and North American interest and curiosity in seeing and learning more about the flora and fauna found in, near, and around the village of A'Ukre. For example, one young Kayapó man approached me and asked what I thought about zoos. I asked why. He commented, "I was in Belém once and saw the Museu Goeldi zoo and how all the animals were there. I remembered how researchers liked to see animals. I thought they would want to come and see animals if I had them here in the village." One important aspect of this relationship has been that the community recognizes that outsiders are willing to assign a market value to the aesthetic consumption of the flora and fauna of the region, and community members want to explore the different valuations of the natural resources the community governs.

As with previous market experimentation, the economic benefits of Pinkaití were mixed. The multiple different cash income sources from the project were diverse. As stated above, the village received a community fee from researchers that was distributed to villagers in the form of cash, food, and other items. Men and women earned money from selling or trading handicrafts with researchers. And finally, different villagers earned salaries or cash income from working as field assistants. Since the village had determined that it was their choice to select different field assistants in customary meetings, this meant that men in the elder age grades were often picked. As a result, some of the younger men interviewed felt as if they never had been able to actively participate in the project. A small minority of villagers expressed criticisms of the project, which included: Pinkaití favors certain families or individuals versus others and does not include the entire community; Pinkaití employs mostly the elder age grades (*meatum* and *mebenget*) and not the younger ones or women at all; and when other revenue activities in the community stopped, the project members salaried by the NGO did not share their resources with other group members. Many consultants reported that CI-salaried positions in the community were not considered a problem until the revenue-generating activities (like timber and the Body Shop project) left the community. Then, the CI-salaried community members were criticized, not for their income per se, but for what they did with that income once other community members did not have a steady cash flow. "They would receive rice and coffee and food from the plane. Everybody was hungry and could see what they had when we had nothing," one community member noted. This quote vividly demonstrates how market integration places the community in new situations where the distribution of wealth is no longer regulated by kin networks, and chiefly (re)allocations often evoke a strong response. The two families that, for a short time, received a salaried payment from the Kayapó project before the project terminated those positions did not hold official leadership positions within the community, and they were only part of the men's elder age grades. Therefore, their role in the distribution of wealth within the community was no different than other community members' within their own age grade; yet, they were held to similar standards as leaders and chiefs. In addition, with market integration, we see that some villagers harbored resentment against villagers who have a long-term relationship or even opportunistic employment with the project. Part of this is from the uneven distribution of monetary wealth and the other part is access to high-quality goods (European- or North American-made tents, water bottles, clothing, etc. that helped with carrying out subsistence tasks). CI recognized this and changed the way they were interacting with community. Despite addressing community concerns, this was an ongoing source of dissatisfaction expressed by many younger men who were not employed by the project and others who saw the project as unevenly benefitting the community.

The younger men I talked with were concerned about raising money for their newly formed families. For this reason, they were often anxious as to why elder men were selected for the project while younger age grades were often not hired. Who the researchers worked with was up to the community during consensual community meetings; however, there may have been other avenues of decision-making that I was not made aware of. Because what is decided in these community meetings is the consensual decision of all politically active adults, individuals that have a conflict with the situation might be overlooked. In this case, the chiefs and elder men community members were part of the hiring contingent. More elder men had an advantage because as an elder in the age-grade system corresponds to a suite of knowledge and practice that relates to subsistence, ceremonial, and political activities. Young men are still learning the vast expertise and knowledge that is only acquired over the course of the lifespan and for this reason often were not frequently picked when researchers needed a specialized field assistant. Finally, some younger men have worked at or with the project, and those that were too young to work when the project was in its best years now hope to become part of NGO projects. In more recent interactions with the community, especially in the context of the short-term field course, elders have expressed their interest in hiring younger men, as well as women, to work as assistants at Pinkaití as a way for the youth to learn the project and, at same time, learn from Kayapó elders.

One final aspect of the community–conservation partnership that I want to highlight is that it is mostly mediated through the men of the community. Community meetings determine key political decisions regarding the project and these meetings initially rarely included women. Men are employed at the ecological research station, and women were not or have infrequently been employed by the project. The exclusion of women from the project and their unfamiliarity with the project space is a result of several barriers in place. Men are more likely to speak Portuguese and be politically active outside of the com- munity. Men also tend to have, but not always, a broader familiarity with the landscape around Pinkaití (it being near a fishing spot) and, thus, more knowl- edge of areas around the project that might be of interest to the researchers. As a consequence, the community members that are most likely to interact with researchers are the men of the community. This gender difference is changing with the field course that takes place at the village, as over the past couple of years women field assistants have been increasingly part of the project.

This does not mean that women are disengaged from the project. While women might be excluded from being field assistants, informally, they have also talked about the benefits from the money and goods the researchers have circulated through A'Ukre. Even though men directly receive cash income or trade items from working at Pinkaití, many of the purchases/goods go to the household. For example, if a husband brings back a tent, this might be used for his family or, if it is a water bottle, he might give it to his wife or sister. In some cases, women might play an active role in how money is spent and request specific items for their family, which husbands will then buy. A typical order to the town will include food and subsistence items, such as rice, beans, sugar, salt, coffee, sandals, tobacco, and fishhooks. In addition, many different researchers started informal handicraft projects with the women in the community, where they would take beaded handicrafts to urban centers in Brazil or European and North American cities to sell. This generated an unreliable but opportunistic cash flow for the women in the community, who were often unable to send their handicrafts outside of the village in any systematic fashion during the project years. Thus, even though women did not directly participate in the project, they did receive some economic benefits from the project in a restricted way, and they engaged with researchers in informal spaces of the project (e.g., daily activities/village life) in what they discussed as meaningful ways. Thus, women remained peripheral to the project, all the while still subject to the community impacts of the partnership as it reverberated through village life.

These difficulties with the program demonstrate some of the complexities with the partnership. While the Pinkaití project was framed by CI as a conservation-development program in the area, the everyday realities and practice of the project and partnership on the ground reveals a more nuanced picture of a partnership associated not only with economic revenues or conservation imperatives but also with language acquisition, place-making practices, and conviviality in the landscape albeit with some limitations in place as to which groups in the village sustains these relationships. One of the criticisms of community–conservation partnerships is that the discourse surrounding conservation science has eclipsed local ways of meaning and knowing the environment, and thus has "produced" people and landscapes in unhelpful frameworks or produced new environmental subjectivities patterned around new governance strategies (Agrawal 2005; Escobar 1995). While not denying this is true in other contexts or rejecting the importance of exposing uneven and often gendered power dynamics and rigid, Western frameworks, for the Kayapó the varied aspects of the project provided a diverse array of opportunities for residents to engage with researchers and conservation practitioners on a variety of levels. The responses of interviewees suggest that villagers are not "passive receivers" of a conservation agenda but "actively shape" the conservation partnership in surprising and unexpected ways while still limited by some of the contested but mutually agreed-upon parameters of the relationship and its manifestations in spatial practice (see Escobar 2001).

Conclusion

A'Ukre's present-day efforts at partnering are part of an ongoing and historically mediated process among the Kayapó to engage with others. The formation and demarcation of the Kayapó Lands are irrevocably tied to the history of the

Brazilian nation-state and the subsequent rapid growth of NGOs and private interests in the Amazon region. A broad understanding of the actors, state and nonstate, confronted by the Kayapó highlights the process whereby the Kayapó peoples have been slowly integrated into state-making agendas and, at the same time, have fortified their efforts at autonomy and partnering. This is the new agenda of making indigenous territorialities. The Kayapó Lands play a part in international and global conversations surrounding biological and cultural diversity and some argue that successful conservation programs should still include *communities* and *participation* (Brosius and Russell 2003, 39).

Offered as a retrospective, the case presented here is a reflection of the prominent interactions between researchers and villagers that are remembered, enacted, and valued in A'Ukre more than twenty years after the partnership began. The Kayapó–CI partnership resulted in a series of social, economic, and place-making exchanges between non-Kayapó researchers and Kayapó villagers employed at Pinkaití and who live in A'Ukre. The results demonstrate that different types of social transactions took place, such as exposure to the international community, researcher participation in ceremonial practices (dance, body painting, song), and Kayapó–researcher informal interactions. The Kayapó–CI partnership provided opportunities for exchange, collaboration and sharing. Accordingly, the relationship villagers have with Pinkaití, and previous researchers at Pinkaití, is one example of the way in which partnerships are performed through interactive experiences and knowledge sharing practices. This partnership resulted in the cultural and physical re-creation of a local place by intensifying the densification of Kayapó social networks and ties to Pinkaití. These ties, as expressed in previous relationships with researchers, storied events that took place in the area, and present use of the site, firmly situate the research station within the local landscape. At the same time, Pinkaití established a circulation of values associated with conservation, friendship, and aesthetics among several different types of actors, values that are intimately linked to the politics of cultural difference where certain types of knowledges are considered legible and legitimate, and others not. However, the production of Pinkaití as a place demonstrates that place-based experiences, and the territorialities they encapsulate, can emerge from prolonged and episodic relationships in a particular locale. Community–conservation relationships have the potential to create naturecultures that incorporate the conviviality of everyday life and customary experiential knowledge transmission processes of indigenous livelihoods into natural resource management programs and projects, in spite of the uneven political economies and discursive fields in which they operate.

At the same time, as noted in the introduction, the Kayapó peoples have been open to incorporating goods, ideas, and practices from non-Kayapó groups (both indigenous and nonindigenous) into their cultural framework for a long time. In addition to Lea's (1986, 2012) work on this subject matter, other Kayapó ethnographers have found similar trends. Fisher (2000) documents how the Xikrin Kayapó adopted the manioc ceremony from the Juruná indigenous group. Vidal and Giannini (1995) observe that several songs and dances of the Xikrin Kayapó originated with neighboring groups. Verswijver (1992a, 142–43) comments on the Mekrãgnoti Kayapó borrowing or taking ornaments, artifacts, and feather work to incorporate into their material culture. Postcontact, Turner (1991a, 1995c) tells us that the Kayapó have also experimented with Brazilian customs, such as Brazilian dance, hairstyles, and clothing. All of these scholars describe the way in which the Kayapó selectively rejected some customs and accepted others, transforming new objects and relationships in a way that is life-giving and supportive to the community. During my time at A'Ukre, I heard similar stories and witnessed comparable events: a body painting that was styled after another indigenous groups' design, a community song that had the same tune as the Brazilian national anthem, and a new design in handicraft production that community members had seen in towns and cities. Acknowledging that the Kayapó have always incorporated other practices, beliefs, and values into their own cultural milieu, it is not hard to discern how community members in A'Ukre approached their relationship with CI with the same flexibility, experimentation, and generosity.

Research suggests that many (but not all) researchers and field assistants were involved in more than purely economic transactions, exchanging ideas about experiential knowledge, language, and humor. While these transactions might not always have been positive, and potential tensions and conflicts may have arisen during the project period, in retrospect, former Kayapó field guides commented most about the meaningful relationships that ensued and not the potential fractured or broken relationships that faltered. As a result, I would argue that individuals in A'Ukre have built upon their understandings of non-Kayapó relationships to the environment and have embedded that experience beyond the research context. I found several Kayapó interviewees discussed Pinkaití and its researchers based on a wide range of characteristics from ceremonial involvement to their ability to climb up hills. Villagers are and will be able to strategically call upon these experiences when appropriate for political rights-based conversations about territorial control and sovereignty.

Community members experienced the partnership differently, however. The distinctions and divisions already in place within Kayapó social institutions were applied to the CI example. Monetization has allowed, if not fostered, for the enlargement of consumptive networks beyond the community. Market integration, when it is approached through market-linked conservation practices and consensus-driven communitywide meetings, can produce village awareness of external perceptions and values of the environment. At the same time, the revenue-generating activities from this project can produce some in-village tensions among different age grades and between men and women. Women from all age grades and men from the lower age grades were the most likely to be excluded from different benefits of Pinkaití.

Furthermore, the performance of the partnership suggests that the social relationships that are formed, shaped, and constructed during partnerships need careful attention. A reconfiguration of the culture–nature binary should not be restricted to unraveling human and nonhuman species assemblages but also inclusive of the human relationships that impact the way in which understandings about the socioecological world are created, contested, and practiced. Scholars have painstakingly documented how divisive traditions concerning naturecultures result in persistent difficulties in the way in which management and conservation ideas travel and circulate in community–conservation relationships that are dominated by non-Indigenous ways of knowing (Brosius and Hitchner 2010). However, a partial erosion of these divisions as experienced through everyday interactions might result in a clearer understanding of the way in which multiple epistemologies are shared, incorporated, and practiced.

Nevertheless, I am wary of suggesting that Kayapó cosmological beliefs and epistemological frames are "hybridized." As emphasized in the introduction and noted above, the incorporation of material and ideological aspects from non-Kayapó groups has been documented as part of Kayapó practice for decades (Lea 2012). Indeed, scholars have suggested that one fundamental problem with hybridity, as proposed by Latour (1993), is the concept is predicated on the process of modernity, where Western and non-Western cultural confluence is heightened (Hannerz 1996)—as in the case study presented in this article. Indigenous and other local groups, including the Kayapó, have borrowed, adapted, and transformed practices from many different, and not necessarily Western, communities. Indigenous knowledge holders repeatedly emphasize that neither culture nor knowledge are stagnant, but rather are dynamic, plastic, and pliable (Berkes 1994). The assertion that hybridity is born out of modernity, then, is found to be limited and does not account for the cultural frameworks, already in place that adeptly incorporate different beliefs, values, and practices into institutions and lifeways, so I suggest indigenous transformative practices as a powerful frame from which to further explore these interactions.

I do, however, contend that the performance and performativity of the partnership enacted out different types of exchanges, as evidenced by the different reactions Marcio, Bento, and Pátricio had during our trip that January afternoon in 2007. Within this context, interactions between multiple individuals, that may have different perceptions of the world based on their positionality or life phase, take place. The result is that "multiple symbolic and political boundaries" are crossed and recrossed during different knowledge-sharing and place-making activities (Ballinger 2004, 34). In this case, the everyday activities that shaped one facet of the Kayapó–CI community–conservation relationship created memories and activities that have persisted in present-day manifestations of the partnership. Despite the mixed results of community and conservation alliances worldwide, I remain optimistic that community-based participation should not be dismissed from conservation agendas (see Brosius and Russell 2003).

In this way, community–conservation partnerships are woven into the larger fabric of making indigenous territorialities, supporting relationships, albeit contested ones, and networks that are key to forging new transactional orders and sharing economies. The Kayapó have defined this partnership through their own social institutions and ways of knowing and being in the landscape and are envisioned as critical to ongoing political strategies in the region, despite broader political economies at work. Today, Kayapó political institutions, dispute resolution, governance strategies, and leadership roles have been tailored to a wide variety of shifting political and economic circumstances. Having a fixed, federally demarcated territorial space that is recognized by international bodies and conservation organizations has spurred the Kayapó peoples to develop and build upon distinct ways of organizing intra- and intercommunity alliances. Communities are flexible in their strategies for partnering, fueled by their own sociospatial histories and other political economic shifts. More than ever, indigenous territories are complex terrains and polysemous homelands that are meant to ensure the preservation of cultural, linguistic, and biological diversity in the face of rapidly changing environmental and social conditions. Accordingly, Tsing (2003a, 167) asks, "Tribal landscapes . . . seem to represent a promising exception to human–nature incompatibility. Is this a crack through which humans might enter a renewed nature?" The example presented in this chapter suggests that rendering visible this "crack" should not only rely upon renewed natures but the mutually beneficial social interactions that result from alliances and the resulting territorialities that comingle in the same locale. As a consequence, communities like A'Ukre are expertly forging new alliances and partnerships to accommodate political, economic, and ecological transformations and to adjust to a rapidly changing geopolitical and ecological terrain.

6

Returns

> Time puts things in their place.
> —García Marquéz, *One Hundred Years of Solitude*

Introduction

When a group of three hundred activists occupied Pimental Island for several days in July of 2012 to protest the construction of the Belo Monte Dam, they spelled out "Pare Belo Monte" (Stop Belo Monte) with their bodies to draw attention to the controversial dam project as the country was preparing for the Rio +20 United Nations Conference on Sustainable Development (UNCED). Activists from fishing and smallholder communities, as well as indigenous groups, including the Kayapó, Kuruaya, Asurini, Juruna, and Munduruku (2012) issued this statement.

> Today we write for those who support us. We write for those who trust in our struggle and agree with our view. We are people who live in the rivers where dams are being built. We are Munduruku, Juruna, Kayapo, Xipaya, Kuruaya, Asurini, Parakanã, Arara, fishermen and riverine [inhabitants]. The river is our supermarket. Our ancestors are older than Jesus Christ. We occupied Belo Monte Dam sites seven days ago. We are against the construction of large projects that destroy our lives. We want to be able to have a dialogue with the government about this. First of all they need to regulate the law about Prior and Informed Consultation, so that they can consult us before doing any study or construction in our lands. The government also needs to stop whatever they are doing in our territory and to take the troops out of it.

Compressed within these lines, activists highlight the complexities of indigenous citizenship in multicultural states, where special provisions for territorial rights are continually undermined by political and economic inequalities, including the logic of late liberal and neodevelopmental markets and the continued militarization of rural and peripheral spaces (Hale 2011; Postero 2007). This letter points to the failures of the democratic state, where a new tide of laws meant to ensure public commentary in development schemes and a series of laws granting distinctive rights to indigenous peoples have not resolved issues of participation, political voice, or recognitional justice. They also show the problematic nature of constitutional reforms that were lauded for granting indigenous peoples and other descendent communities' rights to their lands but also giving the state ultimate control over subsoil rights while retaining FUNAI as the "guardian" of indigenous peoples and their territories.[1] These policies are antagonistic to how many indigenous peoples consider their sovereignty over their lands and futures.

With the successes that the Kayapó peoples have had over the past three decades in territorial consolidation and enforcement, their struggle remains part of sociospatial projects that coalesce around questions regarding indigenous cosmovisions and projects for sovereignty and also inevitably about rights, land, labor, and property. Throughout this book, I illuminated the overlapping and historically sedimented, spatializing pulse of this struggle through the frame of making indigenous territorialities, which I have suggested are radical territorial projects for justice. I stressed the "territorial turn" in Latin American politics (Bryan 2012; Offen 2003), the productive and generative forces that make up local livelihoods, and the politics of indigeneity as key indices from which to examine these issues both locally, as in the Kayapó case, and their relevance to regional, national, and international politics. In making indigenous territorialities legible, I have argued Kayapó communities developed a robust political network of supportive indigenous and conservation NGOs in their area NTFP programs, and a political structure that accommodates for territory-wide leadership that facilitates governance of their homeland and strategic dialogue with different governmental and NGO bodies. Drawing sustenance from indigenous foodways and performative politics, Kayapó communities continue to seek justice when procedural pathways seem to fail. "We continue to fight" is something that I have heard from my Kayapó friends since I began working with them, and it was repeated over and over again in meetings, informal conversations, and in publically issued letters. As John Agnew (1994, 53; 2010) powerfully argued, "territoriality does not necessarily entail the practices of total mutual exclusion which dominant understandings of the modern territorial state attribute to it." In considering territorialities that are attentive to difference and justice making efforts, we see how Kayapó strategies are formulated as political projects that constitute productive, radical counterpublics against dominant discourses surrounding place, region, and home that threaten to erase or dismiss their lifeways.

Moreover, the generative and life-giving practices of making personhood, home, and community remain firmly situated in Kayapó notions of a good life. These are the "small," "intimate," and poetic spaces of everyday life (Canessa 2012). Place and personhood are inevitably relational, generative, and substantive, guided by interactions between human and nonhuman others across space and time. These conceptualizations of being in place are thus orthogonal to but not wholly disconnected from state-centered dominance, disciplinary power, or the reach of transnational networks. As an analytical frame, making indigenous territorialities sharpens our understanding of constant processes of re- and deterritorialization that contour Kayapó lives, bodies, and homes in particular ways, and demonstrates how Kayapó communities enact creative and agentive practices in fields of power that both constrain and enliven projects for current and future generations.[2]

Unsettled Geographies

The neoliberal, neodevelopmental, and multicultural movement in Latin America continues to challenge projects for life, like those put forth by A'Ukre community. The construction of the Belo Monte Dam is only one of several threats that the Kayapó peoples continue to face. Joining a new tide of green politics, including in the agricultural and energy sectors (e.g., hydropower), Baletti (2012, 574) calls the neodevelopmentalist era a moment where "contemporary environmentalist discourses fit within and make possible the emergent, prevailing developmentalist model." Illegal logging, gold mining, and fishing also linger as real dangers to disrupting socioecological landscapes the Kayapó call home. Brazil as a major exporter of soy will retain policies that favor the agro-industrial model that currently dominates the landscape surrounding the Kayapó Lands (Accioli and Monteiro 2011). Moreover, while the Program for the Estimation of Deforestation in the Brazilian Amazon and other initiatives have made great leaps in reduced deforestation in the Brazilian Amazon from 2004 to 2009, work by Fearnside (2013) and Davidson et al. (2012) draw attention to climate change, fire, and droughts as future concerns for further deforestation in the Amazon, especially where the Kayapó live (Jonas et al. 2014, 414). The scalability of rights to land and livelihoods is particularly relevant here, especially as it is able to address national rights provisions, international human rights laws, and indigenous, collective rights.

For the Kayapó peoples, the political, economic, and socioenvironmental programs that have dominated Southern Pará and Northern Mato Grosso for decades have impacted their fight for territorial demarcation, rights-based recognition, and livelihoods. The political and economic timeline of the Brazilian Amazon sharply highlights how successive waves of extractive economies, development plans, socio-natures, and finally, neodevelopmentalism and neo-extractivism have contoured indigenous politics in the region (see Hecht 2012). This has formed the complicated mosaic of protected areas, extractive reserves, agricultural zones, and Indigenous Lands in the Amazon today. The discourses surrounding the delineation of these places plays no small part in the ways in which indigenous peoples, such as the Kayapó, move to enforce their borders, cultivate spaces where they can flourish, and create global landscapes that accommodate radical and alternative visions of indigenous livelihoods.

At the same time, indigenous conceptualizations of place rarely make the front page, and local groups are often stereotypically portrayed as isolated stewards of the forest, ignorant slash-and-burn farmers, or corrupt, acculturated capitalists (e.g., "bad actors"). In contrast, for the Kayapó, the history of their engagement with the region is one that is rooted in long-standing sensibilities to navigate dangerous, foreign, and "Other" beings and forces. Lifeways extend to mythic time through stories passed down from generation to generation: stories that tell how corn first came to communities, the manner in which the Sky Woman passed on her knowledge about growing different types of plants, the tasks of O Òróp and Bira, and the shamans who helped communities form in the very beginning. Landscapes for villagers are choral works and rich repositories of human–animal–plant interactions coproduced by memories, myths, ceremonies, and daily activities. These stories ground Kayapó experiences and simultaneously point to a different perspective than that of territories simply as "containers," a viewpoint that has dominated state-led territorial expansion and global environmental governance of ecosystems (Agnew 2010). As Bessire (2014, 216) makes clear in his ethnography with the Ayoreo peoples in Paraguay, "'culture as becoming' requires meanings that are intrinsically unstable, fluid, and based on rotational time." Mapped on to notions of territory, then, territorialities—their fluid production and sociospatial expression—manifest in complicated ways as the Kayapó peoples struggle to retain their lands alongside radically different cosmovisions of the same place and space.

Yet, through an unyielding commitment to their way of life, Kayapó leaders, such as Raoni, Megaron, Tuira, and Mayalú, have emerged on the political scene to bring their communities together in an effort to fight for a territorial homeland and rights to self-determination over their peoples and lands during this latest wave of capital expansion and environmental stressors. A large part of this struggle is expressed in performative actions that in many ways provide counterspaces to conformist politics. Escobar (2004, 207) describes these spaces as ones that are characterized by a "politics of difference, particular through place-based yet transnational political strategies" and states that "these movements represent the best hope for reworking imperial globality and global coloniality." For the Kayapó these strategies are built upon several decades of indigenous politics and cultivation of public visual vocabularies of resistance. I have argued that the persistence of ceremonies enacted out by Kayapó communities demonstrates alternative ways of interacting with a place, making personhood, and forging political action. Kayapó leaders have drawn strength from these ceremonies and rituals in the political sphere by singing songs, wearing body paint, or performing collective dances—activities that are generative of life forged from the coordinate activities of mothers, brothers, sisters, fathers, and other loved community members. The use of these practices for activist efforts challenge the rationality present in "Western" bureaucratic decision-making processes and offer counterspaces and counternarratives to the dominant models of political action—strategies that ultimately are about recognitional justice (Marion Suiseeya 2015; Marion Suiseeya and Caplow 2013).

Wider viewing publics are not always "fluent" in Kayapó aesthetic and semiotic vocabularies and thus may read the usage of such ceremonial regalia anywhere on the spectrum of "authentic" to "exotic." The Kayapó peoples understand the complexities of what Graham and Penny (2014) have labeled performing indigeneity in order to complicate essentialized understandings of indigenous struggles to make viable political progress within the realm of identity politics while at the same time remaining true to those practices that make them beautiful and whole. In other words, making place is now deeply political given its importance in the broader political-economic landscape of Brazil and the performative aspects of politics that are now commonplace in national and international realms. The entanglement of ceremonial practices and political protests is illustrative of how indigenous politics associated with territorial management and indigenous cosmologies regarding home, people, and place are "a conscious effort to establish social relationships" with Others that have the capacity to generate "new sociopolitical configurations" supportive of Kayapó lifeways (Santos-Granero 2009a, 493).

One of the more politicized conversations in the Brazilian Amazon about being indigenous has centered around regional and local foodways in the region, their contrast with slash and burn techniques used to create commercialized and industrial agricultural and ranching sectors, and their connection with concerns about ongoing land distribution inequality (Tinker, Ingram, and Struwe 1996; Martinelli et al. 2010). Villagers in A'Ukre positioned their engagement with their lands in ways that highlighted food practices linked to making indigenous livelihoods and identities. Swidden agriculture produces some of the main, but not the only, food sources in A'Ukre and agricultural plots are key sites for fortifying social relationships, transmitting knowledge about Kayapó cuisines, and building practice-based skill sets. At the same time, while fields are emblematic of customary foodways, they are also sites of experimentation. Women plant different species depending on preference, access, and kin relations, and a more recent community initiative pays individuals for local produce brought to the school for its food program. Far from simply a vision of the swidden as destructive to forest ecosystems or as producing agroforestry practices congenial to supporting environmental services, Kayapó swidden practices make villages home through different transformative economies, based on social relationships, human and nonhuman interactions, subsistence needs, and market options. As with the previous statement that "the river is our supermarket," villagers also emphasized that their food collection and harvesting strategies were alternative uses of lands and waters that countered large-scale, agro-industrial models prevalent in the state of Pará. These discourses directly engaged with regional conversations about beef and soy production, including the introduction of no-tillage agriculture, crop–pasture–forestry, land-zoning laws, and certification schemes, especially in the ranching sector (Jonas et al. 2014, 414; Nepstad et al. 2006). More importantly, Kayapó seed fairs and other food programs in villages also are aligned with food movements around the Global South that have emphasized food sovereignty, food justice, and food security, the latter which is a platform popular in the World Health Organization, World Trade Organization, and the United Nations.

Just as swidden is many things to residents of A'Ukre, foraging for seasonal fruits and nuts also is evocative of diverse relationships to space, place, and transactional orders. A focus on foraging, especially as it relates to fruits and nuts, offers a lens on past and present use of Amazonian landscapes that demonstrate its anthropogenic character. Foraging practices also highlight place-making strategies that reinforce different socioecological relationships that continue to lie outside of market logics. For example, villagers in A'Ukre identify species that are found in high densities, like Brazil nuts, as characteristics of good landscapes to live in. In this way, local harvesting practices pattern movements across landscapes as villagers orient travels based on historical use, resource distribution, topographical memories, and relationships with human and nonhuman Others, and spending time with friends and family. As Santos-Granero (2006, 66) notes, "the learning process [can be] understood as a quest for knowledge, one in which seekers must prepare both physically and spiritually." Collectively, these practices make indigenous territorialities through embodied skill sets that are cultivated over the course of an individual's lifetime and nurtured through ongoing practice and local worldviews.

Foraging also throws into relief the political economy of NTFPs and the politics behind commoditizing forest goods and services along with the increased commoditization of conservation and natural resource management strategies worldwide. Where the 2012 Rio +20 UNCED conference served as a defining moment from which concerned indigenous and rural residents staged the Pimental occupation, the 1992 UNCED conference twenty years before was a benchmark year that ushered in a several-decade long investment in sustainable development programs. Since that time, NTFP projects have remained popular as market-based strategies alongside the proliferation of payment for ecosystem services as another dominant conservation strategy. Sustainable development markets in A'Ukre have been almost exclusively oriented around NTFPs, the majority of which have centered on Brazil nuts. While NTFP projects are a recent phenomenon, the exchange and trade of Brazil nuts in the Amazon region is not. As the years went by, Brazil nuts went from a traded item to one that was integrated into the community–company partnership and then a community–conservation partnership. While transforming nature into commodities has been a hallmark of neoliberal economic policies, and NTFP projects are an example of this practice, villagers of A'Ukre repeatedly have expressed their preference for this type of market involvement. Their interest in NTFP markets is contrasted against getting involved with highly extractive industries and large-scale, land-use change in the region that the Kayapó of A'Ukre perceive as a detriment to territorial retention because these strategies rely on deforestation and lack of attention to justice issues. Although, engagement with these markets has fluctuated over time, and certainly there has been a pronounced difference in preference of villages over time as to the extent to which they will experiment with or engage in extractivist economies.

With the partnership of local indigenous NGOs and international conservation NGOs, community members hope to continue to forge these types of NTFP projects in the future to create an ongoing cash flow alongside other salaried positions and cash transfer programs in the area. Here we see a vision of the Kayapó Lands that combines global environmental governance norms and poverty alleviation initiatives while simultaneously offering possibilities for local communities to engage with market economies in ways that do not necessarily negatively affect their homeland or lifeways. While these markets do not always challenge dominant industries, they are part of a larger fabric of sustainable forestry and agriculture initiatives that are sweeping the Amazon within an emerging "carbon-biodiversity" framework (Jonas et al. 2014, 414). Under both of these visions, one based on neoliberal logics and the other on global environmental governance regimes, Kayapó peoples are carving out a vision of indigenous territorialities, where residents in A'Ukre emphasize that commodification does not always result in a loss. Rather, market-based projects have the possibility of strengthening, rather than diminishing, their livelihood practices—both in the short-term and also across generations.

Now working alongside AFP, a Kayapó NGO, international conservation interests are hoping to develop new projects of their own; community members in A'Ukre seek to enforce and monitor its borders, build new skill sets integral for self-determination, create sustainable development projects, and govern their land. The Pimental Island occupation highlights this new wave of politics where resistance strategies and activist efforts are fortified by multistakeholder alliances. Whereas previous alliances and factionalism were largely based on the interrelationship between and among fissioned communities and outside groups, alliances are now forged based on territorial management, health care needs, FUNAI requirements, private interests, and nongovernmental involvement in the area. With the devolution of FUNAI as a governing body, NGOs have taken on paragovernmental roles in aiding environmental and social justice programs in the area. Beginning with CI and Pinkaití, A'Ukre's partnership with NGOs has changed and expanded since the 1990s creating an expansive network of short- and long-term alliances supporting a "broad pluralistic approach" to community–outsider partnerships (Berkes 2007, 15188).

Using Pinkaití as a case study, I suggested that local attitudes toward Pinkaití are mainly positive and indicate that the partnership has resulted in Pinkaití as part of their village landscape, a pride in the project area, and highly desired jobs. Tensions that have risen out of the project were based on exclusion from work, where some younger community members and women in the community felt marginalized from the project. Despite criticisms, villagers fondly remember the active years of the project, and the community retains an interest in maintaining and supporting the project area and the network of alliances built from it. Although community goals for alliance and partnering have changed over the years as they navigate intra- and intercommunity dynamics and alliances across their lands. I have argued that this partnership is another example of how the Kayapó have long adopted foreign ideas, practices, or material objects into their lives and "made" them their own, while at the same time drawing attention to the tensions between and among community members about when and the extent to which their peoples should engage in these practices. Through drawing conservation organizations into their realm, A'Ukre villagers have acknowledged the importance of these types of partnerships for political and other purposes. At the same time, a strong vision of community life, one of which is not defined by environmentalist visions of place, remains *tycht*.

In this nexus of events, the rise of community–conservation partnerships, robust indigenous-led social movements, international treaties and conventions linked to global environmental governance, and new energy driven platforms, Kayapó communities have once again risen to the challenge making themselves seen and heard despite major hurdles that still lie ahead.[3] The transnational and national connections between histories of marginalization have recently become amplified, especially in ways in which they connect to sociospatial implications of urban and rural planning, most readily seen in protests against "mega-events," mega projects like the Belo Monte Dam in the Amazon, the 2014 World Cup, and the 2016 summer Olympics in the more industrialized south of the country (Gaffney 2010). The uneven geography of capital in Brazil is certainly expressed in both rural and urban areas, which both have problematic histories of racialized landscapes, police violence, and pacification efforts (Freeman 2012). No one would argue against the fact that Kayapó leaders and communities have unequivocally participated in, and continue to shape, this political landscape. With ongoing issues surrounding carbon emissions, deforestation, and capitalist expansion, the Kayapó peoples of A'Ukre are setting one example on how indigenous livelihood practices that combine conservationist and development concerns can create a shared vision of sustainable Amazonian futures and a *mejkumrei* life. A feminist political ecology approach is essential to these imaginings as it identifies "the point in which ontological difference turned into social inequality . . . [and] . . . when the abstraction of things— nature and human labor—turned into abstract ideas and generalized monetary value. Thus, decolonizing knowledge is an epistemological condition for deconstructing the exploitative trends of the global economy and reviving the ecological and cultural potentials of the people to give life to alternative modes of production, of thinking, of being" (Leff 2012, 7–8).

Belo Monte

The Pimental Island occupation is just one of a series of almost innumerable events in a broader movement against Belo Monte Dam in particular and new infrastructural politics in general. While the scale of the Belo Monte Dam is significantly smaller than previous iterations of the same project, if built, it still would be the world's third largest hydroelectric dam (Santos and Andrade 1990; Turner 2010). It should come to no surprise that the Belo Monte Dam project has been met with large opposition from multi-ethnic alliances, NGOs, and other coalitions over the past several decades based on its projected negative socioenvironmental impacts (Fearnside 2006b; Turner and Fajans Turner 2006). Court battles, large-scale public protests, activist documentaries, online protests, Facebook posts, interactive timelines, public declarations, and visits to governmental offices have marked activity surrounding the dam, from roughly 1989 onward. Activists have appealed to the international community issuing public statements and letters and aligning themselves with organizations like Amazon Watch and International Rivers. Protests have also been ensconced in and drawn strength from international movements for justice and equality, as shown here, such as the Occupy movements that swept Wall Street and in other locations around the globe starting in 2011.

Initiating the Pimental Island occupation at the same time as the Rio +20 UNCED conference also rightly positioned the occupation within conversations about Brazil's sustainable futures, especially as it relates to the privatization of natural resources and multinational investment in green energies and technologies. As the region turns to green energy alternatives (e.g., hydroelectric dams), hydrocarbon development, and ongoing illegal and legal investment in mineral extraction, explosive social and environmental conflicts continue that are now fortified by longstanding, as well as new, "multiclass" movements "made up of the actors with the strongest and most radical attitude toward transnational capital's extractive dynamic" (López and Vértiz 2015, 159). Bebbington (2012, 1154) reports that "among the most striking features of post-1990 investment in extractive industry have been the speed with which it has occurred and the facility with which has occupied new physical and sociopolitical spaces."

Moreover, Brazil is developing "clean" energy sources to reduce its CO2 footprint, as well as maintain its top rating for energy technologies ([MME] Ministry of Mines and Energy 2011). Belo Monte Dam is part of an energy expansion plan of Brazil (2011–2020) where forty-eight projects are proposed to add thirty-six Gigawat to the system (Fearnside 2012). Norte Energia, a public–private consortium of different firms and companies, with Eletrobras is leading the project. The proponents of the dam have promised that the power will develop a region in Brazil that lags behind in infrastructure and reliable power sources suggesting the public good that comes from dam development outweighs local concerns and needs. In 2008 an environmental impact assessment produced by Eletrobras resulted in the Institute of Environment and Renewable Natural Resources (IBAMA) granting a provisional environmental license to dam construction in 2010. Between 2008 and 2010 several public hearings were held, including one in 2009 in Altamira that followed the 2008 Altamira protest. Development plans, such as Belo Monte Dam, vividly draw attention to the spatial marginalization that comes with ongoing capital expansion at the expense of local communities.

The territorial politics involved in projects like Belo Monte Dam also highlight tensions among "pre-existing" indigenous rights to land, the requirement to consult with indigenous peoples in developmental projects, and the limits of land rights in the face of subsoil development (Curi 2014, 115). Major infrastructure projects have been required to conduct an environmental impact study and provide a report on environmental impacts since law 6938 was passed in 1981, and a resolution was passed in 1986 (Fearnside 2006b, 20). This includes an environmental impact assessment (EIA) that addresses social and environmental impacts and a three-stage licensing process (preliminary, installation, and operating) (Cohn 2010). The IBAMA is responsible for authorizing the environmental licenses for projects or activities. Environment impact assessments are often required to include public commentary, thereby offering a space for public "participation" in environmental decision-making. Yet, EIAs, in practice, have repeatedly failed to honor indigenous livelihoods. Indigenous "voices have typically been muted by political pressures from the highest levels of the Brazilian government," making the process far from free, prior, and informed consent (Millikan 2014, 135). Kayapó peoples have countered some of these constraints with their more than three-decade long portfolio of political action that has included a pluralistic governance strategy, a diversity of livelihood strategies, and a strong presence in intergovernmental and international politics.

The social and environmental impacts of Belo Monte will be immense, particularly for the Kayapó peoples. An independent environmental impact statement from forty experts in 2009 found that,

> the Big Bend would receive less water than at any time in its history, fish stocks would be decimated, with some species likely to become extinct. The drying of the Big Bend would make it impossible for indigenous communities to reach the city of Altamira to sell their produce or buy staples. The lowering of the water table would destroy the agricultural production of the region, affecting water

quality. In all probability, the rainforests in this region would not survive. The formation of small, stagnant pools of water would be an ideal environment for proliferation of malaria and other waterborne diseases. Communities upstream, including the Kayapó indigenous people, would suffer the loss of migratory fish species, which are a crucial part of their diet. (International Rivers 2012, np)

Furthermore, many are skeptical of the assessment of how much power it will bring, and it is rumored that the once-national and now-multinational mining corporation Vale will probably benefit the most from the promised energy in nearby aluminum and iron mines rather than the state of Pará as promised (International Rivers 2012). In a 2010 letter against the dam, many leaders, including Kayapó ones, protested, "We, the indigenous people of the Xingu, do not want Belo Monte." Nevertheless, a contract for construction and a partial installation license was granted in 2011. More than ten lawsuits have been filed and federal judges continued to argue against the licensing process on constitutional and environmental concerns, as well as concerns regarding consulting indigenous groups in the area. Some have halted construction for several months. The dam plans, as of 2015, continue to provoke action, as organized and spontaneous grassroots protests against dam development remain firmly entrenched in the region. A recent success took place, when IBAMA revoked the operational license to the dam, which has temporally halted the construction (Amazon Watch 2015).

Yet, a series of decrees, provisions, and bills currently being discussed and debated by the Brazilian government overshadows this success, as these measures, if passed, would make hydroelectric and other development on Indigenous Lands easier and destabilize indigenous territorial claims. New agenda items on the table include PEC 28 and 215, which would change how Indigenous Lands are demarcated and offer the possibility of reversal of demarcation, in the case of 215. Other decrees are directly related to extractivism and hydrodevelopment, giving the government authorization to explore, mine, log, and develop on Indigenous Lands—or to give farmers the ability to claim parts of Indigenous Lands, as with PEC 237 (Curi 2014, 115). The political, economic, ecological, and cultural ramifications of these infrastructural projects and subsoil desires, more than anything, show the stark and seemingly insurmountable legal, political, and economic hurdles Kayapó peoples and other communities in the region will continue to face.

Mejkumrei

I have returned to the village of A'Ukre almost every year since that first visit in 2004 and longer-term work in 2006 and 2007. In many ways, the village has remained the same—the same blue house that became my point of orientation in 2006 continues to be my village-based compass, a marker to trails to a beach behind the houses, routes to fields, and a trail to homes of loved ones. I have stayed in touch with the women and men that became my friends more than a decade ago both professionally and personally. Nhak and others continue to work toward the health and well-being of their families and share different desires about what that future might look like, whether their children become expert filmmakers, leaders in the community, or pursue higher education. When in A'Ukre, I still walk to the river with Nhak and others, where we eat recently harvested and roasted sweet potatoes, fish, joke, and bath their kids and grandkids. We walk to gardens, mourn over elders who have passed, and discuss what was on the news the night before. I sit with elder chiefs and discuss politics—the resurgence in illegal gold mining that has started to go on in their area, a recent trip to Brasília to fight against Belo Monte Dam, or new ideas about a cultural center. The men's house has gone through several iterations of refurbishment, as the roof was replaced twice. New homes and a school have been built to accommodate the growing population. There are plans in the works for an updated water system. A'Ukre has fissioned once again and families from other villages have moved to the area.

As the community TV slowly was abandoned over time, now households and families have their own TVs, DVD players, and cellphones (active in town but serve as small computers in the village), powered by a community generator and also sometimes by household solar power. Music pulses through A'Ukre from curated playlists with a collection of different types of songs: MPB (popular Brazilian music), *forró*, technobrega, hits or classics from the United States, Kayapó biblical hymns, and ceremonial songs. Soccer is still a popular pastime in the late afternoons, and there is a continued interest in learning English and IT skills, while at the same time finding a solid ground from which to navigate two worlds. Back in the United States, I no longer have to wait months before hearing news—I remain connected via Facebook posts (from those friends visiting town) and opportunistic Skype chats. It has become hard to keep up with the Twitter feeds, YouTube videos, Pinterest posts, online marketplaces, and websites that support or promote Kayapó lifeways. The AFP has expanded in its scale and scope, and I continue to be involved in projects, such as a field course and new media center developments in the community, that are considered positive for their lifeways.

Yet the precarity of the future looms on the horizon. While chiefs continue to report their successes, the Belo Monte Dam, an upsurge in illegal gold mining, climate change, a troubled Brazilian and international economy, and changing forestry and indigenous land provisions all show that justice and a continued *mejkumrei* life remains at the forefront of community concerns. For indigenous peoples like the Kayapó, democratic rule and embracement of neodevelopmental policies have not directly translated to meaningful inclusion of indigenous voices in the decision-making process surrounding development in the Amazon region. Marcio would often comment that it was imperative to tell the Kayapó's story in order to raise awareness and activism efforts across the world. Marcio, who met Gordon and Anita Roddick while they were building the Body Shop project in A'Ukre years earlier, was recently in touch with James Cameron and had traveled extensively over Brazil. The most difficult thing for the Kayapó peoples, he said, was trying to raise money for meetings or travel to cities and other important locales. While his statements were not initially related to Belo Monte Dam—because the conflict over its construction had not intensified when I first began to work with him—in subsequent visits to the village, since 2006, Marcio has repeated the same worry to me. As one of many responses, I have found that revisiting conversations and lived experiences amassed over the course of my research, as Marcio suggested, will allow me to tell a small sliver of the story about the meaning that the Kayapó Lands have for communities today.

Concerned by the previous impact that large-scale development initiatives have had on Kayapó villages, the histories of marginalization of indigenous peoples, as well as the immediate and longer-term impact Belo Monte Dam and climatic changes will have, this book in part is a reply to Marcio in support of his hope that Kayapó stories will remain in motion. This book focuses on making indigenous territorialities, a reference that evokes both the poetics of Kayapó daily life, ongoing cosmovisions for the futures of their peoples, and non-Kayapó expressions of territory and territorialities. The Kayapó Lands have become a powerful, porous, and fortified borderland from which radical territories emerge. It is within these territories and territorialities that narratives, ideas, goods, and people cross and circulate for a more just future. Soja (1989, 63) relates, "Social and spatial structures are dialectically intertwined in social life, not just mapped one on the other as categorical projections." Certainly, we cannot begin to unpack the dramatic, politically charged landscape surrounding the Kayapó Lands without taking into consideration the political ecology of the region, as well as how Kayapó peoples continue to "make" and protect their livelihoods and homes from that very same landscape that is generative of life. As one Kayapó friend told me one night, sitting in the fire-lit circle of the village space, "Here is *mejkumrei*; it is good to live here."

Notes

Introduction

1. Originally part of modernization projects, development schemes were considered universal panaceas that would alleviate poverty, inequality, and marginality in what was then referred to as the Third World. In the 1950s many Latin American scholars took a "critical stance" to modernization, offering alternative approaches to development models that emerged as dependency theory and postcolonial theory. These approaches are presented in works by Raúl Prebisch, André Gunder Franck, and Fernando Henrique Cardoso, among others (Vanhulst and Beling 2014, 55).

2. The pillars of developmental thought are rooted in neoclassical economics, deriving first from the Keynesian school followed by a Smith inspired faith in the free reign of markets. The former is generally referred to as modernization and later the neoliberal era of development (Stiglitz 2002). By neoliberalism, I refer to the freeing up of markets "as a structural force that affects people's life chances and as an ideology of governance that shapes subjectivities" (Ganti 2014, 90). Both approaches still consider the North as the political-economic standard that other countries can model themselves after.

3. Also spelled Caiapó, Cayapó, and Kaiapó.

4. The Northern Kayapó peoples are distinguished from the Southern Kayapó, a non-Gê group originally designated as Kayapó around 1825. For their proximity to the gold and slave trade in the São Paulo region in the 16th, 17th, and 18th centuries, the Southern Kayapó were decimated as early as the 1900s. They have no linguistic or cultural relation to the Northern Kayapó but share the same name based on an observational error of an earlier chronicler. The name Southern Kayapó is used at times to designate the Pau D'Arco Kayapó, which were a distinctly different group from the above-mentioned Southern Kayapó. See Bamberger (1967) for a complete discussion of these labels and Hemming (1978) for a discussion on the Southern Kayapó in general. The Northern Kayapó are part of the northwest Gê speaking subgroup. Other large linguistic families in the Amazon are the Arawak-, Pano-, Carib-, Tucano-, and Tupi-speaking groups, although there are numerous medium- and small-sized linguistic groupings as well (Moore 2006).

5. The Body Shop website is available at http://www.thebodyshop-usa.com/

6. Since *buen vivir* attempts to capture diverse worldviews and also work as a political and legal instrument, the concept itself has many faces. For example, Guardiola and García-Quero (2014, 178) suggest there are two positions to *buen vivir*: "the extractive position [also referred to as neoextractivism and republican biosocialism], which views natural resources as tools for achieving *buen vivir*, and secondly the conservationist position, which emphasizes respect for nature and community relations as ways of maintaining *Buen Vivir*."

7. As Graham notes (2014, 312), "Amazonian symbolic economies of alterity privilege connections with the Other and incorporation of the Other as a basis of the self and collective."

8. Anthropologists have arguably always been engaged with and concerned about questions related to territoriality. Perhaps the most established, but also the most dated, approach to this topic derives from materialist and behaviorist theories that dominated the discipline from the 1950s to the 1970s (Binford 1980; Dyson-Hudson and Smith 1978). Proponents of these theories tended to focus on small-scale societies and their past and current relationships to geographical space (Eder 1984, 848). Although different iterations of this model are still being debated today, by the 1980s, the currents of anthropological theory were fundamentally shaped by world events, state-making projects, international conservation regimes, postcolonial conditions, indigenous movements, and intensified global flows, all of which demanded a reconfiguration of theories tied to culture and place (e.g., Clifford 2013; Gupta and Ferguson 1997a, 1997b). Many attribute this renewed scholarly attention to territoriality to the associated interest in space and place, as well as place-based politics, place-making, and placelessness.

9. Interestingly, this phrasing was possibly first used by the anthropologist Ella Cara Deloria in a 1934 letter. She writes, "With my college training, coupled with my Indian background lived in the days when it was a really Indian background, I stand on middle ground, and know both sides" (quoted in Cotera 2008:41).

10. Fenelon and Hall (2008), drawing attention to Coffey and Tsosie (2001), also note the multiple modes of governance indigenous and tribal nations participate in today (tribal, federal, and state). Fenelon and Hall (2008, 1872) further state that cultural sovereignty, or "rights to practice traditional ways of life, including language, religious beliefs, property values, and social systems toward relatives and family," constitutes the grounds from which many indigenous groups enact resistance efforts.

11. In particular, the 1969 landmark publication *Custer Died for Your Sins* by scholar Vine Deloria, Jr. criticized the relationship between the anthropological community and Native American and American Indians. I would add that this criticism extends to anthropological relationships to and history with many indigenous peoples across the globe. Deloria (1969) argued that anthropological scholarship had expertly confined communities within scientific discourse and, through the act of naming and writing, incarcerated communities, individuals, and lives in unproductive ways.

12. I am reminded of Anthony Seeger's research on the Suya, who also live in Central Brazil. Seeger (1981, 1) opens his ethnography thus: "The collection of data in anthropology is almost always the result of the fieldworker at a particular point in his life and theoretical formation and under certain circumstances of health and situation, working with a social group at a certain point in its own processes of change."

13. This is a reference to Jagger's (2008) edited volume by the same title.

14. See Seeger (2004, 93) and Siskind (1973). Anthony Seeger's innovative work with the Suya and songs reminds us of the importance of "doing" ethnography. In the late 1970s and early 1980s Seeger conducted fieldwork that explored why the Suya sing. The rigors of ceremonial singing, in which Seeger participated, answered a portion of these difficult questions and better elucidated what the Suya meant by "strong throat,"

"bad throat," and "beautiful throat," (Seeger 2004, 100) as he recognized through participation the vocal demands of continuous singing.

15. Grenier (1998, 46) defines guided field walks as when "the researcher and key consultants conduct a walking tour through areas of interest to observe, to listen, to identify different zones or conditions, and to ask questions to identify problems and possible solutions. With this method, the outsider can quickly learn about topography, soils, land use, forests, watersheds, and community assets." For more on map biographies, see Berkes et al. (1995).

16. During time spent in A'Ukre, I learned many names of plants, animals, fish, nuts, and fruits that were found around A'Ukre and that community members learned of from living in and traveling to other villages. As my permit did not allow me to collect any specimens, identification of these items by word of mouth posed a difficult task. I relied on several different methods to determine the Portuguese or scientific name to correspond with the Kayapó names. Animals and birds were identified based on their Portuguese names and crosschecked with resources I brought with me to A'Ukre: Emmons and Feer's *Neotropical Field Guide for Mammals*, Hilty's *Birds of Venezuela*, and the respective theses of Darrell Posey and Joan Bamberger (Bamberger 1967; Emmons and Feer 1997; Hilty 2003; Posey 1979). Later, I used photos I developed of different plants, animals, and fish, as well as Amazonian field guides, for interviewees to identify. For turtles and tortoises, I verified my data via personal communications with conservation biologists who have worked in the Kayapó area. I used Calvacante's tropical fruits field guide as well to verify data (Calvacante 1996). All errors in the analysis are my own.

Chapter 1

1. Drawing upon Schlosberg's approach to justice (2007), Sikor (2013, 7) defines distributive justice as "the distribution of goods and bads between different people" and procedural justice as "how decisions are made . . . including the attention to the roles of different people and rules governing decision-making."

2. The term Amazonia refers to the Amazon Basin in South America and encompasses Brazil, Peru, Colombia, Venezuela, Ecuador, Bolivia, Guyana, Suriname, and French Guiana. The Brazilian Amazon includes the states of Acre, Amapá, Amazonas, Pará, Rondônia, Roraima, and Tocantins. While most of the land cover is rainforest, savannah biomes and other vegetation is part of the terrain as well. The Kayapó's territory is currently located in Pará and Mato Grosso states. While Pará is considered part of the Brazilian Amazon, Mato Grosso is not. The Kayapó Lands are comprised of neotropical forest and savannah, so they cannot be characterized as strictly "forested." Equally problematic is that the Kayapó are often depicted as "forest" or "Amazonian" peoples, but their originary territory was vast, as oral histories show that they were in the savannah and other areas in Brazil.

3. Similarly, Alemán (2009, 195) notes that waves of "ecotourists and ethnotourists, evangelical missionaries, state officials, the Guyanese populace, poets and artists, and an international array of biological scientists, ethnographers, and development and NGO personnel" have produced historically contingent imagined cosmographies of

the Guyanese state, which intersect with but are not reflective of indigenous Waiwai cosmologies and senses of place. Also see the other works in this edited volume by Whitehead and Alemán (2009) for additional examples of ontological difference and territorial control in frontier regions.

4. For example, Turner (2008, 17) highlights the Kayapó origin myths this way: "The Kayapo possess a mythical account of the origin of the cosmos as a spatiotemporal continuum. It does presuppose the existence of a timeless and unstructured space as the raw material for the creation of space-time, but then so does the Biblical myth of Genesis presuppose the existence of the waters of the ocean and the spirit of God moving about over them." He refers to the myths about the tapir and the "fire" myth as important origin stories (2008, 18). For example,

> in the Kayapo myth, a primordial tapir (a reasonable stand-in for Jehovah) moves about over the land, gnawing down the trees that held up the disc of the sky, so that its edges fell to earth, creating the dome of the sky we see today . . . The Kayapo conception of the world, however, can best be understood not by starting from the myths of the creation of cosmic space-time, but from the actual source and model of Kayapo cosmological ideas, namely the Kayapo social universe as embodied by the village community and its surrounding region.

And "this fundamental point is succinctly made in the myths that tell of the differentiation of humans from animals and the origin of human culture. The most well-known of these is the story of the origin of cooking fire and its appropriation by humans" (ibid., 52). For the rest of the story see Turner (2008).

5. The Kayapó's spatial sphere is based on the symbolically important concept of a circle and includes horizontal and vertical spatial zones. The vertical aspect of Kayapó villages is an east–west trajectory modeled after the sun's path (Turner 2000, 21–22). Horizontal space is more elaborate in a "series of concentric circles" that spatially define different socioeconomic zones (Turner 1995c, 162).

6. Palm groves are not native to *terre firme* lands, but are found in numerous *terre firme* areas in the Amazonia, and are possibly a product of human disturbance. Palm forests can be found in the semideciduous (*terre firme*) forests near A'Ukre, but these were probably a product of human disturbance by nonindigenous occupants (Salm 2004b).

7. See also Lea's (2012) discussion of these earlier misconceptualizations of indigenous peoples.

8. In this section I focus on the Northern Kayapó. A group, labeled the Southern Kayapó, initially confused scholars as to the migrations and movements of present-day Kayapó communities. However, the Southern Kayapó were determined to be distinct and different from the Northern Kayapó, the group that is the focus of this chapter (Bamberger 1967). Coudreau is recognized as the first explorer to write about the "Cayapos Paraenses" ([or the Kayapó of Pará] Turner 1965; Vidal 1977). Coudreau observed four distinct Kayapó groups in the 1850s: the Pau d'Arco and Chicão, the Purucarus, the Chicris, and the Gorotíres, with an estimated total population size of five thousand (Arnaud 1989, 436; Bamberger 1971). However, the Kayapó are commonly divided historically into three, not four, major subgroupings. These groupings can be confirmed

as early as the 1850s: the Gorotíre, the Irã'ámranhre, (Graduas or Kayapó of the Araguaia, Pau d'Arco, and Chicão), and the Xikrin (also called Djore and Puwu'karwut), with estimated populations of 3,000 in each major subgrouping. This population estimate is on the conservative side, with some demographers calculating a much larger population (Hemming 1978). The Pau d'Arco were the first Kayapó subgroup to be contacted. This sudden and sustained contact with the Portuguese resulted in a drastic decimation of the Pau d'Arco's population in less than forty years (Arnaud 1989, 437). The last known Pau d'Arco Kayapó died in the village of Gorotíre in the 1960s (Arnaud 1989, 437). Today, life-sized black and white photos of Kayapó who visited the Museu Goeldi in Belém during this time period are haunting reminders of their important role in shaping Kayapó connections to research institutions and the tragic decimation that followed their early and sustained contact. Among the three groups, only the Gorotíre and the Xikrin have survived (Fisher 1991).

9. See Giraldin (1997) especially for an interesting discussion between the Panará (Kreen-Akrore) and the Kayapó, including their shared history of outsiders assigning them the same name "Kayapó" or "Caiapó." As noted earlier, scholars have charted the different histories between the Northern and Southern Kayapó.

10. Anthropologist Darrell Posey (2002a, 17–18) outlines a possible scenario of contact during the nineteenth and twentieth centuries. Posey's model is organized around three different types of exchange: indirect, intermediate, and direct.

11. Because of the corruption within the SPI, the SPI was abolished and replaced by FUNAI in 1967–1968.

12. This project, Comissão de Estudos e Planejamento do Problema Índio no Pará, concluded that pacification efforts should be conducted with traditional SPI pacification methods (Schmink and Wood 1992).

13. Gold was found on the reserve as early as the late 1970s, but extraction escalated in the 1980s (Merkens et al. 2002; Schmink and Wood 1992).

14. Brazil's landless population is approximately 4.8 million families, some of which belong to the Movimento dos Trabalhadores Rurais Sem Terra ([MST] National Landless Rural Workers Movement) (Fearnside 2001).

15. Hecht and Cockburn (1990, 161–62) note that a survey conducted in 1988 reported alarming amounts of mercury in Kayapó children. Mercury poisoning and toxicity, although not well documented among the Kayapó, posed a threat in the area as placer mining techniques contaminate rivers and fish—in other words Kayapó food sources—as well as provided other concerning means of direct and indirect contact.

16. Years after the recreation of FUNAI, the 1974 Indian Statute was passed. Like the statute before it, the Indian Statute of 1974 reinforced the concept of *tutela* (guardianship), which continued the paternalistic relationships indigenous groups had with the state.

17. The 1988 Brazilian constitution does not state anything about guardianship (Garfield 2001). The 1916 and subsequent Civil Code still sets precedence on guardianship and the legal rights of indigenous populations. Some indigenous groups have lobbied for the erasure of this clause (Ramos 1998). Groups like the Kayapó have historically been strong proponents of keeping the guardianship clause in place. Those

that are in favor of the clause argue that the concept of tutelage protects indigenous peoples' exceptional legal status that grants them collective land titles. If the clause were dismissed, many indigenous groups including the Kayapó would be unsure of how this translated into land rights. The guardianship clause is still under debate today.

18. The Carajás Iron Ore Project and Programa Integrado de Desenvolvimento do Noroeste do Brasil (Polonoroeste, Northwest Integrated Development Program) received US$2.8 billion in total investments from the World Bank (Redwood 2002, 2).

Chapter 2

1. As Turner (2009b, 164) has elsewhere stated, "there is thus no mutually exclusive distinction between 'society' and nonsocial 'nature' in the sense of a spatial boundary between village and forest; society is built upon, and thus includes, a 'natural' infrastructure."

2. Graham and Penny (2014, 9) also draw attention to a similar concept of "charismatic indigeneity," discussed by Perley in the same volume that emphasizes performance and staging as complicit in generating ideal notions of indigeneity. "Charismatic indigeniety" represents outsiders' imaginings of "real" indigenous groups and ideals that can never be met.

3. The repetitive circulation of these images in the media has the capacity to fuel the stereotype of the "noble savage" that has been dominant since colonization (see Lutz and Collins 1993). The staging of indigenous villages in the World's Fairs, the dehumanizing tour of the Hottentot Venus, and other similar spectacles have for the past several hundred years shaped the varied ways in which popular culture engaged with indigenous peoples (Griffiths 2002; Morton and Edwards 2009). These events, paired with images of noble savages exalted in paintings, narrative descriptions, and films, continue unhelpful stereotyping today (Spitulnik 1993).

4. Creating media "worlds" is certainly fitting phrasing. Ananya Roy and Aiwha Ong (2011, xv) employ "worlding" to suggest it is "a milieu that is in constant formation, one shaped by the multitudinous ongoing activities that by a wedding dream and technique, form the art of being global. Inherently unstable, inevitably subject to intense contestation, and always incomplete, worlding is the art of being global." Although divergent from Roy and Ong's original intention, Kayapó engagements with media and performative politics have certainly created a new "art of being global" that is routinely "subject to intense contestation."

5. As Santos-Granero (2009b, 7) notes, "Persons are not born as such, but must be intentionally manufacture [*sic*] or shape [*sic*] through the input of a variety of substances and affects provided by the parents and the kin (Londoño Sulkin 2005)." Also see Aracy Lopes da Silva's (1986) work on Xavante names and naming, as well as the oft-cited Seeger, da Matta, and Viveiros de Castro's (1979) article on personhood, which also comments on names and naming in Gê societies.

6. See Lea (2012) for a detailed discussion of naming and naming practices. Those described here are a simplified summation of a more complex reality.

7. In addition to names, infants and young children go through a series of different stages, ritually and corporeally expressed over the course of their first years. This is similar to what Fortis (2010, 482) has nicely described in Kuna communities: "When babies are born they are not yet considered fully human by their adult kinspeople.

8. Also see Bamberger (1974, 365–72).

9. See Turner (2009b) for an alternative understanding of *nekrêtch* and the way these valuables are passed down among individuals, households, and villagers.

10. Also important to note is that *nekrêtch* are not just passed on but can be a term that refers to "common" objects. It is contextually important to distinguish the *nekrêtch* that is part of ritual, and use of the term to refer to quotidian objects (Turner 2009b, 161).

11. Graham's (2005, 629) discussion of how Xavante men are proud of "their *a'uwẽ* (Xavante) identity and *a 'uwẽ-höimanazé'* (Xavante way of life, traditions)," and how "'*Auwẽ-höimanazé*' (or the generic form, '*da-höimanazé*') embraces everything that contemporary Xavante associate with their forebears," resonates with how villagers I worked with discussed their lifeways or "culture."

12. As Allard (2013, 545) nicely explains for the Warao, ritual wailing "can be intentionally managed and yet experienced as moving forces." By describing women's crying as wailing or keening here, I am not suggesting that their expression through formalized, ceremonial weeping removes emotion from the experience. See Vanessa Lea (2004) on Kayapó wailing as oratory for a further discussion of this practice in Kayapó communities. Also see Briggs (1992, 1993), Urban (1988), and Graham (1986) for additional commentary on vocal expressions and reported speech in indigenous communities in Latin America.

13. Graham (1995) also has a similar discussion of changing Xavante practices in her ethnography *Performing Dreams*.

14. The 1998 article was an English version of a 1996 Portuguese publication on the same subject. Several of Viveiros de Castro's lectures on this topic in 1998 were published in volume 1 of *HAU*'s 2012 Masterclass Series entitled Cosmological Perspective in Amazonia and Elsewhere: Four Lectures Given in the Department of Social Anthropology, Cambridge University, February–March 1998. These lectures now join a corpus of work on this issue that Viveiros de Castro has published widely on.

15. Or more appropriately, drawing on Ingold, Viveiros de Castro (1998, 479) notes that Western scientific notions of humanity both place us within the animal kingdom and distinguish humans as distinct moral beings from animality. These distinctions, although ambiguous, place humans (culture) and nature as antinomies.

16. For more recent engagements with multinatural perspectivism and its limitations see Turner (2009a), Ramos (2012), Sáez (2012), and Rosengren (2015). For additional critiques see Descola (2013) and his other works.

17. Turner (2009b, 165) further explains, "the socialized (painted, coiffured, and ornamented) human body, as the form of the social person, is the site where the animal or 'natural' aspects of human existence and the 'cultural' aspects of social personhood associated with gender, generation, kinship, and other social roles converge."

18. Some interviewees noted that only certain individuals or households could hunt for or care for macaws; others thought this practice was more open to all community members.

19. For example, in thinking about soundscapes of villages, Graham (1995, 64) describes the sounds in an indigenous Xavante community this way, "If you stop to listen, you hear the din of dogs barking, chickens clucking, babies crying, the thump of wooden mortars as women pound the husks from rice, children's laughter, and voices; above all you hear voices, the murmur of people talking, conversing inside and outside of houses." In this same chapter, Graham also describes other vocalizations and soundscapes that animate daily and seasonal cycles of village life.

Chapter 3

1. Hames (1983) has developed the notion of polyvarieties in swidden systems. Boster (1985) has furthered our understanding of the selection criteria of cultivars, especially in relationship to manioc. In this same article, Boster (1985) provides an overview of research conducted on cultivar selection and taxonomic characteristics.

2. See Berlin (1992:5) and his description of "why it is notable that nonliterates 'know so much' about nature" and Boster (1985: 315) on why "humans are natural historians by nature."

3. See Rosaldo's (1989, 114) comments on Conklin's work.

4. Some suggest ethnobiology was practiced as early as 1935 and that it was Johnson in 1974 who solidified ethnoecology as a subfield in its own right (Hunn 2007).

5. Also see Ellen's (2006, S1); Ellen describes the field as a biological, archeohistorical, and sociocultural pursuit that is an "important intellectual junction between biology, culture, and sociality." Ellen (2006, S1) defines ethnobiology as follows: "Today, ethnobiology is, first and foremost, the study of how people of all, and of any, cultural tradition interpret, conceptualize, represent, cope with, utilize, and generally manage their knowledge of those domains of environmental experience, which encompass living organisms, and whose scientific study we demarcate as botany, zoology, and ecology."

6. This project generated many publications, such as Anderson and Posey (1985), Elizabetsky and Posey (1986), Posey (1983, 1986, 1987), Camargo and Posey (1990), Hecht and Posey (1990), and Overal and Posey (1990). The coauthored paper by a Kayapó chief and a Western-trained scientist is an interesting publication that emerged out of Posey's dedication to pushing forward ethnobiological knowledge (Megaron-Txukarramãe and Stout 1990). However, indigenous authorship is notably absent in other scholarly papers produced from this project. Research topics covered the ethnoentomology of several key species that the Kayapó use in their agricultural fields ([Azteca ants] Overal and Posey 1990), food procuring strategies ([honey from Meliponinae, *Apidae Hymenoptera*] Camargo and Posey 1990), ceremonial practices ([wasps]) Overal and Posey 1984), and possible protein sources. Elizabetsky and Posey (1986) explored

the pharmaceutical properties of plants utilized by the Kayapó, characteristic of the first wave of ethnoecological research.

7. See Posey (1992) for his reply to Parker. Also see Hecht (2009) for a reappraisal of the debate.

8. The critiques of Posey's work should also be a warning to researchers to reevaluate ideas about indigenous conservationism (commonly referred to as the "Ecological Indian" debate) and distinguish between voluntary conservationism and indirect biodiversity preservation while at the same time recognizing indigenous cosmovisions (Kretch 1999; Smith and Wishnie 2000).

9. Posey (1985) argued that species in these trails or wild domesticates are planted by the Kayapó; although, no consultant in A'Ukre would corroborate this claim. What is more likely is that agricultural practices yield a diverse array of intentionally and unintentionally planted crops in the disturbed areas. Many of these areas fringe the garden trails and might perhaps be the source of this claim.

10. Lathrap (1970), Wilson and Dufour (2002), and Wilson (2003) discuss preferences among Amazonian groups for growing more of the toxic bitter manioc than its nontoxic relative, sweet manioc.

11. Prytupi's sister's kids. According to Kayapó kinship terms, female ego's kids and female ego's sister's kids are all called *kra*.

12. For the evolutionary characteristics of manioc (also commonly referred to as cassava or yucca), see Sambatti, Martins, and Ando (2001, 93), who argue that manioc "is perhaps the most important crop in swidden cultivation in the lowland tropical Americas."

13. In addition to baskets, women would also recycle woven plastic sacks (from urban supermarkets) to increase the volume of their load. The sack method was especially useful to add more to already full loads. Alternatively, some households with closer gardens started to use wheelbarrows to transport harvests; however, using baskets was the dominant method. In the case of transporting bananas, on the other hand, they would line their backs with banana leaves when carrying sappy bundles of bananas.

14. *Terra preta*'s fertility is often juxtaposed with other soils found in *terra firme* lands that are "highly weathered, acidic, [and have] low carbon-exchange capacity . . . low fertility and, consequently, low crop production potential" (Novotny et al. 2009, 1003; see also Cunha et al. 2009).

15. See Hecht (2009) and Hecht and Posey (1989) for an in-depth analysis of Kayapó fire ecology practices.

16. In that vein, anthropologists working in a nearby area in Brazil, the Xingu National Park, just south of the Kayapó Lands, have recently presented interesting research findings that might help with understanding Kayapó practices. The Kuikuro, a Xingu indigenous group, also prefer to plant a diversity of crops in soils identified as *terra preta* and to plant staple crops in the close-by red soils. Additionally, the Kuikuro find ceramics and structures from previous settlements in and around their agricultural fields (Schmidt and Heckenberger 2009, 163).

17. Also note the rattan–swidden system described by Weinstock (1983).

Chapter 4

1. Portions of this chapter appear in Zanotti (2009).

2. Shackleton (2014, 696) provides an especially useful definition of NTFPs, which he notes "can include floral products such as grasses, roots, flower, fruits, and bamboo, which people use for a variety of purposes . . . as well as faunal products such as insects, birds, fish, or game."

3. *Pidjô* is a general term for fruit (*pi* means "tree" or "wood").

4. Consumers are receptive to this type of product (Igoe 2010; O'Dougherty 2002). Culturally and environmentally sensitive products have become more mainstream since the 1990s. Rubenstein (2009, 137) relates, "Consumers do not see their individual identities as mediated by the marketplace, their choices manufactured by the world economy in response to shifts in labor and capital. Rather, they see consumption as mediated by their individuality, with the result that consumption becomes 'the production of personal style.'" The "production of personal style" is part of the way in which different, desired subjectivities are developed by metrospiritual consumers.

5. For more on the Body Shop, see Morsello (2002, 2006), Ros-Tonen et al. (2008), and Terence Turner (1995b). The most recent manifestation of this includes beauty bags decorated by the Kayapó available for purchase through companies like Teadora (http://www.teadorabeauty.com/kayapo).

6. Crumley (1993, 378) defines historical ecology as "the study of past ecosystems by charting the change in landscape over time" and as tracing "the ongoing dialectical relations between human acts and acts of nature, made manifest in the *landscape*" (Crumley 1994, 9, italics in original).

7. Balée (1994, 1) emphasizes that a historical ecological approach is "a powerful paradigm for comprehending interrelationships between Amazonian environments and associated indigenous societies because it focuses on the interpenetration of culture and the environment rather than on the adaptation of human beings to the environment."

8. For instance, recently found geoglyphs in Brazil's Acre state are shown to extend into the Peruvian Amazon and represent previously unknown, large-scale landscape modifications that took place across geopolitical borders and new information on the ways in which past inhabitants have used the land. In another site, irrigation works found in Llanos de Moxos, Bolivia, which borders the Amazon, are thought to have played a critical role in sustainable agricultural production and large-scale landscape modification strategies (Ranzi, Feres, and Brown 2007; Schaan et al. 2007). In the Xingu area of the Central Brazilian Amazon, archaeological and ethnohistorical research has found that polities, or what look like vast regional trade networks among different groups, existed and left indelible marks on the land (Heckenberger 2006).

9. According to Fuentes (2010, 600) "'Structural ecology' involves the study of the biotic landscape and physical environment in which creatures, such as humans and macaques live. 'Social ecology' asks after how different agents navigate and create social networks, sometimes across species lines (Latour 1993; see also Popielarz and Neal 2007); it keeps the forces of history, political economy, interindividual relationships and culture clearly in view."

10. See also Nadasdy (2003) for a more detailed discussion of Western notions of property and rights and how they can be mismatched with indigenous considerations of the same landscapes.

11. Clement (2006, 2009) discusses fruit tree distribution as it affects landscape composition over time.

12. Brazil nuts are technically seeds, but the common usage name remains *nut* in both English and Portuguese. In Kayapó, *y* translates to "seed."

13. Fisher (2000) and Gordon (2006) provide a detailed description of the Xikrin relationship with Vale.

Chapter 5

1. This chapter draws from Zanotti (2014a).

2. Hybridity is a capacious term, which has been described by Marwan Kraidy (2002, 318) as one of "conceptual ambiguity" and "epistemological uncertainty," and it has strongholds in cultural studies, indigenous studies, postcolonial theory, anthropology, and other disciplines. Gilroy (1993), Bhabha (1994), and others, are often considered some of the main and influential thinkers that critically addressed hybridity as a conceptual frame. A review of hybridity is beyond the scope of this chapter, although I do address it here as applicable to the confluence of political ecology work and science and technology studies. Other seminal work, for example, Hutnyk (2005) who critiques hybridity as a concept that often does not address racial and ethnic identities in the context of politics and economics, have also challenged hybridity on its colonial underpinnings. On the other hand, Kraidy (2002, 319) explains that seminal work from Werbner and Modood (1997), Joseph and Fink (1999), and Gómez-Peña (1996) have challenged this stance, highlighting Joseph's (1991, 1) description of hybridity "as a disruptive democratic discourse of cultural citizenship" that is a "distinctly anti-imperial and antiauthoritarian development." For one review of hybridity see Rubdy and Alsagoff (2014).

3. Topics include data on economically valuable tree species, market participation among the Kayapó, the effect of logging on mammal communities, ecology of species that have subsistence and ceremonial value to the Kayapó, and other important species in neotropical environments (Baider 2000; Salm 2004a; Scheffler 2002).

4. For example, villagers in A'Ukre are part of a Plano Básico Ambiental (Basic Environmental Plan) with Onça Puma, a mining company based out of Ourilândia do Norte.

5. The Environmental Defense Fund has played a role in the area since its efforts are linked with the Paraná indigenous group. The Paraná inhabit Indigenous Lands adjacent to the southwest border of the Kayapó territories.

Chapter 6

1. Article 231 (1) 1988 constitution grants indigenous peoples "original right to the lands traditionally occupied by them," but "indigenous lands are federal lands forming part of the Union's exclusive domain, and . . . the exploitation of water resources on these lands is subject to previous legislative authorization, which entitles indigenous

communities to be heard at specific public hearings (Article 231[3])" (da Costa 2014, 18). The constitution also "requires public participation in decision-making processes, decisions on the construction of dams and the flooding of land are now taken jointly by society, a number of government institutions and especially the population affected" (da Costa 2014, 14). The protection of indigenous groups' rights lie with FUNAI and the Ministry of Justice.

2. See McLean (2009) for a discussion on creativity as it relates to nature-culture debates and capitalist engagement.

3. Although I emphasize the importance of Rio +20 here, a multitude of other convention and multilateral agreements also dominate the current landscape of environmental governance on the international stage. Too numerous to outline here, some other prominent agreements or protocols have been the Millennium Ecosystem Assessment, Convention on Biological Diversity, Convention on International Trade in Endangered Species of Wild Fauna and Flora, and the UNFCCC.

Bibliography

Accioli, C., and S. Monteiro. 2011. "Brazil: World's Breadbasket." *The Brazilian Economy* 3 (11): 14–21.

Agarwal, Bina. 1992. "The Gender and Environment Debate: Lessons from India." *Feminist Studies* 18 (1): 119–158.

Agnew, J. 1994. "The Territorial Trap: The Geographical Assumptions of International Relations Theory." *Review of International Political Economy* 1 (1): 53–80.

———. 2010. "Still Trapped in Territory?" *Geopolitics* 15 (4): 779–84.

Agrawal, Arun. 1995. "Dismantling the Divide Between Indigenous and Scientific Knowledge." *Development and Change* 26 (3): 413–39.

———. 2005. "Environmentality." *Current Anthropology* 46 (2): 161–90.

Alemán, Stephanie W. 2009. "Inhabiting the Imagined Space: Constructing Waiwai Identity in the Deep South of Guyana." In *Anthropologies of Guayana: Cultural Spaces in Northeastern Amazonia*, edited by Neil Whitehead and Stephanie W. Alemán, 194–206. Tucson: University of Arizona Press.

Alkon, Alison Hope, and Julian Agyeman. 2011. *Cultivating Food Justice: Race, Class, and Sustainability*. Boston: The MIT Press.

Alkon, Alison Hope, and Teresa Marie Mares. 2012. "Sovereignty in US Food Movements: Radical Visions and Neoliberal Constraints." *Agriculture and Human Values* 29 (3): 347–59.

Allard, O. 2013. "To Cry One's Distress: Death, Emotion, and Ethics Among the Warao of the Orinoco Delta." *Journal of the Royal Anthropological Institute* 19 (3): 545–61.

Altieri, Miguel A. 1987. *Agroecology: The Scientific Basis of Alternative Agriculture*. Boulder, CO: Westview Press.

———. 1989. "Agroecology: A New Research and Development Paradigm for World Agriculture." *Agriculture, Ecosystems and Environment* 27 (1-4): 37–46.

———. 1993. "Ethnoscience and Biodiversity: Key Elements in the Design of Sustainable Pest Management Systems for Small Farmers in Developing Countries." *Agriculture, Ecosystems and Environment* 46 (1–4): 257–72.

Altieri, Miguel, and Victor Manuel Toledo. 2011. "The Agroecological Revolution in Latin America: Rescuing Nature, Ensuring Food Sovereignty and Empowering Peasants." *Journal of Peasant Studies* 38 (3): 587–612.

Amazon Watch. 2013. "Welcome Mayalú!" Available at http://amazonwatch.org/news/2013/0918-welcome-mayalu, accessed March 10, 2014.

———. 2015. "Victory on the Xingu: Belo Monte Denied Operational License." Available at http://amazonwatch.org/news/2015/0923-victory-on-the-xingu-belo-monte-denied-operational-license, accessed September 23, 2015.

Anderson, Anthony B., and Edviges M. Ioris. 1992. "Valuing the Rain Forest: Economic Strategies by Small-Scale Forest Extractivists in the Amazon Estuary." *Human Ecology* 20 (3): 337–69.

Anderson, Anthony. B., and Darrell A. Posey. 1985. "Manejo de Cerrado Pelos Índios Kayapó." *Museu Paranes Emílio Goeldi, Series Boletim* 2 (1): 77–98.

Anderson, Eugene N. 1974. "The Life and Culture of Ecotopia." In *Reinventing Anthropology*, edited by Dell Hymes, 264–83. New York: Vintage Books.

Anderson, Eugene N., Deborah Pearsall, Eugene Hunn, and Nancy Turner. 2011. *Ethnobiology*. Hoboken, NJ: John Wiley and Sons.

Anguelovski I., and Martínez Alier J. 2014. "The 'Environmentalism of the Poor' Revisited: Territory and Place in Disconnected Global Struggles." *Ecological Economics* 10 (2): 167–76.

Appadurai, A. 1996. *Modernity at Large: Cultural Dimensions of Globalization*. Minneapolis: University of Minnesota Press.

Arnaud, Expedito. 1989. *O Índio e a Expansão Nacional*. Belém: Editora Cejup.

Arnold, J. E. Michael, and M. Ruiz Pérez. 2001. "Can Non-Timber Forest Products Match Tropical Forest Conservation and Development Objectives?" *Ecological Economics* 39 (3): 437–47.

Asad, Talal. 1975. *Anthropology and the Colonial Encounter*. London: Ithaca Press.

Asara, V., I. Otero, F. Demaria, and E. Corbera. 2015. "Socially Sustainable Degrowth as a Social–Ecological Transformation: Repoliticizing Sustainability." *Sustainability Science* 103 (3): 375–84.

Augé, M. 2008. *Non-Places: An Introduction to Supermodernity*, translated by John Howe. New York: Verso.

Baider, Claudia. 2000. "Demografia e ecologia de dispersão de frutos de Bertolletia Excelsa Humb. and Bonpl. (Lecythidacea) em castanhais silvestres da Amazônia Oriental." PhD diss., Departamento de Ecologia, Instituto de Biociências, Universidade de São Paulo.

Balée, William. 1989. "The Culture of Amazonian Forests." In *Resource Management in Amazonia: Indigenous and Folk Strategies*, edited by Darrell A. Posey and William Balée, 1–21. Bronx, NY: New York Botanical Garden.

———. 1992. "People of the Fallow: A Historical Ecology of Foraging in Lowland South America." In *Conservation of Neotropical Forests: Working from Traditional Resource Use*, edited by K. H. Redford and C. Padoch, 35–57. New York: Columbia University Press.

———. 1994. *Footprints of the Forest: Ka'apor Ethnobotany—The Historical Ecology of Plant Utilization by an Amazonian People*. New York: Columbia University Press.

———. 2006 "The Research Program of Historical Ecology." *Annual Review of Anthropology* 35: 75–98.

Baletti, Brenda. 2012. "Ordenamento Territorial: Neo-developmentalism and the Struggle for Territory in the Lower Brazilian Amazon." *The Journal of Peasant Studies* 39 (2): 573–98.

Ballinger, Pamela. 2004. "'Authentic Hybrids' in the Balkan Borderlands." *Current Anthropology* 45 (1): 31–60.

Bamberger, Joan. 1967. "Environment and Cultural Classification: A Study of the Northern Cayapo." PhD diss., Harvard University.

———. 1971. "The Adequacy of Kayapó Ecological Adjustment." Proceedings, *International Conference of Americanists* 38 (3): 373–79.

———. 1974. "Names and the Transmission of Status in a Central Brazilian Society." *Ethnology* 13 (4): 362–78.

Banks, Marcus, and Jay Ruby. 2011. *Made to Be Seen: Perspectives on the History of Visual Anthropology*. Chicago: University of Chicago Press.

Barham, Bradford L., and Oliver T. Coomes. 1994. "Reinterpreting the Amazon Rubber Boom: Investment, the State, and Dutch Disease." *Latin American Research Review* 29 (2): 73–109.

Barreto, Paulo, Carlos S. Jr., Anthony Anderson, Rodney Salomão, Janice Wiles, and Ruth Noguerón. 2005. "Human Pressure on the Brazilian Amazon—Report 3." IMAZON *State of the Amazon Report* 3: 1–6.

Barrionuevo, Alexei. 2007. "To Fortify China, Soybean Harvest Grows in Brazil." *New York Times*, April 6. Available at http://www.nytimes.com/2007/04/06/business/world business/06soy.html?oref=slogin&_r=0, accessed December 10, 2014.

Basso, Keith H. 1996. *Wisdom Sits in Places: Landscape and Language Among the Western Apache*. Albuquerque: University of New Mexico Press.

Bebbington, Anthony. 2000. "Reencountering Development: Livelihood Transitions and Place Transformations in the Andes." *Annals of the Association of American Geographers* 90 (3): 495–520.

———. 2012. "Underground Political Ecologies: The Second Annual Lecture of the Cultural and Political Ecology Specialty Group of the Association of American Geographers." *Geoforum* 43 (6): 1152–62.

Beck, Ulrich. 1992. *Risk Society: Towards a New Modernity*. Thousand Oaks, CA: Sage Publications.

Beckerman, Stephen. 1983a. "Does the Swidden Ape the Jungle?" *Human Ecology* 11 (1): 1–12.

———. 1983b. "Barí Swidden Gardens: Crop Segregation Patterns." *Human Ecology* 11 (1): 85–101.

Behar, Ruth. 1996. *Vulnerable Observer: Anthropology that Breaks your Heart*. Boston: Beacon Press.

Berkes, Fikret. 1999. *Sacred Ecology: Traditional Ecological Knowledge and Resource Management*. Ann Arbor: Taylor and Francis.

———. 2004. "Rethinking Community-Based Conservation." *Conservation Biology* 18 (3): 621–30.

———. 2007. "Community-Based Conservation in a Globalized World." *Proceedings of the National Academy of Sciences of the United States* 104 (39): 15188–93.

Berkes, Fikret, A. Hughes, P. J. George, R. J. Preston, B. D. Cummins, and J. Turner. 1995. "The Persistence of Aboriginal Land Use: Fish and Wildlife Harvest Areas in the Hudson and James Bay Lowland, Ontario." *Arctic* 48 (1): 81–93.

Berlin, B. 1992. *Ethnobiological Classification: Principles of Categorization of Plants and Animals in Traditional Societies*. Princeton, NJ: Princeton University Press.

Bernard, H. Russell. 2011. *Research Methods in Anthropology: Qualitative and Quantitative Approaches*, 5th edition. Lanham, MD: AltaMira Press.

Besky, Sarah. 2008. "Can a Plantation be Fair? Paradoxes and Possibilities in Fair Trade Darjeeling Tea Certification." *Anthropology of Work Review* 29 (1): 1–9.

Bessire, Lucas. 2014. *Behold the Black Caiman: A Chronicle of Ayoreo Life*. Chicago: University of Chicago Press.

Bessire, Lucas, and David Bond. 2014. "Ontological Anthropology and the Deferral of Critique. *American Ethnologist* 41: 440–56.

Bessire, Lucas, and Daniel Fisher. 2012. *Radio Fields Anthropology and Wireless Sound in the 21st Century*. New York, NY: NYU Press.

Bhabha, Homi. 1994. *The Location of Culture*. London: Routledge.

Biersack, Aletta. 2006. "Reimaging Political Ecology Culture/Power/History/Nature." In *Reimagining Political Ecology*, edited by Aletta Biersack and James B. Greenburg, 3–42. Durham, NC: Duke University Press.

Binford, Lewis R. 1980. "Willow Smoke and Dogs' Tails: Hunter-Gatherer Settlement Systems and Archaeological Site Formation." *American Antiquity* 45 (1): 4–20.

Biolsi, Thomas, ed. 1997. *Indians and Anthropologists: Vine Deloria, Jr. and the Critique of Anthropology*. Tucson: University of Arizona Press.

Bird Rose, Deborah. 1996. *Nourishing Terrains*. Canberra: Australia Heritage Commission.

Blaikie, P. M., and H. Brookfield, eds. 1987. *Land Degradation and Society*. London and New York: Methuen.

Blanco, Michel. 2006. "Entrevista: Paulinho Paiakan, Longe do Silêncio." *Indígena* 3 (4): 2–7.

Blaser, Mario, Ravi de Costa, Deborah McGregor, and William D. Coleman. 2010. "Reconfiguring the Web of Life: Indigenous Peoples, Relationality, and Globalization." In *Indigenous Peoples and Autonomy: Insights for a Global Age*, edited by Mario Blaser, Ravi de Costa, Deborah McGregor, and William D. Coleman, 3–26. Vancouver: University of British Columbia Press.

Bodirsky, Monica, and Jon Johnson. 2008. "Decolonizing Diet: Healing by Reclaiming Traditional Indigenous Foodways." *Cuizine* 1 (1). Available at: https://www.erudit.org/revue/cuizine/2008/v1/n1/019373ar.html, accessed March 22, 2016.

Boster, James Shilts. 1985. "Selection for Perceptual Distinctiveness: Evidence from Aguaruna Cultivars of Manihot Esculenta." *Economic Botany* 39 (3): 310–25.

Briggs, C. L. 1992. "'Since I Am a Woman, I Will Chastise My Relatives': Gender, Reported Speech, and the (Re)Production of Social Relations in Warao Ritual Wailing." *American Ethnologist* 19 (2): 337–61.

———. 1993. "Personal Sentiments and Polyphonic Voices in Warao Women's Ritual Wailing: Music and Poetics in a Critical and Collective Discourse." *American Anthropologist* 95 (4): 929–57.

Brody, Hugh. 1985. *Maps and Dreams: Indians and the British Columbian Frontier*. London: J. Norman and Hobhouse.

Brondizío, Eduardo. 2008. *The Amazonian Caboclo and the Açaí Palm: Forest Farmers in the Global Market*. New York: New York Botanical Garden.

———. 2009. "Agriculture Intensification, Economic Identity, and Shared Invisibility in Amazonian Peasantry: Caboclos and Colonists in Comparative Perspective." In *Amazon Peasant Societies in a Changing Environment: Political Ecology, Invisibility and Modernity in the Rainforest*, edited by Cristina Adams, Rui Murrieta, Walter Neves, and Mark Harris, 181–214. Dordrecht, The Netherlands: Springer.

Brondizío, Eduardo, C. C. M. Safar, and A. D. Siqueira. 2002. "The Urban Market of Açaí Fruit (Euterpe Oleracea Mart.) and Rural Land Use Change: Ethnographic Insights into the Role of Price and Land Tenure Constraining Agricultural Choices in the Amazon Estuary." *Urban Ecosystems* 6 (1–2): 67–98.

Brosius, J. Peter, and Sarah L. Hitchner. 2010. "Cultural Diversity and Conservation." *International Social Science Journal* 61 (199): 141–68.

Brosius, J. Peter, and D. Russell. 2003. "Conservation from Above: An Anthropological Perspective on Transboundary Protected Areas and Ecoregional Planning." *Journal of Sustainable Forestry* 17 (1–2): 39–66.

Brosius, J. Peter, Anna Tsing, and Charles Zerner. 1998. "Representing Communities: Histories and Politics of Community-Based Natural Resource Management." *Society and Natural Resources* 11 (2): 157–68.

Browder, John O., and Brian J Godfrey. 1997. *Rainforest Cities: Urbanization, Development, and Globalization of the Brazilian Amazon*. New York: Columbia University Press.

Brown, Michael F. 1998. "Can Culture be Copyrighted?" *Current Anthropology* 39 (2): 193–222.

———. 2003. *Who Owns Native Culture?* Cambridge, MA: Harvard University Press.

Bruni, Frank. 2010. "Nordic Chef Explores Backyard." *New York Times*, July 7, 2010: D1. Available at http://www.nytimes.com/2010/07/07/dining/07chef.html?pagewanted=all &_r=0, accessed January 12, 2015.

Brush, Stephan B. 1975. "The Concept of Carrying Capacity for Systems of Cultivation." *American Anthropologist* 77 (4): 799–810.

———. 1993. "Indigenous Knowledge of Biological Resources and Intellectual Property Rights: The Role of Anthropology." *American Anthropologist* 95 (3): 653–86.

Bryan, Joe. 2012. "Rethinking Territory: Social Justice and Neoliberalism in Latin America's Territorial Turn." *Geography Compass* 6 (4): 215–26.

Büscher, Bram, Sian Sullivan, Katja Neves, Jim Igoe, and Dan Brockington. 2012. "Towards a Synthesized Critique of Neoliberal Biodiversity Conservation." *Capitalism Nature Socialism* 23 (2): 4–30.

Byrd, Jodi A. 2014. "Tribal 2.0: Digital Natives, Political Players, and the Power of Stories." *Studies in American Indian Literatures* 26 (2): 55–64.

Cadieux, K. V., and R. Slocum. 2015. "What Does it Mean to do Food Justice." *Journal of Political Ecology* 22 (1): 1–26.

Cajete, Gregory. 2000. *Native Science: Natural Laws of Interdependence*, 1st edition. Santa Fe, NM: Clear Light Publishers.

Callon, M. 1986. "Some Elements of a Sociology of Translation: Domestication of the Scallops and the Fishermen of St. Brieuc Bay." In *Power, Action and Belief: A New Sociology of Knowledge?*, edited by J. Law, 196–223. London: Routledge.

Callon, M., and J. Law. 1995. "Agency and the Hybrid Collectif." *South Atlantic Quarterly* 94 (2): 481–507.

Calvacante, Paulo B. 1996. *Frutas Comestíveis da Amazônia*. Belém: Museu Paraense Emílio Goeldi.

Camargo, Isabel, and Monica Hitatchi Mekaru. 2006. *Plano de Negócios Castanha do Brasil: Aukre, Moikarako, Kikretum*. São Paulo: Instituto Brasileiro de Educação em Negócios Sustanaveis.

Camargo, J. M. F., and Darrell A. Posey. 1990. "O Conhecimento dos Kayapó sobre as Abelhas Sociais sem Ferrão (Meliponinae, Apidae Hymenoptera); Notas Adicionais." *Boletim Museu Paranese Emílio Goeldi, Série Zoologia* 6 (1): 17–42.

Campbell, Jeremy M. 2015. "Indigenous Urbanization in Amazonia: Interpretive Challenges and Opportunities." *The Journal of Latin American and Caribbean Anthropology* 20 (1): 80–86.

Canessa, Andrew. 2012. *Intimate Indigeneities: Race, Sex, and History in the Small Spaces of Andean Life*. Durham NC: Duke University Press.

Cardoso, Catarina. 2002. *Extractive Reserves in the Brazilian Amazon: Local Resource Management and the Global Political Economy*. Burlington, VT: Ashgate.

Carneiro, Robert L. 1960. "Slash and Burn Agriculture: A Closer Look at its Implications for Settlement Patterns." In *Men and Cultures*, edited by A. F. C. Wallace, 229–34. Philadelphia: University of Pennsylvania Press.

Cepek, Michael. 2012. *A Future of Amazonia: Randy Borman and Cofán Environmental Politics*. Austin: University of Texas Press.

Chakrabarty, D. 2000. *Provincializing Europe: Postcolonial Thought and Historical Difference*. Princeton, NJ: Princeton University Press.

Chapin, Mac, Zachary Lamb, and Bill Threlkeld. 2005. "Mapping Indigenous Lands." *Annual Review of Anthropology* 34: 619–38.

Charnley, Susan, and Melissa R. Poe. 2007. "Community Forestry in Theory and Practice: Where Are We Now?" *Annual Review of Anthropology* 36: 301–36.

Chernela, Janet. 1986. "Os Cultivares de Mandioca na Área do Uapés (Tukano)." In *Suma Ethnológica Brasileira*, vol. 1, edited by Berta G. Ribeiro, 151–58. Petrópolis: Vozes, FINEP.

———. 2005. "The Politics of Mediation: Local-Global Interactions in the Central Amazon of Brazil." *American Anthropologist* 107 (4): 620–31.

———. 2006. "Actualidades, Lex Talionis: Recent Advances and Retreats in Indigenous Rights in Brazil." *Journal of Latin American Anthropology* 11 (1): 138–53.

Chernela, Janet, and Laura Zanotti. 2014. "Limits to Knowledge: Indigenous Peoples, NGOs, and the Moral Economy in the Eastern Amazon of Brazil." *Conservation and Society* 12 (3): 306–17.

Choy, Timothy K., Lieba Faier, Michael J. Hathaway, Miyako Inoue, Shiho Satsuka, and Anna Tsing. 2009. "A New Form of Collaboration in Cultural Anthropology: Matsutake Worlds." *American Ethnologist* 36 (2): 380–403.

Clement, Charles R. 2006. "Fruit Trees and the Transition to Food Production in Amazonia." *In Time, Complexity, and Historical Ecology*, edited by W. Balée and Clark L. Erickson, 165–86. New York: Columbia University Press.

———. 2009. "Domestication of Amazonian Fruit Crops—Past, Present, Future." In *Diversidade Biologica e Cultural da Amazonia*, 2nd edition, edited by Ima Celia Guimaraes Vieira, Jose Maria Cardoso da Silva, David Conway Oren, and Maria Angela D'Incao, 351–72. Belém: Museu Paraense Emilio Goeldi.

Clendenning, Alan. 2008. "Indians Attack Brazil Official with Machetes in Protest." *National Geographic.* http://news.nationalgeographic.com/news/2008/05/080521-AP-indians-dam .htm, accessed January 15, 2015.

Clifford, James. 1988. *The Predicament of Culture.* Boston: Harvard University Press.

———. 1997. *Routes: Travel and Translation in the Late Twentieth Century.* Boston: Harvard University Press.

———. 2013. *Returns.* Cambridge, MA: Harvard University Press.

Coelho de Souza, Marcela. 2002. "O Traço e o Círculo: O Conceito de Parentesco entre os Jê e seus Anthropólogos." PhD diss., Federal University of Rio de Janeiro.

———. 2010. "A Vida Material das Coiasa Intangíveis." In *Conhecimento e Cultural*, edited by Marcela Coelho de Souza and Edine Coffaci de Lima, 97–118. Brasília: Programa Nacional de Cooperação Acadêmica/ Coordenação de Aperfeiçoamento de Pessoal de Nível Superior.

Coffey, Wallace, and Rebecca Tsosie. 2001. "Rethinking the Tribal Sovereignty Doctrine: Cultural Sovereignty and the Collective Future of Indian Nations." *Stanford Law and Policy Review* 12 (2): 191–221.

Cohn, Clarice. 2010. "Belo Monte e Processos de Licenciamento Ambiental: As Percepções e As Atuações dos Xikrin e dos seus Antropólogos." *Revista de Antropologia Social dos Alunos do PPGAS-UFSCar* 2 (2): 224–51.

Conklin, Beth. 1997. "Body Paint, Feathers, and VCRs: Aesthetics and Authenticity in Amazonian Activist." *American Ethnologist* 24 (4): 711–34.

———. 2002. "Shamans versus Pirates in the Amazonian Treasure Chest." *American Anthropologist* 104 (4): 1050–61.

Conklin, Beth, and Laura R. Graham. 1995. "The Shifting Middle Ground: Amazonian Indians and Eco-Politics." *American Anthropologist* 97 (4): 695–710.

Conklin, Harold. 1954. "An Ethnoecological Approach to Shifting Agriculture." *Transactions of the New York Academy of Sciences* 17 (2): 133–42.

———. 1957. "Hanunóo Agriculture: A Report on an Integral System of Shifting Cultivation in the Philippines." F. A. O. Forest Development Paper No. 12. Rome.

———. 1969. "An Ethnoecological Approach to Shifting Agriculture." In *Environment and Cultural Behavior*, edited by A. Vayda, 221–33. New York: Natural History Press.

Conquergood, Dwight. 1991. "Rethinking Ethnography: Towards a Critical Cultural Politics." *Communication Monographs* 58 (2): 174–94.

Coombes, Brad, Jay T. Johnson, and Richard Howitt. 2014. "Indigenous Geographies III: Methodological Innovation and the Unsettling of Participatory Research." *Progress in Human Geography* 38 (6): 845–54.

Cotera, María Eugenia. 2008. *Native Speakers: Ella Deloria, Zora Neale Hurston, Jovita González and the Poetics of Culture*. Austin: University of Texas Press.

Cotton, C. M. 1996. *Ethnobotany: Principles and Applications*. Chichester, NY: John Wiley and Sons.

Cresswell, T. 2013. *Place: A Short Introduction*. Malden, MA: John Wiley and Sons.

Cruikshank, J. 2005. *Do Glaciers Listen? Local Knowledge, Colonial Encounters, and Social Imagination*. Vancouver: University of British Columbia Press.

Crumley, Carol. 1993. "Analyzing Historic Ecotonal Shifts." *Ecological Applications* 3 (3): 377–84.

———. 1994. *Historical Ecology: Cultural Knowledge and Changing Landscapes*. Santa Fe, NM: School of American Research Press.

Cunha, Manuela Carneiro da, and Mauro W. B. de Almeida. 2000. "Indigenous People, Traditional People, and Conservation in the Amazon." *Daedalus* 129 (2): 315–38.

Cunha, Tony Jarbas Ferreira, Beata Emoke Madari, Luciano Pasqualoto Canellas, Lucedino Paixão Ribeiro, Vinicius de Melo Benites, and Gabriel de Araújo Santos. 2009. "Soil Organic Matter and Fertility of Anthropogenic Dark Earths (Terra Preta de Índio) in the Brazilian Amazon Basin." *Revista Brasileira de Ciência do Solo* 33 (1): 85–93.

Curi, Melissa Volpato. 2014. "Moving Foward or Backwards? Indigenous Peoples, Development and Democracy in Brazil." *Tipití: Journal of the Society for the Anthropology of Lowland South America* 12 (2): 113–17.

Da Col, Giovanni, and David Graeber. 2011. "Forward: The Return of Ethnographic Theory." *HAU* 1 (1): vi–xxxv.

Da Costa, Agnes. 2014. "Sustainable Dam Development in Brazil: The Roles of Environmentalism, Participation and Planning." In *Evolution of Dam Policies*, edited by W. Scheumann and O. Hensengerth, 13–53. Berlin Heidelberg: Springer.

Davidson, Eric A., Alessandro C. De Araújo, Paulo Artaxo, Jennifer K. Balch, I. Foster Brown, Mercedes M. C. Bustamante, Michael T. Coe, Ruth S. Defries, Michael Keller, Marcos Longo, J. William Munger, Wilfrid Schroeder, Britaldo S. Soares-Filho, Carlos M. Souza, and Steven C. Wofsy. 2012. "The Amazon Basin in Transition." *Nature* 481 (7381): 321–28.

De la Cadena, Marisol. 2015. *Earth Beings: Ecologies of Practice Across Andean Worlds*. Durham: Duke University Press.

Declaration. 2010. "Indigenous Declaration after the Belo Monte Dam Auction." Available at http://www.internationalrivers.org/resources/indigenous-declaration-after-the-belo-monte-dam-auction-4297, accessed January 29, 2015.

DeHart, Monica C. 2010. *Ethnic Entrepreneurs: Identity and Development Politics in Latin America*. Stanford, CA: Stanford University Press.

Deleuze, Gilles, and Félix Guatarri. 1987. *A Thousand Plateaus: Capitalism and Schizophrenia*, translated by Brian Massumi. Minneapolis: University of Minnesota Press.

Deloria Jr., Vine. 1969. *Custer Died for Your Sins: An Indian Manifesto*. New York: Macmillan Publishing.

———. 2003. *God is Red: A Native View of Religion*. Golden, CO: Fulcrum Publishing.

———. 2004. "Marginal and Submarginal." In *Indigenizing the Academy: Transforming Scholarship and Empowering Communities*, edited by Devon Abbott Mihesuah and Angela Cavender Wilson, 16–30. Lincoln: University of Nebraska Press.

Denevan, William. 1992. "The Pristine Myth: The Landscape of the Americas in 1492." *Annals of the Association of American Geographers* 82 (3): 369–85.

———. 2001. *Cultivated Landscapes of Native Amazonia and the Andes*. Oxford: Oxford University Press.

———. 2006. "Pre-European Cultivation in Amazonia." In *Time, Complexity, and Historical Ecology*, edited by William Balée and Clark L. Erickson, 153–64. New York: Columbia University Press.

Dennison, Jean. 2012. *Colonial Entanglement: Constituting a Twenty-First Century Osage Nation*. Chapel Hill: University of North Carolina Press.

Descola, P. 2013. *Beyond Nature and Culture*, translated by Janet Lloyd. Chicago: University of Chicago Press.

Descola, P., and G. Pálsson, eds. 1996. *Nature and Society: Anthropological Perspectives*. London: Routledge.

Di Leonardo, Michela. 1998. *Exotics at Home: Anthropologies, Others and American Modernity*. Chicago: University of Chicago Press.

Diniz, Edson Soares. 2005. "Os Kayapó Gorotíre: Aspectos Sócio-Culturais do Momento Atual." In *Etnologia Indígena da Amazônia Brasileira*, 19–70. Belém, Pará: Gráfica Editora Meridional.

Dirlik, A. 2011. "Globalization, Indigenism, Social Movements, and the Politics of Place." *Localities* 1: 47–90.

Dos Santos, Sales Augusto, and Laurence Hallewell (transl.). 2002. "Historical Roots of the 'Whitening' of Brazil." *Latin American Perspectives* 29 (1): 61–82.

Dove, Michael. 1993. "Smallholder Rubber and Swidden Agriculture in Borneo: A Sustainable Adaptation to the Ecology and Economy of the Tropical Forest." *Economic Botany* 47 (2): 136–47.

———. 2011. *The Banana Tree at the Gate*. New Haven, CT: Yale University Press.

Dowie, Mark. 2009. *Conservation Refugees: The Hundred-Year Conflict between Global Conservation and Native Peoples*. Boston: Massachusetts Institute of Technology Press.

Dressler, Wolfram, and Robin Roth. 2011. "The Good, the Bad, and the Contradictory: Neoliberal Conservation Governance in Rural Southeast Asia." *World Development* 39 (5): 851–62.

Dyson-Hudson, Rada, and Eric Smith. 1978. "Human Territoriality: An Ecological Reassessment." *American Anthropologist* 80 (1): 21–41.

Eden, Michael J. 1993. "Swidden Cultivation in Forest and Savanna in Lowland Southwest Papua New Guinea." *Human Ecology* 21 (2): 145–66.

Eder, James F. 1984. "The Impact of Subsistence Change on Mobility and Settlement Pattern in a Tropical Forest Foraging Economy: Some Implications for Archeology." *American Anthropologist* 86 (4): 837–53.

Elden, Stuart. 2006. "The State of Territory under Globalization." *Thamyris/Intersection* 12: 47–66.

Elisabetsky, E., and Darrell A. Posey. 1986. "Pesquisa Etnofarmacológica e Recursos Naturais no Trópico Úmido: O Caso dos Índios Kayapó do Brasil e suas Implicações para a Ciência

Médica." In *Anais do Primeiro Simpósio do Trópico Úmido*, vol. 2: Flora e Flores, 85–93. Belém, Empresa Brasileira de Pesquisa Agropecuária, Centro de Pesquisa Agropecuária do Trópico Úmido.

Ellen, Roy. 2006. "Introduction." *Journal of the Royal Anthropological Institute* 12: S1–S22.

Elmhirst, Rebecca. 2011. "Introducing New Feminist Political Ecologies." *Geoforum* 42 (2): 129–32.

Emmons, Louise H., and François Feer. 1997. *Neotropical Rainforest Mammals*. Chicago: University of Chicago Press.

Emperaire, Laure, and Nivaldo Peroni. 2007. "Traditional Management of Agrobiodiversity in Brazil: A Case Study of Manioc." *Human Ecology* 35 (6): 761–68.

Erazo, Juliet. 2013. *Governing Indigenous Territory: Enacting Sovereignty in the Ecuadorian Amazon*. Durham, NC: Duke University Press.

Erikson, Clark. 2008. "Amazonia: The Historical Ecology of a Domesticated Landscape." In *The Handbook of South American Archaeology*, edited by Helaine Silverman and William Isbell, 157–83. New York: Springer.

Escobar, Arturo. 1995. *Encountering Development: The Making and Unmaking of the Third World*. Princeton, NJ: Princeton University Press.

———. 1998. "Whose Knowledge? Whose Nature? Biodiversity, Conservation, and the Political Ecology of Social Movements." *Journal of Political Ecology* 5 (1): 54–82.

———. 1999 "After Nature: Steps to an Antiessentialist Political Ecology." *Current Anthropology* 40 (1): 1–30.

———. 2001. "Culture Sits in Places: Reflections on Globalism and Subaltern Strategies of Localization." *Political Geography* 20 (2): 139–74.

———. 2004. "Beyond the Third World: Imperial Globality, Global Coloniality and Anti-Globalisation Social Movements." *Third World Quarterly* 25 (1): 207–30.

———. 2008. *Territories of Difference: Place, Movements, Life, Redes*. Durham, NC: Duke University Press.

———. 2015. "Degrowth, Postdevelopment, and Transitions: A Preliminary Conversation." *Sustainability Science* 10 (3): 451–62.

Ewart, Elizabeth. 2003. "Lines and Circles: Images of Time in a Panará Village." *Journal of the Royal Anthropological Institute* 9 (2): 261–79.

———. 2014. *Space and Society in Central Brazil: A Panara Ethnography*. New York: Bloomsbury Academic.

Fabian, Michael. 1992. *Space and Time of the Bororo*. Gainesville: University Press of Florida.

Fairhead, James, and Melissa Leach. 1996. *Misreading the African Landscape: Society and Ecology in a Forest-Savanna Mosaic*. Cambridge: Cambridge University Press.

Fairhead, James, Melissa Leach, and Ian Scoones. 2012. "Green Grabbing: A New Appropriation of Nature?" *Journal of Peasant Studies* 39 (2): 237–61.

Fausto, Carlos. 2008. "Too Many Owners: Mastery and Ownership in Amazonia," translated by David Rodgers. *Mana* 4 [online]. Available at http://socialsciences.scielo.org/scielo.php?script=sci_arttext&pid=S0104-93132008000100001, accessed March 12, 2016.

Fearnside, P. M. 2001. "Land-Tenure Issues as Factors in Environmental Destruction in the Brazilian Amazonia: The Case of Southern Pará." *World Development* 29 (8): 1361–72.

———. 2003. "Conservation Policy in Brazilian Amazonia: Understanding the Dilemmas." *World Development* 31 (5): 757–79.

———. 2006a. "Avança Brasil: Environmental and Social Consequences of Brazil's Planned Infrastructure in Amazonia." *Environmental Management* 30 (6): 735–47.

———. 2006b. "Dams in the Amazon: Belo Monte and Brazil's Hydroelectric Development of the Xingu River Basin." *Environmental Management* 38 (1): 16–27.

———. 2007 "Brazil's Cuiabá-Santarém (BR-163) Highway: The Environmental Cost of Paving a Soybean Corridor through the Amazon." *Environmental Management* 39 (5): 601–14.

———. 2012. "Brazil's Amazon Forest in Mitigating Global Warming: Unresolved Controversies." *Climate Policy* 12 (1): 70–81.

———. 2013. "What is at Stake for Brazilian Amazonia in the Climate Negotiations." *Climatic Change* 118 (3): 509–19.

Feld, Steven, and Keith Basso. 1996. "Introduction." In *Senses of Place*, edited by Steven Feld and Keith Basso, 3–12. Santa Fe, NM: School of American Research Press.

Fenelon, James V., and Thomas D. Hall. 2008. "Revitalization and Indigenous Resistance to Globalization and Neoliberalism." *American Behavioral Scientist* 51: 1867–1900.

Field, Les. 2009. "Global Indigenous Movements: Convergence and Differentiation in the Face of the Twenty-First-Century State." In *Border Crossings: Transnational Americanist Anthropology*, edited by Kathleen Fine-Dare and Steven L. Rubenstein, 230–246. Lincoln: University of Nebraska Press.

Fine-Dare, Kathleen, and Steven L. Rubenstein, eds. 2009. *Border Crossings: Transnational Americanist Anthropology*. Lincoln: University of Nebraska Press.

Fisher, William H. 1991. "Dualism and its Discontents: Social Process and Village Fissioning among the Xikrin-Kayapo of Central Brazil." PhD diss., Cornell University.

———. 1994. "Megadevelopment, Environmentalism and Resistance: The Institutional Context of Kayapó Indigenous Politics in Central Brazil." *Human Organization* 53 (3): 220–32.

———. 2000. *Rain Forest Exchanges: Industry and Community on an Amazonian Frontier*. Washington, DC: Smithsonian Press.

———. 2003. "Name Rituals and Acts of Feeling among the Kayapó (Mebengokre)." *Journal of the Royal Anthropological Institute* 9 (1): 117–36.

Flowers, Nancy M., Daniel R. Gross, Madeline L. Ritter, and Dennis W. Werner. 1982. "Variation in Swidden Practices in Four Central Brazilian Indian Societies." *Human Ecology* 10 (2): 203–17.

Freeman, James. 2012. "Neoliberal Accumulation Strategies and the Visible Hand of Police Pacification in Rio de Janeiro." *Revista de Estudos Universitários* 38 (1): 95–126.

Forsyth, Tim. 2003. *Critical Political Ecology: The Politics of Environmental Science*. London: Routledge.

Fortis, P. 2010. "The Birth of Design: A Kuna Theory of Body and Personhood." *Journal of the Royal Anthropological Institute* 16: 480–95.

Foucault, Michel. 1986. "Of Other Spaces." *Diacritics* 16 (1): 22–27.

Fuentes, A. 2010. "Naturalcultural Encounters in Bali: Monkeys, Temples, Tourists, and Ethnoprimatology." *Cultural Anthropology* 25: 600–24.

Gaffney, C. 2010. "Mega-Events and Socio-Spatial Dynamics in Rio de Janeiro, 1919–2016." *Journal of Latin American Geography* 9 (1): 7–29.

Ganti, Tejaswini. 2014. "Neoliberalism." *Annual Review of Anthropology* 43 (1): 89–104.

Garfield, Seth. 2001. *Indigenous Struggle at the Heart of Brazil: State Policy, Frontier Expansion, and the Xavante Indians 1937–1988*. Durham, NC: Duke University Press.

German, Laura A. 2004. "Ecological Praxis and Blackwater Ecosystems: A Case Study from the Brazilian Amazon." *Human Ecology* 32 (6): 653–83.

Gibson-Graham, J. K. 2008. "Diverse Economies: Performative Practices for Other Worlds." *Progress in Human Geography* 32 (5): 613–32.

Gilroy, P. 1993. *The Black Atlantic: Modernity and Double Consciousness.* London: Verso.

Ginsburg, Faye, Lila Abu-Lughod, and Brian Larken. 2002. *Media Worlds: Anthropology on New Terrain.* Berkeley: University of California Press.

Giraldin, O. 1997. *Cayapó e Panará: Luta e Sobrevivência de um Povo Jê no Brasil Central.* Campinas: Editora da Unicamp.

Glaser, Bruno, Ludwig Haumaier, Georg Guggenberger, and Wolfgang Zech. 2001 "The 'Terra Preta' Phenomenon: A Model for Sustainable Agriculture in the Humid Tropics." *Naturwissenschaften* 88: 37–41.

Godoy, Ricardo A., and Kamaljit S. Bawa. 1993. "The Economic Value and Sustainable Harvest of Plants and Animals from the Tropical Forest: Assumptions, Hypotheses, and Methods." *Economic Botany* 47 (3): 215–19.

Goeman, Mishuana. 2013. *Mark My Words: Native Women Mapping our Nations.* Minneapolis: University of Minnesota Press.

Goldman, Mara J., Paul Nadasdy, and Matthew D. Turner, eds. 2011. *Knowing Nature: Conversations at the Intersection of Political Ecology and Science Studies.* Chicago: University of Chicago Press.

Goldman, Michael. 2006. Imperial Nature: *The World Bank and Struggles for Social Justice in the Age of Globalization.* New Haven, CT: Yale University Press.

Gómez-Peña, G. 1996. *The New World Border: Prophecies, Poems and Loqueras for the End of the Century.* San Francisco: City Lights.

González-Pérez, Sol, Pascale de Robert, and Márlia Coelho-Ferreira. 2013. "Seed Use and Socioeconomic Significance in Kayapó Handicrafts: A Case Study from Pará State, Brazil." *Economic Botany* 67 (1): 1–16.

Gordillo, Gaston. 2014. *Rubble: The Afterlife of Destruction.* Durham, NC: Duke University Press.

Gordon, Cesar. 2006. *Economia Selvagem: Ritual e Mercadoria entre os Índios Xikrin Mebêngôkre.* São Paulo: Fundação Editora da UNESP (FEU).

Gragson, Ted L., and Ben G. Blount. 1999. *Ethnoecology: Knowledge, Resources, and Rights.* Athens, GA: University of Georgia Press.

Graham, Elizabeth. 2006. "A Neotropical Framework for Terra Preta." In *Time and Complexity in Historical Ecology,* edited by William Balée and Clark L. Erickson, 57–86. New York: Columbia University Press.

Graham, Laura. 1986. "Three Modes of Shavante Vocal Expression: Wailing, Collective Singing, and Political Oratory." In *Native South American Discourses,* edited by J. Sherzer and G. Urban, 83–118. Berlin: Mouton de Gruyter.

———. 1995. *Performing Dreams: Discoveries of Immortality Among the Xavante of Central Brazil.* Austin: University of Texas Press.

———. 2002. "Amazonian Indians and the Symbolic Politics of Language in the Global Public Sphere." In *Indigenous Movements, Self-representation, and the State in Latin America,* edited by Kay B. Warren and Jean E. Jackson, 181–227. Austin: University of Texas Press.

———. 2005. "Image and Instrumentality in a Xavante Politics of Existential Recognition: The Public Outreach Work of Eténhiritipa Pimentel Barbosa." *American Ethnologist* 32 (4): 622–41.

———. 2014. "Genders of Xavante Ethnographic Spectacle: Cultural Politics of Inclusion and Exclusion in Brazil." In *Performing Indigeneity: Global Histories and Contemporary*

Experiences, edited by Laura Graham and Glenn Penny, 305–350. Lincoln, NE: University of Nebraska Press.

Graham, Laura, and Glenn Penny, eds. 2014. *Performing Indigeneity: Global Histories and Contemporary Experiences*. Lincoln: University of Nebraska Press.

Graveline, Fyre Jean. 2000. "Circle as Methodology: Enacting an Aboriginal Paradigm." *International Journal of Qualitative Studies in Education* 13 (4): 361–70.

Greene, Shane. 2009. *Customizing Indigeneity Paths to a Visionary Politics in Peru*. Stanford: Stanford University Press.

Grenier, L. 1998. *Working with Indigenous Knowledge: A Guide for Researchers*. Ottawa: International Development Research Centre.

Griffiths, Alison. 2002. *Wondrous Difference: Cinema, Anthropology & Turn-of-the-Century Visual Culture*. New York: Columbia University Press.

Guardiola, Jorge, and Fernando García-Quero. 2014. "Buen Vivir (living well) in Ecuador: Community and Environmental Satisfaction without Household Material Prosperity?" *Ecological Economics* 107: 177–84.

Guariguata, M.R., C. Garcia-Fernandez, D. Sheil, R. Nasi, C. Herrero-Jáuregui, P. Cronkleton, and V. Ingram. 2010. "Compatibility of Timber and Non-Timber Forest Product Management in Natural Tropical Forests: Perspectives, Challenges, and Opportunities." *Forest Ecology and Management* 259 (3): 237–45.

Gudynas, Eduardo. 2009. "Diez Tesis Urgentes sobre el Nuevo Extractivismo: Contextos y Demandas Bajo el Progresismo Sudamericano Actual." In *Extractivismo, Política y Sociedad*, edited by Jürgen Schuldt, Alberto Acosta, Alberto Barandiará, Anthony Bebbington, Mauricio Folchi, CEDLA, Alejandra Alayza and Eduardo Gudynas, 187–225. Quito: Centro Andino de Acción Popular – Ecuador/ Centro Latino Americano de Ecología Social.

Gupta, Akhil, and James Ferguson, eds. 1997a. *Anthropological Locations: Boundaries and Grounds of a Field Science*. Berkeley: University of California Press.

———, eds. 1997b. *Culture, Power, Place: Explorations in Critical Anthropology*. Durham, NC: Duke University Press.

Gupta, Akhil. 1998. *Postcolonial Developments: Agriculture in the Making of Modern India*. Durham, NC: Duke University Press.

Guthman, Julie. 2004. *Agrarian Dreams the Paradox of Organic Farming in California*. Berkeley: University of California Press.

Haig-Brown, Celia. 2003. "Creating Spaces: Testimonio, Impossible Knowledge, and Academe." *International Journal of Qualitative Studies in Education* 16 (3): 415–33.

Hale, Charles R. 2011. "Resistencia para que? Territory, Autonomy and Neoliberal Entanglements in the 'Empty Spaces' of Central America." *Economy and Society* 40 (2): 184–210.

Hall, Anthony L. 1989. *Developing Amazonia: Deforestation and Social Conflict in Brazil's Carajas Programme*. New York: Manchester University Press.

———. 2013. "Combating Deforestation through REDD+ in the Brazilian Amazon: A New Social Contract?" *Sustenabilidade em Debate* 4 (1): 79–98.

Hames, Raymond. 1983. "Monoculture, Polyculture, and Polyvariety in Tropical Forest Swidden Cultivation." *Human Ecology* 11 (1): 13–34.

Hames, Raymond, and William T. Vickers. 1983. "Introduction." In *Adaptive Responses of Native Amazonians*, edited by William T. Vickers and Raymond B. Hames, 1–26. New York: Academic Press.

Hammond, D. S., P. M. Dolman, and A. R. Watkinson. 1995. "Modern Ticuna Swidden-Fallow Management in the Colombian Amazon: Ecologically Integrating Market Strategies and Subsistence-Driven Economies?" *Human Ecology* 23 (3): 335–56.

Hannerz, Ulf. 1996. *Transnational Connections: Culture, People, Places.* London: Routledge.

Haraway, D. 1988. "Situated Knowledges: The Science Question in Feminism and the Privilege of Partial Perspective." *Feminist Studies* 14 (3): 575–99.

———. 1992. "The Promises of Monsters: A Regenerative Politics for Inappropriate/d Others." In *Cultural Studies*, edited by Lawrence Grossberg, Cary Nelson, and Paula A. Treichler, 295–337. New York: Routledge.

———. 2003. *The Companion Species Manifesto: Dogs, People, and Significant Otherness.* Chicago: Prickly Paradigm.

———. 2008. *When Species Meet.* Minneapolis: University of Minnesota Press.

Harris, David R. 1971. "The Ecology of Swidden Cultivation in the Upper Orinoco Rain Forest, Venezuela." *Geographical Review* 61 (4): 475–95.

Harris, Leila M., and María Cecilia Roa-García. 2013. "Recent Waves of Water Governance: Constitutional Reform and Resistance to Neoliberalization in Latin America (1990–2012)." *Geoforum* 50: 20–30.

Harvey, David. 1990. *The Condition of Postmodernity: An Enquiry into the Origins of Cultural Change.* Cambridge: Blackwell.

———. 2003. *The New Imperialism.* New York: Oxford University Press.

Heatherington, Tracey. 2010. *Wild Sardinia: Indigeneity and the Global Dreamtimes of Environmentalism.* Seattle: University of Washington Press.

Hecht, Susanna B. 2003. "Indigenous Soil Management and the Creation of Amazonian Dark Earths: Implications of Kayapó Practice." In *Amazonian Dark Earths: Origins, Properties, Management*, edited by Johannes Lehmann, Dirse C. Kern, Bruno Glaser, and William I. Woods, 355–72. Dordrecht, The Netherlands: Springer.

———. 2009. "Kayapó Savanna Management: Fire, Soils, and Forest Islands in a Threatened Biome." In *Amazonian Dark Earths: Wim Sombroek's Vision*, edited by William I. Woods, Wenceslau G. Teixeira, Johannes Lehmann, Christoph Steiner, Antoinette WinklerPrins, and Lilian Rebellato, 143–62. Dordrecht, The Netherlands: Springer.

———. 2011. "The New Amazon Geographies: Insurgent Citizenship, 'Amazon Nation' and the Politics of Environmentalisms." *Journal of Cultural Geography* 28 (1): 203–23.

———. 2012. "From Eco-catastrophe to Zero Deforestation? Interdisciplinarities, Politics, Environmentalisms and Reduced Clearing in Amazonia." *Environmental Conservation* 39 (1): 4–19.

Hecht, Susanna B., and A. Cockburn. 1990. *The Fate of the Forest: Developers, Destroyers, and Defenders of the Amazon.* New York: Harper Perennial.

Hecht, Susanna B., and Darrell A. Posey. 1989. "Preliminary Findings on Soil Management of the Kayapó Indians." In *Resource Management in Amazônia: Indigenous and Folk Strategies*, edited by D. A. Posey and W. L. Balée, 174–88. New York: New York Botanical Garden.

Heckenberger, Michael. 2005. *The Ecology of Power: Culture, Place and Personhood in the Southern Amazon, AD 1000–2000.* New York: Routledge.

———. 2006. "History, Ecology, and Alterity: Visualizing Polity in Ancient Amazonia." In *Time and Complexity in Historical Ecology*, edited by William Balée and Clark L. Erickson, 311–40. New York: Columbia UniversityPress.

Heckenberger, Michael, James B. Peterson, and Eduardo G. Neves. 1999. "Village Size and Permanence in Amazonia: Two Archaeological Examples from Brazil." *Latin American Antiquity* 10 (4): 353–76.

Hemming, John. 1978. *Red Gold: The Conquest of the Brazilian Indians.* London: Macmillan.

Hermes, M. 1998. "Research Methods as a Situated Response: Towards a First Nations' Methodology." *International Journal of Qualitative Studies in Education* 11 (1): 155–68.

Hilty, Steven L. 2003. *Birds of Venezuela*. Princeton: Princeton University Press.

Himley, Matthew. 2008. *Geographies of Environmental Governance: The Nexus of Nature and Neoliberalism*. *Geography Compass* 2 (2): 433–51.

Holbraad, Martin, Morten Axel Pedersen, and Eduardo Viveiros de Castro. 2014. "The Politics of Ontology: Anthropological Positions." *Theorizing the Contemporary, Cultural Anthropology*. Available at http://culanth.org/fieldsights/462-the-politics-of-ontology -anthropological-positions, access January 13, 2014.

Holmes, Leilani. 2000. "Heart Knowledge, Blood Memory, and the Voice of the Land: Implications for Research among Hawaiian Elders." In *Indigenous Knowledges in Global Contexts: Multiple Readings of Our World*, edited by George Jerry Sefa Dei, Budd L. Hall, and Dorothy Goldin Rosenberg, 37–53. Toronto: University of Toronto Press.

Holt-Gímenez, Eric. 2006. *Campesino a Campesino: Voices from Latin America's Farmer to Farmer Movement for Sustainable Agriculture*. Oakland: Food First Books.

Hornburg, A. 2005. "Ethnogenesis, Regional Integration, and Ecology in Prehistoric Amazonia." *Current Anthropology* 46 (4): 589–620.

Horton, L. 2006. "Contesting State Multiculturalisms: Indigenous Land Struggles in Eastern Panama." *Journal of Latin American Studies* 38: 829–858.

Howe, Cymene. 2015. "Life Above Earth: An Introduction." *Cultural Anthropology* 30 (2): 203–9.

Hubbard, P., R. Kitchin, and G. Valentine. 2004. "Introduction." In *Key Thinkers on Space and Place*, edited by P. Hubbard, R. Kitchin, and G. Valentine, 1–15. London: Sage.

Hunn, Eugene. 2007. "Four Phases of Ethnobiology." *Journal of Ethnobiology* 27 (1): 1–10.

Hutnyk, John. 2005. "Hybridity." *Ethnic and Racial Studies* 28 (1): 79–102.

Hymes, Dell H. 1974. *Reinventing Anthropology*. New York: Vintage Books.

Igoe, Jim. 2010. "The Spectacle of Nature in the Global Economy of Appearances: Conservation." *Critique of Anthropology* 30 (4): 375–97.

Ingold, Tim. 1993. "The Temporality of the Landscape." *World Archaeology* 25 (2): 152–74.

———. 2000. *The Perception of the Environment: Essays in Livelihood, Dwelling and Skill*. London: Routledge.

———. 2007. *Lines: A Brief History*. New York: Routledge. International Rivers

International Rivers. 2008. "A Knife in the Water." Available at, http://www.international rivers.org/blogs/232/a-knife-in-the-water, accessed January 4, 2014.

———. 2012. "Belo Monte: Massive Dam Project Strikes at the Heart of the Amazon." Available at: http://www.internationalrivers.org/files/attached-files/Belo_Monte_FactSheet_ May2012.pdf

IUCN (International Union for Conservation of Nature). 1994. *Guidelines for Protected Area Management Categories*. IUCN Commission on National Parks and Protected Areas with the Assistance of the World Conservation Monitoring Centre. Gland: IUCN.

Jagger, Alison, ed. 2008. *Just Methods: An Interdisciplinary Feminist Reader*. Boulder: Paradigm Publishers.

Jameson, F. 1991. *Postmodernism, or the Cultural Logic of Late Capitalism*. Durham, NC: Duke University Press.

Jefferson, Kathleen. (1974) 2009. *Semantic Clause Analysis in Focus for Learning Kayapó*. Brasilia: Summer Institute of Linguistics.

Johnson, Jay T. 2012. "Place-Based Learning and Knowing: Critical Pedagogies Grounded in Indigeneity." *GeoJournal* 77 (6): 829–36.

Johnson, Jay T., and Soren C. Larsen. 2013. "Introduction: A Deeper Sense of Place." In *Deeper Sense of Place: Stories and Journeys of Indigenous-Academic Collaboration*, edited by Jay Johnson and Soren C. Larsen, 7–18. Corvallis: Oregon State University Press.

Johnson, Jeffrey, Christine Avenarius, and Jack Weatherford. 2006. "The Active Participant-Observer: Applying Social Role Analysis to Participant Observation." *Field Methods* 18 (2): 111–34.

Jonas, M., J. P. Ometto, M. Batistella, O. Franklin, M. Hall, D. M. Lapola, E. F. Moran, S. Tramberend, B. L. Queiroz, A. Schaffartzik, A. Shvidenko, S. Nilsson, and C. A. Nobre. 2014. "Sustaining Ecosystem Services: Overcoming the Dilemma posed by Local Actions and Planetary Boundaries." *Earth's Future* 2 (8): 407–20.

Jorge, Malu S. P., and Carlos A. Peres. 2005. "Population Density and Home Range Size of Red-Rumped Agoutis (*Dasyprocta leporina*) Within and Outside a Natural Brazil Nut Stand in Southeastern Amazonia." *Biotropica* 37 (2): 317–21.

Joseph, M. 1999. "Introduction: New Hybrid Identities and Performance." In *Performing Hybridity*, edited by M. Joseph and J. N. Fink, 1–27. Minneapolis: University of Minnesota Press.

Joseph, M., and J. N. Fink, eds. 1999. *Performing Hybridity*. Minneapolis: University of Minnesota Press.

Kahn, Miriam. 2000. "Tahiti Intertwined: Ancestral Land, Tourist Postcard, and Nuclear Test Site." *American Anthropologist* 102 (1): 7–26.

Kallis, Giorgos, Erik Gómez-Baggethun, and Christos Zografos. 2013. "To Value or Not to Value? That is Not the Question." *Ecological Economics* 94: 97–105.

Kallis, Giorgios, Federico Demaria, and Giacomo D'Alisa. 2015. "Introduction." In *Degrowth: A Vocabulary for a New Era*, edited by G. D'Alisa, F. Demaria, and G. Kallis, 1–17. New York: Routledge, Taylor and Francis Group.

Kamenka, Eugene, ed. 1983. *The Portable Karl Marx*. Selected, translated in part, and with an introduction by Eugene Kamenka. New York: Penguin Books.

Katz, Cindi. 2001. "On the Grounds of Globalization: A Topography for Feminist Political Engagement." *Signs* 26 (4): 1213–34.

Kayapó. 1989. "Kayapó Bring Their Case to the United States." *Cultural Survival Quarterly* 31 (1): 18–19.

King, Thomas. 2003. *The Truth about Stories: A Native Narrative*. Toronto: House of Anansi Press.

Komarinksy, Sara. 2009. "Suitcases Full of Mole: Traveling Food and the Connections Between Mexico and Alaska." *Alaska Journal of Anthropology* 7 (1): 41–56.

Kopenawa, D., and Bruce Albert. 2013. *The Falling Sky: Words of a Yanomami Shaman*. Cambridge, MA: The Belknap Press of Harvard University Press.

Kraidy, M. M. 2002. "Hybridity in Cultural Globalization." *Communication Theory* 12 (3): 316–339.

Kramer, J. 2006. *Switchbacks: Art, Ownership, and Nuxalk National Identity*. Vancouver: University of British Columbia Press.

Krech, Shepard. 1999. *The Ecological Indian: Myth and History*. New York: W&W Norton and Co.

Kremen, Claire, Adina M. Merenlender, and Dennis D. Murphy. 1994. "Ecological Monitoring: A Vital Need for Integrated Conservation and Development Programs in the Tropics." *Conservation Biology* 8 (2): 388–97.

LaDuke, Winona. 2013. "In the Time of Sacred Places." Seven Pillars Houses of Wisdom. Available at: http://www.sevenpillarshouse.org/article/in_the_time_of_the_sacred_places, accessed March 12, 2016.

Lagrou, Els. 2009. *Arte Indígena no Brasil: Agência, Alteridade e Relação*. Belo Horizonte: C/Arte.

Larson, Anne, and Fernanda Soto. 2008. "Decentralization of Natural Resource Governance Regimes." *Annual Review of Environmental Resources* 33: 213–39. Available at http://ssrn.com/abstract=1319919, accessed February 10, 2010.

Larson, Brooke. 1998. "Andean Communities, Political Cultures, and Markets: The Changing Contours of a Field." In *Ethnicities and Markets in the Andes*, edited by Brooke Larson, Olivia Harris, and Enrique Tandeter, 5–53. Durham, NC: Duke University Press.

Larsen, S. C., and J. T. Johnson. 2012. "In Between Worlds: Place, Experience, and Research in Indigenous Geography." *Journal of Cultural Geography* 29 (1): 1–13.

Lathrap, D. W. 1970. *The Upper Amazon*. New York: Praeger.

———. 1977. "Our Father the Cayman, Our Mother the Gourd: Spinden Revisited, or a Unitary Model for the Emergence of Agriculture in the New World." In *Origins of Agriculture*, edited by C. A. Reed, 713–15. The Hague: Mouton.

Latour, Bruno. 1993. *We Have Never Been Modern*. Cambridge, MA: Harvard University Press.

———. 2004. *Politics of Nature: How to Bring the Sciences back into Democracy*. Cambridge, MA: Harvard University Press.

———. 2005. *Reassembling the Social: An Introduction to Actor-Network Theory*. Oxford and New York: Oxford University Press.

Lauer, Matthew. 2012. "Oral Traditions or Situated Practices? Understanding How Indigenous Communities Respond to Environmental Disasters." *Human Organization* 71 (2): 176–87.

Lauer, Matthew, and Shankar Aswani. 2009. "Indigenous Ecological Knowledge as Situated Practices: Understanding Fishers' Knowledge in the Western Solomon Islands." *American Anthropologist* 111 (3): 317–29.

Laurance, William F., A. J. Albernaz, and Carlos Da Costa. 2001. "Is Deforestation Accelerating in the Brazilian Amazon?" *Environmental Conservation* 28 (4): 305–311.

Laurance, William F., Mark A. Cochrane, Scott Bergen, Philip M. Fearnside, Patricia Delamonica, Christopher Barber, Sammya D'Angelo, and Tito Fernandes. 2001. "The Future of the Brazilian Amazon." *Science* 291 (5503): 438–39.

Law, J., and J. Hassard. 1999. *Actor-Network Theory and After*. Oxford: Blackwell.

Lawson, V. 2007. *Making Development Geography*. London: Hodder Arnold.

Lea, Vanessa R. 1986. "Nomes e Nekrets Kayapó: Uma Concepção de Riqueza." PhD diss., Universidade Federal do Rio de Janeiro, Rio de Janeiro.

———. 1995 "The Houses of the Mebengokre (Kayapó) of Central Brazil—A New Door to their Social Organization." In *About the House Lévi-Strauss and Beyond*, edited by Janet Carsten and Stephen Hugh-Jones, 206–25. Cambridge: Cambridge University Press.

———. 2001. "The Composition of Mebengokre (Kayapó) Households in Central Brazil." In *Beyond the Visible and the Material: The Amerindianization of Society in the Work of Peter Rivière*, edited by Laura Rival and Neil Whitehead, 157–76. Oxford: Oxford University Press.

———. 2004. "Mẽbengokre Ritual Wailing and Flagellation: A Performative Outlet for Emotional Self-Expression." *Indiana* 21: 113–25.

————. 2012. *Riquezas Intangíveis de Pessoas Partíveis: os Mébêngôkre (Kayapó) do Brasil Central.* São Paulo: Editora da Universidade de São Paulo.

Lefebvre, Henri. 1991. *The Production of Space*, translated by Donald Nicholson-Smith. Oxford: Blackwell.

Leff, Enrique. 2012. "Political Ecology: A Latin American Perspective." In *Encyclopedia of Life Support Systems EOLSS—Encyclopedia of Social Sciences and Humanities–Culture, Civilization and Human Society*, edited by UNESCO-EOLSS Joint Committee. Oxford, UK: UNESCO, Encyclopedia of Life Support Systems Publishers.

Lévi-Strauss, Claude. 1966. *The Savage Mind*. Chicago: University of Chicago Press.

————. 1967. *Les Structures Élémentaires de la Parenté*. Paris, La Haye: Mouton et Co.

Li, Tania Murray. 2000. "Articulating Indigenous Identity in Indonesia: Resource Politics and the Tribal Slot." *Comparative Studies in Society and History* 42 (1): 149–79.

————. 2014. *Land's End Capitalist Relations on an Indigenous Frontier*. Durham, NC: Duke University Press.

Lievesley, G. A., and S. Ludlam. 2009. *Reclaiming Latin America: Experiments in Radical Social Democracy*. New York: Zed Books.

Little, P. E. 2001. *Amazonia: Territorial Struggles on Perennial Frontiers*. Baltimore: Johns Hopkins University Press.

Long, William. 1995. "How Gold Led Tribe Astray." *Los Angeles Times*, August 29: A1.

Lopes da Silva, A. 1986. *Nomes e Amigos da Prática Xavante a uma Reflexão sobre os Jê*. São Paulo: Faculdade de Filosofia, Letras e Ciências Humanas, Universidade de São Paulo.

Londoño-Sulkin, Carlos. 2012. *People of Substance*. Toronto: University of Toronto Press.

López, Emiliano, and Francisco Vértiz. 2015. "Extractivism, Transnational Capital, and Subaltern Struggles in Latin America." *Latin American Perspectives* 42 (5): 152–68.

Lowe, Celia. 2006. *Wild Profusion: Biodiversity Conservation in an Indonesian Archipelago*. Princeton, NJ: Princeton University Press.

Lowie, Robert. 1963. "The Northwestern and Central Ge." In *Handbook of South American Indians*, edited by Julian H. Steward, 477–517. New York: Cooper Square Publishers, Inc.

Lutz, Catherine, and James Collins. 1993. *Reading National Geographic*. Chicago: University of Chicago Press.

Lyon, Sarah M., and Mark Moberg, eds. 2010. *Fair Trade and Social Justice Global Ethnographies*. New York: New York University Press.

Malcolm, J., B. Zimmerman, R. Cavalcanti, F. Ahern, and R. W. Pietsch. 1999. "Use of RAADARSAT in the Design and Implementation of Sustainable Development in the Kayapó Indigenous Area, Para, Brazil." *Canadian Journal of Remote Sensing* 24 (4): 360–66.

Manathunga, C. 2009. "Research as an Intercultural 'Contact Zone.'" *Discourse: Studies in the Cultural Politics of Education* 30 (2): 165–77.

Mann, C. 2002. "1491." *The Atlantic Monthly* 289 (3): 41–53.

Banks, Marcus, and Jay Ruby, eds. 2011. *Made to be Seen: Perspectives on the History of Visual Anthropology*. Chicago: University of Chicago Press.

Mares, Teresa, and Devon G. Peña. 2011. "Environmental and Food Justice: Toward Local, Slow, and Deep Food Systems." In *Cultivating Food Justice: Race, Class, and Julien Agyeman*, 197–220. Boston: The MIT Press.

Marimán, Pablo, Sergio Caniuqueo, Jose Millalén, and Rodrigo Levil. 2014. "Epilogue to ¡ . . . Escucha Winka . . . !" *E-Misférica Decolonial Gesture* 11 (1). Available at http://hemispheric institute.org/hemi/en/emisferica-111-decolonial-gesture/carcamo, March 12, 2016.

Marion Suiseeya, Kimberly. 2015. "REDD+ and the 'Do No Harm' Principle: A Retreat from Justice?" Paper presented at the Workshop on Equity, Justice, and Well-being in Ecosystem Governance. March 27, 2015. London: International Institute for Environment and Development

Marion Suiseeya, Kimberly, and Susan Caplow. 2013. "In Pursuit of Procedural Justice: Lessons from an Analysis of 56 Forest Carbon Project Designs." *Global Environmental Change* 23 (5): 986–79.

Martinelli, Luiz A., Rosamond Naylor, Peyer M. Vitoseuk, and Paulo Moutinho. 2010. "Agriculture in Brazil: Impacts, Costs, and Opportunities for a Sustainable Future." *Current Opinion in Environmental Sustainability* 2 (5–6): 431–38.

Martinez-Alier, Joan, Giuseppe Munda, and John O'Neill. 1998. "Weak Comparability of Values as a Foundation for Ecological Economics." *Ecological Economics* 26 (3): 277–86.

Martins, José de Souza. 1984. "The State and the Militarization of the Agrarian Question in Brazil." In *Frontier Expansion in Amazonia*, edited by Susanna B. Hecht and A. Cockburn, 463–90. Gainesville: University Press of Florida.

Massey, Doreen. 1994. *Space, Place and Gender*. Minneapolis: University of Minnesota Press.

———. 2005. *For Space*. Thousand Oaks, CA: Sage Publications.

Maybury-Lewis, David, ed. 1979. *Dialectical Societies: The Gê and Bororo of Central Brazil*. Cambridge, MA: Harvard University Press.

Megaron-Txukarramãe, and Mick Stout. 1990. "A Expedição Venatória dos Kayapó e Animais Importantes." In *Ethnobiology: Implications and Applications. Proceedings of the First International Congress of Ethnobiology*, edited by Darrell A. Posey and W. L. Overal, 227–41. Vol. 1. Belém: Museu Paraense Emílio Goeldi.

McCarthy, Julie. 2008. Brazilian Tribes Say Dam Threatens Way of Life. Available at http://www.npr.org/templates/story/story.php?storyId=91007395, accessed August 28, 2014.

McGregor, D. 2004. "Coming Full Circle: Indigenous Knowledge, Environment, and Our Future." *The American Indian Quarterly* 38 (3/4): 385–410.

McLean, Stuart. 2009. "Stories and Cosmogonies: Imagining Creativity Beyond 'Nature' and 'Culture.'" *Cultural Anthropology* 24 (2): 213–45.

Merkens, B., R. Poccard-Chapuis, M. Pikkety, A. Lacques, and A. Venturieri. 2002. "Crossing Spatial Analyses and Livestock Economics to Understand Deforestation Processes in the Brazilian Amazon: The Case of São Félix do Xingú in South Pará." *Agricultural Economics* 27 (3): 269–94.

Miller, Joanna. 2013. "Things as Persons: Body Ornaments and Alterity Among the Mamaindê (Nambikwara)." In *The Occult Life of Things: Native Amazonian Theories of Materiality and Personhood*, edited by Fernando Santos-Granero, 60–80. Tucson: University of Arizona Press.

Millikan, Brent. 2014. "The Amazon: Dirty Dams, Dirty Politics and the Myth of Clean Energy." *Tipití: Journal of the Society for the Anthropology of Lowland South America* 12 (2): 134–38.

Mintz, Sidney W., and Christine M. Du Bois. 2002. "The Anthropology of Food and Eating." *Annual Review of Anthropology* 31 (1): 99–119.

MME (Ministry of Mines and Energy). 2011. "Projeto de Usina Hidrelétrica Belo Monte: Fatos e Dados." Available at: http://www.mme.gov.br/documents/10584/1590364/BELO_MONTE_-_Fatos_e_Dados.pdf/94303fc2-d171-45be-a2d3-1029d7ae5aad, accessed March 11, 2012.

Moberg, Mark. 2014. "Certification and Neoliberal Governance: Moral Economies of Fair Trade in the Eastern Caribbean." *American Anthropologist* 116 (1): 8–22.

Momsen, Richard P. 1979. "Projeto RADAM: A Better Look at the Brazilian Tropics." *Geo-Journal* 3 (1): 3–14.

Montagnini, F., and R. Mendelsohn. 1997. "Managing Forest Fallows: Improving the Economics of Swidden Agriculture." *Ambio* 26 (2): 118–23.

Moore, Denny. 2006. "Brazil: Language Situation." In *Encyclopedia of Language and Linguistics*, edited by Keith Brown, 117–28. Oxford: Elsevier.

Moore, Donald S. 1998. "Subaltern Struggles and the Politics of Place: Remapping Resistance in Zimbabwe's Eastern Highlands." *Cultural Anthropology* 13 (3): 344–81.

———. 2005. *Suffering for Territory: Race, Place, and Power in Zimbabwe.* Durham, NC: Duke University Press.

Moore, Donald, Anand Pandian, and Jake Kosek. 2003. "Introduction. The Cultural Politics of Race and Nature: Terrains of Power and Practice." In *Race, Nature, and the Politics of Difference*, edited by Donald Moore, Jake Kosek, and Anand Pandian, 1–70. Durham, NC: Duke University Press.

Morsello, Carla. 2002. "Market Integration and Sustainability in Amazonian Indigenous Livelihoods: The Case of the Kayapó." PhD diss., University of East Anglia, Norwich.

———. 2006. "Company-Community Non-Timber Forest Product Deals in the Brazilian Amazon: A Review of Opportunities and Problems." *Forest Policy and Economics* 8 (4): 485–94.

Morsello, Carla, Juliana Aparecida da Silva Delgado, Thiago Fonseca-Morello, and Alice Dantas Brites. 2014. "Does Trading Non-Timber Forest Products Drive Specialisation in Products Gathered for Consumption? Evidence from the Brazilian Amazon." *Ecological Economics* 100 (C): 140-49.

Morton, Christopher A., and Elizabeth Edwards, eds. 2009. *Photography, Anthropology and History: Expanding the Frame.* Farnham: Ashgate Publishing.

Mukerji, Chandra. 2002. "Material Practices of Domination: Christian Humanism, the Built Environment, and Techniques of Western Power." *Theory and Society* 31 (1): 1–34.

Muehlbach, Andrea. 2001. "'Making Place' at the United Nations: Indigenous Cultural Politics at the U.N. Working Group on Indigenous Populations. *Cultural Anthropology* 16 (3): 415–48.

Muraca, Barbara. 2012. "Towards a Fair Degrowth-Society: Justice and the Right to a 'Good Life' Beyond Growth." *Futures* 44 (6): 535–45.

Murphy, Isabel. 2004. *And I in My Turn, Will Pass It On: Knowledge Transmission Among the Kayapó.* Dallas: Summer Institute of Linguistics International.

Nadasdy, Paul. 1999. "The Politics of Tek: Power and the 'Integration' of Knowledge." *Arctic Anthropology* 36 (1/2): 1–18.

———. 2003 *Hunters and Bureaucrats: Power, Knowledge, and Aboriginal-state Relations in the Southwest Yukon.* Vancouver: University of British Columbia Press.

———. 2007 "Adaptive Co-Management and the Gospel of Resilience." In *Adaptive Co-Management: Collaborating, Leaning, and Multi-Level Governance*, edited by Derek Armitage, Fikret Berkes, and Nancy Doubleday, 208–27. Vancouver: University of British Columbia Press.

Nagar, Richa, Victoria Lawson, Linda McDowell, and Susan Hanson. 2002. "Locating Globalization: Feminist (Re)readings of the Subjects and Spaces of Globalization." *Economic Geography* 78 (3): 257–84.

Nazarea, Virginia D, ed. 1999. *Ethnoecology: Situated Knowledge/Located Lives*. Tucson: University of Arizona Press.

———. 2006. "Local Knowledge and Memory in Biodiversity Conservation." *Annual Review of Anthropology* 35: 317–35.

Nelson, Diane. 1999. *A Finger in the Wound: Body Politics in Quincentennial Guatemala*. Berkeley: University of California Press.

Nepstad, D., S. Schwartzman, B. Bamberger, M. Santilli, D. Ray, P. Schlesinger, P. Lefebvre, A. Alencar, E. Prinz, Greg Fiske, and Alicia Rolla. 2006. "Inhibition of Amazon Deforestation and Fire by Parks and Indigenous Lands." *Conservation Biology* 20 (1): 65–73.

Nepstad, D., and S. Schwartzman. 1992. *Advances in Economic Botany, vol. 9: Non-Timber Forest Products from Tropical Forests. Evaluation of a Conservation and Development Strategy*. New York: New York Botanical Garden Press Department.

Neumann, Roderick P. 1998. *Imposing Wilderness: Struggles over Livelihood and Nature Preservation in Africa*. Berkeley: University of California Press.

Neves, Eduardo G., and James B. Peterson. 2006. "Political Economy and Pre-Columbian Landscape Transformations in Central Amazonia." In *Time and Complexity in Historical Ecology*, edited by William Balée and Clark L. Erickson, 279–311. New York: Columbia Press.

Niezen, Ronald. 2003. *The Origins of Indigenism: Human Rights and the Politics of Identity*. Berkeley: University of California Press.

Noronha Inglez de Sousa, Cássio. 2000. "Vantagens, Vícios e Desafios. Os Kayapó Gorotire em Tempos de Desenvolvimento." PhD diss., Universidade de São Paulo.

Novotny, Etelvino H., Michael H. B. Hayes, Beáta E. Madari, Tito J. Bonagamba, Eduardo R. de Azevedo, André A. de Souza, Guixue Song, Christiane M. Nogueiraf, and Antonio S. Mangrich. 2009. "Lessons from the *Terra Preta de Índios* of the Amazon Region for the Utilisation of Charcoal for Soil Amendment." *Brazilian Chemical Society* 20 (6): 1003–10.

Nyéléni. 2007. "Declaration of Nyéléni: Declaration of the Forum for Food Sovereignty." Sélingué, Mali. Available at: http://nyeleni.org/spip.php?article290, accessed May 5, 2013.

O'Dougherty, M. 2002. *Consumption Intensified: The Politics of Middle-Class Daily Life in Brazil*. Durham, NC: Duke University Press.

Offen, Karl H. 2003. "The Territorial Turn: Making Black Territories in Pacific Colombia." *Journal of Latin American Geography* 2 (1): 43–73.

Orlove, Ben. 2007 "Editorial: Current Approaches to Hybridity." *Current Anthropology* 48 (5): 631–32.

Overal, W., and Darrell A. Posey. 1984. "Uso de Formigas do Gênero *Azteca* para Controle de Saúvas entre os Caiapó do Brasil." *Ciência e Cultura* 36 (Suplemento), 935.

Overal, W., and Darrell A. Posey, eds. 1990. *Ethnobiology: Implications and Applications. Proceedings of the First International Congress of Ethnobiology*, vol. 1. Belém: Museu Paraense Emílio Goeldi.

Overing, Joanna. 2003. "In Praise of the Everyday: Trust and the Art of Social Living in an Amazonian Community." *Ethnos* 68 (3): 293–316.

Pacheco, Pablo. 2009. "Agrarian Reform in the Brazilian Amazon: Its Implications for Land Distribution and Deforestation." *World Development* 37 (8): 1337–47.

Padoch, Christine, Emily Harwell, and Adi Susanto. 1998. "Swidden, Sawah, and In-between: Agricultural Transformation in Borneo." *Human Ecology* 26 (1): 3–20.

Pálsson, Gisli. 1994, "Enskilment at Sea." *Man* 29 (4): 901–27.

Parker, Eugdene. 1992. "Forest Islands and Kayapó Resource Management in Amazonia: The Apete." *American Anthropologist* 94 (2): 406–28.

————.1993. "Fact and Fiction in Amazonia: The Case of the Apete." *American Anthropologist* 95 (3): 715–23.

Paulson, Susan, and Lisa L. Gezon, eds. 2005. *Political Ecology across Spaces, Scales, and Social Groups*. New Brunswick: Rutgers University Press.

Peña, Guillermo de la. 2005. "Social and Cultural Policies Toward Indigenous Peoples: Perspectives from Latin America." *Annual Review of Anthropology* 34 (1): 717–39.

Pereley, Bernard. 2014. "Living Traditions: A Manifesto for Critical Indigeneity." In *Performing Indigeneity: Global Histories and Contemporary Experiences*, edited by Laura Graham and H. Glenn Penny, 32–54. Lincoln: University of Nebraska Press.

Pimentel, David, Michael McNair, Louise Buck, Marcia Pimentel, and Jeremy Kamil. 1997. "The Value of Forests to World Food Security." *Human Ecology* 25 (1): 91–120.

Pokorny, Benno, James Johnson, Gabriel Medina, and Lisa Hoch. 2012. "Market-based Conservation of the Amazonian Forests: Revisiting Win–Win Expectations." *Geoforum* 43 (3): 387–401.

Popielarz, Pamela A., and Zachary P. Neal. 2007. "The Niche as a Theoretical Tool." *Annual Review of Sociology* 33 (1): 65–84.

Posey, Darrell Addison. 1979. "Ethnoentomology of the Gorotire Kayapó of Central Brazil." PhD diss., University of Georgia.

————. 1983. Folk Apiculture of the Kayapó Indians of Brazil. *Biotropica* 15 (2): 154–158.

————. 1985 "Indigenous Management of Tropical Forest Ecosyetems: The Case of the Kayapó Indians of the Brazilian Amazon." *Agroforestry Systems* 3 (2): 139–58.

————. 1986. *Ethnoecology and the Investigation of Resource Management by the Kayapó Indians of Gorotire, Brazil*. Simposío do Trópico Úmido, 1. Belém, Embrapa.

————. 1987. "An Ethnoentomological Survey of Brazilian Indians." *Entomologia Generalis* 12 (2/3): 191–202.

————. 1992. "Reply to Parker." *American Anthropologist* 94 (2): 441–43.

————. 1999. "Safeguarding Traditional Resource Rights of Indigenous People." In *Ethnoecology: Situated Knowledge/Located Lives*, edited by Virginia Nazarea, 217–30. Tucson: The University of Arizona Press.

————. 2002a "Contact Before Contact: Typology of Post-Colombian Interaction with the Northern Kayapó of the Amazon." In *Kayapó Ethnoecology and Culture*, edited by Kristina Plenderleith, 14–24. London: Routledge.

————. 2002b. "Time, Space, and the Interface of Divergent Cultures: The Kayapó Indians of the Amazon Face the Future." In *Kayapó Ethnoecology and Culture*, edited by Kristina Plenderleith, 33–41. London: Routledge.

————. 2002c. "Report from Gorotire: Will Kayapó Traditions Survive?" In *Kayapó Ethnoecology and Culture*, edited by Kristina Plenderleith, 55–57. London: Routledge.

Posey, Darrell Addison, John Frechione, John Eddins, Luiz Francelino Da Silva, Debbie Myers, Diane Case, and Peter Macbeath. 1984. "Ethnoecology as Applied Anthropology in Amazonian Development." *Human Organization* 43 (2): 95–107.

Posey, Darrell Addison, and Susanna B. Hecht. 1990. "Indigenous Soil Management in the Latin American Tropics: Some Implications for the Amazon Basin." In *Ethnobiology: Implications and Applications. Proceedings for the First International Congress of Ethnobiology (Belém, Pará)*, edited by Darrell Addison Posey and W. L. Overal, 73–86. Belém: Museu Paraense Emílio Goeldi.

Postero, Nancy Grey. 2007. *Now we are Citizens: Indigenous Politics in Postmulticultural Bolivia*. Stanford: Stanford University Press.

Povinelli, Elizabeth. 2011. *Economies of Abandonment*. Durham, NC: Duke University Press.

Prins, Harald. 2004. "Visual Anthropology." In *A Companion to the Anthropology of American Indians*, edited by T. Biolsi, 506–25. Malden, MA: Blackwell.

Rabben, Linda. 2004. *Brazil's Indians and the Onslaught of Civilization: The Yanomami and the Kayapó*. Seattle: University of Washington Press.

Rabinow, Paul. 1996. *Essays on the Anthropology of Reason*. Princeton, NJ: Princeton University Press.

Raffles, Hugh. 2002. "Intimate Knowledge." *International Social Science Journal* 54 (173): 325–35.

Ramos, Alcida. 1984. "Frontier Expansion and Indian Peoples in the Brazilian Amazon." In *Frontier Expansion in Amazonia*, edited by Susanna B. Hecht and A. Cockburn, 83–104. Gainesville: University Press of Florida.

———. 1994 "The Hyperreal Indian." *Critique of Anthropology* 14 (2): 153–71.

———. 2009. "Pulp Fictions of Indigenism." In *Race, Nature, and the Politics of Difference*, edited by Donald Moore, Jake Kosek, and Anand Pandian, 356–79. Durham, NC: Duke University Press.

———. 1998. *Indigenism: Ethnic Politics in Brazil*. Madison: University of Wisconsin Press.

———. 2012. "The Politics of Perspectivism." *Annual Review of Anthropology* 41: 484–94.

Ranzi, A., R. Feres, and F. Brown. 2007. "Internet Software Programs Aid in Search for Amazonian Geoglyphs." *Eos* 88 (21): 226–29.

Rebellato L., W. I. Woods, and E. G. Neves. 2009. "Pre-Columbian Settlement Dynamics in the Central Amazon." In *Amazonian Dark Earths: Wim Sombroek's Vision*, edited by W. I. Woods, W. G. Teixeira, J. Lehmann, C. Steiner, A. WinklerPrins, and L. Rebellato, 15–31. Dordrecht, The Netherlands: Springer.

Redwood, J. 2002. *World Bank Approaches to the Brazilian Amazon: The Bumpy Road Towards Sustainable Development*. Latin America and Caribbean Region: World Bank.

Ribeiro, Maria Beatriz N., Adriano Jerozolimski, Pascale de Robert, and William E. Magnusson. 2014. "Brazil Nut Stock and Harvesting at Different Spatial Scales in Southeastern Amazonia." *Forest Ecology and Management* 319: 67–74.

Rival, Laura. 2002. *Trekking Through History: The Huaorani of Amazonian Ecuador*. New York: Columbia University Press.

———. 2006. "Amazonian Historical Ecologies." *Journal of the Royal Anthropological Institute* 12 (s1): S79–S94.

Robbins, P. 2012. *Political Ecology: A Critical Introduction*. 2nd edition. Critical Introductions to Geography. Malden, MA: J. Wiley and Sons.

Robbins, P., K. McSweeny, T. Waite, and J. Rice. 2006. "Even Conservation Rules are made to be Broken: Implications for Biodiversity." *Environmental Management* 37 (2): 162–69.

Rocheleau, Dianne, and Robin Roth. 2007. "Rooted Networks, Relational Webs and Powers of Connection: Rethinking Human and Political Ecologies." *Geoforum* 38 (3): 433–37.

Rocheleau, Diane, and David Edmonds. 1997. "Women, Men and Trees: Gender, Power and Property in Forest and Agrarian Landscapes." *World Development* 25 (8): 1351–71.

Roosevelt, Anna. 1989. "Resource Management in Amazonia Before the Conquest: Beyond Ethnographic Projection." *Advances in Economic Botany* 7: 30–62.

———. 2000. "The Lower Amazon: A Dynamic Human Habitat." In *Imperfect Balance: Landscape Transformations in the Precolumbian Americas*, edited by D. L. Lentz, 455–91. New York: Columbia University Press.

Ros-Tonen, A. F. Mirjam, Tinde van Andel, Carla Morsello, Kei Otsuki, Sergio Rosendo, and Imme Scholz. 2008. "Forest-Related Partnerships in Brazilian Amazonia: There is

More to Sustainable Forest Management than Reduced Impact Logging." *Forest Ecology and Management* 256 (7): 1482–97.

Rosaldo, Renato. 1989. *Culture and Truth*. Boston: Beacon Press.

Roth, Christopher Fritz. 2008. *Becoming Tsimshian: The Social Life of Names*. Seattle: University of Washington Press.

Rosengren, Dan. 2015. "Being and Becoming: On Conditions of Existence in the Amazon." *Tipití: Journal of the Society for the Anthropology of Lowland South America* 13 (1): 80–94.

Roy, Ananya, and Aihwa Ong, eds. 2011. *Worlding Cities Asian Experiments and the Art of Being Global*. Malden, MA: Wiley-Blackwell.

Royce, Anya Peterson. 2011. *Becoming an Ancestor: The Isthmus Zapotec Way of Death*. Albany: State University of New York Press.

Rubdy, Rani, and Lubna Alasgoff, eds. 2014. *The Global-Local Interface and Hybridity: Exploring Language and Identity*. Ontario: Multilingual Matters.

Rubenstein, Steven. 2001. "Colonialism, the Shuar Federation, and the Ecuadorian State, Environment and Planning D." *Society and Space* 19 (3): 263–93.

———. 2009. "Crossing Boundaries with Shrunken Heads." In *Border Crossings: Transnational Americanist Anthropology*, edited by Kathleen S. Fine-Dare and Steven L. Rubenstein, 119–70. Lincoln: University of Nebraska Press.

Rupp, Stephanie. 2011. *Forests of Belonging: Identities, Ethnicities, and Stereotypes in the Congo River Basin*. Seattle: University of Washington Press.

Russell, W. M. S. 1988. "Population, Swidden Farming and the Tropical Environment." *Population and Environment* 10 (2): 77–94.

Rylands, Anthony B., and Katrina Brandon. 2005. "Brazilian Protected Areas." *Conservation Biology* 19 (3): 612–18.

Sáez, Oscar C. 2012. "Do Perspectivismo Ameríndio ao Índio Real." *Campos—Revista de Antropologia Social* 13 (2): 7–23.

Sage, Colin. 2014. "The Transition Movement and Food Sovereignty: From Local Resilience to Global Engagement in Food System Transformation." *Journal of Consumer Culture* 14 (2): 254–75.

Salm, Rodolfo. 2004a. "Densidade do Caule e Crescimento de Attalea maripa e Astrocaryum aculeatum: Implicações para a Distribuição de Palmeiras Arborescentes na Floresta Amazônica." *Biota Neotropica* 4 (1): 1–11.

———. 2004b. "Tree Species Diversity in a Seasonally-dry Forest: The Case of the Pinkaití Site, in the Kayapó Indigenous Area, Southeastern Limits of the Amazon." *Acta Amazônica* 34 (3): 435–43.

Sambatti, J. B. M., P. S. Martins, and A. Ando. 2001. "Folk Taxonomy and Evolutionary Dynamics of Cassava: A Case Study in Ubatuba, Brazil." *Economic Botany* 55 (1): 93–105.

Santos, Robert. 1984. "Law and Social Change: The Problem of Land in the Brazilian Amazon." In *Frontier Expansion in Amazonia*, edited by Marianne Schmink and Charles H. Wood, 439–62. Gainesville: University Press of Florida.

Santos-Granero, F. 1998. "Writing History into the Landscape: Space, Myth, and Ritual in Contemporary Amazonia." *American Ethnologist* 25 (2): 128–48.

———. 2006. "Sensual Vitalities: Noncorporeal Modes of Sensing and Knowing in Native Amazonia." *Tipití: Journal of the Society for the Anthropology of Lowland South America* 4 (1): 57–80.

———. 2009a. "Hybrid Bodyscapes." *Current Anthropology* 50 (4): 477–512.

————. 2009b. "Introduction: Amerindian Constructional Views of the World." In *The Occult Life of Things*, edited by F. Santos-Granero, 1–32. Tucson: University of Arizona Press.

Sawyer, Donald. 1984. "Frontier Expansion and Retraction in Brazil." In *Frontier Expansion in Amazonia*, edited by Susanna B. Hecht and A. Cockburn, 180–203. Gainesville: University Press of Florida.

Santos, Leinad Ayer De O., and Lúcia M. M. de Andrade. 1990. *Hydroelectric Dams on Brazil's Xingu River and Indigenous Peoples*. Cambridge: Cultural Survival.

Schaan, Denise P. 2011. *Sacred Geographies of Ancient Amazonia: Historical Ecology of Social Complexity*. Walnut Creek, CA: Left Coast Press.

Schaan, D., M. Pärssinen, A. Ranzi, and J. Piccoli. 2007. "Geoglifos da Amazônia Ocidental: Evidência de Complexidade Social entre Povos da Terra Firme." *Revista de Arqueologia da Sociedade de Arqueologia Brasileira* 20: 67–82.

Scheffler, Pamela. 2002. "Dung Beetle (*Coloeoptera: Scarabaeidae*) Ecology in the Intact and Modified Landscape of Eastern Amazonia." PhD diss., Pennsylvania State University and Universidade Federal de Viçosa.

Schiffer, Sueli Ramos. 2002. "São Paulo: Articulating a Cross Border Region." In *Global Networks: Linked*, edited by Saskia Sassen, 209–36. New York: Routledge.

Schmidt-Vogt, D. 1998. Secondary Forest in Swidden Agriculture in the Highlands of Thailand. *Journal of Tropical Forest Science* 13 (4): 748–67.

Schmidt, M., and M. J. Heckenberger. 2009. "Amerindian Anthrosols: Amazonian Dark Earth Formation in the Upper Xingu." In *Amazonian Dark Earths: Wim Sombroek's Vision*, edited by W. I. Woods, W. G. Teixeira, J. Lehmann, C. Steiner, A. WinklerPrins, and L. Rebellato, 163–90. Dordrecht, The Netherlands: Springer.

Schmink, Marianne, and Charles H. Wood. 1992. *Contested Frontiers in Amazonia*. New York: Columbia University Press.

Scholsberg, David. 2007. *Defining Environmental Justice: Theories, Movements, and Nature*. Oxford: Oxford University Press.

Schuler Zea, Evelyn. 2010. "On-Yesamarî and Laterality: Waiwai Meanderings." *Tipití: Journal of the Society for the Anthropology of Lowland South America* 8 (1): 1–20.

Schwartzman, Stephan, and Barbara Zimmerman. 2005. "Conservation Alliances with Indigenous Peoples of the Amazon." *Conservation Biology* 19 (3): 721–27.

Scott, James. 1998. *Seeing Like a State: How Certain Schemes to Improve the Human Condition Have Failed*. New Haven: Yale University Press.

Seeger, Anthony. 1981. *Nature and Society in Central Brazil: The Suya Indians of Mato Grosso*. Cambridge, MA: Harvard University Press.

————. 2004. *Why the Suya Sing: A Musical Anthropology of an Amazonian People*. Urbana: University of Illinois Press.

Seeger, Anthony, Roberto da Matta, and Eduardo B. V. de Castro. 1979. "A construção da pessoa nas sociedades indígenas brasileiras." *Boletim do Museu Nacional, Série Antropologia* 32: 2–19.

Shackleton, Charle M., and Ashok K. Pandey. 2014. "Positioning Non-Timber Forest Products on the Development Agenda." *Forest Policy and Economics* 38: 1–7.

Shackleton, Sheona. 2014. "Impacts of Climate Change on Food Availability: Non-Timber Forest Products." In *Global Environmental Change*, edited by Bill Freedman, 695–700. New York: Springer Science and Business Media.

Shanly, Kathryn W. 2015. "'Mapping:' Indigenous Presence: The Declaration of the Rights of Indigenous Peoples at Rhetorical Turns and Tipping Points." In *Mapping Indigenous*

Presence: North Scandinavian and North American Perspectives, edited by Kathryn W. Shanley and Bjørg Evjen, 5–26. Tucson: The University of Arizona Press.

Shepherd, C. J. 2010. "Mobilizing Local Knowledge and Asserting Culture: The Cultural Politics of In Situ Conservation of Agricultural Biodiversity." *Current Anthropology* 51 (5): 629–54.

Shiva, Vandana. 2005. *Earth Democracy: Justice, Sustainability, and Peace*. Cambridge, MA: South End Press.

Sikor, Thomas, ed. 2013. *The Justices and Injustices of Ecosystem Services*. New York: Routledge, Taylor and Francis Group.

Simmons, Cynthia S., with Stephen Perz, Marcos A. Pedlowski and Luiz Guilherme Teixeira Silva. 2002. "The Changing Dynamics of Land Conflict in the Brazilian Amazon: The Rural-Urban Complex and its Environmental Implications." *Urban Ecosystems* 6 (1): 99–121.

Simpson, Audra. 2014. *Mohawk Interruptus: Political Life Across the Borders of Settler States*. Durham, NC: Duke University Press.

Siskind, Janet. 1973. *To Hunt in the Morning*. Oxford: Oxford University Press.

Slater, Candace. 2002. *Entangled Edens: Visions of the Amazon*. Berkeley: University of California Press.

Smith, Eric, and Mark Wishnie. 2000. "Conservation and Subsistence in Small-Scale Societies." *Annual Review of Anthropology* 29: 493–524.

Smith, Laurel. 2012. "Decolonizing Hybridity: Indigenous Video, Knowledge, and Diffraction." *Cultural Geographies* 19 (3): 329–48.

Smith, Neil. 2008. *Uneven Development Nature, Capital, and the Production of Space*. 3rd edition. Athens: University of Georgia Press.

Smith, Nigel. 1980. "Anthrosols and Human Carrying Capacity in Amazonia." *Annals of the Association of American Geographers* 70 (4): 553–66.

Soares da Silveira, Diego. 2012. *Redes Sociotécnicas na Amazônia: Tradução de Saberes no Campo da Biodiversidade*. Rio de Janeiro: Multifoco.

Soja, Edward. 1989. *Postmodern Geographies: The Reassertion of Space in Critical Social Theory*. London: Verso.

———. 1996. *Thirdspace: Journeys to Los Angeles and Other Real-and-Imagined Places*. Cambridge, MA: Blackwell.

Sommer, Barbara A. 2005. "Colony of the Sertão: Amazonian Expeditions and the Indian Slave Trade." *The Americas* 61 (3): 401–28.

Spitulnik, Debra. 1993. "Anthropology and Mass Media." *Annual Review of Anthropology* 22: 293–315.

Spoon, J. 2011. "The Heterogeneity of Khumbu Sherpa Ecological Knowledge and Understanding in Sagarmatha (Mount Everest) National Park and Buffer Zone, Nepal." *Human Ecology* 39 (5): 657–72.

Spyer, Patricia. 2000. *The Memory of Trade: Modernity's Entanglements on an Eastern Indonesian Island*. Durham, NC: Duke University Press.

Stepp, John Richard. 2005. "Advances in Ethnobiological Field Methods." *Field Methods* 17 (3): 211–18.

Steward, Julian. 1955. *Theory of Culture Change: The Methodology of Multilineal Evolution*. Urbana: University of Illinois Press.

Stiglitz, J. 2002. *Globalization and its Discontents*. New York: W.W. Norton.

Subramanian, Ajantha. 2009. *Shorelines: Space and Rights in South India*. Stanford, CA: Stanford University Press.

Sulkin, Carlos David Londoño. 2012. *People of Substance—An Ethnography of Morality in the Colombian Amazon*. Toronto: University of Toronto Press.

Sutton, D. E. 2010. "Food and the Senses." *Annual Review of Anthropology* 39: 209–23.

Taussig, M. 1997. *The Magic of the State*. New York: Routledge.

Taylor, D. 2003. *The Archive and the Repertoire: Performing Cultural Memory in the Americas*. Durham, NC: Duke University Press.

Thomson, Ruth, and Stout, Mickey. 1974 *Modalidade em Kayapó*. (Série Lingüística, 3.) Brasilia: Summer Institute of Linguistics.

Thrupp, L. A. 2000. "Linking Agricultural Biodiversity and Food Security: The Valuable Role of Agrobiodiversity for Sustainable Agriculture." *International Affairs* 76 (2): 283–97.

Tinker, P. B., J. S. Ingram, and S. Struwe. 1996. "Effects of Slash-and-Burn Agriculture and Deforestation on Climate Change." *Agriculture, Ecosystems and Environment* 58 (1): 13–22.

Todd, Zoe. 2014. "An Indigenous Feminist's take on the Ontological Turn: 'Ontology' is Just Another Word for Colonialism." Available at http://zoeandthecity.wordpress.com/2014/10/24/an-indigenous-feminists-take-on-the-ontological-turn-ontology-is-just-another-word-for-colonialism/, accessed November 5, 2014.

Toni, Fabiano. 2003. "Forest Management in Brazil's Amazonian Municipalities." In *Municipal Forest Management in Latin America*, edited by Lyes Ferroukhi, 145–78. Jakarta: Center for International Forestry Research.

Tsing, Anna. 2003a. "Agrarian Allegory and Global Futures." In *Nature in the Global South*, edited by Paul R. Greenough and Anna Lowenhaupt Tsing, 124–69. Durham, NC: Duke University Press.

———. 2003b. "Cultivating the Wild: Honey-Hunting and Forest Management in Southeast Kalimantan." In *Culture and the Question of Rights: Forests, Coasts, and Seas in Southeast Asia*, edited by Charles Zerner, 24–55. Durham, NC: Duke University Press.

———. 2005. *Friction: An Ethnography of Global Connection*. Princeton, NJ: Princeton University Press.

———. 2015. *The Mushroom at the End of the World: On the Possibility of Life in Capitalist Ruins*. Princeton, NJ: Princeton University Press.

Tuan, Yu Fu. 1977. *Space and Place: The Perspective of Experience*. Minneapolis: University of Minnesota Press.

Tuhiwai Smith, Linda. 1999. *Decolonizing Methodologies*. London: Zed Books.

Turner, Nancy, Marianne Boelscher Ignace, and Ronald Ignace. 2000. "Traditional Ecological Knowledge and Wisdom of Aboriginal Peoples in British Columbia." *Ecological Applications* 10 (5): 1275–87

Turner, Terence. 1965. "Social Structure and Political Organization Among the Northern Cayapo." PhD diss., Harvard University.

———. 1991a. "Representing, Resisting, Rethinking: Historical Transformations of Kayapó Culture and Anthropological Consciousness." In *Colonial Situations: Essays on the Contextualization of Ethnographic Knowledge*, edited by George W. Stocking Jr., 285–313. Madison: University of Wisconsin Press.

———. 1991b. "'We are Parrots,' 'Twins are Birds': Play of Tropes as Operational Structure." In *Beyond Metaphor: The Theory of Tropes in Anthropology*, edited by J. W. Fernandez, 121–58. Stanford, CA: Stanford University Press.

———. 1993. "The Role of Indigenous Peoples in the Environmental Crisis: The Case of the Brazilian Kayapó." *Perspectives in Biology and Medicine* 36 (3): 526–45.

————. 1995a. "An Indigenous People's Struggle for Socially Equitable and Ecologically Sustainable Production: The Kayapó Revolt against Extractivism." *Journal of Latin American Anthropology* 1 (1): 98–121.

————. 1995b. "Neoliberal Ecopolitics and Indigenous Peoples: The Kayapó, the 'Rainforest Harvest' and the Body Shop." *Yale School of Forestry and Environmental Studies Bulletin* 98: 113–23.

————. 1995c. "Social Body and Embodied Subject: Bodiliness, Subjectivity, and Sociality Among the Kayapó." *Cultural Anthropology* 10 (2): 143–70.

————. 2003a. "Representation, Polyphony, and the Construction of Power in a Kayapó Video." In *Indigenous Movement, Self-Representation, and the State in Latin America*, edited by Kay Warren and J. E. Jackson, 229–50. Austin: University of Texas Press.

————. 2003b. "The Beautiful and the Common: Inequalities of Value and Revolving Hierarchy Among the Kayapó." *Tipití: Journal of the Society for the Anthropology of Lowland South America* 1 (1): 11–26.

————. 2008. "Cosmology, Objectification and Animism in Indigenous Amazonia." Keynote address presented to the Nordic Network for Amerindian Studies. Copenhagen, Denmark, November 9.

————. 2009a. "The Crisis of Late Structuralism. Perspectivism and Animism: Rethinking Culture, Nature, Spirit, and Bodiliness." *Tipití: Journal of the Society for the Anthropology of Lowland South America* 7 (1): 3–40.

————. 2009b. "Valuables, Value, and Commodities among the Kayapó of Central Brazil." In *The Occult Life of Things: Native Amazonian Theories of Materiality and Personhood*, edited by Fernando Santos-Granero, 152–69. London: Routledge.

————. 2010. "From Ecological Disaster to Constitutional Crisis." Guest Post, *Anthropology Works*. Available at: http://anthropologyworks.com/2010/05/12/from-ecological-disaster -to-constitutional-crisis-3/, accessed July 5, 2012.

————. (1980) 2012. "The Social Skin." *HAU: Journal of Ethnographic Theory* 2 (2): 486–504. Reprinted from *Not Work Alone: A Cross-Cultural Study of Activities Superfluous to Survival*, edited by Jeremy Cherfas and Roger Lewin, 111–40. Beverley Hills: Temple Smith.

Turner, Terence, and Vanessa Fajans-Turner. 2006. "Political Innovation and Inter-Ethnic Alliance: Kayapo Resistance to the Developmentalist State." *Anthropology Today* 22 (5): 3–10.

Uhl, Christopher, and I. C. Guimaraes Viera. 1989. "Ecological Impacts of Selective Logging in the Brazilian Amazon: A Case Study from the Paragominas Region of the State of Para." *Biotropica* 21 (2): 98–106.

Urban, Chris. 1988. "Ritual Wailing in Amerindian Brazil." *American Anthropologist* 90 (2): 385–400.

Vaccaro, Ismael, and Oriol Beltran. 2010. "Conservationist Governmental Technologies in the Western European Mountains: The Unfinished Transformation of the Pyrenees." *Journal of Political Ecology* 17: 29–41.

Vaccaro, Ismael, Oriol Beltran, and P. A. Paquet. 2013. "Political Ecology and Conservation Policies: Some Theoretical Genealogies." *Journal of Political Ecology* 20: 255–72.

Vaccaro, Ismael, Allan Charles Dawson, and Laura Zanotti. 2014. "Introduction: Negotiating Territoriality Spatial Dialogues Between State and Tradition." In *Negotiating Territoriality: Spatial Dialogues Between State and Tradition*, edited by Allan Dawson, Laura Zanotti, and Ismael Vaccaro, 1–20. New York: Routledge.

Vandergeest, Peter, and Nancy Peluso. 1995. "Territorialization and State Power in Thailand." *Theory and Society* 24 (3): 385–85.

Vanhulst, J., and A. E. Beling. 2014. "Buen Vivir: Emergent Discourse Within or Beyond Sustainable Development?" *Ecological Economics* 101: 54–63.

Veríssimo, Alberto, Carlos Souza Júnior, Steve Stone, and Christopher Uhl. 1998. "Zoning of Timber Extraction in the Brazilian Amazon." *Conservation Biology* 12 (1): 128–36.

Verswijver, Gustaaf, ed. 1992a. *Kaiapó Amazonia: The Art of Body Decoration.* Royal Museum for Central Africa: Snoeck-Ducaju and Zoon.

———. 1992b. *The Club—Fighters of the Amazon: Warfare Among the Kaiapo Indians of Central Brazil.* Gent: Rijksuniversiteit te Gent.

Vidal, Lux. 1977. *Morte e Vida de uma Sociedade Indígena Brasileira: Os Kayapó Xikrin do Rio Cateté.* São Paulo: Editora da Universidade de São Paulo.

———. 1981. "Contribution to the Concept of Person and Self in Lowland South American Societies: Body Painting Among the Kayapo-Xikrin." *Dispositio* 6 (17/18): 169–81.

Vidal, Lux B., and Isabelle Giannini. 1995. "Ritual Music of the Kayapó-Xikrin, Brazil." In *Ritual Music of the Kayapó-Xikrin* [CD booklet]. The International Institute for Traditional Music, Berlin, in cooperation with the International Council for Traditional Music, eds. Washington DC: Smithsonian/Folkways Recordings.

Vilaça, Aparecida. 2002. "Making Kin out of Others in Amazonia." *Journal of the Royal Anthropological Institute* 8 (2): 347–65.

Visweswaran, Kamala. 1994. *Fictions of Feminist Ethnography.* Minneapolis: University of Minnesota Press.

Viveiros de Castro, E. 1992. *From the Enemy's Point of View: Humanity and Divinity in an Amazonian Society.* Chicago: University of Chicago Press.

———. 1998. "Cosmological Deixis and Amerindian Perspectivism." *Journal of the Royal Anthropological Institute* 4 (3): 469–88.

Vom Bruck, Gabriele, and Barbara Bodenhorn, eds. 2006. *The Anthropology of Names and Naming.* New York: Cambridge University Press.

Wagamese, Richard. 2011. *One Story, One Song.* Vancouver: Douglas & McIntyre

Wagley, Charles. 1977. *Welcome of Tears: The Tapirapé Indians of Central Brazil.* New York: Oxford University Press.

Walker, Wayne, Alessandro Baccini, Stephan Schwartzman, Sandra Ríos, María A. Oliveira-Miranda, Cicero Augusto, Milton Romero Ruiz, Carla Soria Arrasco, Beto Ricardo, Richard Smith, Chris Meyer, Juan Carlos Jintiach, and Edwin Vasquez Campos. 2014. "Forest Carbon in Amazonia: The Unrecognized Contribution of Indigenous Territories and Protected Natural Areas." *Carbon Management.* Available at: http://www.tandfonline.com/doi/abs/10.1080/17583004.2014.990680#.VMweL8boMwR.

Warren, Jonathan W. 2001. *Racial Revolutions: Antiracism and Indian Resurgence in Brazil.* Durham, NC: Duke University Press.

Weinstein, Barbara. 1983. *The Amazon Rubber Boom, 1850–1920.* Stanford, CA: Stanford University Press.

Weinstock, Joseph A. 1983. "Rattan: Ecological Balance in a Borneo Rainforest Swidden." *Economic Botany* 37 (1): 58–68.

Wells, M. P., and K. E. Brandon. 1993. "The Principles and Practice of Buffer Zones and Local Participation in Biodiversity Conservation." *Ambio* 22 (2–3): 57–162.

Werbner, P., and T. Modood, eds. 1997. *Debating Cultural Hybridity: Multi-Cultural Identities and the Politics of Anti-Racism.* London: Zed Books.

Werner, Dennis W. 1983. "Why Do the Mekranoti Trek?" In *Adaptive Responses of Native Amazonians,* edited by Raymond Hames and William Taylor Vickers, 225–38. New York: Academic Press.

Werner, Dennis W., N. M. Flowers, M. L. Ritter, and D. R. Gross. 1979. "Subsistence Productivity and Hunting Effort in Native South America." *Human Ecology* 7 (4): 303–315.

Werner, Oswald. 1969. "The Basic Assumptions of Ethnoscience." *Semiotica* 1 (3): 329–38.

West, Paige. 2006. *Conservation is Our Government Now: The Politics of Ecology in Papua New Guinea.* Durham, NC: Duke University Press.

———. 2012. *From Modern Production to Imagined Primitive: The Social World of Coffee from Papua New Guinea.* Durham, NC: Duke University Press.

West, Paige, James Igoe, and Dan Brockington. 2006. "Parks and Peoples: The Social Impact of Protected Areas." *Annual Review of Anthropology* 35: 251–77.

Whatmore, S., and L. Thorne. 1997. "Nourishing Networks: Alternative Geographies of Food." In *Globalizing Food: Agrarian Questions and Global Restructuring,* edited by D. J. Goodman and M. J. Watts, 287–304. London: Routledge.

Whitehead, Neil. 2002. *Dark Shamans.* Durham, NC: Duke University Press.

Whitehead, Neil, and Stephanie W. Alemán. 2009. *Anthropologies of Guayana: Cultural Spaces in Northeastern Amazonia.* Tucson: University of Arizona Press.

Wilbert, Johannes, and Karin Simoneau. 1978. *Folk Literature of the Gê Indians,* vol. 1. Los Angeles: University of California Los Angeles Latin American Center Publications.

Wilson, W. M. 2003. "Cassava (Manihot esculenta Crantz), Cyanogenic Potential, and Predation in Northwestern Amazonia: The Tukanoan Perspective." *Human Ecology* 31 (3): 403–16.

Wilson, Warren M., and D. L. Dufour. 2002. "Why 'Bitter' Cassava? Productivity of 'Bitter' and 'Sweet' Cassava in a Tukanoan Indian Settlement in the Northwest Amazon." *Economic Botany* 56 (1): 49–57.

Wolf, Eric. 1982. *Europe and the People Without History.* Berkeley: University of California Press.

Wollenberg, E. 1998. "Conclusion." In *Incomes from the Forest: Methods for the Development and Conservation of Forest Products for Local Communities,* edited by E. Wollenberg and A. Ingles, 221–27. Bogor, Indonesia: Center for International Forestry Research.

Woods W. 1995. "Comments on the Black Earths of Amazonia. *Papers and Proceedings of Applied Geography Conference* 18: 159–65.

Woods, W., and J. M. McCann. 1999. "The Anthropogenic Origin and Persistence of Amazonian Dark Earths." *Yearbook. Conference of Latin Americanist Geographers* 25: 7–14.

Woods, W., and William M. Denevan. 2009. "Amazonian Darth Earths: The First Century of Reports." In *Amazonian Dark Earths: Wim Sombroek's Vision,* edited by William I. Woods, Wenceslau G. Teixeira, Johannes Lehmann, Christoph Steiner, Antoinette WinklerPrins, and Lilian Rebellato, 1–14. Dordrecht, The Netherlands: Springer.

Wood, Charles, and John Wilson. 1984. "The Magnitude of Migration to the Brazilian Frontier." In *Frontier Expansion in Amazonia,* edited by Marianne Schmink and Charles Wood. 142–52. Gainesville: University of Florida Press.

Zaks, D., C. C. Barford, N. Ramankutty, and J. A. Foley. 2009. "Producer and Consumer Responsibility for Greenhouse Gas Emissions from Agricultural Production—A Perspective from the Brazilian Amazon." *Environmental Research Letters* 4 (4): 1–12.

Zanotti, Laura, and Janet Chernela. 2008. "Conflicting Cultures of Nature: Ecotourism, Education and the Kayapó of the Brazilian Amazon." *Journal of Tourism Geographies* 10 (4): 495–521.

Zanotti, Laura. 2009. "Economic Diversification and Sustainable Development: The Role Non-Timber Forest Products Play in the Monetization of Kayapó Livelihoods." *Journal of Ecological Anthropology* 13 (1): 26–41.

———. 2014a. "Hybrid Natures? Community Conservation Partnerships in the Kayapó Lands." *Anthropological Quarterly* 87 (3): 665–93.

———. 2014b. "Political Ecology of Movement and Travel: Territorialities and Place-Making among the Kayapó." *Journal of Political Ecology* 21. Available at jpe.library.arizona.edu/volume_21/Zanotti.pdf

———. 2015. "Water and Life: Hydroelectric Development and Indigenous Pathways to Justice in the Brazilian Amazon." *Politics, Groups, and Identities* 3 (4): 666–72.

Zanotti, Laura, and Marcela Palomino-Schalscha. 2015. "Taking Different Ways of Knowing Seriously: Implications and Challenges for Non-Indigenous Researchers Working with Indigenous Peoples." *Sustainability Science* 11 (1): 139–52.

Zimmerer, Karl S. 2006. *Globalization and New Geographies of Conservation*. Chicago: University of Chicago Press.

Zimmerer, Karl S., Ryan E. Galt, and Margaret Buck. 2004. "Globalization and Multi-Spatial Trends in the Coverage of Protected-Area Conservation (1980–2000)." *Ambio* 33 (8): 520–29.

Zimmerman, Barbara. 2010. "Beauty, Power, and Conservation in the Southeast Amazon: How Traditional Social Organization of the Kayapó Leads to Forest Protection." In *Indigenous Peoples and Conservation—from Rights to Resource Management*, edited by Kristen Walker Painemilla, Anthony B. Rylands, Alisa Woofter, and Cassie Hughes, 63–72. Arlington, VA: Conservation International.

Zimmerman, Barbara, C. A. Peres, J. R. Malcolm, and T. Turner. 2001. "Conservation and Development Alliances with the Kayapó of South-Eastern Amazonia, a Tropical Forest Indigenous People." *Environmental Conservation* 28 (1): 10–22.

Index

In this index, references to images and photographs are in *italics*. Information located in the notes is indicated thus: 203n76, meaning note 76 on page 203.

About the Author

Laura Zanotti is an Associate Professor in the Department of Anthropology at Purdue University. Zanotti completed her PhD at the University of Washington in 2008 and joined the Anthropology faculty at Purdue University in fall of 2009. She specializes in collaborative research, feminist political ecology, indigenous studies, environmental justice, and media anthropology. Since 2004 she has carried out participatory research with the Kayapó peoples. More recent work has emphasized water security issues in the Amazon region with a focus on co-building digital media "worlds" in Kayapó communities, highlighting leadership, strengthening communities in coastal Alaska, and exploring Electronic Life Histories in the Midwest. The focus of these projects is on mapping spatial inequalities and injustices experienced by communities that depend upon healthy landscapes for sustainable and sovereign futures. Zanotti's research is currently funded by National Science Foundation and Purdue University's College of Liberal Arts. Her work has resulted in ten published articles and an edited volume with Routledge.